# The Anthropology of Time

EXPLORATIONS IN ANTHROPOLOGY
A University College London Series

Series Editors:   Barbara Bender, John Gledhill and Bruce Kapferer

# The Anthropology of Time

*Cultural Constructions of Temporal Maps and Images*

**Alfred Gell**

BERG

*Oxford • Washington, D.C.*

First published in 1992 by
**Berg**.
Editorial offices:
150 Cowley Road, Oxford, OX4 1JJ, UK
22883 Quicksilver Drive, Dulles, VA 20166, USA

Reprinted in 1996.

Berg is the imprint of Oxford International Publishers Ltd.


**Library of Congress Cataloging-in-Publication Data**

A catalogue record for this book is available from the Library of
Congress.


**British Library Cataloguing-in-Publication Data**

Gell, Alfred
  The anthropology of time: cultural constructions of temporal
  maps and images. – (Explorations in anthropology)
  I. Title   II. Series
  115


ISBN  0 85496 717 6
      0 85496 890 3 (pb)


Printed and bound in the UK by WBC Book Manufacturers,
Bridgend, Mid-Glamorgan.

# Contents

# Figures and Tables

## Figures

## Tables

# Acknowledgements

The composition of this book has occupied me, off and on, for more years than I care to contemplate, and over the course of this time I have amassed a number of debts. Of these, perhaps the most outstanding is the debt I owe to Bruce Kapferer, the editor of the series 'Explorations in Anthropology', who encouraged me to revise and publish the original manuscript of this book, which I had sadly concluded was not likely to appeal to anyone outside my immediate circle. Latterly, reading over the completed manuscript, I am more sanguine than hitherto, that among these pages there will be some capable of beguiling, even instructing, a more diverse audience than I feared in my more despondent moments. Bruce Kapferer's editorial stimulus has been all the more noteworthy in that I am well aware that on theoretical questions I have frequently taken positions which are diametrically opposed to his own. His comments I have taken into account as best I could, and very useful they were too, but I am also particularly conscious of his editorial forbearance, and grateful for it. I can say the same for Jadran Mimica, who brought my manuscript to his attention initially. I can only conclude that these two have behaved in a genuinely altruistic manner throughout, and what framer of 'Acknowledgements' can say more than that?

Among my other debts are those I owe to present and past colleagues at the London School of Economics, notably Maurice Bloch, whom I have repaid in typical departmental fashion with a bouquet of criticism and carping. He read the original manuscript and discussed many detailed points with me. Christina Toren also read the original version, and advised me on psychological questions. She is not, however to be held responsible in any way for my discussion of cognition. I am also particularly grateful to Ward Keeler, who provided me with the data on Bali which I have reported (I hope correctly) on pages 74–5, in the course of one of the most memorable anthropological conversations I have been privileged to enjoy. Needless to add, any deficiencies in my account of Bali are not attributable to him. Nancy Munn read the complete final draft, and though she was too much under pressure with her own forthcoming review of the 'Anthropology of Time' literature to make detailed comments, I drew enormous reassurance from her generally favourable reaction. Sections of this work have also been presented at seminars at the L.S.E., the University of Oxford, and New York University, where audiences made a number of useful comments.

I am grateful to the London School of Economics and my department for granting me a sabbatical year during which I was able to revise and substantially rewrite this book.

Finally I must thank Simeran Gell, and Rohan for putting up with me while I got on with my solitary labours. I hope it has all been worthwhile.

# Part I

# Differences in the Cognition of Time Attributed to Society and Culture

# Chapter 1

## Durkheim

The anthropology of time, in its contemporary form, can be traced to a well-known passage in the introductory chapter of Durkheim's *The Elementary Forms of the Religious Life* (1915: 9–11):

> what philosophers call the categories of the understanding, the ideas of time, space, class, number, cause, personality . . . correspond to the most universal properties of things . . . they are like the solid frame surrounding all thought [which] does not seem to be able to liberate itself from them without destroying itself, for it seems that we cannot think of objects which are not in time and space, that have no number, etc. . . . Now when primitive beliefs are systematically analysed, the principal categories are naturally found. They are born in religion and of religion, they are a product of religious thought. . . . Religious representations are collective representations which express collective realities . . . so if the categories are of religious origin they ought to participate in this nature common to all religious facts . . . it is allowable to suppose that they are rich in social elements.
>
> For example, try to represent what the notion of time would be without the processes by which we divide it, measure it, or express it with objective signs, a time which is not a succession of years, months, weeks, days and hours. . . . We cannot conceive of time except by distinguishing its different moments. Now what is the origin of this differentiation? [*Durkheim at this point briefly disposes of the idea that private intuitions of successive experiences are adequate for this.*] . . . in reality, observation proves that these indispensable guidelines [which provide] . . . an abstract and impersonal frame . . . like an endless chart, where all duration is spread out before the mind, and upon which all possible events can be located in relation to fixed and determined guidelines . . . are taken from social life. The divisions into days, weeks, months, years, etc. correspond to the periodical recurrence of feasts and public ceremonies. A calendar expresses the rhythm of collective activities, while at the same time its function is to assure their regularity . . . what the category of

3

time expresses is the time common to the group, a social time, so to speak.

This remarkably forthright theoretical statement does two things: first, it places the problem of the sociology of time in an explicit philosophical framework; and second, it brings out the circularity inherent in interpretative sociology of the kind Durkheim initiated, in that collective representations (of time, space, etc.) are both *derived from* society and also *dictate to* society. Not that this circularity is necessarily·vicious; it may be described as cybernetic, dialectical or hermeneutic, from different points of view. In embracing this circularity, Durkheim initiated a distinctive phase in the history of thought, to which, needless to say, Marx, Weber, Pareto and Simmel also contributed, namely, the era of sociological interpretation and sociological explanation.

Durkheim raises the issue of time in a philosophical (metaphysical) context, and links his notion of 'social time' to the philosophical tradition of Kantian rationalism. He rejects the 'naive realist' assumption that time just is what it is, and that time-reckoning concepts enable people to 'grasp' time as if it were one more external fact of nature among many. This marks a crucial step forward. It is only at this point, many anthropologists would feel, that the 'time' problem becomes interesting at all, i.e. when the possibility is raised that collective representations of time do not passively reflect time, but actually *create* time as a phenomenon apprehended by sentient human beings. This is an intrinsically exciting proposition for at least two reasons. First of all, it suggests a way of resolving the feelings of perplexity which the notion of time itself has always seemed to generate, ever since the days of St Augustine. The mystery of time will be dissolved, it is implied, once sociology has uncovered its origins in the familiar domain of communal life. Sociological understanding is presented as a path towards rational transcendence, providing the existential benefits of religious faith without the need for faith itself. And second, the thesis of the social origination of human temporal experience offers the prospect of a limitless variety of vicarious experiences of unfamiliar, exotic, temporal worlds, to be gained through the study of the myriad forms of society which have evolved and sustained their distinctive temporalities at different places and during different historical epochs. This is a dazzling, tempting vision.

It would be a most unimaginative reader who failed to respond to the powerful allure of Durkheim's doctrine of the social origin of 'time' as a category of the mind. He directly or indirectly inspired many notable ethnographic analyses of social time, only a tiny handful of which I shall be able to sample here. He also inspired further theoretical work on social time, (e.g. Halbwachs 1925) up to and including the present work, which, without Durkheim, would have no subject-matter. Even Durkheim's most formidable critics, such as Bloch (1977), work within the field of enquiry he defined, and reason according to the parameters of sociological interpretation which he initially laid down.

But, despite the fact that it would be hard to exaggerate the importance of *Elementary Forms of the Religious Life* as a contribution to the development of sociological theory in general, and the study of social time in particular, there is a fatal defect in Durkheim's argument, which needs to be brought to light. This arises from Durkheim's attempt to promote sociological analysis to the level of metaphysics, by identifying collective representations of time with Kantian 'categories'. In later chapters I shall demonstrate that this move opens the door to a variety of relativist interpretations of social time, which can be shown to be incoherent and misleading. But the first task is to unpick the details of Durkheim's argument.

Durkheim's thesis is that time exists for us because we are social beings. The pervasiveness of time, the mysterious way in which time seems to encompass everything without exception, so that it is not possible for us to think our way around it, reveals the social origins of time, because society is also like this, i.e. all-encompassing and not to be comprehended by the unaided individual. In approaching time in this way, Durkheim is applying to it his more general theory of the social determination of concepts. But with a difference. It is one thing to argue that 'society' is responsible for the formation of concepts such as 'dog' or 'cat' or 'uncle' or 'sacred' or 'profane', for these are particular objects and qualities, and we can imagine the world existing without them, i.e. being without uncles, dogs or cats, or entities designated as possessing sacred or profane qualities. But there is a class of very general concepts which are held by many philosophers to underlie all discursive thought, concepts such as time, space, number, cause, and so on, without which it is impossible to think of any world whatsoever existing. These concepts are promoted in Kantian parlance to the status of 'categories', and the essential question in philosophy is to determine whence the categories, the basic framework of all thinking and experiencing, originate.

Durkheim's purpose is to supply a novel answer to this enduring topic of philosophical speculation. He is therefore not seeking merely to clarify the empirical questions as to how, through collective representations, human beings have sought to codify time, but he is also raising the much more problematic issue of how it comes about that time exists to be codified.

Let me briefly sketch in some aspects of the philosophical background. Philosophers have advanced two kinds of solution to the problem of accounting for the origin of the categories. Ignoring a multitude of important but subtle variations in points of view, one group of philosophers have denied that there is anything about the categories which cannot be derived from experience. The world is real, it is out there, we are aware of it through our senses as it really is, and it really is temporal, spatial, pervaded by relations of cause and effect, and it is populated by objective beings which can be classified into 'natural' kinds through resemblance, contiguity in space and time, etc. This is the doctrine of realist empiricism, and in its extreme form it denies that the categories are in any way special or distinct from empirical concepts. Category concepts are very high-level generalizations from experience. They are based on inductions that have turned out true so invariably that they are accepted as absolutely true, but that might none the less turn out to be false. J. S. Mill, in the half-century leading up to the publication of Durkheim's works, maintained that the truths of logic were like this, i.e. generalizations of frequently successful lines of thought, not fundamentally different from empirical truths. The realist–empiricist approach in epistemology is historically allied with individualism and Utilitarianism in social matters. If the truths of logic could, in principle, be arrived at by a single ultra-methodical individual, by reflection on the repetitive character of experience, then so could such an individual singlehandedly determine appropriate criteria for judging actions to be right or wrong, or judging laws to be just or unjust. Actions and laws can be judged objectively by their contribution to the sum of human happiness, and the furtherance of order and progress in society. Moreover, such an individual could assume complete personal responsibility for the conduct of his social behaviour in relation to others, through *contracts* explicitly and accountably entered into with them.

All this is anathema to Durkheim, as it always has been to most continental philosophers. Since one of the major motivating factors behind Durkheim's sociology was hostility towards the social views of nineteenth-century Utilitarians, he was naturally disinclined to accept the empiricist epistemology which the Utilitarians simultaneously advocated. This is perhaps unfortunate, since Empiricism is a more permissive philosophy than Durkheim allows. The coupling of Empiricism and Utilitarianism versus Rationalism and anti-Utilitarianism was taken for granted in Durkheim's era, and it is not at all surprising that Durkheim, whose ambition was to formulate a non-Utilitarian basis for a just and morally united social order, propounded views on cognition which explicitly turned away from Empiricism in favour of a form of Rationalism. But first, I must say something about Rationalism in general.

Rationalism is opposed to Empiricism in maintaining that it is reason, not experience, that provides the guarantee of truth, and that the categories are not arrived at by induction from experience, but are basic thought-forms, which enable us to *have* experiences in the first place. The continental philosophers Descartes, Leibniz and Kant are prototype rationalists, just as the Anglo-Scottish philosophers Hume and Mill are prototype empiricists, the English Channel, as usual, playing the decisive role in the epidemiology of philosophical convictions (Sperber 1985). Durkheim's Rationalism is the outcome of tradition and pedagogy rather than argument and debate – which is only what a good Durkheimian might suppose. At the same time, his brand of Rationalism is, in truth, a highly revisionist one, in that he identifies reason, the guarantor of truth, with collective representations, grounded in transitory social and historical conditions. The impersonal 'reason' is really society, which obliges people to think their thoughts in common because their lives are lived in common. This view of the matter is diametrically opposed to orthodox Rationalism of the Cartesian variety, where the emphasis is placed on the private, apodeictic certainty of the lone *cogito*, set in opposition to everything else, including the body, the external world of appearances, other animate or sentient beings, etc., all of which are doubtful and possibly illusory.

Durkheim's Rationalism is not of the solitary variety, the kind that toys with the forbidden fruit of solipsism. His views are derived not from Descartes but from Kant, and his whole doctrine, both the secular religiosity of his social and ethical programme, and the rationalist tone of his cognitive theory resemble the equivalent portions of Kant's output quite closely, with the single outstanding difference that whereas, for Kant, reason is an aspect of nature, for Durkheim reason is an aspect of society.

The Kantian doctrines we need to consider are two in number (Kant 1929; Wilkerson 1976):

(1) *Transcendental idealism*: The world of sensory appearances, for which Kant's term is translated as 'representations' in English and French (cf. collective representations) belong to the order of phenomena. The phenomenal world is wholly distinct from the substrate of noumena, the ultimately real world of things-in-themselves. We cannot speculate about the noumenal order because our thought and experience are confined to the world of phenomena; but the final truth of the world and the definitive moral law are noumenal rather than phenomenal.

(2) *The dependence of intuitions (sense experiences) on concepts* (i.e. categories): 'Representations' cannot cohere except in conjunction with a 'transcendental aesthetic', i.e. certain ground-conditions, contributed by a faculty inherent in the perceiving subject, which bind together the raw materials of intuitions so that they manifest themselves as spatio-temporally confined external objects. The appearance of an external universe of objects arrayed in space and time is produced 'subjectively', not in the sense that the external universe is determined by the subject's private whim, but in the sense that only the 'faculty' present in the percipient, imposing the categorial prerequisites for phenomenal status (i.e. spatiality, temporality, number, etc.) on the noumenal order, can make possible the manifestation of the noumenal as the phenomenal.

Time and space are 'pure concepts of the understanding'. By this Kant means not only that they are contributed by the understanding to the process of representing the noumenal as the phenomenal, but also that they belong to the understanding alone, and that they are not derived from the world of appearances which they permit the understanding to represent to itself. One of Kant's most important points is that pure concepts of the understanding, and logical manipulations of these pure concepts (e.g. mathematics, metaphysics, logic) do not incorporate, and cannot by themselves be made to dispense, positive knowledge concerning the contingent nature of the noumenal truth of the world. ˜

We can now reconsider these points while sketching in Durkheim's 'sociological' reworking of Kantian rationalism.

(1) Durkheim is a rationalist in denying that the senses can provide the input needed to form a representation of the world, without the additional contribution of organizing ideas. To this extent he follows Kant. But though Durkheim is operating with a two-tier notion of 'reality', a preconceptual substrate overlaid by a postconceptual 'phenomenal reality', just as Kant is, the crucial gap between the two tiers is very differently positioned in each case. In Kant's theory, the categories (or pure concepts of the understanding) mediate the transition between the noumenal and the 'natural', whereas for Durkheim the categories mediate the transition between the natural and the social. Durkheim has nothing to say about the noumenal realm of things-in-themselves imagined by Kant; the equivalent place in his theory of cognition is played by a realm of natural appearances prior to all conceptual ordering, something akin, perhaps, to the 'blooming, buzzing, confusion' evoked by William James in his own not dissimilar account of the nature of cognitive processes (James 1963). For Kant, the primordial stratum is not only unseen, it is prior to all seeing; not only unrepresented, it is wholly unrepresentable. Quite different is the primordial stratum presupposed by Durkheim, which is manifest to the senses and to the mind, but which is featureless and chaotic, devoid of the familiar landmarks and guidelines which make reality intelligible to us.

Collective representations, in their categorial role, bring it about that 'nature' is placed 'inside society', as Durkheim puts it. By this he does not mean that the sun or the moon, or tables and chairs, are members of this or that society, but that the sun-that-I-know, the moon-that-I-know, etc. would not exist as the objects-of-knowledge they actually are in the minds of perceiving subjects were these subjects not capable of bringing to bear on them a series of conceptual schemes which are socially derived. Kant and Durkheim, therefore, share the view that the phenomenal world is structured by mind-contrived conceptual underpinnings. The 'real' world is created by our ideas; this is the essential point, and the one denied by Empiricism.

(2) Durkheim is quite explicit in identifying the primary reality-circumscribing concepts provided for in his theory with the Kantian categories, including time, the category we are primarily interested in. The substrate of pre-categorial nature is timeless, or at least devoid of time as we would recognize it. But Durkheim opposes his conception of the category time to Kant's (at least by implication; cf. the passage on space which immediately follows the passage on time, quoted above, p. 3). He says that the Kantian categories of space and time are 'homogeneous', but space and time as cognized by human beings via collective representations are far from featureless; if not time and space would remain uncognizable still.

Actually, Durkheim is wrong in saying that time and space as envisaged by Kant (as 'pure concepts of the understanding') are homogeneous. Kant, following Newton rather than Leibniz, regarded time and space as absolute rather than purely relational. There is every indication that Kant understood time to be absolutely directional with respect to before and after. The distinction between temporally anterior and temporally posterior events is a function of the asymmetry of time as a category, not a function of the properties of events themselves. Durkheim's unfounded claim that Kant believed categorial time to be 'homogeneous' rather than ordered with respect to before and after plays an important part in his argument, because it gives him added leverage in introducing 'social' time discriminations in the place of the overly featureless Kantian category. In fact, in Kantian category time, every possible event is ordered with respect to every other possible event, either as preceding it, accompanying it or following it. This is not to say that we automatically know, or may ever be able to find out, in what order any set of events occurred. But it is never an intrinsically impossible question to ask, which is Kant's point.

Durkheim meanwhile, having rejected the Kantian alternatives, enriches space and time, even in their most basic categorial forms, with a complex grid of distinctions, which can have no origin in the isolated psyche, in the faculty of cognition 'hidden deep within the human soul' invoked by his rationalist predecessor. The distinctions Durkheim has in mind must be traced to the social and organizational necessities of collective life.

However meritorious the influence of Durkheim's thoughts on 'social time' may have been in directing attention towards the role of collective action in shaping human temporal awareness (a theme that will presently be explored in considerable detail), it is impossible to proceed any further without remarking that Durkheim is being disingenuous at this point. His line of argument is:

1. The objective world cannot be experienced except via the categories.
2. Time is one such category.
3. Can we think of time except in terms of periods? (Answer: No)
4. Are conventional time periodizations socially derived? (Answer: Yes)
5. Therefore, we cannot have any experience of the objective world except in the light of socially derived periods of duration which constitute the category 'time'. (And ditto for space, cause and the other categories.)
6. Therefore, all experience of the objective world is socially derived.

Even if one admits, for debating purposes, steps 1 and 2 of the argument, not one of steps 3–6 either follows from steps 1 and 2 or is compelling on its own.

Against 3: There is no reason to say that we cannot think of temporal relationships other than in terms of periodizations. Suppose we go back to Kantian time, which is asymmetric with respect to before and after, but is otherwise featureless. If we then single out an event *e*, we can say, *a priori*, that event *e* occurs at T *e*. If time is asymmetric, we know that for any *e'*, any event that is not *e* itself, T *e'* is simultaneous with, or before, or after, T *e*. All events are semi-ordered (only 'semi-ordered' because events can be simultaneous with one another as well as before/after one another) with respect to all other events. This conclusion follows tautologously given the asymmetry built into the Kantian category time. Thus, far from not providing any means to conceptualize temporal relationships between events, the category of time envisaged by Kant has all the definition required to specify *all* the temporal relationships between *all* possible events, quite without reference to any concept of a regular periodic scheme whatsoever.

Against 4: Descending from these abstract considerations, we can note that the empirical case for 4 is not overwhelming. Most people would say that the common social periodicities (days, months and years) are derived from the behaviour of the sun and moon, which exercise a contingent effect on both social life and timekeeping. And even periodicities which do not have astronomical determinants, such as the market-week, are arranged as they are for reasons which are inescapably bound up with material considerations, storage and transport constraints, and the like. This is not to express disagreement with the proposition that social life dictates which periodicities are regarded as socially salient, but to claim that these periodicities are entirely socially derived is another matter. Thus, seasons may be conventionally indicated by means of religious feasts rather than by reference to natural phenomena, i.e. Christmastime, Lent, Easter, etc., but why are these feasts and fasts held in the particular seasons they are? Historically, the answers are straightforwardly ecological ones. At the very least, it has to be said that the sources of socially salient periodicities are not themselves pure inventions of the human mind, but adaptations to the physical ambience within which social life has to take place.

Against 5: The kernel of Durkheim's argument is reached in this step. Durkheim says, in effect, that the fact that it is impossible to think about temporal relationships in terms of any but socially derived periodizations means that when 'time' figures as one of the constitutive categories of all cognitive representations of the phenomenal world, as it does in Kant's Transcendental Aesthetic, it must do so in a pre-given 'social' guise. Kant's claim is that it is impossible to conceive of an external object, e.g. an elephant, except that it be an elephant in space and time. But it is not at all part of Kant's claim that to conceive of an elephant one has to conceive of it as positioned at *some specifiable point-location* in space and time. It just has to be an elephant which is not outside the bounds of space and time altogether. But it is just this stipulation that Durkheim introduces here to lend plausibility to his metaphysical argument. Having already posited the idea that in order to specify a temporal location, a periodization scheme must be made use of, and that periodization schemes are social in origin, he feels enabled to say that the temporal foundations of cognition are socially derived because temporal cognition of external objects consists in giving them point locations in time. And ditto for space, cause, number, etc.

But his reasoning is invalid. In the first instance, it is perfectly easy to demonstrate that the temporal location of an object, or more precisely the events in which an object participates, can be specified with or without reference to a periodic scheme, e.g. I can say that the battle of Borodino took place on 7 September 1811 (making use of the periodic scheme of the calendar), or alternatively that it occurred after Austerlitz and before Waterloo (i.e. somewhere in the non-periodic sequence of famous battles of the Napoleonic Wars). Secondly, even if it were true that temporal locations could only be specified in terms of periodizations, periodic schemes are often based on natural phenomena which contingently affect social life but are by no means socially determined, being dependent on the mechanical properties of the universe as an assemblage of matter. And finally, the specifiability of the temporal location of an object/ event has no bearing on the Kantian argument that there are no non-temporal, non-spatial objects or events.

I believe that there is no real connection at all between what Kant wishes to demonstrate in the *Critique of Pure Reason* and what Durkheim wishes to demonstrate in the passage from *Elementary Forms of the Religious Life*, cited at the beginning of this chapter. In effect, Durkheim is representing a programme of sociological inquiry, i.e. research into the multiplicity of social institutions and forms of ideas having to do with time, as if that would at once coincide with the results of metaphysical inquiry and also render metaphysics as a distinct activity unnecessary. Neither of these promises can be made good. Sociology is being oversold as a substitute (if that were needed) for the intellectual activity of philosophy. Sociology (and its sister subject, social anthropology) has been much harmed by Durkheim's plausible mimicry of the forms of philosophical argument. Sociology became unduly aggrandized as an independent source of philosophical truth, and at the same time threatened to displace the only intellectual discipline capable of exercising some restraint over the resultant flow of paradoxical and confusing utterances, i.e. philosophy itself.

Metaphysical and sociological arguments, though capable of being articulated one to another, belong to separate domains. Sociologists can, of course, say things from a sociological standpoint, about philosophers and what they do, including offering sociological explanations for the popularity of certain views among philosophers working in the context of particular social/ historical settings. Conversely, philosophers can pronounce on the validity of the reasoning advanced by sociologists. But this is not at all the same as saying that sociological analysis uncovers the kinds of truths that philosophers are interested in, or vice versa.

By claiming that sociological analysis constituted an independent route towards the strictly metaphysical goals of rationalist philosophizing, Durkheim opens a door through which all manner of demons are able to crowd in. We shall meet one or two of these demons later. But although it is essential to highlight Durkheim's malign influence as the encourager of a certain type of quasi-metaphysical sociological speculation, it is equally essential to recognize the imaginative stimulus his work gave to perfectly valid lines of sociological and anthropological inquiry. Among Durkheim's more notable anthropological successors were Evans-Prichard, Lévi-Strauss and Leach. None of these authors is wholly immune to criticism on the score of making excessive metaphysical claims for the Durkheimian approach to time, but equally, none of them could have arrived at his perfectly valid insights without Durkheim's example.

# Chapter 2

## Evans-Pritchard

In his early account of *Nuer Time Reckoning* (1939: 209), Evans-Pritchard commits himself to the following statement: 'Perceptions of time, in our opinion, are functions of time reckoning, and are hence socially determined.' This exemplifies perfectly the besetting post-Durkheimian urge to make unnecessarily sweeping metaphysical claims. But the author may have had second thoughts, because the sentence does not recur in the reworking of the material in the 'Time Reckoning' article which was later incorporated into *The Nuer* (1940). Here, Evans-Pritchard makes a sensible distinction between what he calls 'œcological time' and 'structural time'. (Œcological time is the set of time concepts derived from the Nuer environment and the adaptation the Nuer have made to it. Structural time is time geared to the organizational forms of Nuer social structure, defined by Evans-Pritchard as institutionalized relationships between political groups.)

Both of these kinds of time concepts can be described as 'social'. Œcological time is social in that Nuer society, like almost any other, is largely organized around the fulfilment of productive tasks, and can be seen, in many of its aspects at least, as an adaptation to an ecological niche maintained by socially co-ordinated collective action. Structural time is even more obviously social, in that it is geared to the genealogical charters for lineage, clan and tribal political affiliations; but it also has a 'natural' component in that the idiom of genealogy is the symbolic form imposed by the Nuer on the demographic reproduction of successive generations, and hence of Nuer society as a natural entity.

The treatment given to temporal ideas in *The Nuer* has rightly been held up as a brilliant and exemplary demonstration of the linkages between social factors and temporality. In so lucidly identifying the resonances between temporal and social forms, Evans-Pritchard can be said to have singlehandedly justified Durkheim's programmatic statements about social time. But famous as it is, I am not sure that certain peculiarities in Evans-Pritchard's exposition have been sufficiently noticed, thereby obscuring to some degree the highly original approach the author adopts.

*The Nuer* opens with a lengthy account of Nuer ecology and production at the level of the isolated productive unit (the household, cattle-camp, etc.), while the second part of the book deals with the large-scale organization of Nuer society (the lineage system, the political system and the age organization). This design has caused confusion ever since the book appeared, so that undergraduates are often advised to skip the 'Œcology' part altogether, or read it after reading part II, on the grounds that, given his Durkheimian views, Evans-Pritchard cannot possibly have intended to give to ecological factors the kind of prominence or causal priority the layout of the book seems to suggest. But this advice is based on a misinterpretation of the actual role Evans-Pritchard attributed to ecological factors. The natural propensity of cultural ecologists is to assume that the outermost constraints on the structure of social systems are set by ecological variables in conjunction with the technological factors. Within these encompassing constraints, institutional forms, such as lineages, clans and households, are regarded as subordinate. Evans-Pritchard has this all the other way about; treating ecological constraints in terms of the smallest units of Nuer society and their cycles of activity, units which are encompassed by the framework of political units of differing genealogical definition and territorial scope, and causally subservient to them.

We can look at the way in which this argument sequence emerges in Evans-Pritchard's treatment of Nuer time concepts. The opposition between the ecological and the social can also be viewed as an opposition between the microcosm and the macrocosm. At the microcosmic level, Nuer society is an ecology, whereas at the macrocosmic level Nuer society is an arrangement of political units related to one another in idealized genealogical space–time. And turning to Nuer modes of 'time-reckoning' as such, we can see that these can also be opposed as microcosmic/ecological and macrocosmic/structural.

The author documents the dependence of Nuer time-reckoning at the microcosmic (domestic) level on the daily cycle of the 'cattle clock' and the annual cycle of seasonal activities. His account confirms the idea that, for pre-technological people, the passage of time and the carrying out of a regular sequence of productive tasks and social activities cannot be dissociated from one another. Time is concrete, immanent and process-linked, rather than being abstract, homogeneous and transcendent.

But when we turn to macrocosmic time (and by macrocosmic time I mean durations longer than a single ecological cycle), the picture alters somewhat. The social processes by which macrocosmic time is calibrated are themselves abstract rather than concrete.

Time of long duration in pre-literate societies is most frequently associated with the concept of generations, reigns of kings, successions to various offices in kinship or territorial units, i.e. with processes whose cycles are roughly coterminous with the human lifespan, or with stages in the developmental cycle of the domestic unit or units of wider scope, attendant on reaching a certain stage within the lifecycle. Although these developmental and generational cycles are associated in various ways with biological events, they are by no means biological phenomena in themselves, in the obvious way that 'generations' of crops are sown and harvested in a regular seasonal cycle, or the annual 'crop' of offspring of domesticated animals which have a definite breeding season and a relatively short lifespan.

It has been pointed out that the much utilized concept of a human generation is essentially a 'fiction' (Needham 1974). None the less, many societies distribute social roles according to generational criteria, and in forming collective representations of the time-depth of a socially constructed universe, rely heavily on generational successions as the primary calibrating device. Many societies (e.g. the Tallensi; Fortes 1945) practise adelphic succession, requiring that offices be inherited by each surviving member of a set of real or classificatory brothers in turn before being passed on to any of their sons, with the result that the latest born among the senior generation and the first born among the junior generation are likely to pass their entire lives without achieving office.

More notable still are the societies that maintain official age/ generation set systems, of which the best known are those of east Africa, including the Nuer. I would say more about these systems, which are clearly salient in the context of the present work, were there not already in existence a number of articles and monographs which make this task superfluous, notably the elegant and comprehensive comparative analysis by Stewart (1977), and detailed ethnographic accounts of individual systems by Spencer (1965) and Hallpike (1972), to name only a selection. The point to note is simply that demographic logic demands that if one assigns all the individuals forming an age cohort the arbitrary generational index of 0 in year 1, by the time there are children's children's children of these individuals around, the chronological age-range of the intervening generations will be approaching a distribution which mirrors the age distribution of the population as a whole, and after a few more 'generations' actually will be so distributed. Many generation set systems operate on the assumption that there are living members of only three or four generations in existence at once: if these generation sets were not adjusted in some way there would be no relation at all between chronological age and 'generational' status. As it is, generation sets often embrace individuals of widely differing age, but usually there exist additional devices to ensure that entirely random age distributions in 'generations' do not persist. (The reader is referred to the works cited for further elucidation of these mechanisms.)

I mention these systems only in order to reinforce the point that Nuer macrocosmic time concepts, in being linked to generations, i.e. to the age organization and to the branching nodes in genealogical charters, are linked to processes which are 'abstract' in the sense of having no real-world counterpart, although they are articulated to real-world events (births and deaths).

Evans-Pritchard shows how the hierarchy of agnatic units, represented in the form of a genealogical charter, determines the structural distance between any two Nuer, which is proportional to the number of ascending and descending nodes separating them in the agnatic genealogy. But besides specifying agnatic relatedness, the genealogy also has spatio-temporal implications. Temporal implications arise from the fact that nodes occur at generational intervals, and spatial implications from the fact that each agnatic unit at each level of segmentation is associated with a territorial division. In fact, the celebrated diagram, which Evans-Pritchard later used to illustrate the principle of segmentary opposition, could be read as an ultra-schematic map of Nuerland (Figure 2.1a), and it can equally well be used to represent the branching of a genealogical tree (Figure 2.1b), which is at the same time a representation of the temporal passage of the generations. Using these elements one can construct a composite diagram which expresses the coincidence of genealogy, territoriality and temporality, as conceptualized by the Nuer and described by Evans-Pritchard (Figure 2.1c)

Thus, if ego (in Figure 2.1) encounters a fellow Nuer who belongs to a distantly related tribal section, which is associated with a spatially distant part of Nuerland, then the encounter takes place through a maximum 'thickness' of space and time in the structural sense, with corresponding modifications in the institutional and moral aspects of the relationships, even though these two Nuer are only three feet apart and are strictly contemporaries. 'Structural time' appertains to ideas and their consequences, not to physical facts and their consequences.

The actual social arrangements in space and time in which Nuer participate can run counter to the ideal scheme I have depicted, but Evans-Pritchard maintains, to the puzzlement of some (Schneider 1963) and the enlightenment of others, that it is the very abstractness and idealization of the Nuer scheme of genealogical/spatial/temporal co-ordination that makes possible the laxity found in their real-world practice.

In a fascinating passage, he contrasts the stabilized, eternalized space-time framework of Nuer social categories with the time that pervades the microcosmic world, the time that actually passes, in which events are pushed back into the past rather than remaining suspended forever at a certain node in an unchanging hierarchical structure.

> We have remarked that the movement of structural time is, in a sense, an illusion, for the structure remains fairly constant and the perception of time is no more than the movement of persons, often as groups, through the structure. Thus age-sets succeed one another for ever, but there are never more than six sets in existence and the relative positions occupied by these six sets are fixed structural points through which actual sets of persons pass in endless succession. Similarly . . . the Nuer system of lineages may be considered as a fixed system, there being a constant number of steps between living persons and the founder of their clan and the lineages having a constant relation to one another. However many generations succeed one another the depth and range of lineages does not increase . . .
> If we are right in supposing that the lineage structure never grows,

**Figure 2.1   Space, genealogy and time**

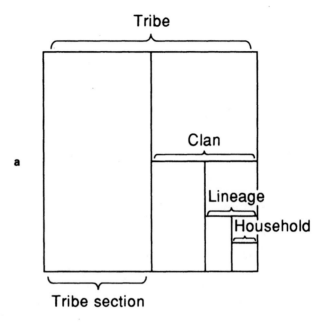

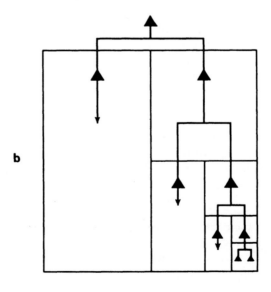

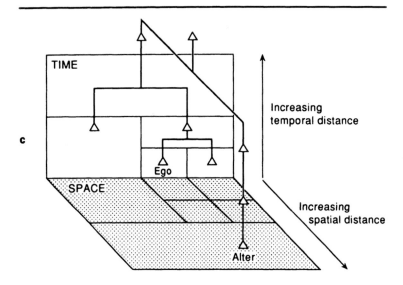

it follows that the distance between the beginning of the world and the present day remains unalterable. Time is not thus a continuum but a constant structural relation between two points, the first and last persons in a line of agnatic descent. Evans-Pritchard 1940: 107, 108)

In this way, just as the ecological order is encapsulated in the social order within the overall design of Evans-Pritchard's argument, so microcosmic/ecological time, which passes, is encapsulated within structural time, which does not. But does this idea, however appealing, really stand up to critical scrutiny? First of all, we can note that there is nothing illogical or metaphysically aberrant about the well-known phenomenon of 'telescoping' genealogies, i.e. silently revising the content of accepted beliefs about the identities of ancestors, so that the line of descent from the founding ancestor to presently living individuals does not exceed a certain number of generations, generally around 8–10. The Nuer's genealogical beliefs may be false, but they are not held in defiance of compelling evidence to the contrary, and moreover they are false beliefs which have innumerable true consequences in the form of actual social observances which are predictable in the light of the current genealogical consensus. The Nuer do not have to have any particular ideas at all about the nature of time in order to persist in a genealogical consensus which, *de facto* but not *de jure*, alters with the passage of time in incorporating a set of newcomer-ancestors at lower nodes in the

structure and discarding a proportion of no longer socially relevant ancestors located at nodes in the middle reaches of the
structure. 'Motionless structural time' is, from this point of
view, Evans-Pritchard's idea, not a Nuer idea. But none the less
I think that Evans-Pritchard's account is illuminating in that it
suggests that the Nuer, at least when they are thinking about
temporal relationships in the genealogical idiom, operate with
temporal concepts which are entirely non-metrical in character.
In other words, he may be correct in saying that so far as the
Nuer are concerned, the temporal relationship between founding ancestors and present-day people does not alter as one
generation succeeds another in the here-and-now. We have
copious ethnographic testimony to the effect that various cultures do not consider that the temporal relationship of the present to the mythic/ancestral past is one that is affected by the
passage of time: perhaps the best-known instance of this being
the Australian Aborigines' beliefs about dream-time vs. the present. But it is misleading to imagine that the evidence which
exists on this score proves anything about non-standard concepts of duration. We have only to look at traditional Christian
beliefs. The religious significance of the events recorded in the
New Testament remain utterly unaffected with the passage of
time, even though these events are attributed to a datable period
in the history of the world, which grows more distant with
every passing year. It is wholly beside the point to introduce the
issue of the increasing durational interval between the epoch of
the founding ancestors, or the New Testament epoch, and the
present day, when the symbolic salience of the events attributed
to these epochs depends precisely on the fact that they are
unaffected by the intervening lapse of time. I suggest that it
would be more precise to say that what the Nuer, or the Aborigines, or the Christians believe is that there are relationships
between events or epochs which are temporal to the extent that
epoch A precedes epoch B in time, but that the relationship
between the events of epochs A and B is unaffected by the
durational interval A/B. There is priority, there is order, but
there is no measure. In order to hold beliefs in this form there is
no reason to assume heterodoxy in temporal belief-systems,
logic, 'perception', etc.

# Chapter 3

## Lévi-Strauss

The theme introduced in the preceding chapter, of a structural or mythic time, which, by contrast to run-of-the-mill or 'œcologicical' time does not pass or change, reappears in many guises in the work of Lévi-Strauss (1963, 1966, 1969). He uses a rather similar distinction to contrast, not only the kinds of time found coexisting in a single society, but to oppose whole classes of societies.

Societies which share our conception of historical time as an enormous file into which historical events are entered, never to be expunged, are called 'hot' societies, i.e. societies which have internalized their own historicity. 'Cold' societies are those whose fundamental cognitive schemes are static and unreceptive to change; societies which externalize their historicity as an influence foreign to their continued well-being. Cold societies have as their ideal the perpetuation of a closed system impervious to external influence and not dependent on external sources of power. Lévi-Strauss (1948, 1969) compares hot societies to open systems like pumps, whereas cold societies are compared to closed systems like clocks (ignoring the fact that clocks, even so, have to be wound up). When cold societies are overtaken by history, as they all must be eventually, they try to make it seem as if this historically contingent transformation was one foreseen from the beginning of time, and had, in essence if not in actuality, always been the case.

It would require an extensive analysis, which I do not propose to undertake here, to trace the many ramifications of this theme throughout Lévi-Strauss's works. Meanwhile, it is true to say that, on the whole, this author discusses time – most frequently making use of the Saussurean distinction between 'diachrony' and 'synchrony' – not directly as an anthropological topic, but as a by-product of model-building exercises arising from the analysis of data which do not, on the surface, have to do with time at all, i.e. kinship systems, rituals, myths, etc. Lévi-Strauss is not concerned with either 'real' time or indigenous time concepts, but with time in abstract anthropological models. Indeed, it emerges clearly from the intellectual autobiography incorporated into *Tristes tropiques* (1961) that the original stimulus which led him to develop his structuralist position in the 1940s was his negative reaction to the time-and-history obsessed philosophy of his French contemporaries – Sartre in particular – who were in turn influenced by Husserl's analysis of 'internal time-consciousness', which will be examined later (Chapters 23 and 26, below).

Lévi-Strauss is essentially an anti-time man. His interest in the sociology of time is focused primarily, and perhaps with a degree of envious nostalgia, on the ways in which societies can annul time and its effects. Faithful to the traditions of Durkheimian social theory, his ideal is for order achieved without authoritarianism, and the image of 'cold' societies which so regulate their affairs that historically contingent events do not make 'a difference which makes a difference', thereby removing at a stroke the basis and motivation for power politics, has undeniable attractions. But Lévi-Strauss's successors have certainly not been slow in pointing out that the temporal anaesthesia he describes cannot be realized without mystification or logical sleight-of-hand.

Even a friendly critic, such as John Barnes (1971), notes that Lévi-Strauss's account of the well-ordered time of 'synchronous models' is ambiguous between being genuinely immobile and merely cyclical (i.e. periodic). He has in mind the very familiar type of synchronic model of cycles of affinal alliance, which Lévi-Strauss certainly did not invent, but which he did much to popularize, such that group A gives women to group B, who give women to group C, who (in the simplest case) give women to group A, thus closing the cycle. A similar pattern is repeated in the next generation, and so on indefinitely. The question Barnes raises is, in what sense should such a model be considered 'synchronic'? After all, time is represented here, because it is not an extraneous fact about such cyclical exchange-models that they represent a series of repetitions of the same exchanges, occurring over the lapse of time (generations). Indeed, this constitutes their very essence. As I shall demonstrate in slightly more detail in Chapter 4, the idea of periodic 'repetition' unavoidably implies the idea of linear temporal extension. What 'synchronic structural models' of the Lévi-Strauss type display is not immobile 'synchronic time, present contemporaneously in all its parts, but the diachronic recurrence of structurally identical but numerically and chronologically distinct exchange-events, i.e. diachronic non-change.

The 'synchronous' time of which Lévi-Strauss speaks is in fact quite conventionally linear and irreversible, and hence in no way distinct from 'diachronic' time. The contrast between synchrony and diachrony in Lévi-Strauss's writings has less to do with distinct types of 'time' than with the contrast between models and reality, structure and events, essence and accident. All these can be perfectly intelligibly discussed without invoking the concepts of synchrony and diachrony at all, still less any need for the revision of any orthodox temporal metaphysics. A 'mechanical model' shows the 'history' of the unfolding of a certain sequence of events (e.g. the formation of alliances between groups) as it is predicated by the overt or covert institutional arrangements of a given society. The result may be orderly or disorderly. If it is orderly, then a 'mechanical model' can express this fact; if not, then a 'statistical model' may reveal orderliness at a probabilistic level (e.g. the regularities in the statistical pattern of alliance demonstrated by Héritier (1981) among the Biami, or Kelly (1977) among the Etoro). In either case, time is not abolished, nor is the result any less 'diachronic' for not incorporating the actual historical (recorded or potentially recordable) data concerning the relevant transactions as they occur in real time.

Time is as inescapable in models as it is in real life; what is different about models is only the attenuated version of reality they supply, reduced to its logical, relational core. Models can be manipulated in ways that reality cannot, but a manipulated model which diverges from the real-world facts from which the model is ultimately derived corresponds to a set of counterfactual propositions, not intended to be true as they stand, but only to be of use for purposes of hypothetico-deductive reasoning. Because models provide an abstract, manipulable version of reality, it does not mean that the canons of temporal logic applicable to events represented in models are different from the ones applicable to the events represented in the model as they occur in real or historical time. In particular, time does not become 'motionless' in the model-context in any sense in which it can be regarded as not 'motionless' in other contexts.

What seems to be meant by calling time 'motionless' – and this applies to the motionless 'structural time' of the Nuer as well as to Lévi-Strauss's synchronic time – is the imperviousness of some process or institutional form to systemic change. A cyclic mechanical model of a process envisages a finite set of identifiable event types which are not added to, or subtracted from, as the result of the postulated occurrence of an event or subset of events envisaged in the model. In linear time, a cyclical event-sequence is repetitious and non-branching. But this characteristic is not 'timelessness'; all that is involved is a strict restriction on the order and identity of the event types falling within the scope of the model.

However damaging the outcome of any serious attempt to subject Lévi-Strauss's opposition between synchrony and diachrony to logical scrutiny, I would be doing less than justice to the most inspiring of modern anthropologists if I let matters rest here. It is necessary to convey also some idea of the way in which the opposition I have just described is actually exploited analytically in Lévi-Strauss's writings, which I can best do by summarizing part of one of his texts. An instructive example is provided by his discussion of the 'never ending struggle' between synchrony and diachrony manifested among the Australian Aborigines, which is to be found in the second half of the chapter 'Time regained' in *The Savage Mind* (1966).

The 'struggle' arises from the nature of the 'totemic thought', which is the subject of that book, which shows itself as a propensity to classify out the natural and social environment by means of a series of 'totemic operators', a combinatorial grid of distinction-marking oppositions whose root metaphor is 'the species'. This classificatory propensity in itself has nothing to do with time, but it has two outgrowths which do: (1) a system of origin myths which relate the present, tangible world to an ancestral creative epoch in the past; and (2) a ritual system which brings the present world into line with the mythic past by periodically re-enacting it in the here-and-now.

Among the Australian Aborigines this mutual interaction of the 'noumenal' ancestral creator-beings and their living 'phenomenal' counterparts, who ritually recapitulate the creative epoch, is particularly marked. Lévi-Strauss quotes a long passage from Strehlow (1947) to the effect that all the daily activities of Aborigines living in the traditional way are both re-

enactments of the long-past prototypical activities of the ancestors in the dream-time (the noumenal, mythic period) and at the
same time are contemporaneous with these same ancestral
doings, in that the ancestors are considered *still* to be engaging,
invisibly, in these activities at all the relevant sacred sites specified in the myths. The totemic past and the real world coalesce,
but are also distinct from one another, in that the phenomenal
order of things, the non-dream-time life, is only a pale shadow
of the 'real' world of the dream-time ancestral beings.

> Mythic history thus presents the paradox of being both disjoined
> from and conjoined to the present. It is disjoined from it because the
> original ancestors were of a nature different from contemporary men:
> they were creators and these are imitators. It is conjoined with it
> because nothing has been going on since the appearance of the
> ancestors, except events whose recurrence periodically effaces their
> particularity. . . . the savage mind succeeds in overcoming this two-
> fold contradiction [by means of] a coherent system in which dia-
> chrony, in some sort mastered, collaborates with synchrony. (Lévi-
> Strauss 1966: 236).

According to Lévi-Strauss this contradiction is overcome by
three kinds of ritual performances: (1) *Historical rites*, which recreate
the past so that it becomes present (Past → Present); (2) *Death
rituals*, which recreate the present so that it is integral with the past
(Present → Past); (3) *Rites of control*, which adjust the periodic
increase/decrease of totemic species in the here-and-now to the
fixed scheme of relationships between men and totemic species
established in the mythic past (Present = Past). Hence, as Lévi-
Strauss concludes elsewhere, 'ritual is a machine for the destruc-
tion of time', though we are entitled to object that this is hyperbole,
since it is not time that is destroyed, but its effects.

Lévi-Strauss recognizes that the reconciliation of the 'timeless'
order of things as they are *sub specie aeternitatis*, and the messy
here-and-now order of things, is only something that is to be
aimed at, not something that can be fully achieved by ritual
means. Concluding his analysis he points to the important role
of the *chirunga*, the totemic objects of stone or carved wood
which, when produced from their hiding-places at the sacred
sites, provide physical proof of the interpenetration of the
mythic and mundane time-frames during the rituals held there.
These objects are held to be actually coeval with the ancestral
beings, palpable traces of their presence on earth at one time.

Lévi-Strauss compares them to our historical archives, whose contents are mainly published, and consist of documents whose historic significance would survive into the present even if the documents themselves did not, but which we none the less jealously preserve simply because these *are* the original documents and as such are irreplaceable.

Why are we interested in preserving the original of the Magna Carta, scrawled notes from Elizabeth to Essex, the actual yellow chair Van Gogh is supposed to have painted? Lévi-Strauss says that this is our only way of coming into contact 'synchronously' with *our* ancestors, whom we otherwise know from history books, but whom we find it hard to think of as being one flesh with ourselves without such physical symbols. This is undoubtedly true. But it needs to be said also that the sensation of copresence with the past, which we gain from the contemplation of historic relics, is an illusion. The original of·the Magna Carta, which is available for inspection at Canterbury, is not a fragment of the world of 1215 which has somehow become displaced in time and has strayed into the twentieth century. The Magna Carta is an object, present in the world of today, which has an authenticated history including events which took place in 1215. But those events and the Magna Carta of 1215 which participated in them are gone for good, and the availability of the self-same piece of parchment, present today, called the 'Magna Carta', will not bring them back, because any events which *that* piece of parchment participates in will be events of today, not events of 1215. In other words, it is a category-mistake to attribute dates to objects at all; because only events have dates. What objects have is *histories*, including many dated events, and we think that objects have dates only because we often identify objects by associating them with the events surrounding their creation, events which, in the case of the Magna Carta, took place in 1215.

One has to admit that the illusion of time-travel engendered by the contemplation of ancient objects is a strong one, stronger perhaps than mere logic. But nothing will enable the Magna Carta, once it has lasted up to today, ever to get *back* to 1215, and the *chirunga*-illusion is just this, i.e. that by handling the ancient stones and engraved boards, made smooth by prolonged use, the ritual operators are physically transported into a different temporal realm contemporaneous with the making of the *chirunga* and populated by their makers, just as we feel so transported when we enter an ancient and well-preserved cathedral.

However compelling the illusion, an illusion it remains. I have no quarrel with Lévi-Strauss's analysis of the manipulation of time, which lies at the heart of so many of the ritual performances described by ethnographers. It is only necessary to draw back at the point where the attempt to interpret symbolic action degenerates into a rash attempt to rewrite the laws of logic or physics so as to make ritual claims come out 'true' in some absolute sense. But if these laws were not as they are, if time and history were not as destructive of all the orderly schemes we cling to as they manifestly are, there would be no *sense* in holding rituals anyway. This point, I think, is one that Lévi-Strauss never loses sight of, so that he never claims that the 'timeless' order evoked by Australian Aborigine myth and ritual is a culturally constituted sub-universe on its own, with its own distinct and culturally relative temporality. He is, in other words, not a cultural relativist, but one who, as he says, 'observes from afar', a standpoint incompatible with cultural relativism.

Indeed, in terms of current theory, Lévi-Strauss's main weakness is precisely this Olympian detachment, and in particular his unwillingness to consider 'history' on a par with 'structure'. Sahlins (1985) has argued the case for seeing the 'contingent', even unique, historical events which Lévi-Strauss consigns to diachrony, as just as much the product of 'synchronic' cultural schemes as predictable, periodic events such as repetitions of alliances or the performance of increase rituals. Lévi-Strauss's unsatisfactory attitude towards history, and the now much-criticized dichotomization between 'hot' and 'cold' societies which underlies it, stem from his confusions concerning synchrony and diachrony, mentioned earlier. It is because Lévi-Strauss was under the illusion that 'the time of models' (synchronic time) was somehow essentially different from the 'chronological' time in which the events of history transpire that he assumed his characteristically blinkered attitude towards the applicability of the cultural/structural approach to the study of the contingencies of history. After Sahlins, it is only too apparent that in so doing he unduly and gratuitously restricted the scope of anthropological enquiry. Now, liberated from the Procrustean bed of synchrony vs. diachrony, much that originally belonged to Lévi-Straussian structuralism lives on, not as the special-purpose theory of 'cold' societies, but as a component of a far more general 'anthropological history' applicable to all societies.

# Chapter 4

## Leach

In 1961, Leach republished two short essays, which have since exercised a considerable influence on the treatment of time in social anthropology. Taking his cue from Durkheim and Van Gennep, Leach begins by suggesting that the English word 'time' embraces many meanings, not all of which would be thought to have anything to do with one another by speakers of other languages. He argues that this heterogeneity can be traced to the fact that there are two logically quite distinct 'basic experiences' of time. There are (1) that certain natural phenomena repeat themselves; and (2) that for the individual organism life-changes are irreversible and death inevitable. He goes on to say that the invariable strategy of religious thought is to try to convince us that the kind of 'time' we live in is along the lines suggested by (1) rather than by (2). We are immortal because time repeats itself:

> One of the commonest devices . . . is to assert that death and birth are the same thing, that birth follows death just as death follows birth. This seems to amount to denying the second aspect of time by equating it with the first.
>
> I would go further. It seems to me that if it were not for religion we should not attempt to embrace the two aspects of time under one category at all. Repetitive and non-repetitive events are not, after all, logically the same. We treat them both as aspects of 'one thing', *time*, not because it is rational to do so, but because of religious prejudice. The idea of Time, like the idea of God, is one of those categories we find necessary because we are social animals rather than because of anything empirical in our objective experience of the world'. (Leach 1961: 125)

Even making adjustments for Leach's customarily assertive style, we are being asked to accept some very sweeping and paradoxical-seeming statements more or less on trust. Could it really be that there is nothing the least 'empirical' about the experience of time, and that it is only lingering religious preju-dice which persuades us, or other people, to the contrary? And what is the apparently self-evident 'logical difference' between repeating and non-repeating events?

Without pausing to offer any further reasons for accepting these particularly strong initial assumptions, Leach proceeds to make his major claim. Primitive peoples, up to and including the ancient Greeks, think of time as a simple, discontinuous oscillation between 'opposites'. The 'time process', he says, is experienced as 'a repetition of repeated reversals, a sequence of oscillations between polar opposites: night and day, winter and summer, drought and flood, age and youth, life and death. In such a scheme the past has no "depth" to it, all past is equally past, it is simply the opposite of now' (ibid.: 126).

This flattened time is not even cyclical, it is simply alternating. The flow of time is like the flow of current in an AC electrical circuit. Leach is at some pains to emphasize the non-cyclical nature of alternating time, insisting that time 'as an aspect of motion in a circle' is a geometrical metaphor foreign to the thought of 'unsophisticated communities', where images of a more homely nature are selected in order to capture time's fleeting passage; eating and vomiting, the giving and receiving of brides in marriage, or the alternating sequence of agricultural tasks.

Leach develops his conception in terms of two examples. In the first of his essays, 'Cronus and Chronos', he examines the mythological details surrounding Cronus, the father (and vic-tim) of Zeus, whom Aristotle maintained to be a representation of Chronos, 'eternal time'. There is no real etymological rela-tionship between the name 'Cronus' and the word for time 'Chronos', so the whole exercise may rest on the rather shaky foundation of an academician's pun, long post-dating the time at which the Greeks could have been called 'unsophisticated' in their cosmological beliefs. Nevertheless, Leach has no difficulty in demonstrating a striking sequence of reversals in the Cronos myth: Cronos is born of the separation Sky and Earth; he begets children on his sister Rhea, but swallows them (except Zeus). Later, he vomits up his swallowed children, who become the gods Hades, Hestia, Poseidon, Hera, Demeter, etc. Eventually, Zeus overthrows his father and castrates him. Leach's analysis of the myth carries a good deal of conviction, in so far as it

shows the prevalence of 'reversal' motifs in Greek cosmogony.
However, the same might be said of many more Greek myths
than this one, and the part of Leach's argument which links the
Cronos myth specifically to the expression of a distinctive notion
of temporality is far less convincingly demonstrated.

The analysis of the Chronus myth paves the way for the
second of the two essays, in which he exemplifies 'alternating
time' in the context of ritual rather than myth (ibid.: 132–6). In
this essay, entitled 'Time and False Noses', Leach proposes a
model of the 'general flow of time' in primitive society, based on
a combination of the idea of repetitious time already introduced,
and the well-known three-stage model of 'rites of passage' devised by Van Gennep. He suggests that there is a basic distinction between secular or 'profane' time, when time goes
forwards, and 'sacred' time, the time of world-restoring rituals,
when time goes backwards, in order to return us to square one.
Sacred time has a structure which derives from Van Gennep's
model of initiation rituals, themselves most frequently regarded
as rituals of 'rebirth'. The three phases of sacred time commence
with sacralization, which is the 'death' of the profane individual
and his removal to a higher moral plane. Then follows an
anomalous phase of 'marginality' ('ordinary social time has
stopped'; ibid.: 134), which comes to an end with the 'rebirth' of
the individual into the profane world. Leach notes that in ritual
it is common to mark each of these three stages with unusual
behaviour. The three he isolates are (1) formality, i.e. slow,
measured behaviour, strong stress on differential social status,
etiquette, etc.; (2) masquerade, i.e. fancy dress, disguised
identity, breaking rules of normal social etiquette; and (3) role-
reversal, which is in a sense the union of (1) and (2), in that
everybody has to behave in a way which is the opposite of
normal, e.g. committing obligatory sacrilege, *lèse-majesté*, trans-
vestism, etc. Leach argues that formality goes with the
'sacralization' phase of sacred time, masquerade with 'desacra-
lization', and role-reversal with the anomalous period in between the two when time is going backwards. This explains the
back-to-front role-behaviour: 'sacred time is played in reverse,
death is converted into birth' (ibid.: 136).

This is a brilliant idea, for which ethnographic documentation
can easily be produced, although it cannot be said that Leach
does this himself. I shall shortly discuss one relevant example,
which is provided by the Umeda 'Ida' ritual (Gell 1975),

although, as will become clear, I no longer believe, as I did at one time, that such 'ritual inversions' are really evidence of the presence of notions of backwards-running time in anybody's mind except the anthropologist's. But before turning to this material it is convenient to deal with the objections which have been made against Leach's 'alternating time' by an anthropologist who shares his allegiance to a generally Durkheimian viewpoint.

The anthropologist in question is Robert Barnes (not to be confused with John Barnes, Lévi-Strauss's critic, mentioned previously). Barnes (1974), in the course of a discussion of collective representations of time among the Kédang of eastern Indonesia, takes particular exception to Leach's claim that 'cyclical' time is a modern notion, and that primitive time is alternating. Barnes says that the geometric image of a circle is not an essential property or diagnostic feature of 'cyclical' notions of time. Speaking of the annual cycle, he remarks that all that is necessary is that the phases of a process should be both distinguished from one another, and identified with the equivalent phases of the same process in previous and subsequent cycles. 'Time, as it is represented in Kédang', he states, 'is oriented, irreversible, and repetitive' (ibid.: 198). He bears out his criticisms of Leach's view that primitive time is alternating rather than cyclical by showing how the Kédang are at great pains to ensure that the life–death cycle does *not* reverse itself. The great concern of the Kédang is to ensure that the dead do *not* return, and much ritual activity is directed towards ensuring that the dead stay safely dead. In other words, though it may be true that in ritual contexts some societies may represent processes occurring in reverse direction (e.g. the Umedas, described in Chapter 5) this is a quite separate issue from the far more general propensity we have for recognizing an element of repetitiveness in the natural and social events which go on around us. Forming collective representations of these observable regularities is not an activity confined to primitive societies or ritual contexts. Barnes is surely correct in arguing that the typical form taken by collective representations of 'time' in pre-technological societies is not zig-zag alternation but cyclical in his non-geometric sense (i.e. periodic). He says that the Kédang have a 'holistic' (cyclical) view of time; that they see time synoptically, all at once, not as an endless stream which loses itself in a limitless past and future lying beyond their ken. Thus he agrees with Leach in maintaining the general Durkheimian thesis of the social determination of collective representations of time, but he disagrees with Leach as to the formal properties of 'primitive' conceptions of time. For Barnes, the defining feature of primitive temporality is non-cumulative repetitiveness, rather than to-and-fro alternation.

In fact, the alternating time which Leach is at pains to contrast with cyclical time would be correctly described as 'cyclical' in terms of the topology of time, whereas Barnes' so-called 'cyclical' time is not cyclical at all, but linear (though containing repeated sequences of events). Let me attempt to make this clear. It is conceivable that time should be cyclical, and that moments in time should recur. But were the topology of time to assume this form, it would never be possible to distinguish the occurrence of an event *e*, from the recurrence of the same event *e* the next time round the cycle. We would not have 'another summer' coming round again, i.e. another *token* of the *type* of events we call 'summers' but simply 'summer' full-stop. There would be only one summer because the event 'summer' would occur only once in the whole of time – it would only have only *one token* as well as only *one type*. Leach, in his more radical moments, seems to be arguing towards precisely this conception of time, for instance, when he claims that for the early Greeks, time was 'without depth'. However, this type of time has to be represented as a circle (or a loop of some kind) because otherwise there is no other way of representing the idea that time consists of a movement from A (birth, say) to B (death) *and back again*, because a purely linear representation A ↔ B cannot indicate that these are two separate movements, one from life to death (A → B) and another from death to life (B → A). The logical property of cyclicity is built into the concept of alternating time, whatever its geometrical or metaphorical embodiment.

But there is no reason to think that alternating/cyclical time is really what Leach has in mind, even granted that it is not a logically incoherent idea in itself (Newton-Smith 1980). Leach is quite clear that the underlying rationale for 'alternating time' is the religious notion of eternal recurrence, and in particular the 'psychological' comfort people derive from the idea that they die only to be born, and live, again. It is the 'again-ness' property of 'repeating events' which is important from Leach's point of view, but this is exactly the property that they would lack if time were topologically cyclic or 'alternating' in Leach's sense of the word. The recurrence of events, as opposed to the simple occurrence of events, presupposes that repeated event-tokens of any event type can be temporally indexed. Repeated events form an ordered series; the occurrence of event *e*, followed in time by its first recurrence as event *e'*, followed by its second recurrence as event *e"*, followed by its third as event *e'''*, and so on, *ad infinitum*, or until the cycle is concluded for the last time. Indexing events as the 1st, 2nd, 3rd, *n*th recurrences (tokens) of a given event-type necessitates the introduction of a linear time dimension along whose length the recurrent tokens of event type *e* can be arranged. The psychological comfort afforded by the religious doctrine of recurrence, or the metaphorization of human life – actually a linear progression from birth to death – 'as if' it were an oscillation like day/night/day/night . . ., etc. depends crucially on the 'again-ness' property of repeating event tokens, which in turn depends crucially on indexicality of events strung out along a linear time-axis.

In short, for Leach to infer what he wishes to infer concerning the founding metaphors of religious thought, viz. that they make non-recurrent events (such as the birth and life-events of individuals) look like recurrent events (successive dawns and sunsets) he has to assume a linear time-axis, because it is only with respect to such a linear time-axis that any event could ever be said to have 'repeated' itself.

But how do these considerations apply to Barnes (1974)? I wholly agree with his strictures against Leach's 'alternating' time. Outside the ritual context, which will be discussed later, I know of no evidence that any collective representations of time involve the idea of returning to the *status quo ante* by reversing the sequence of events or 'inverting time'. I am equally in agreement with his claim that the Kédang are typical in having collective representations of socially established periodicities (the seasons, the human lifecycle, etc.), and that they orient themselves in time with reference to these socially established periodicities. Where I would part company with him, though, is in assuming that the possession of such an array of collective representations is tantamount to having a distinct 'cyclical' notion of time (distinct from our own linear-progressive time). He produces no evidence to show that the Kédang talk about time as such in an unusual or distinctive way. What really seems to be the case is that the Kédang, like much of the rest of human-kind, manage their affairs by means of a set of collective

representation of social and natural processes which are characteristically fixed, of limited durational extent and (relatively)
impervious to change. The Kédang, as described by Barnes, are
conservative folk who do not reckon on ever encountering any
radically novel event-types, only recurrent tokens of event-
types that are familiar and occur according to well-known
periodicities. The collective representations of 'time' are not
representations of the topology of the time-dimension, but are
representations of what characteristically goes on in the temporal world, i.e. the periodic realization of expectable sequences
of events. The only 'form' of time which will accommodate these
collective representations, these standardized expectations, is
linear-progressive time, no different, in its logical layout, from
the temporal forms that underlie our own collective representations appertaining to time. The relevant distinction does not lie
between different 'concepts of time', but different conceptions
of the world and its workings. The Kédang do not believe that
the world changes much or in very important ways, by contrast
to ourselves, who are perhaps inclined to believe that the world
changes constantly and in ways that matter a great deal. But it is
equally essential, both to the belief that 'the world goes on and
on being the same', and to the contrary belief that 'the world
goes on and on becoming different', that one believes that the
world goes on and on.

# Chapter 5

## Time-reversal in Umeda Ritual

Bearing in mind Barnes' criticisms of Leach's conflation of cyclical and reversing time, I want now to introduce an extended example in order to give some idea of the way in which an analysis of the ritual manipulation of time in the ritual context in the Durkheim–Leach manner really works. The example I shall discuss is the Umeda *ida* ritual, on which I have already published an analytical monograph, which falls squarely into this tradition (Gell 1975). Since I have undertaken the task of criticizing my Durkheimian forebears, mentors and contemporaries, I can hardly make an exception of myself. So I shall summarize the relevant part of my analysis, without seeking to extenuate its faults.

The Umeda, numbering some 400, occupy an extensive tract of broken, infertile and densely forested country adjoining the border between Papua-New Guinea and West Irian. They live at very low densities and are demographically marginal, subsisting on sago, bamboo shoots, forest leaves and the produce of their small and unkempt gardens. Such meat as they consume (very little) is hunted in the forest, and small fish are taken from the rivers. They are undernourished and disease-ridden. Being pig-less, shell-less and Big Man-less, they resemble hunter-gatherers more than they do the more typical and more prosperous New Guinea societies of the highlands and the maritime fringe. Their village, a string of hamlets only distinguishable from afar by the waving tops of the coconut palms planted there, is the focus of their leisure and ritual activity, but for the most part their daily lives are lived out in the vast and rather gloomy forest. Here they eke out a living in bush encampments, perpetually at the mercy of the very real hazards of disease, injury and violence, as well as the mystical hazards, no less salient in their eyes, presented by sorcerers and evil spirits.

The village, with its ancestral coconut palms, is the central point around which the productive nuclear family units revolve, like moons, only to congregate there *en masse* for the annual performance of *ida*, which is the temporal focus of the Umeda year, just as the village is the spatial focus in Umeda territory. Despite the dispersed, fragmentary nature of their day-to-day existence, or perhaps because of it, the Umedas are particularly concerned to create order and pattern in their society, and this is achieved through ritual co-ordination via the *ida* ritual.

The *ida* ritual provides for the temporal orderliness of Umeda existence, because it is no exaggeration to say that the productive activity of a whole year (sago processing, hunting, fishing, gardening, manufacture of artefacts, etc.) is oriented towards amassing a surplus against the ritual time. That these surpluses are not very impressive, nor the ritual a very protracted affair (a fortnight at most, and only four days of actual dancing), does not matter; it is the idea of working throughout the year with a definite temporal goal in mind which is significant. The Umeda annual cycle is shown in Figure 5.1.

Figure 5.1 can serve as a representation of the schema of repetitive event-types internalized by Umedas, but of course, no Umeda ever suggested to me that time was circular, nor indeed did I ever uncover an Umeda 'concept' of time in that sense at all. The Umedas do incidentally consider that the cosmos as a whole, not just the annual cycle, is repetitious. The belief, or more precisely the fear, is that eventually a cataclysm will happen which will completely destroy the world. The waters in the rivers will rise up and simultaneously the sky will fall, crushing all living beings out of existence. Then the water will fall again, and the sky resume its normal position, and the corpses of the Umedas will lie rotting. When the corpses have rotted away altogether, and only fleshless bones are left, then the plants and animals and human beings will revive, and the world will be created again from the beginning, only to go through exactly the same cycle once again – a notion of cosmic recurrence which invites immediate comparison with that maintained by the Stoic philosophers, though the Umedas refrain from deriving comparable inferences concerning the transcyclical identity of living individuals and particular events.

The *ida* ritual, which is performed twice, consists of the appearance of a series of masked and painted dancers over the course of a night and two days of dancing. The ritual is overtly

**Figure 5.1  The Umeda annual cycle**

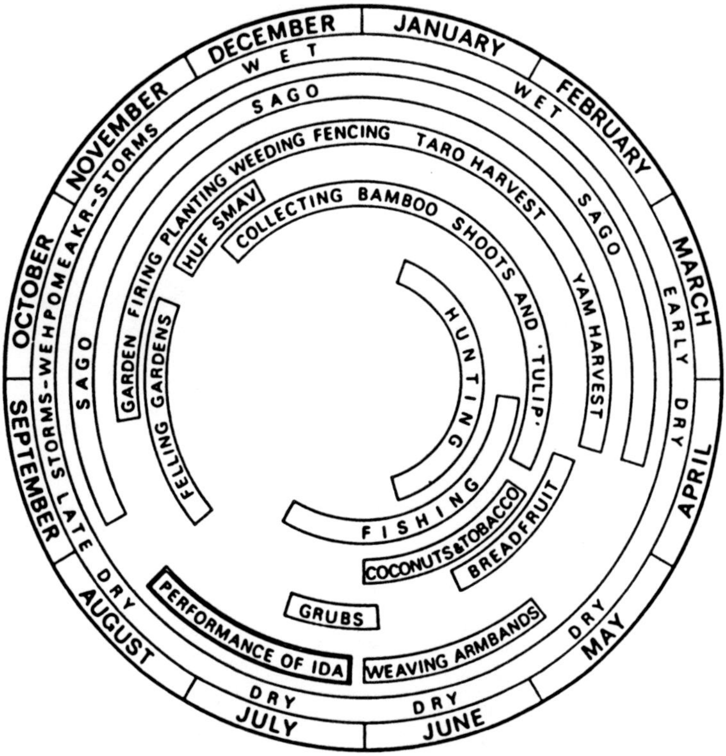

aimed at increasing the supply of sago, though it is clear that the 'regeneration' of the human population, rather than their staple food resource, is the underlying theme of the drama.

The meaning of the ritual is best approached by studying the attributes of the masked dancers indicated in Table 5.1. The dancers appear in a fixed sequence, commencing with the most senior role, the cassowary-dancers, and concluding with the appearance of the red bowmen (*ipele*) who are 'new men' who have been produced by the ritual itself. In between the cassowaries and the red bowmen, who are each others' polar opposites, there appears a series of figures whose attributes are intermediate between the two. The ritual as a whole can thus be treated as the mediation of the antithetical relationship between the cassowary and the red bowmen.

Table 5.1 needs a certain amount of explanation in order to

**Table 5.1** Synoptic table of the Ida ritual

| Ritual role | Time of appearance | Age-status of dancer | Body-paint |
|---|---|---|---|
| Cassowary (2 dancers) | Night (the first dancers to appear) | Senior man (married, with children) | Black 'old skin' associated with war-paint, smoked meat, corpses |
| Sago (2 dancers) | Dawn (transition between night and day) | Fairly senior | Stripes of black and red |
| Firewood (2 dancers) | After the sago dancers | Young men | Stripes similar to sago-dancers, but less black |
| Fish (many dancers) | First fish (early morning) are senior men, during the main daytime dance, young men | Senior men followed by young men | Initially black (senior men) followed by polychrome designs representing animal and fish markings, bark, creepers, etc. |
| Neophyte fish | Daytime | Adolescent | All-red paint (birth: 'new' skin) |
| Termite (many) | Afternoon, evening | Senior men | Complex polychrome designs |
| Preceptor (2 dancers) | Sunset (with red bowmen) | Old men | None |

| Penis | Mask | Dance | Mythic attributes |
|-------|------|-------|-------------------|
| Large gourd sexually active | Large, efflorescent with large fringe, fruits branches | Wild | Associated with the wild, the bush, affines, senior status, social autonomy |
| Large gourd sexually active | Same as cassowary | Wild | Associated with 'death' of natural substances produced by fire, and their re-generation as cultural things (bush → garden, raw sago → cooked sago pudding) |
| Large gourd | Similar to cassowary mask but with tall central pole | Wild | Associated with fire, cookery, the decay of trees and their replacement |
| Large gourd | Tall mask made of coconut fibre. 'New growth' | Leaping dance in single file. 'Warrior' style | Associated with reproduction. Dreaming of fish thought to indicate conception of children. Children identified ritually with fish, especially the red variety |
| Small gourd sexual restraint | Same as fish | One circuit; shuffling gait | Youngsters being initiated |
| Small gourd sexual restraint | Miniature version of the cassowary mask | Restrained dance followed by children | Associated with excessive reproduction. Debilitation of men as a result of having children |
| No gourd (impotent) | None | One circuit restrained | Secular role, like women and children |

become intelligible. The column marked 'time of appearance' is explanatory enough; the moment in the day/night cycle of the appearance of a dancer in a given ritual role encodes (1) the temporal relationship between that ritual role and the other ritual roles in *ida*, and (2) the temporal relationship between that ritual role and the various cyclical phenomena (notably the human lifecycle) which are metaphorically evoked by the dancers' various attributes. Thus the cassowary comes before all the other dancers and also during the night, symbolically evoking the powers of the night (violence, sexuality, removal of normal social restraints) and the 'night' of the human lifecycle, which corresponds to socially mature middle age. The sago-dancer comes after the cassowary (night) and before the fish (day) at dawn, the period of transitions. The symbolic associations of the sago-dancer are with the transitions mediated by fire – cooking, creating gardens by burning the forest – and with marginal experiences (pain and orgasm) – the dancers have to leap over a fire and then, before departing, plunge their hands into boiling-hot sago jelly, flinging it up into the air, an action explicitly associated with ejaculation of semen.

The fish dominate the morning, the 'debilitated' termite-dancers (representing reproductive men) the afternoon, until both are eclipsed by the red bowmen, whose arrival concludes the ritual and also prepares for its re-enactment, because the red bowmen are also 'cassowary-chicks', and sunset is followed by night. The temporal references contained in the ritual roles are reinforced by the restrictions on the age-category of dancers eligible to play particular roles.

How body paint relates to time requires some more detailed comment. The Umeda ritual system uses colour to encode age on the basis of two powerful analogies drawn from nature. The most important of these is human skin and hair. Melanesian babies are born with reddish-golden skin which darkens progressively, and as infants they also have coppery hair, which gradually turns black. The same red → black transition is also seen in the development of plants, notably the colour changes in the spathes of palm trees (an important raw material in Umeda technology; Gell 1975: 315ff). The cassowary is the quintessence of black, in the ritual as in nature. Here black stands for maturity and social autonomy; the cassowary is anti-social. And it is in fact true that as Umedas grow older they become more and more like cassowaries, living an independent life with their wives and children in the deep bush. It is to counteract this tendency for Umeda society to dissolve into its constituents, to revert to nature, that the *ida* ritual is mounted, because it is only by establishing its cultural and social hegemony over the wild that Umeda society can perpetuate itself. Black is admired, in a negative way, as the colour associated with warfare, ancestral ghosts and above all the untrammelled freedom of the forest, away from society and man. The Umedas admire the cassowary figure without conferring moral approbation. Playing the cassowary is the great event, which occurs only once in a man's biography, because it is only in this ritual disguise that he can be, or at least can pretend to be, absolutely free.

Looking down the 'body paint' column, it can be seen that no other actor in the drama achieves 'blackness' to the extent the cassowaries do. In fact, as the ritual proceeds, the proportions of black to red in the body paint of the major performers steadily diminish, until we reach the red bowmen whose body paint is all red, with the exception of black decorative lines. The general point to be borne in mind is that the body paint progression in *ida* goes from black to red, from age to youth.

Just as the colours used in body paint encode references to the lifecycle, so do masks, though only the outlines of this system can be indicated here. Figure 5.2 shows traditional age-related hair-styles and for comparison various kinds of masks.

The cassowary mask corresponds to the bushy hair-style of senior men. This contrasts with the tall column of tightly bound hair on the top of the head adopted by younger men in traditional times. The mask-analogue of this hair-style is the tall fish mask. The termite mask is a miniaturized version of the cassowary mask and the red bowman's mask is a miniaturized version of the fish mask. All these masks form a transformation set, as shown in Figure 5.2. The phases of the male lifecycle are expressed via the mask sequence: (1) red bowman (competitive hunting, bachelorhood, asceticism) → (2) fish mask (sexual display) → (3) cassowary mask (efflorescent sexuality) → (4) termite mask (reproductivity, domesticity) → (5) preceptor (no mask, infancy/old age).

The dance-styles adopted by each ritual role further reinforce these points about lifecycle stages. The cassowary, as befits the 'autonomous' mature male, dances in a wild, structureless way. As the ritual progresses the dances become more and more controlled and shorter in duration, until at the very end the red

**Figure 5.2   Umeda hair-styles and Masks**

a   *hairstyles*

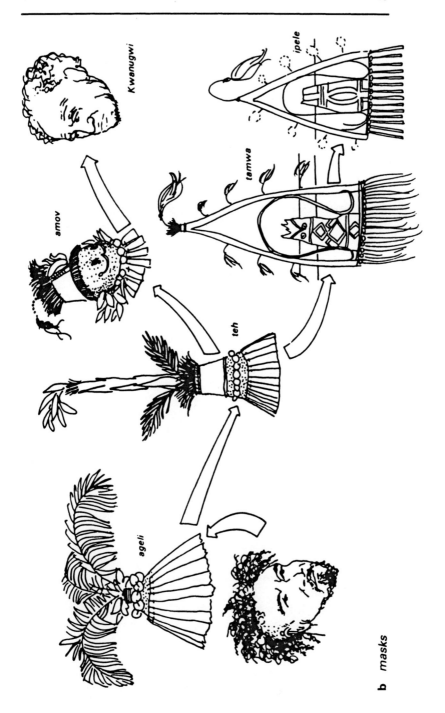

b masks

bowmen emerge only to make one loping, almost furtive, circuit of the arena before firing off their arrows and making a hurried departure. The impression of ever-increasing suppression of spontaneity in the interests of the hegemony of the social is vividly conveyed by these means (Gell 1985a).

The general interpretation of the *ida* ritual I put forward in *Metamorphosis of the Cassowaries* was that the ritual enacts a process of bio-social regeneration. The Umedas are rightly worried about keeping their fragile society viable; and every year they mount a splendid performance, the objective of which is the provision of some degree of collective assurance that they can indeed do so, on condition that they hold fast to the principles underlying their social order, keeping ever-encroaching nature at bay or, better still, pre-empting nature by cultural means. The cassowaries are the Lords of Misrule, representing man in 'natural' guise, fertile but disorderly, free but anti-social. The scenario of the ritual is the subjugation of this natural spontaneity, which alone can ensure the perpetuation of Umeda society but which at the same time threatens its very essence. After the orgiastic night dance of the cassowaries with which the ritual begins, this regeneration process is put in motion, by their replacement, at dawn, by the sago-dancers. These are 'cooked' over a fire, and raw sago is cooked into sago-jelly, whereupon the hand-plunging ritual mentioned earlier takes place and a climactic transition occurs. After an interlude (the firewood dancers, who are important mainly for their masks, which are intermediate between the cassowary-type and the fish-type) the fish themselves arrive. The presence of these, the most numerous dancers, indicates the impregnation of women; for it is believed that if a woman dreams of a fish that means she will bear a child, and fish are associated with reproduction and children in other ways as well. Then, in the afternoon, real children appear in the arena, following the by now debilitated termite dancers. Finally, the ritual produces 'new men' in the form of the red bowmen, *hunters*, whose arrows, made potent by their users' sexual abstinence, kill the cassowaries and impregnate the bush for the following year. But these bowmen are also nascent cassowaries, since their stripes mimic the stripes on cassowary chicks:

> At the next performance of *ida* the cassowary chick will have become the cassowary . . . red will have turned to black. And the 'black' of

the unpainted [preceptors] will have turned to the red of unpainted children, the redness of the neophytes. Thus the circularity renews itself, the dialectic of Black and Red. The Heraclitean struggle of senior and junior generations, autonomy and repression, spontaneity and order, nature and culture, will never cease to be joined only to resolve itself in such a way that it renews itself indefinitely. (ibid.: 346)

Let this suffice as an account of *ida*. The question now to be tackled is the way in which *ida* can be said to attain its effect, as a ritual, by the manipulation of time. Does *ida* invert time? The patterned relationship between age-categories (as implied by the status of the dancers) and the symbolism of their attributes (mask in relation to hair-style) laid out below suggests that it does:

| Age category | youths → | young → adults | older married man |
|---|---|---|---|
| Hairstyle | short/ → controlled | long/ → controlled | long/ uncontrolled |
| Derivative mask | red bowman ← | fish ← | cassowary |

That is, the ritual figures appear in the inverse order to that in which the corresponding age categories are attained in real life. Black precedes red, age precedes youth.

But is this really 'inversion' in the sense required to support Leach's argument, discussed earlier, to the effect that in primitive societies time is ritually 'reversed' during a sacred liminal period, so as to start anew subsequently? Not necessarily. The cassowary is senior and comes first, the red bowman is junior and comes last; there is no 'inversion' here because this is the normal order of things. The senior naturally takes precedence in time over the junior.

But if one examines the course of the ritual as a whole, it is clear that the opposition, in itself total, between the cassowaries and the red bowmen is bridged by degrees, so that there is a smooth transition between them. Each of the more important figures to appear represents a progressively more marked departure from the 'cassowary' end of the spectrum and a progressive approximation towards the 'bowman' end of the spectrum.

It would seem that the demonstration of the underlying continuity between the cassowary and the bowman, despite their
apparently irreconcilable stereotypes, is one of the deeper purposes of the ritual. And this psychologically is compelling, since
if one turns from ritual to real life, it is evident that there is no
Umeda paterfamilias who is so far gone in individualism, in
cassowary-like autonomy, as to set no store by the values of
hunting, asceticism and self-adornment practised by bachelors;
nor yet is there a bachelor, however careful in his behaviour,
who never indulges his cassowary-like nature.

So cassowary and bowman are really one and the same in
being aspects of a single, multifaceted Umeda masculine persona. This Janus-faced image of idealized masculinity is 'ro-
tated' before the enchanted spectators at *ida*, but in a direction
which is the inverse of the one in which these facets of the
masculine persona are normally displayed during lifecycle development.

Having established this point, I argue that it is possible to see
the *ida* ritual as a ritual representation of lifecycle phases occurring in 'reversed (symbolic) time' as in Figure 5.3, and the
accompanying explanation:

> Three kinds of time are here distinguished: the central arrow is
> 'duration' – the actual time in which the ritual is performed. The
> lower-most arrow is 'process' time: the time continuum established
> by organic processes, e.g. the red–black continuum or, on a larger
> scale, the human lifecycle. The upper arrow is 'symbolic' time, here
> shown as the 'inversion' of both 'duration' and 'process' time. The
> 'inversion' of symbolic time is achieved by taking the sequence of
> events in process time (T' T'' T''') and reproducing them symbolically
> in inverse order (T''' T'' T') relative to the absolute standard provided
> by duration (D' D'' D'''). (ibid.: 335)

The analysis of *ida* concludes with a complicated argument,
which I shall summarize only in part, to the effect that the ritual
can be understood as the 'mediation' of certain 'contradictions'
inherent in the notion of time itself, i.e. the 'conflict between
synchrony and diachrony' – an idea I borrowed directly from
Lévi-Strauss and Leach. Time, I argue, has two ways of mani-
festing itself, diachronically, through the 'before and after'
sequence of events, and 'synchronically' through the non-
changing temporal oppositions which exist between old and
new, senior and junior, and so on. In sociological terms, there is

**Figure 5.3   Time inversion**

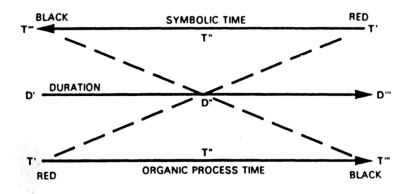

a basic paradox arising from the fact that social life consists of
transitory events, but social structure has an abiding temporal
organization, i.e. age-categories, lifecycle phases, generations,
etc. These temporal statuses do not change, although the individuals who occupy them do. The intellectual difficulty or
'contradiction' involved here, if there is one, which is open to
question, is akin to the difficulty we have in trying to understand how the plume of water sent up by a well-designed
fountain, apparently so stable in its overall shape, is none the
less composed of water droplets all undergoing motions of the
most violent kind. 'Everything passes, BUT everything remains
the same' (ibid.: 343).

> It seems to me that the idea of cyclic or repetitive time, far from
> being, as Leach argues, a religious fiction designed to make the
> prospect of death less terrifying . . . – is an attempt to resolve this
> ambiguity of time, which is both a continuous process and a synchro-
> nic opposition between old and young.
>   The idea of time as an oscillation or cycle, continually repeating
> itself, mediates between these two inextricably related but mutually
> contradictory experiences of time, i.e. between social process and
> social structure, diachrony and synchrony. In periodic ritual, media-
> tion is sought, and found, between the pressures of diachrony (the
> processes which continually submit organisms to irreversible change)
> and the constraints of synchrony (the intelligible structure which
> survives all changes). This is achieved by a mutual accommodation
> between the two: diachrony submits to synchrony by becoming an
> oscillation which never departs too far from the axis of the synchron-
> ous 'now': synchrony submits to diachrony in admitting the regular

induction of fresh cohorts into the categories it provides; inductions which are generally marked by *rites de passage*. (ibid.: 343–4)

What second thoughts do I have to offer at this stage? I continue to adhere to the position I arrived at in 1975 concerning the general interpretation of the *ida* ritual, despite some penetrating criticisms from Brunton (1980), Juillerat (1980), Werbner (1984) and others. Juillerat (forthcoming) is about to publish a rival analysis of the ritual as a whole, based on his fieldwork in the nearby village of Yafar where a largely identical ritual is performed. The issues that I want to raise at present have to do neither with ethnographic analysis nor the methodology of the symbolic interpretation of ritual representations. I am concerned only with the consequences of the Durkheim/Lévi-Strauss/ Leach-derived ideas on time, synchrony vs. diachrony and 'time reversal', which I incorporated into the analysis without examining them very critically. I was, I think, trapped in an idiom of 'temporal cultural relativism' (see below), which distorted the analysis and generated metaphysical pseudo-problems where none really exists.

I would not now write of ritual as if it had the power to modify the nature or directionality of 'time' as a category, nor would I commit myself to statements to the effect that for the Umedas there are two, three or $n$ kinds of 'time'. The ritual manipulations of collective representations of natural and social processes, which is what is really taking place in *ida*, can be understood without constructing a metaphysical scenario involving either inverted time, or stabilized 'synchronic' time, which lead to logical contradictions, which then have to be 'overcome' by ritual dialectic. Moreover, though I was unfortunately not aware of this at the time, the metaphysical scenario of inverted ritual time I proposed has the effect of precisely cancelling out the very symbolic manipulations of natural and social processes which are essential to the meaning of the ritual.

For instance Figure 5.3 shows 'three kinds of time': symbolic time, duration and organic process time. There is no reason to distinguish, first of all, between duration and organic process time 'as kinds of time'. The ritual in 'duration' consists of a series of events (ERit = 'ritual event') between which before-and-after temporal relationships can be defined in terms of a linear series (T1, T2, T3). Thus:

ERit 1 (T1) → ERit 2 (T2) → ERit 3 (T3), etc.

These ritual events metaphorically or analogically refer to events or phases in the lifecycle processes as represented by the Umedas (ELc = 'lifecycle event'):

ERit (ELc1), ERit (ELc2), ERit (ELc3)

Lifecycle events occur in a fixed before-and-after sequence, as do ritual events:

ELc1 (T1) → ELc2 (T2) → ELc3 (T3)

But the order in which lifecycle events occur is not mirrored by the order in which the ritual events representing these lifecycle events occur:

ERit 1 (T1 (ELc3 (T3))) → ERit 2 (T2 (ELc2 (T2)))
→ ERit 3 (T3 (ELc1 (T1)))

But this is not to distinguish between more than one kind of 'time'. We only need one symbol T plus an index indicating where T is positioned in a before-and-after sequence, T1, T2, . . . Tn, to represent any kind of time whatsoever. There is no need at all to introduce temporal continua with non-standard topologies in order to analyse ritual manipulations of the ordering of events within processes. Moreover, it is easy to see that if the 'inverted' sequence of lifecycle events represented in *ida* actually took place in reversed time, they would in fact be taking place in the right order, not the reversed one:

ERit 1 (T3 (ELc3 (T3))) → ERit 2 (T2 (ELc2 (T2)))
→ ERit 3 (T1 (ELc1 (T1)))

That is, if the 'reversed' sequence of lifecycle events in *ida* took place in 'reversed' time, the sequence would no longer be reversed in terms of lifecycle events.

In short, *ida* represents a process undoing itself in normal, forwards-running time, not a process going forwards normally in backwards-running time. We are only tempted to conceptualize matters in the latter way, because, if time went backwards, events would go backwards too, and the Umedas would be 'metaphysically justified' in *showing* them go backwards. But this is to miss the point entirely: what the Umedas want to do is regenerate their world in real time, not have it continue inexorably on its degenerative course, but in inverted time.

Secondly, there is the supposed 'contradiction' between diachrony and synchrony to be considered. This contradiction does not arise, because diachrony and synchrony are not two kinds of time but necessary consequences of their being only one kind of time. Synchronic time is something of a misnomer: synchronous relationships are relations between categories in a classification system which are unaffected by time, even though the criteria on which certain categories may be based can include various kinds of temporal relationships (e.g. an age hierarchy used for purposes of social classification). An age-category of, say, 'mature married men' is a category whose membership is exclusive to individuals who have certain biographical qualifications. These individuals have a right to belong because their (diachronic) histories contain events (being married, begetting children), which the histories of more junior men do not contain. There is a relationship between the membership of this category at time T and the membership of more junior categories at time T-minus and more senior categories at time T-plus, because these very men belonged to more junior categories previously and will belong to more senior categories by-and-by. But at time T, there is no temporal relationship of anteriority or posteriority between the membership of the categories 'senior elders'/'mature married men'/'bachelors' because the members of the various age categories are simply contemporaneous with one another. Synchronic time, as manifested in a collective representation such as an age hierarchy therefore boils down to the fact that different things (in this case, different men) have different histories, and things can be classified according to their histories. Bachelors are men with no history of having been married, more senior men have histories which include this event, and others indicative of social maturity such as having children, heading an independent household, and so on. Synchronic time is therefore just the classificatory mechanism which arranges entities according to the real or putative events in their histories.

If this is so, then there is no reason to believe that there are any but diachronic temporal relationships, i.e. the relationship between events in histories.

There is no contradiction between synchrony and diachrony, because synchronic classification does not conflict with diachronic historicity. One can classify entities (synchronically) according to the events in their diachronic histories, just as one can synchronically classify entities according to their colour, size, price at market, how many of them there are etc. There is no intellectual puzzle here, nor, I think, is there really any evidence the Umedas thought there was one. The 'struggle between synchrony and diachrony', evoked by Lévi-Strauss, is not a struggle between different kinds of time, but the struggle between classification systems and the real world. All classification systems have their difficulties, which stem from tendencies of real-world objects to fail to conform to the criteria laid down for them. When Lévi-Strauss writes, very tellingly, of societies with an attitude towards history which denies, not that history has taken place, but simply that it has made any difference to *them*, he surely gets to the heart of the matter (1968). The 'conflict' is between this attitude, faith in the ability of a certain set of event-and-process classifications to embrace all foreseeable events, and the unfortunate tendency of real events not to occur normatively. The clash is between classifications and reality, not between irreconcilable features of reality.

And where the Umedas are concerned, the purpose of the ritual is not the reconciliation of synchronic and diachronic time, but the attempt to ensure that diachrony only throws up the normatively approved kinds of events, as defined by the synchronic classificatory scheme. The *ida* ceremony does not 're-verse' time; what it does, instead, is to manipulate processes in a symbolic way in order to indicate a certain normative path for events, thereby reinforcing the Umedas' confidence in the viability of their society.

# Chapter 6

## Cultural Relativism

In Chapter 5 I remarked that while writing my original account of the Umeda ritual I was to some extent misled by the doctrine of 'temporal cultural relativity', which I had inherited from my predecessors in structuralist anthropology, among whom Durkheim's influence remains very strong. 'Cultural relativity' is obviously a subject which has to be discussed in any work on the anthropology of time. The difficulty is that there are many different points of view which can be categorized as 'cultural relativist' ones, some of which are mistaken, while others are not only innocuous, but essential to any kind of anthropological understanding. It would be difficult indeed to justify most of the activities anthropologists engage in unless cultural experience made a great deal of difference to every aspect of thought and behaviour, and one way of defining anthropology would be that it is empirically the study of the differences between cultures, and theoretically the study of the differences these differences make. And within this general definition of the scope of anthropology must inevitably be included the study of cultural differences in the conceptualization of temporal relationships.

But it might be considered that it is contradictory to define anthropology in this way, and at the same time put forward the kind of arguments I have advanced up to now, which have tended to suggest that 'time' is entirely uniform from culture to culture. This is the issue which must now be confronted head-on. What I want to affirm is that temporal cultural relativism is in fact justified, but that it can only be successfully defended against the reductionist positions which deny cultural relativities due recognition, on condition that the specific form of cultural relativist theory adopted is not presented as if it were a contribution to metaphysics, in the manner initiated by Durkheim.

The point of view which undermines the case for temporal cultural relativism in the very act of seeking to affirm it, is the doctrine of temporal 'mentalities' or 'world-views', i.e. distinct, culturally constituted temporal frames of reference of equivalent status to rationally argued metaphysical theses, such as those defended by Kant in the *Critique of Pure Reason*. Ethnographically, cultural temporal relativities consist of differential sets of contingent beliefs, held by different cultures and subcultures, as to the historical facticity and anticipated possibilities of the world. There is a big difference between 'metaphysical' postulates and systems of contingent beliefs. Very dissimilar contingent beliefs can be expressed, understood and acted upon, in the light of uniform, but implicit, logico-metaphysical premises, and indeed only in the light of these premises. What is mistaken, I think, is to suppose that cultural systems of transmitted beliefs and representations are pervaded with a deep 'cultural logic', which sets the outermost limits on the 'thinkable', for members of a given culture. These outer limits on the 'thinkable' exist, but they are not properties of this or that cultural system. And they are quite distinct from the constraints of a *de facto* kind which limit the range of beliefs which members of a given culture actually entertain, or the kinds of thoughts which would 'naturally' occur to them.

The problem with Durkheimian anthropology is that in discussing this or that culturally constituted world, anthropologists have tended to seek a level of analysis which would imply that their findings have a bearing on the constitution of the world in general, on what kind of a place the world in general must be considered to be, and not just on the culturally constituted world they are investigating. The formulation of defensible views about what the world is like in general or categorical terms (the promulgation and defence of metaphysical postulates of one sort or another) is the province of philosophy and metaphysics, not anthropology. In particular, it is unwise for anthropologists to think that ethnography is the kind of enterprise which could result in the discovery of new ways of construing the world in its general or categorical aspect which would amount, in themselves, to useful additions to the spectrum of potentially valid metaphysical points of view. The consequences of overstepping the inherent limitations of ethnography as a descriptive genre is the promulgation of inherently self-defeating metaphysical claims (such as the claim that ritual is designed to make time go into reverse) or becoming mired in non-problems such as the fictitious 'contradiction' between diachrony and synchrony.

The effect of the methodological position I advocate is that it permits anthropologists to assert whatsoever they see fit, concerning the content of exotic belief systems, short of claiming that in so doing they are contributing to our understanding of truth, necessity, logic, meaning, etc., i.e. questions of a general philosophical or metaphysical nature. And that is what anthropologists inevitably seek to do, once they go beyond the task of attempting to convey the content of beliefs and representations current in particular cultural systems, by taking it upon themselves to explain these beliefs and representations by showing that they *could be true*, in some absolute sense, in a world in which certain non-standard metaphysical truths also held. Let me give an example of the malign consequences of looking for differences in 'underlying' metaphysical postulates when seeking to explain exotic contingent beliefs.

An early and influential writer in the vein of metaphysical apologetics for exotic belief-systems was Lévy-Bruhl. Not only did Lévy-Bruhl exercise a powerful influence over the development of cognitive anthropology, which continues to the present day (Evans-Pritchard 1965; Horton and Finnegan 1973), but his influence over Piaget's developmentalist theories in child psychology is also very marked, with knock-on effects in Piaget-inspired cross-cultural psychology (Piaget 1970; Hallpike 1979; cf. Chapter 12 this volume). It is instructive to consider at this point one of the instances of 'pre-logical mentality' which he analysed most carefully, and which also has to do with spatio-temporal relationships. The example in question is the puzzling case of the missionary Grubb and the purloined pumpkins (Lévy-Bruhl 1922).

Grubb, a missionary among the Leguna Indians of Grand Chaco, Brazil, was one day accosted by an Indian, who accused him of stealing pumpkins from his garden. This Indian was personally known to Grubb, but the missionary had not seen him in a long while, and his village was 150 miles from the mission station. The Indian demanded compensation for the stolen pumpkins with every appearance of genuine grievance. He was not mollified when Grubb protested that he had not visited the Indian's village recently, and could not therefore have stolen pumpkins from his garden. Grubb thought the man

must be joking to begin with, but as the scene developed he
became increasingly aware that the man was perfectly serious,
and inwardly convinced of the soundness of his case. Grubb's
puzzlement only became more complete when the Indian, in the
course of their argument, freely conceded that Grubb had *not*
visited the garden, but he none the less persisted in his demands for compensation:

> I should have lost patience with him [Grubb wrote] had he not
> evidently been in real earnest and I became deeply interested in-
> stead. Eventually I discovered that he had dreamed that he was out
> in his garden one night, and saw me, from behind some tall plants,
> break off and carry away three pumpkins, and it was payment for
> these that he wanted. 'Yes', I said,' but you have just admitted that I
> had not taken them.' He again assented, but replied immediately, 'If
> you had been there you would have taken them.' (W. Grubb 'An
> unknown people in an unknown land', p. 275, cited in Lévy-Bruhl,
> *Primitive Mentality*, 106–7)

Grubb concluded that the Indian's grounds for his accusation
were that dreams reveal the 'will' of the dreamed-about person,
so that in so far as Grubb figured in the Indian's dream as a
pumpkin-thief, he ought to be punished for harbouring thieving
intentions, even though the attempt to remove the pumpkins
was never actually made and in fact no pumpkins were missing.

Lévy-Bruhl is not satisfied with this explanation. He focuses
on what he takes to be the logical incongruity of two assertions
made by the Indian:

1. You, Grubb, stole my pumpkins.
2. You, Grubb, have not been near my garden for a long time.

He argues that the Indian accepts both of these assertions as
literally and simultaneously true, and can do so because he has
different canons of 'logic' from those of civilized men.

> He prefers admitting implicitly what the schoolmen call the 'multi-
> presence' of a person to doubting what seems a certainty. That is the
> necessary result of his experience which, beyond and above the
> realities which we term objective, contains an infinity of other beings
> in an unseen world. Neither time, nor space, nor logical theory are of
> any use to us here, and this is one of the reasons which cause us to
> regard the primitive mind as 'pre-logical'. (ibid.: 107)

It seems to me that Grubb's explanation is much closer to the mark than Lévy-Bruhl's, or, more accurately, Grubb's conjecture is, rightly or wrongly, an *explanation* consistent with the fact of the case, while what Lévy-Bruhl has to say turns out, on closer inspection, not to be an explanation at all. But in one respect Lévy-Bruhl is not to be blamed for assuming that 'logical theory' would be at a loss to elucidate the workings of the Indian's mind, in that in his day the branch of logic nowadays called 'modal logic', the logic of possible worlds rather than necessarily actual ones, was much less well understood than it is at present. What the Indian is doing, if Grubb is correct, is claiming compensation for a wrong which could have possibly happened, not one that actually did happen. In so doing, the Indian is not reasoning in a way that lacks parallels in our own legal system, which punishes people for 'loitering with intent', 'conspiracy', 'attempted' crimes of murder, theft, arson, etc., even when no significant damage of any kind has been inflicted on anybody or anything. Where Leguna law differs from our own is in admitting the uncorroborated testimony of a plaintiff in the form of dream-experience as adequate evidence of the criminal intentions of a defendant. The basis of this legal principle must be a belief in the veridical character of dreams, not as representations of the real world, but as representations of counterfactual worlds (non-actual worlds) sufficiently closely related to the original to permit reasonable inferences as to the moral proclivities of individuals in this (actual) world being drawn on the basis of the behaviour of their counterparts recognized in dreams. In other words, the Leguna believe contingently (1) that the nature of dreaming is such that individuals act 'in character' morally speaking, when dreamed about; and (2) that people are sufficiently trustworthy to report their dreams honestly. Possibly both these beliefs are false, though it would be very difficult to prove that either of them is, and certainly both can be held without any deviation from logical orthodoxy.

This Grubb explanation does not require any very great leap of the imagination. Lévy-Bruhl's, on the other hand, has very far-reaching implications indeed. What he says, in effect, is that the Leguna Indians have heterodox logical criteria for so-called 'first-order objects' (Lyons 1977), i.e. tables, chairs, people, missionaries, pumpkins, etc., such that any particular first-order object can exist simultaneously at different spatial co-ordinates, instead of being restricted to unique spatio-temporal co-ordinates. According to the proposed assumption of a metaphysic of 'multipresence' a first-order object does not have to be at one place at any one time, but can be in many places at once. Under this assumption, the Indian can, according to Lévy-Bruhl, hold without being aware of contradicting himself, that Mr Grubb stole the pumpkins from the Indian's garden, and that Mr Grubb did not visit the Indian's garden and could not have stolen the pumpkins. This is a prime example of the tactic employed by post-Durkheimians of 'explaining' ethnographic facts which are anomalous in terms of our contingent belief-system, by constructing a metaphysical scenario which removes the contradiction at the level of contingent beliefs by reformulating it as a contrast in implicit metaphysical categories. Because the exotic metaphysics thus produced seem self-consistent, it can then be asserted that fundamental metaphysical categories are culturally relative and socially determined. But the reasoning involved in this case, and in all the analogous ones, does not stand up.

There is no way, even granting the possibility that the Indian believes in multipresence, that assertions (1) and (2) can be other than mutually contradictory. If the Indian believes in multipresence he will deny (2) (that Grubb has not visited his garden) because a multipresent Mr Grubb certainly *has* visited his multipresent garden and stolen his multipresent pumpkins in such a case. But if so, then Mr Grubb's best move is to fall in with the Indian's way of looking at things and claim, instead, that it was some other Mr Grubb who did the deed, and that the Indian must seek compensation from him, not from the here-present missionary of impeccable honesty, or alternatively admit that he really did steal the pumpkins, but that he has already paid compensation to another multipresent Indian. Moreover, he can question the necessity for the payment of any compensation at all, for however many pumpkins are stolen from however many gardens, enough multipresent pumpkins will remain to supply all needs.

In short, unless the Indian and Mr Grubb share standard metaphysical assumptions about the spatio-temporal confinement of first-order objects such as missionaries, gardens and pumpkins, it is impossible for there to be identifiable thefts of identifiable pumpkins from identifiable gardens by identifiable missionaries. The notion of assigning guilt for specific crimes to specific individuals loses all meaning in such a context. Lévy-

Bruhl's argument overcomes the problem of cultural interpretation posed by the Indian's apparently aberrant behaviour, by imagining a logical context in which this behaviour would *not* be anomalous, i.e. if missionaries can be at more than one place at a time, one missionary can both steal and not steal some pumpkins. But this does not account for the Indian's behaviour within the framework of assumptions wherein it actually *is* anomalous (i.e. the framework operated by the likes of Grubb and Lévy-Bruhl), but transposes the situation to a different world where, because different metaphysical assumptions hold, the very facts of the case are different, and are not anomalous any longer. Lévy-Bruhl's explanation explains a different set of facts from the set of facts reported by Grubb, i.e. the facts that would be the case were first-order objects multipresent. But these are not the reported facts, for which, it follows, Lévy-Bruhl has actually no explanation at all. His argument is self-defeating: it 'solves' the explanatory problems present in ethnography by metaphysically recontextualizing them so that they cease to be problems. But in that case they cannot be explained either. The oddness of the Indian's behaviour cannot be specified, except in the light of the assumption that objects are not multipresent, and that the world (this actual world) does not contain an 'infinity of other beings' absolutely on a par with the objectively real first-order objects of the kind Grubb and Lévy-Bruhl are prepared to recognize. It is only in the light of such presuppositions that there is anything to explain, and it must be in the light of such presuppositions that the explanation must be formulated. As we have seen, it is not difficult to do this, by identifying the culturally-specific beliefs entertained by Leguna Indians, but not shared by Grubb or Lévy-Bruhl, concerning the reliability of dreams as a source of evidence in legal disputes.

Our 'logic' and their 'logic' are identical, our objective world and their objective world are identical too; where we differ is only in the contingent beliefs we hold about the workings of the world we otherwise share. And these differences are sufficient both to generate and explain the interminable sagas of mutual misunderstandings which fill the library shelves.

# Chapter 7

## Transcendental Temporal Cultural Relativism

Lévy-Bruhl's work is only marginally of concern to time-anthropology, and moreover has many merits to which I have hardly done justice in the preceding pages. He was aware of the difficulties inherent in his idea of a 'pre-logical mentality', and however much one may disagree with his Durkheimian approach, he always remains in contact with the spirit of his ethnographic sources, honestly perplexed as to what they may imply in terms of the cognitive processes of 'primitive' men. I turn next to Durkheimianism in its most hypertrophied form, as it appears in the work of Gurvich (1961).

Gurvich, at one time a dominant figure in French sociology and the holder of Durkheim's Chair in Sociology at the University of Paris, wrote, among many other books, *Spectrum of Social Time* (1961), which may be said to carry to fruition the metaphysical ambitions of his predecessor. This work is particularly of concern to me in that it is the most self-consciously theoretical treatise on the sociology of time by a Durkheimian sociologist. Zerubavel's works, which one might cite in this connection, are certainly Durkheimian in tone, but are much more empirical, and all the better for that (Zerubavel 1981).

Gurvich believes that time is multiple, that it is determined by sociological factors, and that this is empirically demonstrable. Time, we are informed, is a 'convergency and divergency of movements which persist in discontinuous succession and change in a continuity of heterogeneous moments' – tolerance of contradictions does not seem to be exclusively a characteristic of the pre-logical mentality! In another place, time is defined as 'converging and diverging movements of total social phenomena giving birth to time and also elapsing in time'. Gurvich is saying that it is the processes ('movements') that go on in time

61

which are responsible for there being time at all, and moreover, that corresponding to the different characteristics of the processes which go on in time, time itself is different in each particular instance. Time is thus constituted out of a dynamic movement whose rhythms, expansions, contractions and irregular pulsations are generated by the patterns of events occurring in time, these events constituting 'total social phenomena', i.e. the processes of production, reproduction, exchange, class struggle, and so on.

Gurvich reduces the suggested multiplicity of time to eight typological variants, which are local distortions of regular or cosmic time, produced by sociological 'relativity' (the reference to Einstein's theory is made explicitly). But as we are not dealing with events on the relativistic scale, Gurvich's time distortions are really distortions of Newtonian cosmic time, i.e. what the knife-edge of Absolute Time would look like if bent out of shape by local factors of sociological origin. The eight variants are:

1. Enduring time of slowed duration (slowed-down time).
2. Deceptive time (slowed time with irregular and unexpected speeded-up stretches).
3. Erratic time (slowed-down and speeded-up by turns, neither predominating, without predictable rhythms).
4. Cyclical time (Gurvich equates cyclical time with 'motionless' of 'static' time).
5. Retarded time (in which a given moment T1 in retarded time equals a later moment. T1 + $n$ in non-retarded time).
6. Time in advance (the inverse of retarded time, in which T1 in time-in-in-advance equals T1 − $n$ in non-advanced time).
7. Alternating time (time alternating between being retarded and in advance).
8. Explosive time (time very much advanced and also speeded-up).

In what follows I shall deal with only three of these eight typological variants of time, those manifested by the 'peasant class', but before doing so I must briefly look at Gurvich's philosophical justification of his system of multiple times.

In principle, n + 1 times can exist: this is a question of the reality of the facts and of the construction of these facts by the different sciences. All of these times [i.e. not only Gurvich's eight, but those of the other natural sciences as well] in spite of their profound differences possess the same formal characteristics of convergent and divergent movements and thus enter into the general category of time. (Gurvich 1961: 21)

According to this author the sociologist has to understand any social phenomenon in the light of the appropriate typological variant of time, if he is to achieve the 'relative unification' of social phenomena stemming from different sociological milieux, historical periods, class conditions, and so forth, within the framework of general sociological theory. He argues that the same is the case for the natural sciences: the time of Newtonian mechanics differs from that of relativity theory, which differs in turn from the time of thermodynamics, chemistry, the life-sciences, etc. (A similar view is put forward in the work of Frazer 1978.) In other words, he seems to think that for each kind of causal process and the associated theory, there is a different kind of 'time', rather ignoring the fact that, for example, we can tell how different thermodynamic cosmological models are from Newtonian ones precisely because the moving bodies in a Newtonian solar system can be made to go into reverse relative to absolute space-time without difficulties arising for the theory, whereas this is not so in the case of thermodynamic models involving the idea of increasing entropy. It is because different branches of natural-scientific theory do not depend on different notions of time that we can determine in what respects they differ, otherwise they would not merely be different but wholly incommensurable.

Gurvich goes on to say that one or more of the eight kinds of time he has identified will be manifested particularly in any given sociological milieu, such as modern mass society, classical nineteenth-century bourgeois society, feudalism, the peasant milieu and the archaic or primitive milieu. Each of these will impose its specific vector on regular time; speeding it up, slowing it down or otherwise distorting it. What is not clear, however, is how the standard tempo is set, relative to which others are deemed fast or slow, regular or irregular, since in Gurvich's scheme of things no total social phenomenon generates standard time. One has to assume that standard time is the sociologist's own time.

Let us turn to a specific application of Gurvich's theory of multiple times. The 'peasant class' are defined as those who work their own land in small family farms, showing class loyalty to one another and antipathy towards the urban working class and the rich bourgeoisie and techno-bureaucrats. In the spectrum of social time they manifest, primarily, (1) enduring time of long duration and slow motion, (5) retarded time, and (4) cyclical time related to the seasons. 'This class', says Gurvich, 'tends to remain faithful to traditional patterns and symbols which supports the peasant's inclination to move in retarded time turned in on itself, because traditional patterns [of activity] and symbols unfold in this time.' There is thus a dialectical relationship, or positive feedback, between enduring and/or retarded time which are expressed in certain patterns of symbolic behaviour, which tend, in turn, to reinforce these types of social time.

My initial reaction to this characterization of the peasant class and the temporal rhythm of peasant life is to protest vigorously against the false stereotype it perpetuates. The dilatory, backwards-looking peasant is a creature of fiction, particularly fiction produced by landlords and urban intellectuals. In my experience, peasants are as harried by the demands of time and fleeting opportunity as urbanites of any description, in fact more so, because the nature of the agricultural work process imposes heavy opportunity costs on any kind of delay or *ad hoc* restructuring of the work schedule. Ploughing, sowing, weeding and harvesting must be done at the appropriate time or not at all, with labour resources and animal capital resources stretched to their utmost, incurring heavy marginal penalties for inefficient use. In the next chapter I shall discuss the 'opportunity cost notion of time', which is really much closer to the peasant's true way of thinking about time than 'traditional patterns and symbols'.

But let us, for the sake of theoretical argument, concede that peasants really do conduct their business at a snail's pace, really do spend inordinate amounts of time on unproductive activities such as superstitious ritual observances, leaning over five-barred gates, and conducting aimless, slow-paced conversations about nothing very much.

What would the world be like if the peasant class lived in 'slower time' than the urban intellectual class, from whose standpoint it appears that a unit of peasant time takes longer to pass than the equivalent unit of standard, non-peasant, time? In 'enduring time of long duration' a peasant hour of 60 peasant minutes is equal to, say, an hour-and-a-half of non-peasant time, each peasant minute being slowed down so that it takes 90 seconds, standard time, to pass. We can first of all imagine this on the relativistic analogy favoured by the author. We can imagine ourselves (up at the great house) looking out of a window, which gives a view of the peasant world outside. We have a watch which gives standard time, and we can see the clock on the church spire in the village, which we shall imagine, for the moment, gives peasant time. If we synchronize our watch with the church clock at 12 noon, by the time our watch says the time is 1 o'clock, the church clock will be saying that the time is 12.45, and the peasants will only have got as much work done as we would have managed to do in three-quarters of an hour, our time. This is the strict analogy with time-dilation in relativity. But it cannot be what Gurvich has in mind because in relativistically dilated time all causal processes are slowed down (from the point of view of an observer in a different inertial frame) which is why the village clock is running slow. Consequently, it has nothing to do with the peasants' supposedly dilatory habits that they appear to get so little done; we could despatch battalion after battalion of agricultural shock-workers to the village without effecting any speeding-up of the tempo of village life. Moreover, if we were to leave our observation-post up at the great house and were to go down to the village ourselves, we would be astonished to find that work was proceeding at a brisk pace. In the village, perfectly normal time would have been restored, and, on the contrary, it would be life up at the great house which would appear to be going very slowly. So in this case we would find that we had no reason to say that in the peasant milieu time is slowed down.

But there is another interpretation of the idea of slowed-down time which is possibly closer to what Gurvich has in mind. Perhaps the observer's watch and the village clock will always keep pace with one another, so that when the watch says the time is 1 o'clock, the village clock also says 1 o'clock. But there is somehow *more time* between 12 noon and 1 o'clock down in the village than up at the great house, despite the formal synchrony of clocks. There is only one way to do this, namely to compress events into smaller intervals of time so that more of them can be accommodated within one synchronous clock interval in slow (expanded) time than in standard time. This would be like playing a film at one-and-a-half times normal speed, showing scenes from a world in which all clocks have been set to run slow. We can imagine that shots of clocks in the film would show them running slow if the film were played at normal speed, but would show them keeping good time, by the standard of a clock installed in the viewing theatre, if the film were run at the faster speed. In this way we would expand time and slow it down, because we could cram an hour and a half's worth of thrills and spills into only an hour's worth of screen time. But of course, in such a film the actors would seem to race around like the demented characters in an old-time silent comedy played at the inappropriate speed on modern projection equipment. Which is hardly the image of peasant life that Gurvich wishes to evoke. Perhaps the peasants, as well as their clocks, have been set to run slow? But they would not *seem* to run slow, neither to themselves, since one peasant hour cannot be slowed down relative to another peasant hour, but only relative to a non-peasant or standard hour, nor would they seem to run slow to us, because although there were 90 of our (fast) minutes in one (slow) peasant hour, the slowed-down peasants would appear to be behaving at the same tempo as they would be if their time and our time were identical. So we would never know.

It would seem that if Gurvich wishes to say that peasants conduct their business in an apparently slowed-down tempo, then peasant time is speeded up, rather than slowed down, with respect to standard time. This would mean that there was less time, not more time, in a peasant hour than in a standard hour, which in turn would explain why the peasants manage to get so little done in one of 'their' hours. But this would hardly be the fault of the peasants. And in this case, also, the original objection to relativistically slowed-down time would apply. From the peasant's own point of view, everything would be proceeding at a normal pace, and there would be no occasion for anyone situated in the peasant temporal milieu, observing the events taking place in the vicinity, to notice anything odd about the time at all.

In short, if you want to get across the idea that affairs in the peasant milieu move rather slowly, as Gurvich does, the one assumption you must adhere to is that 'time' is *not* moving slowly, too. If you do this, then by inexorable logic the peasants are speeded up once more. Saying that the peasants are a slow lot, living in slow time, amounts to saying two things which precisely cancel one another out.

Let me give another example to show Gurvich-type reasoning applied to a situation in which it appears, at first glance, to be quite reasonable. Social geographers have noted the way in which respondents tend to overestimate the relative distance between locations in their own neighbourhood, by comparison with distances between locations in far-off parts of the country or the world (Gould and Whyte 1974). Thus (geographically ill-informed) Londoners may believe that the distance between two cities in the crowded southeast (London and Brighton) is the same as the distance between cities 'up north' (Birmingham and York) which are in actuality more than twice as many miles apart. Given that the same kind of distortions can be detected in the geographical belief-systems entertained by ill-informed individuals anywhere in the country, or the world, we can generalize these findings by constructing a model of 'subjective' 'local' or 'personal' space, as opposed to 'objective' or 'Ordnance Survey' space. Subjective space is expanded in ego's own neighbourhood, and contracted elsewhere.

It might then be argued, apparently with good reason, that people who hold the spatial beliefs which generate distorted maps do not live in 'objective' space but in 'subjective' space, and this is the reason for their peculiar spatial beliefs. It is because 'lived space' is expanded in ego's own neighbourhood, that ego's beliefs about the locations of cities in Britain conflict with their positions as shown on Ordnance Survey maps. But this cannot be so. For if we were to superimpose a distorted grid of 'subjective' or 'lived' space onto an identically distorted map of Britain we would simply re-create a map of Britain which *is identical in its propositional content* with the Ordnance Survey map, because the large distances in ego's neighbourhood in 'subjective space' are metrically equivalent to smaller distances further away. The propositional content of the Londoner's distorted map of Britain is only preserved if this map is drawn in Ordnance Survey space, not in 'subjective' space, centred on London.

That is to say, we can attribute to people non-standard ideas about 'space', or non-standard beliefs about the locations of places in standard space, but we cannot do both simultaneously without these two exactly cancelling one another out. And in fact, people who hold map-beliefs which are geographically incorrect do not hold beliefs about space at all. They simply operate on the basis of non-standard notions about the geography of Britain. The view that non-standard spatial beliefs about the relative distances between close-lying and far-away places can be 'explained' by attributing to people non-standard notions of 'space' is a further instance of the tactic, employed by Durkheimian anthropologists, of constructing a metaphysical scenario in which non-standard contingent beliefs become the equivalent of standard contingent beliefs.

Let me return to Gurvich and his views on peasants after this brief digression, which was designed to make clear the self-defeating nature of the kind of metaphysical argument he espouses. We can very easily see that the second kind of 'time' aberration he attributes to peasants is just as meaningless as the first. This is 'retarded' time, by which he means, presumably, that peasants behave anachronistically, preserving the manners and customs of bygone ages, while the rest of us have acquired more up-to-date habits. I hope, in the light of the preceding discussion, that it will be obvious why anachronistic behaviour is the one failing of which people in 'retarded time' can never justly be accused. If the peasants do not merely *behave* as if the date were 1850, but actually *belong* to 1850, then they are as up-to-date as we are. Either time is retarded, or the peasants are retarded in their old-fashioned ways, but not both at once. But the fact is that we identify behaviour as 'anachronistic' not by attaching a by gone date to it, in which case it would not be anachronistic, but because we must attach today's date to it. The phenomenon of anachronism therefore argues in favour of the unity of time, not its multiplicity.

As for the claim that the peasant class lives in 'cyclical' time, that has perhaps already been refuted by the observations made earlier (Chapter 5) with respect to Leach and Barnes. Cyclical time is the one kind of time in which events which seem to us (in linear-progressive time) to repeat themselves, happen only once. The repetitiveness, as well as the slow tempo and anachronistic semblance of peasant life, are all equally dependent on the 'time dimension' of the peasant milieu conforming rigorously to the linear-progressive one we ourselves recognize.

# Chapter 8

## Bali: the 'Motionless Present'

Gurvich's form of transcendental temporal cultural relativism, with its unfortunate analogies to contemporary relativistic physics, is self-contradictory in rather obvious ways. But not all cultural relativists are so self-evidently the victims of their own rhetoric, nor are all cultural analyses cast in the 'relativist' manner as superficial and stereotyped as his. One can draw a distinction between 'transcendental' cultural relativism, which seeks to explain cultural differences in terms of differently constituted 'realities' or (cultural) 'universes', and non-transcendental relativism, which highlights inter-cultural differences in beliefs, attitudes and values within one encompassing reality. Unfortunately, though it is quite easy to draw a formal distinction between transcendental and non-transcendental cultural relativism, as I have just done, it is not so easy to certain in many instances into which of these two categories particular anthropological texts should be placed. This difficulty arises because cultural-relativist statements are commonly made within implied inverted commas ('in a manner of speaking') for rhetorical or expressive purposes.

A case in point is Geertz's deservedly admired and influential essay 'Person Time and Conduct in Bali' (1973). Hostile critics of Geertz's work such as Bloch (1977) have no difficulty in portraying Geertz as a transcendental relativist of the deepest dye, on a par with Gurvich, and it is true that he risks a number of very Gurvich-like remarks. But the real intellectual debt in Geertz's essay is to Schutz and Weber mediated via Schutz (Schutz 1962, 1966). Schutz certainly never promulgated cultural relativism or associated himself with the idea that categorial forms like space, time, causality, etc. were 'socially derived' in the Durkheimian sense. Schutz was not concerned at all with different cultures or societies as self-contained entities or 'universes' but with the properties of 'the social world' conceived universalistically. His major point is that the kind of 'interpretation' carried on by sociologists is theoretically feasible (i.e. can result in objective knowledge) because this interpretative process is essentially identical to the ongoing process of interpretation or 'meaning-giving' engaged in by agents in the course of their own daily lives. The principle of congruence (or 'reciprocity of perspectives') between observer's meaning-giving and agent's meaning-giving acts – which is the underlying principle behind Geertz's 'interpretative' approach in anthropology (Marcus and Fischer 1986) – is incompatible with the notion that observer and agent (subject, informant, etc.) occupy incommensurate 'cultural universes'. So there is reason to think that Geertz should not be categorized as a relativist in terms of his underlying theoretical standpoint, even though he often sounds like one, as in his more impassioned moments as a prose stylist. But let us consider what he has to say in more detail.

Geertz's essay is not primarily about time as such, but about the concept of the person. However, it contains a number of remarkable statements about Balinese time. His major thesis is that the Balinese conceptualize one another, in terms of personal identities, as 'generalized contemporaries', as exemplars of types, holders of titles, kinship statuses, religious offices, etc. rather than as 'consociates' (Schutz 1967). 'Consociates' in Schutz's terminology are individuals with shared, intimate biographical experiences, as distinct from contemporaries, and unknowable predecessors or successors, who cannot share in each others' biographies by reason of their non-coincidence in time. Geertz argues that for the Balinese, all conceivable people are present 'simultaneously' on Bali, in that all person-types are permanently represented by their tokens. But because persons in Bali are person-tokens of person-types which can have more than one token (just as an office can have more than one holder), persons are not as individualized as they are among ourselves, and they are not seen as living historically unique lives in non-repeating 'durational' time.

This, I think, is the main thrust of Geertz's argument, and it is one which is surely sociologically illuminating outside the limited ethnographic context of Bali; i.e. in many societies 'being a person' and 'holding an office' (in respect of kinship, religious, political, statuses, etc.), i.e. being a token of a certain, permanently represented person-type, are difficult to distinguish

from one another in the idiom of indigenous collective representations. We make an implicit connection between the idea of
'personality' and the ideas of individuality, idiosyncrasy, uniqueness, etc., linkages which are quite foreign to the thought
processes of many other cultures (especially ones with historical
connections to the religion of Hinduism, as is the case with Bali).
However, just as we do not need to assume a heterodox
metaphysical system to 'explain' curious ideas about temporality, there is no need to assume that the Balinese have non-
standard metaphysical notions about 'identifiable individuals' in
order to understand their view that any given Balinese is a token
of a permanently represented person-type. Individuals are identifiable on logical and metaphysical criteria (objective space-time
co-ordinates, occupancy of a unique niche in the web of causal
relationships surrounding them, etc.) – which have nothing to
do with social rules and classifications. Apples or individual
grains of sand are equally identifiable 'individuals' in this logical
sense. But when we buy a pound of apples we are only interested
in their type-characteristics as 'Cox's pippins, grade A', not in
the token-characteristics which make each apple unique, the
precise 'biography' of each apple, the flecks of red, yellow and
green, which are special to each particular one, and so on. These
features are not denied, but they are not salient. Geertz is saying
that the Balinese tend to treat everybody as we treat apples, or
postmen, i.e. as individuals whose type-characteristics are
much more salient than their idiosyncratic features as tokens of
these types, which include the features which make them 'identifiable individuals' in the logical sense.

Geertz calls this a 'depersonalizing' notion of the person,
though a 'de-individualizing' notion of the person would be a
more accurate way of expressing the same idea. The Balinese do
not lack a notion of personhood, but their concept of 'person'
proves, on examination, to be the performance of a socially
prescribed office, part of a system of such person-offices which
the Balinese have developed to an enormous degree.

He links this concept of the person to a 'detemporalizing'
notion of time. Balinese time, he writes, is 'a motionless present,
a vectorless now' (ibid.: 404), – produced out of the 'anony-
mized encounter of sheer contemporaries' (ibid.: 391). It is these
utterances which seem to align Geertz with the out-and-out
cultural temporal relativists like Gurvich. But, viewed dispassionately, it is not really a question of the Balinese living in a

different kind of 'time' from ourselves. Rather, it is a question of the Balinese refusing to regard as salient certain aspects of temporal reality which we regard as much more important, such as the cumulative effects of historical time.

The cultural evidence for Balinese detemporalization comes in a paradoxical form, namely, the luxuriant proliferation of Balinese calendars, of which there are two, a 'permutational' calendar and a luni-solar one, not counting the modern Gregorian calendar which is also in use. The evidence for Balinese detemporalization is specifically connected with the permutational calendar, which has a very interesting property (for a calendar), viz. that it does not generate regular periodicities (such as solar years subdivided into lunar months, subdivided into market weeks, etc.). Instead, the permutational calendar specifies quantum units (days) in terms of the combined product of independent five-, six- and seven-day cycles. Thus beginning at an arbitrary trinomial expression, we get an apparently random pattern:

$$
\begin{array}{llll}
1/5/6 & 1/4/4 & 1/3/2 & 1/2/7 \\
2/6/7 & 2/5/5 & 2/4/3 & 2/3/1 \\
3/1/1 & 3/6/6 & 3/5/4 & 3/4/2 \\
4/2/2 & 4/1/7 & 4/6/5 & 4/5/3 \\
5/3/3 & 5/2/1 & 5/1/6 & 5/6/4 \ldots \text{etc.}
\end{array}
$$

To complete the entire pattern takes 210 days in all, but there are binomial combinations which occur more frequently, i.e. between the five- and seven-day cycles every 35 days, and between the six- and seven-day cycles every 42 days, and between the five- and six-day cycles every 30 days. Each of these 'lesser' conjunctions, resulting in regular binomial days, is inflected, or modulated, by the presence of the third (variable) member of the trinomial set. The end result is that the calendar, far from slicing up time into convenient chunks of duration, has the effect of imposing a fine grid of distinctiveness over 'days' as qualitatively unique exponents of the combinatorial system, not particularly connected to the days in its immediate vicinity (as, for us, 18, 19 and 20 June run into one another by virtue of being 'adjacent weekdays' in this year's Gregorian calendar). As Geertz explains, the purpose of the permutational calendar is not to tell you 'what day it is', but to tell you 'what *kind* of day it is'. The calendar is not a scheme of time measurement, but a component of a system of action; a system of ritual observances (temple festivals, which occur sporadically throughout the year, not at recognized festival seasons and not on any recognized sabbath) and personal actions dictated by the conjunction of 'personal days' (birthdays, auspicious days) and days recognized as being 'good' for particular activities, such as getting married, making a beginning on an important project, and so on. Geertz goes on to say that the other Balinese calendar, the luni-solar one derived from the Indian Hindu calendar (which in India is firmly articulated to astronomical observations), has in Bali become almost equally formulaic, and although the Balinese luni-solar calendar does actually keep track both of the solar year and twelve lunar months (by means of intercalary days – occasional lunar-month days which count as two, every 63 days) the Balinese regulate this by referring to the permutational calendar, not by observation of the heavens. In other words, a perfectly functional 'astronomical' calendar is treated as if it were just as arbitrary a creation as the permutational calendar. In short, both Balinese calendars are non-metrical and 'non-durational', and thus correspond to the climaxless 'steady state' and non-progressive tenor of Balinese social life.

It is surely indisputable that Geertz's account of the Balinese calendar conveys a vivid sense of the guiding principles informing the culture as a whole, and I am sure that he is correct in drawing attention, as he does throughout his essay, to the deep interconnections between the Balinese sociological 'steady state' (etiquette determined by an unchanging regime of 'social placement', underpinned by kinship terminology and the teknonym* naming-system) and the equally non-progressive cycling of the day-naming system. If ever one could hope to see a cultural/ interpretative approach to notions of temporality vindicated, one may see them vindicated here. None the less, in order to communicate his sense of the cultural singularity of Bali, Geertz's has rather exaggerated the degree to which the Balinese calendar is useless for the purposes to which calendars are put elsewhere (i.e. for co-ordinating actions on a regular basis) and the practical use made by the Balinese of their calendars for this specific purpose.

---

* Teknonymy is a system of personal naming whereby individuals are known not by their given name, but by the name of a close relative, whose relation to them is specified in the naming expression, thus: 'Mother-of-John'.

According to a subsequent critic (Howe 1981: 22ff), ordinary
Balinese use the permutational calendar for practical organizational purposes, which need have nothing to do with the
qualitative characteristics of particular 'days'. The qualitative
distinctness of each 'day' does not mean that days cannot be
counted for time-measuring purposes. The calendar is invoked
in order to co-ordinate secular activities and the Balinese are
'very adept at doing this in their heads, and are capable of
computing large intervals (over 100 days)'. Howe disagrees with
Geertz that Balinese attitudes to time are non-durational. All
days are 'different', having different mystical qualities, being
associated with different temple festivals, and so on, but this
does not mean that the Balinese do not count and measure
temporal intervals with precision; on the contrary, unless they
could do this efficiently, their 'frenetic' ritual life would hardly
be feasible.

Howe argues that Balinese are perfectly capable of thinking in
terms of linear/progressive time even when they are utilizing
their traditional calendrical system. When thinking about cycles
as wholes they are thinking in terms of 'cyclical duration'; when
thinking about sequences of events within a cycle they deal in
terms of 'linear duration'. Howe says that there is really no
conflict between 'linear' and 'cyclical' (i.e. non-durational) time.
Temporal cycles return to the same 'logical' point (by which he
means the same point in terms of a cyclical scheme of classification), but not to the same 'temporal' point, in that time is
understood to have passed as the cycle repeats itself. I think that
here Howe is making the same point that was made earlier (see
Chapter 4) that the notion of cyclical recurrence is logically
dependent on the idea of linear time, because only in linear time
can cyclical event sequences be said to recur.

I can also draw here on a discussion of Balinese time concepts
I had with Dr Ward Keeler, an expert in the area. He said that
the Balinese make use of a variety of temporal classifications in
different contexts and for different purposes. Long-term planning makes use of the luni-solar calendar and/or the official
Gregorian one. Local short-term planning makes use of the
five-day market week in rural areas, or a three-day market week
in the vicinity of large markets which operate on a three-day
cycle. Lucky days are determined by another three-day cycle,
one of the three days being appropriate for initiating any given
activity (e.g. lighting a new lamp for the first time, starting

house-building, or cutting the first sheaf at harvest-time, etc.). Ritual events are determined by the 210-day cycle of thirty *uku* (weeks) of seven days. More expert Balinese can combine the seven-day ritual week with the five- and six-day weeks so as to specify ritual days as trinomial expressions, in the way Geertz describes, but for most purposes the *uku* by itself is sufficient. And even experts make use of aids in the form of published almanacs which print, for each day, the phase of the moon, the luni-solar date, the day name in terms of all ten weekly cycles, the activities for which the day is propitious, plus the date according to the Gregorian calendar, the Chinese calendar and the Islamic calendar. Before the arrival of printed almanacs, the timing of rituals was computed with the assistance of carved calendar-boards of traditional design. Dr Keeler expressed the view that Geertz's article gives a rather foreshortened view of Balinese practical time-keeping, suggesting a tremendous piling-up of superimposed systems; in fact, not all systems are in use at once, and some are in use very little at all.

Finally, there is a different kind of critical point which can be made against Geertz's presentation of Balinese temporal notions, short of accusing him of incoherent metaphysical relativism. A calendrical system of the degree of complexity exhibited by the Balinese one is an instrument of power and influence in society, not simply a neutral item of 'culture' accessible to all. Bloch (whose criticisms of Geertz will be considered in Chapter 9) accuses Geertz of concentrating on 'ritual' time-handling schemes, at the expense of practical/secular schemes, which lack the properties which Geertz attributes to Balinese time-conceptualizations as a whole. This criticism is unfounded, to the extent that although the permutational calendar is used for computing important ritual days (such as the island-wide festival *gulungan*, every 210 days) it is also used for determining auspicious days for purely secular enterprises, such as initiating commercial ventures, building houses, and so on. Overriding concern with identifying 'lucky' days cannot be quarantined as a matter of 'ritual' since it pervades the whole spectrum of life and mundane activities. But it does tend to concentrate secular influence in the hands of 'ritual' specialists, i.e. the 'experts' who can give authoritative verdicts on auspicious days, which vary from activity to activity, and from individual to individual.

The best ethnography dealing with this kind of nexus between social influence and calendrical expertise (which in turn depends on the nature of the traditional calendar) comes not from Bali, but from recent studies made in northern Thailand, among Thai (Davis 1976) and among Shan (Tannenbaum 1988). Among these communities (both Buddhist) there exists a variety of calendrical-prognosticatory schemes based on the four-phase lunar cycle, the planetary (seven-day) week, the cycle of twelve animals (familiar to us from Chinese year-names like the year of the dragon, monkey, ox, etc.), which apply to years and also days, and esoteric cycles to do with the times at which certain spirits need to be fed, and the orientation of a giant subterranean dragon which turns on its axis as the year proceeds. These schemes of good and bad days are available to all, in widely circulated printed almanacs and wall-charts. However, Davis is able to show, making use of seven of the available schemes, all of which are in principle complementary and equally valid, that in one randomly selected month (17 December – 15 January 1972) there were, in fact, absolutely no days at all on which it would have been wholly safe for a young, fit Thai man to leave home. But this is precisely the time of year at which young northern Thai men set out for seasonal migrant labour, and consequently the 'rules' were consistently and flagrantly violated. Yet the system as a whole persists, and the sale of almanacs remains as buoyant as ever (Davis 1976: 22).

Davis discusses the many kinds of secondary rationalizations available to those whose pragmatic interests require the infringement of this or that calendrical stipulation, and he also makes the point that the near inevitability of any given activity taking place on a day deemed unpropitious according to some calendrical scheme, provides an intelligible cultural explanation for any kind of failure or disappointment (ibid.: 22–3). I suspect that the Balinese calendar persists, at least in part, because it provides the kind of *post hoc* explanation for misfortune (exonerating the victim of personal responsibility for his enterprise should it miscarry), which Davis describes so well in relation to the structurally similar Thai calendar. But there is also another, more political, aspect to this.

The calendrical system (in the form of printed almanacs, wall-charts, etc.) is not esoteric, and is available to all with a knowledge of written Thai, in which most northern Thai and Shan are literate. But the 'advice' available in this form is patently impossible to adhere to. Consequently second-order expertise is needed in order to select, from among the range of prognosticatory schemes, the one most significant in relation to any specific activity or project which a particular individual might contemplate. Tannenbaum (1988) describes the way in which, among the Shan, this kind of wisdom is ascribed only to precept-keeping Buddhist ascetics, who have 'power' which can be derived, ultimately, only from succession from a long line of Buddhist teachers. The social importance of calendrical experts is not a matter of the imposition of elite power (conferred by literacy) on a cowed, subservient populace. Instead, there is spontaneous demand for an authoritative verdict stemming from a populace, all of whom have access to 'level-one' calendrical expertise, without being able to derive from this expertise unequivocal prescriptions as to their most advantageous courses of action. That is to say, it is the very plurality and complexity of the calendrical system, and the fact that this system is truly democratic and available to all, which motivates the emergence of elite calendrical experts who can provide authoritative advice. And of course, there is a carry-over between the 'power' of the Buddhist expert to 'avoid mistakes' in offering calendrical advice, and the more generalized social influence of Buddhist religious virtuosi regarding the very important matter of donations to the *sangha* and religious intervention in political and social affairs generally.

Issues of the kind examined by Davis (1976) and Tannenbaum (1988) hardly surface in Geertz's account of the Balinese calendar. Even making allowances for the different institutionalization of religious power in Thailand and Bali respectively, they clearly could have been. It is Geertz's turning aside from pragmatic or political considerations which forms the basis of Bloch's critique, which I shall consider next.

# Chapter 9

## Anti-Durkheimian Anti-relativism

In his lecture 'The Past and the Present in the Present' (1977) Bloch makes a two-pronged attack on Geertz's position. First of all, he identifies Geertz as a cultural relativist, and objects to what he says on the grounds that cultural relativism is wrong in principle. Secondly, he maintains that Geertz has confused ideology with cognition, that is to say, he has accepted as a guide to 'how the Balinese think' a particular sub-set of the messages flowing back and forth in the Balinese universe of communication, namely, the messages which are promulgated in 'ritual' contexts. But this is fatal, because these ritual messages are only intended to legitimize authority, and are systematically misleading. Geertz and other anthropologists who advance similar views 'have presented as cultural variation what are in fact differences in the ritual communication view of the world and *our* everyday practical one. In doing this . . . they have confounded the systems by which we know the world with the systems by which we hide it.'

I shall deal with the two prongs of Bloch's argument in turn. First, let us look at his attack on relativism. Bloch traces the origins of cultural relativism to Durkheim, who developed the theory of the social determination of concepts (cf. Chapter 1) in the form in which it appears in the writings of anthropologists like Geertz. (Other influences have been at work as well, notably German Romanticism, mediated via Boas: ibid.: 279.) Bloch (1989) argues that Durkheim's 'sociological' version of Kantianism was motivated by his opposition to naive empiricist theories of cognition, derived from Hume. But, he says, since the eighteenth century, cognitive theory in psychology has made tremendous advances, and the intellectual basis of the Kantian/rationalist premiss that cognition (i.e. the application of categorial forms) precedes perception, experience and action, can no longer be sustained. Anthropologists who belong to the Durkheimian tradition are therefore reliant on a 'sociological' theory of cognition whose claims to superiority over competing (modern) psychological theories of cognition can no longer be intellectually justified. Anthropologists who being to the Durkheimian tradition (which includes most anthropologists) operate what he calls the 'anthropological theory of cognition', which is out-of-date and demonstrably untrue. It is this anthropological theory of cognition which tempts anthropologists into making cultural relativist claims about basic thought-forms, such as time. But he remarks, if the 'notion of time' were really culturally relative, 'physics should really become a sub-trade of anthropology' (Bloch 1989: 282).

Instead of making inflated claims, he continues, anthropologists should make a clear distinction between cognition and ideology. Cognition is a human universal in the sense that all human beings go through a developmental process during which they learn to apply schemata, originally derived from interaction with the world, to structure experiences and grasp relations (such as temporal relations between events). Cognitive time is universal perceptual time. Ideologies, on the other hand, are ideas which are presented in contexts in which authority is being imposed in some way, usually in the course of ritual events such as initiation ceremonies, the installation of sacred rulers, the celebration of ancestors, and so on. In these types of situation the anthropologist is liable to encounter collective representations which strikingly contradict ordinary, everyday notions about the world – representations, for instance, which imply that time goes round and round rather than on and on, or that time is wholly immobilized, past, present and future are identical, and nothing can ever change. It is not hard to see how the purposes of 'traditional legitimization' are well served by collective representations which communicate the fusion of the past, ancestral precedent, and the present, in which these ancestral precedents are mobilized to ensure the continuity of the ruling group in society. But the anthropologists' mistake, according to Bloch, is to have taken these 'ritual' communications, because of their cultural distinctiveness and the intriguing way in which they subvert our common-sense notions of cognitive normality, as if they set the cognitive standard in all contexts, not just ritual ones. They do not reflect cognition at all; they are there to mask, from cognitive scrutiny, certain aspects of the real world which would otherwise be open to it.

The standpoint of cultural relativity stems from misplaced literalism in interpreting ritual communications as if they directly expressed 'alternative' metaphysical postulates. In order to puncture this willing complicity in the deceptions practised in the ritual context, Bloch enumerates certain principled objections to relativism as such. First (as noted previously), the 'hard' sciences have consistently failed to pay any attention to 'culture' in constructing scientific models of the world. Second, Bloch says that if other cultures had profoundly different notions about time from our own, we would not be able to communicate with them. Third, he says that, as a matter of fact, the study of 'the syntax and semantics of natural languages' has shown that all natural languages operate on fundamentally identical logical premises, and 'if all syntax is based on the same logic, then all speakers must apprehend time the same way' (Bloch 1989: 283). Fourth, and finally, he refers to the work of cognitive psychologists, ethnoscientists and psycholinguists, who have demonstrated the empirical existence of cognitive universals (e.g. of intrinsic perceptual salience of 'focal' colours in colour classifications: Berlin and Kay 1969, etc.). (I shall discuss the psychological and linguistic aspects of the anti-relativist position in Chapters 11–15.)

Having made these general points against 'the anthropological theory of cognition' and the anti-scientific relativism which it leads to, he embarks on the second prong of his two-pronged attack, which is this time more specifically aimed at Geertz, rather than at post-Durkheimian anthropology in general. He has to show that the evidence for the idiosyncratic, cultural, 'Balinese' concept of time stems from the social context of the promulgation of strictly 'ideological' (i.e. legitimizing) ritual discourse, and that these concepts do not reflect 'how the Balinese think' about time in 'everyday' (or politically 'oppositional') contexts, outside the ritual frame of reference.

Bloch uses two separate but interconnected arguments in order to make these criticisms of Geertz stick. The first set of arguments relate to the ethnography of time on Bali, which Geertz has presented (he claims) in a very distorted way. The second argument is of a more general, comparative nature, and amounts to a demonstration that Bali belongs to a broad category of 'hierarchical' societies, all of which have comparable ideologies, and comparable collective representations of time, and which can all be contrasted with 'non-hierarchical' societies which lack comparable representations and ideologies for predictable, sociological reasons.

The nature of Bloch's objections to Geertz's ethnographic depiction of Balinese time will already have become clear. Bloch cites Hobart (1975) to the effect that only priests, in their official capacity, use the permutational calendar, while cultivators use 'the seasons' (presumably the luni-solar calendar, which Geertz himself says is relied on by farmers in calendrical computations because it keeps track of seasonal changes: Geertz 1973: 398). This particular assertion of Hobart's is not corroborated by Howe (1981) however, and it does seem that the permutational calendar is more in use in pragmatic contexts than Bloch would have us believe (especially if one includes everyday prognostication of 'lucky' days under the rubric of 'pragmatic calendar use', as I believe is correct; cf. Chapter 8 above). Nor is Geertz wholly silent about the increasing use of the Gregorian calendar in bureaucratic and other contemporary contexts. But whereas Geertz sees this as an aspect of 'change', Bloch interprets this as evidence that Balinese thought-processes are not pervasively influenced by the traditional permutational calendar at all, which is restricted to the ritual contexts. Finally, he notes that the Balinese have been subject to a long series of political and social upheavals throughout this century, culminating in the ending of Dutch colonialism, and the paroxysms engendered by Sukarno's rise to power. The non-periodic sequence of epoch-marking events (wars, volcanic eruptions, etc.) is used in Bali (just as here) to calibrate the times-of-occurrence of less public events (such as the year in which children were born). Geertz, once again, has not failed to notice this fact, but he interprets it quite differently. Geertz sees in this only the limitless individualization of 'punctual' moments of time, which are wholly discontinuous, and hence not articulated to any sense of historical time as a regulated, homogeneous flow. While for Bloch, on the other hand, the consensual recognition of the non-periodic 'calendar' of historic events demolishes Geertz's claim as to the 'timelessness' of Balinese life: the Balinese are consciously in the thick of history and change, and use historical landmarks in order to orient themselves in time generally.

Having disposed of these matters, Bloch introduces his comparative argument, which is to underline the formal coincidence between 'immobilized time' (which he associates with the ritual use of the permutational calendar) and social hierarchy as a world-wide phenomenon. This he contrasts with the pragmatic orientation towards time observable among non-hierarchical people, such as the Hadza (a self-consciously egalitarian tribe of African hunter-gatherers with a 'present focused' temporal orientation: Woodburn (1980). Temporal orientation is, indeed, a function of social structure, as Durkheim would have argued, but only if 'social structure' is made strictly equivalent to 'hierarchy', i.e. social domination buttressed by ritual ideology – forms of communication which are framed in such a way as to render them immune from rational criticism and argument. Thus Bloch can conclude:

> the Balinese evidence does not support the view that notions of time vary from culture to culture, it only shows that, in ritual contexts, the Balinese use a different notion of time from that in more mundane contexts and that in these mundane contexts categories and classifications are . . . based on cognitive universals. (Bloch 1989: 285)

How just are Bloch's criticisms of Geertz? This depends very much on what, exactly, Geertz is understood to be saying. Geertz's text can be read as a cultural-relativist apology for traditional Balinese hierarchy – the reading Bloch has chosen to make – but it is not clear to me that Geertz's text *has* to be read that way. It is equally possible to read Geertz's essay without concluding that Geertz intends to imply cultural relativity in its pseudo-metaphysical form. Geertz is providing an interpretation of certain prominent themes in Balinese culture, not a positive account of Balinese psychology and cognition. The most that Geertz can be accused of in this respect is not having made greater efforts to exclude the reading of his work which would construe it as supportive of hard-line 'metaphysical' relativism of the kind exemplified by Gurvich (or Whorf, whose views I will outline in Chapter 14). Geertz's relativism is not a matter of dogma, but a by-product of literary artifice. As Marcus and Fischer (1986) have noted, Geertz's style of interpretative anthropology aims at a particular literary effect, which they call 'defamiliarization', i.e. the world is presented in a recognizable but transformed manner so that we attain a new perspective on 'normal' understanding of the world by viewing it from unusual co-ordinates. Geertz heightens the defamiliarization effect by using ethnography very selectively, and by piling up details so as to create the impression of a private Balinese reality. But I think one can draw a distinction between Geertz's 'literary' relativism, which is explicitly concerned with the textual representation of cultures, and which views cultures as texts 'read over the shoulder' of the native inhabitants, and the more naive forms of relativism.

The weakness in Geertz's approach is not that he is imposing a positive theory of (cognitive) cultural relativity, but that his exclusively cultural/interpretative frame of reference allows him to avoid the question as to why, of all possible cultural representations, these particular ones should thrive on Bali. Moreover, in order to achieve the brilliant effect of interpretative defamiliarization, which is such a distinctive feature of Geertz's style, the whole cultural system has to be compressed and totalized in a way that is unfaithful to the real character of such systems, both as 'lived' from within, and as encountered from without. Perhaps Geertz can be legitimately accused of suffering from the 'synoptic illusion' identified by Bourdieu (1977; Chapters 28–29 below) in his parallel discussion of ethnographic analyses of the Kybele calendar, i.e. the false totalization of cultural conceptual schemes. And because he engages in this artificial totalization of Balinese 'culture', he cannot handle the kinds of pragmatic issues concerning the ways in which calendrical schemes are deployed and appealed to in practice which Davis (1976) and Tannenbaum (1988) have illuminated in their more down-to-earth accounts of the structurally similar Thai calendar(s). But this distortion of ethnographic reality arises from the logic of literary presentation, not from dogmatic adherence to a false conception of the psychology of cognition.

In Bloch's eyes, Geertz's major failing is that he gives undue respectability to conservative ideologies, by discouraging any tampering with traditional, legitimizing, symbolic forms on the grounds that these constitute the 'total' culture. In assessing this verdict we may begin to take leave of the Balinese material and bring into consideration some of the wider implications of Bloch's critique.

# Chapter 10

## Contrasted Regimes

Is it true, as Bloch says, that there are really only two 'kinds' of time: (1) cognitively universal time, and (2) cyclic, 'immobilized' ritual time. And is it true that 'cyclic' time is exclusively confined to the ritual legitimization of authority in hierarchical societies? I shall defer consideration of Bloch's psychological thesis of cognitively universal pragmatic time to Chapters 11–12. But the question of the purported confinement of 'cyclical' notions of time to the ritual frame of reference is one which can be answered with reference to anthropological material in isolation, and is therefore more conveniently considered first. I do not think that Bloch's claim that 'cyclic' ideas of time are exclusively confined to ritual contexts and are produced only in hierarchical societies can be sustained. This criticism can be supported not just by citing counterexamples (which I shall produce later), but also by following through the implications of Bloch's own views about 'practical' (non-ritual) time. Where does 'practical' time come from?

> it is in contexts where man is most directly in contact with nature that we find universal concepts, [thus] the hypothesis that it is something in the world, but beyond society, which constrains at least some of our categories is strengthened, though this need not be nature as an independent entity to man, but as I believe is suggested by Berlin and Kay's data and foreshadowed by Marx, nature as the subject of human activity. (Bloch 1989: 285)

Cyclic time is produced by ritual, but 'nature as the subject of human activity' produces practical time, about which we are told little more than that it is linear. But here there is a difficulty. 'Nature as the subject of human activity' is pervasively periodic. There is ample evidence to suggest that concepts of 'duration' are, in most agrarian societies, centred on periodicity and recurrence, a point made convincingly by Barnes (1974) in relation to the Kédang. In fact, it is difficult to express the idea of 'linear' progressive time without appealing to the idea of discrete intervals of time being added to one another serially, days succeeding days, months succeeding months, years succeeding years, and so on. The recognizability factor of recurrent cycles is critical to 'practical' temporality. It is not religious dogma, but the closed nature of the agricultural productive cycle, and the opportunity costs incurred by undue delay in completing the phases of this cycle, which focalize 'recurrence' as the most salient feature of 'time' in agrarian communities. There is nothing at all mystical about this, and it has nothing intrinsically to do with hierarchy.

Bloch implies that cognitively universal time stems from the uniform characteristics of human interactions with nature as the subject of human activity, or more specifically, labour. In this section I shall sketch in the cultural time-handling system of the two societies of which I have had direct experience as an ethnographer, the Umeda of New Guinea, and the Muria Gonds, a 'tribal' (*adivasi*) society of central India. Neither of these societies would be described as hierarchical, and though both mount elaborate rituals (the major Umeda ritual, *ida*, has already been described) in neither case would it be true to say that ritual is primarily concerned with legitimizing authority. Moreover, although both the Umeda and the Muria think about natural and social processes in terms of established cycles or periodicities, there are structural differences between 'cyclical time' (i.e. cyclical processes) in the two instances, which I would trace to differences in their respective regimes of production. In other words, although I agree with Bloch when he says that ideas of 'time' (i.e. socially recognized processual schemes) arise through interaction with 'nature as the subject of human activity', I believe that the contexts in which nature becomes the subject of human activity are insufficiently uniform to give rise to universals of time cognition.

The Umeda, like many lowland New Guinea societies, subsist primarily on sago. Processing sago is a year-round activity, which is only suspended briefly during the ritual season, but which is perfectly feasible at any time of year, except during rare and unpredictable droughts, when water for leaching starch from sago logs becomes termporarily scarce. The Muria Gonds

of central India are rice growers on dyked but otherwise unirri-
gated fields, dependent for their main crop on the monsoon
rains. To this simple but essential difference in productive
regimes profound differences in temporal attitudes and time
concepts can be traced. The temporal regime of Umeda, ritual
considerations apart, is essentially homogeneous and equable,
with only slight seasonal variations; among the Muria, on the
other hand, each season is associated with sharply distinct activities, so that at different seasons of the year one might as well
be living in a completely different place. Were a stranger to visit
Muria country in July, and leave before the rains ended, he
would have no means of forming a mental image of Muria
country in March, when the mud would have turned to dust,
the lush, green, waterlogged paddy fields to broken red wastes,
silence and intense industry to noise, leisure, merriment. A
visitor to the Umeda would be at no such disadvantage.

Paddy cultivation pits man against nature and the inexorable
passage of the seasons in a way that sago production never
does. Certain processes, notably sowing, weeding and harvesting, have to be performed within temporal parameters set by the
biological requirements and growth pattern of the rice plant.
The seed rice must fall onto waterlogged earth, weeding must
be complete before the grain-bearing shoots mature, harvesting
before the grain begins to be shed. These demands, emanating
from the nature of the cultigen, and the fact that it is being
grown in an artificial environment rather than where it would
occur naturally, place exceptional demands on labour resources
and management skills at 'life-crisis' stages in the life of the rice
plant. In the cultivation, or more precisely, the exploitation, of
sago there is nothing comparable to the tension generated in dry
grain agriculture at all seasons except the slack period between
harvesting and planting. Sago is a wild plant in Umeda country,
though sago stands can be artificially created by planting suckers in
suitable places. Moreover, sago palms once felled spontaneously
regenerate in the same place. The tension involved in sago
production is of a different kind. Sago palms take up to fifteen
years to mature, although some may be ready for felling after
about seven years. The maturation of rice plants is a process
which can be observed on a week-to-week basis, almost a day-
to-day basis, whereas months and even years go by with little
discernible effect on a sago palm. The Umedas' worries about
sago palms are of a diffuse, long-term kind; worries that the

palms are maturing too slowly, or that when, after years of slow growth, they are felled, they will be nothing but wood inside. The Muria farmer contemplates imminent, short-term disaster, with the prospect of a better or luckier season to follow; the Umeda think in terms of apocalyptic doom lurking as a background possibility, but have few short-term worries.

These are the contrasts in productive regimes as between the Muria and the Umedas: now let us turn to the contrasts in temporal regimes. In essence, the whole matter can be summed up in one Muria Gondi word which does not have a counterpart in the Umeda vocabulary. The word in question is *pabe*, meaning 'disposable time, opportunity'. This word is most frequently encountered as part of the expression *pabe mayon*. This is the stock excuse for refusing any form of assistance and means, 'I have not got time'. The notion of time as a scarce resource is one which, to the best of my knowledge, is simply not encountered in Umeda. I sometimes had to solicit labour for carrying from the Umedas. As time went by, they discovered that I was not, as they had imagined, an eccentric patrol officer, but an ordinary human being whose requests could safely be refused. What used to puzzle me was the way in which the Umedas, when making their excuses, never cited pressing duties elsewhere, as we would ourselves. They simply stated that they had no wish to do as I desired. To our way of thinking, that hardly counts as an 'excuse'; but given the elasticity of time-demand in Umeda none other is culturally available to them. It is not that the Umedas were idle; far from it. Their economy only left them a slim margin in terms of food, and in order to subsist they had to work regularly and often quite hard. But they had no reason to develop the opportunity-cost notion of time which is found among the Muria and people like them, in which the non-performance of activity during a specific 'window of opportunity' was tantamount to its non-performance at any time. For the Umedas, the non-performance of an activity at some specified time merely means that it has been deferred to some other time, with the consequent loss of whatever benefit might have accrued had it been performed rather than deferred, but not the additional loss of the 'opportunity' to perform it.

The Umedas have no names for months, nor any idea of how many months there are in a year. Their ritual cycle is entirely lacking in first-fruits ceremonies; there is no 'new' sago. The seasons are only weakly distinguished as wet and dry, though

some other Umeda comestibles than sago, notably bamboo
shoots, taro and *gnetum gnemon* leaves have distinct times of
appearance. They lack weeks, weekly markets or a sabbath day.
However, they are not incapable of co-ordinating short-term
activities by day-counting. But instead of having a fixed weekly
cycle, they make use of a set of seven words articulated to
'today', i.e. the day before the day before yesterday/the day
before yesterday/yesterday/today/tomorrow/the day after
tomorrow/the day after the day after tomorrow.

In the Umeda 'week', today, so to speak, is always Wednesday. This shifting, barrierless time corresponds to the shifting,
improvisatory and uncoordinated nature of the Umeda productive process; the meanderings of autonomous family groups
from one sago stand to another in the dense forest, punctuated
by sporadic excitements of an unpredictable kind (collective
running-down of a wounded wild pig, the performance of
curing rituals for the sick, or staking out the paths into the
village to catch and kill a sorcerer), all without reference to any
overall schedule. Only the ritual cycle gives any coherence to
the pattern, and the ritual cycle is imposed, one is inclined to
say, in defiance of the facts of nature and productive processes,
rather than because of them.

Among the Muria, we encounter an entirely different temporal regime. The Muria have named months, borrowed, along
with their present agricultural technology, from the Hindus of
Bastar. They are capable of detailing, with precision, the annual
cycle of activities, and those who are literate make use, like
other Indian peasants, of the published agricultural almanacs
which give advice as to astrologically propitious moments for
initiating different kinds of work. Their traditional calendar is
articulated by first-fruits ceremonies, all the major ceremonies
celebrating village and clan divinities falling into this category.
Life-crisis ceremonies, of which the most important are naming
ceremonies, betrothals, marriages and entombments, also fall at
predetermined times of year, rather than at irregular times
throughout the year. The calendar of ritual events is co-
ordinated at the district level, so that the gods of particular
villages and clans, together with their devotees, can assemble in
large numbers and visit each village in turn. This progression of
calendrical feasts of the gods from place to place throughout the
district is recapitulated, on a smaller scale, by the institution of
the market week, the seven days of the week being named both

by their Hindi names and by the names of the markets held on particular days of the week: Thursday is Pharasgaon market day, Friday is Dhorai market day, Saturday is Chhote Dongar market day, Sunday Narayanpur market day, and so on (Gell 1982). At these markets men from different villages meet and co-ordinate the affairs of the district. Despite being illiterate, Muria can and frequently do make arrangements for social and ritual events months or even years in advance within a rigid calendrical framework.

It is significant that one of the three words from English which have entered the Muria vocabulary is 'time' (the others are 'power' and 'officer'). Time, power, authority, scheduling are all linked together in a single complex of meanings, whose basis, I would argue, lies in the nature of the established regime of peasant production. Farming, anywhere in the world, is a gamble, wherein the odds always favour those who can afford to plan in the longer term over those who are obliged to plan in the short term only. Exercising 'power' in the peasant milieu is equivalent to having control over time, being able, in other words, to organize (i.e. schedule) the activities of a productive household so as not to be left behind by events, which proceed according to the inexorable but never entirely predictable timetable set by the interaction between seasonal weather conditions and the biological needs of the various crops. The enduring popularity of farming almanacs in India and elsewhere in the peasant world is to be attributed to the fact that these documents, whose stipulations are more honoured in the breach than the observance (cf. Chapter 8) none the less epitomize the essential – temporal – form of the farmer's predicament, offering a magical surrogate for control over time and chance which the peasant, always on the horns of some planning dilemma, never has.

These two examples show, I think, that Bloch is correct in believing that human interaction with 'nature beyond society' profoundly influences time cognition. But this interaction is by no means standardized. Different societies or social strata, operating under different ecological circumstances, employing different technologies and faced with different kinds of long-term and short-term planning problems, construct quite different cultural vocabularies for handling temporal relationships. Temporal cognitive universals of a substantive kind, i.e. universal contingent belief systems appertaining to the way the world works as a complex of temporal relationships between events, are just as mythical as post-Durkheimian culture-specific temporal metaphysical systems. Everything that we could want to say about time, culture and cognition can be said without embracing either of these unpalatable alternatives.

Having established the Umedas and the Murias as examples of contrasted types of temporal regime, with the suggestion that it is the system of subsistence production which is primarily responsible for the differences between them, it may be of interest to pursue the argument a little further in relation to the distinction between 'ideological' time and 'practical' time, suggested by Bloch. It will be recalled that Bloch believes that practical time (deriving from perceptual cognitive universals) is linear, whereas ideological time, found only in ritual contexts and designed to 'hide' reality, is static and/or cyclic.

At first glance, the form taken by the ritual representations of time among both the Muria and the Umeda seems to support Bloch. The Muria ritual system is, as mentioned previously, an elaborate series of first-fruits ceremonies, sacrifices honouring the gods at the completion of each stage in the agricultural year, after which the new crop may be eaten and preparations for the production of next year's crops may begin. The Muria cult of the gods is a cycle of calendrical feasts. It would be not at all inaccurate, therefore, to say that the Muria ritualize time in cyclical form, and that the purpose of ritual is to celebrate both the hierarchy (mortals vs. gods) and the established order of things in fixed, immobilized time. On the other hand, Muria calendrical feasts do not legitimize hierarchical relationships among mortals themselves. These calendrical feasts are all-Muria affairs, and the Muria are 'egalitarian' in the same way that the New Guinea Highlanders are 'egalitarian', i.e. their villages are presided over by a clique of Big Men (*siyan*, wise ones) whose positions of influence are based on achievement principles, not ascribed status. Where other castes participate in Muria calendrical feasts, as they did in the village where I stayed, then these castes, even if they are officially higher than the Muria in the caste hierarchy (not eating beef, and so on) attend under Muria patronage, as their ritual clients. This is because the Muria are the original owners of the land, and it is their local clan gods, not the Hindu ones, who ensure its fertility. Muria rituals are the occasions, not for demonstrations of hierarchy, but, quite the converse, for obligatory, sustained and inclusive commensality and gift exchange between all component households in the village. This is not a Saturnalia, an occasion for subverting hierarchy for the duration of a limited 'ritual season' after which it is reimposed (Bloch 1989: 127). On the contrary, it is the dramatization of the ideal egalitarian social order. This ideal order is founded on unstinting generosity and fellow-feeling towards all co-villagers, and through its enactment the Muria hope to win the favour of their democratic gods, who hate exclusiveness, and will always cast down the mean or over-mighty from their place. Muria ritual is not, in other words, a device for the legitimization of hierarchy, but the means of collectively renouncing it.

The 'cyclical' view of time is not, in origin, a ritual attitude, but an attitude which stems from a certain *type* of practicality, the practicality of the peasant or subsistence farmer. Transmuted into ritual, this attitude is expressed in the celebration of calendrical feasts which represent the agrarian year in ideal form as regular, repetitive and presided over by more or less reliable and beneficent gods, who must be thanked and propitiated. I do not deny that ritual in peasant/subsistence societies can have overtones supportive of established social hierarchy, but it also has to be acknowledged that in so far as elements of resistance to social hierarchy exist in such societies – these sentiments are particularly marked among the Muria, but they are not unique in this respect – then these, too, are brought to the fore in calendrical rites. And in general it is true to say that such calendrical celebrations confirm and perpetuate the peasant cultivator's belief that he is in control of his situation, that the world is a predictable place, and that his knowledge of its workings is adequate to his needs. We can call this 'ideological' in that it is the socially approved manner of whistling in the dark, but there is no need to attribute it to the mystificatory strategies of a privileged elite.

The next point which needs to be made is that granted the fact that Muria ritual represents the world in the form of an idealized cyclical temporal scheme, there is a profound difference between the form of 'cyclic' ritual representations of time among the Muria, and the ritual representation of time found among the Umedas, who, according to Bloch's scheme, would be placed in just the same bracket. Here I may refer to the earlier discussion of the difference between alternating event-sequences of the $A \rightarrow B \rightarrow C \rightarrow B \rightarrow A$ type and recurrent event-sequences of the $A \rightarrow B \rightarrow C \rightarrow A \rightarrow B \rightarrow C$ type. These are lumped together by many writers including Lévi-Strauss, Gurvich and Bloch, but (here I concur with Leach) they are very different and give rise to distinct types of collective representations of cosmological/ritual processes (see Chapter 4 above). But it is not a matter of choosing which of these two types of event-sequence is most characteristic of 'primitive notions of time' (as in the conflict of opinions between Leach and Barnes; cf. Chapter 4 above). As processual schemes – not metaphysical dogmas about time, but general conceptions of natural and social processes – both kinds of model are equally possible and may indeed coexist.

In order to make this clear, an analogy may help. The London underground system includes two kinds of lines. Most, like the Bakerloo Line, have two termini (Baker Street and the Elephant and Castle are the termini on the Bakerloo Line) between which the trains run back and forth. However, one line (the Circle Line) has no terminus, but it does have two important stations, Victoria to the south and Edgeware Road to the north, where the trains stop to be cleaned and take on fresh crews etc. Umeda ritual, the *ida* ceremony in particular, represents the cosmos on the Bakerloo Line principle. Before the ceremony begins, the world, so to speak, is at the Elephant and Castle, in a mess, about to succumb to the natural but fertile disorder represented by the cassowaries (cf. Chapter 5). Then, as the ritual progresses, via a systematic exploitation of metaphors of natural and social processes thrown into reverse, the world is gradually restored to Baker Street, pristine and renewed.

The principle underlying Muria ritual, on the other hand, is the Circle Line principle; Circle Line trains never go into reverse – and there are no metaphors for reversed time in Muria ritual – instead, they arrive at *thresholds* marking new stages in their continuous forward movement. The calendrical rituals of the Muria are not restorative, like the *ida* ceremony, but celebratory, like life-crisis rituals. Thus although Muria and Umeda rituals both invite analysis in terms of 'cyclic' conceptions of time, the varieties of 'cycles' in either case are distinctly different. And this implies, in turn, that Bloch's global distinction between ritual/ cyclic and pragmatic/linear concepts of time is oversimplified.

# Chapter 11

# Psychological Evidence for the Universality of Time Cognition

One of the major points made by Bloch in his critique of cultural relativism was, it will be recalled, that contemporary psychology has moved beyond naive realism, and is now in a position to chart the development of categories of thought, such as time, in the ontogenetic development of cognition at the individual level. In this section I shall briefly look at the psychological evidence concerning time cognition in order to see how well Bloch's claim stands up.

There are two branches of psychological theory which have to be considered here. First, there is the body of psychological experimentation on so-called 'time-perception', which should perhaps better be called time-estimation, in which subjects, usually adults, are asked to estimate 'elapsed time' under a variety of experimental settings. And second, there is the work on the development of the ability to handle temporal relationships during infancy and childhood, work which is primarily associated with Piaget and his school. Bloch attaches particular importance to Piagetian work in the area of cognition as forming the basis for a replacement to the outmoded 'anthropological theory of cognition' (1989: 113). I shall deal with the psychological evidence for time perception in this chapter, and with Piaget developmental psychology in Chapter 12.

We have no dedicated sense-organ for the measurement of elapsed time, as we have for the measurement of vibrations in the air (forming sounds) or the wavelengths and relative positions of light-waves striking the retinas of our eyes. To speak of the 'perception' of time is already to speak metaphorically. Hence it is somewhat disingenuous on Bloch's part to argue that because Berlin and Kay (1969) were able to demonstrate, in a

famous cross-cultural survey, that human beings were universally liable to perceive certain certain colours (corresponding to
particular wavelengths) as 'focal', the same kind of argument
must apply to the perception of time. In effect, what Berlin and
Kay found was that colours like bright red are singled out in all
languages and provided with a primary taxonomic label, while
colours like turquoise (which we think of as intermediate between two 'primary' colours, blue and green) are never singled
out in the same way, and are commonly named, as turquoise is
in English, by a 'secondary' colour-taxon based on some exemp-
lar in the real world, in this case a well-known semi-precious
stone. Berlin and Kay's findings have won almost universal
acceptance (cf. Gell 1975: 310ff), but it is impossible to apply
their work in any direct way to the perception of time. The
significance of their work is that it strongly suggests that every
human being sees colours in the same way; the sensation I get
from a patch of bright red is exactly the same as the sensation
that an Amazonian gets, or a Mayan Indian, or whoever. But the
whole thrust of the work done by experimental psychologists on
'time-perception' points in exactly the opposite direction. The
primary topic of experimental work on time has been the immense variability of estimates of durations made by experimental subjects placed in different settings, allotted different tasks, given different drugs, suffering from different
physical and mental diseases, belonging to different classes,
different chronological ages, and so on (Fraisse 1964; Cottle
1974; Ornstein 1969). Psychological studies of 'subjective' time
are no less 'relativist' than cultural studies of differences in
temporal saliences, such as Geertz (1973), indeed, that is the
whole point of conducting them.

    Meanwhile, it is always possible for us to distinguish how
long an interval 'seemed' to last (our perception of its duration)
and how long it actually did last (the cognitive judgement we
arrive at on the basis of all the information at our disposal,
including, for example, making use of a clock). The psychological study of time-perception consists precisely in the analysis
and explanation of the *variable* relationship between 'perceived'
and 'clock' durations. In fact, our organic sense of durations is
relatively unreliable, and in arriving at cognitive durational
judgements we mainly rely on cues derived from clock-like
cyclical processes in the external environment, in default of
actual clocks, not on perceptions of duration *per se*.

Ornstein's (1969) influential study of the psychology of durational judgements suggests very strongly that the estimated duration of experimental tasks assigned to subjects in the laboratory is a function of the processing load imposed by each task individually, i.e. the greater the amount of information processing per unit of clock time, the greater the estimated duration of the task relative to the estimated durations of other tasks demanding less processing. Because in real-world situations tasks vary randomly in the amount of central information processing they require, we can legitimately assume that estimated durations in real world situations vary randomly, within limits, relative to clock time. On the analogy with judgements of colour, this would be like judging colours in a world where the colour of incident light varied randomly.

Perceived duration and cognized duration vary with respect to one another, and cognized duration (what we 'know' the time to be, or the amount of time we 'know' a particular task has taken) always takes precedence over 'perceived' duration (what we 'feel' the time to be). We may certainly perceive time, but we place no reliance on these perceptions. We rely instead on a system of inferences based not on the perception of duration as such, but on the perception of clock-like processes in the outside world. The functional utility of perceived duration to the organism is not the provision of an internal clock measuring time, but the provision of internal feedback relative to the loading imposed on the organism by a particular task or activity, whether it is physical or mental, at least in so far as we are only considering relatively short durations, well within the limits of endogenous circadian rythms.

Because there is systematic variance between cognized duration (the length of a duration according to our beliefs about the measurement of durations) and perceived duration (the measure of a duration sensed internally) there are no grounds for supposing that cognized duration is ultimately founded on perceived duration. Time cognition is a function of the beliefs we hold about the world, not a direct outgrowth of primitive processes of time-perception monitored by an internal clock mechanism. For this reason, I do not think that Bloch is correct in arguing for a clear distinction between 'basic' time perception-cum-cognition, what he calls 'the perception of duration' vs. the 'cultural' apparatus of belief-systems and/or classification systems appertaining to time, what he calls 'the way time is divided up or metaphorically represented' (1977: 282). Temporal cognitions are based on inferential schemes whose input data do not come in the form of estimated durations, but in the form of significant events in the outside world which have temporal meanings: '*if* X is the case (and I can see that it is), *then* in terms of such-and-such a temporal/processual schema, we are at time T.' In arriving at temporal judgements calendars and clocks are essential, not, as Bloch would have it, merely cultural frills without cognitive significance.

Here I include cattle-clocks, and the like. The whole world is just one big clock, but it is one which different people can read very differently – because what we can see, out there in the objective world, is only, so to speak, the hands of the clock, but not the clock-face in relation to which, and to which alone, the configuration of the hands assumes its particular temporal meaning.

# Chapter 12

## Piagetian Developmental Psychology

Bloch's claim that modern experimental psychology has uncovered substantive universals of temporal cognition is not, however, based on the experimental work on 'subjective' time which has just been alluded to. The only experimental psychologist he cites, other than psycholinguists (see Chapter 13 below) is Piaget. And this is eminently justifiable, since Piaget's (1970) important series of experiments on the development of the sense of time among children is without a doubt the most elaborated cognitive exploration of temporal thinking yet to have been produced. In this section I shall briefly outline the relevant parts of Piaget's work on time, and offer some comments on its applicability to the anthropological question of the cross-cultural psychic universality of conceptions of time.

As is well known, Piaget elaborates a series of 'stages' in the growth of the mind. There are three stages, the second of which is divided into two. I list them below, with notes to indicate the kinds of time-conceptions which emerge at the various stages.

1.  The sensori-motor stage (before the age of 2, language not developed, child entirely bound up with his immediate environment). At this stage the child is unable to classify processes at all.
2a. Pre-operatory stage I (ages 3–6 approximately). At this stage the child learns to order events into series. Recurrent events are recognized and phases in processes are articulated by means of 'punctual' time indicators.
2b. Pre-operator stage II (ages 7–11). At this stage the child learns not only to recognize series of events, but to co-ordinate series one with another. However, in doing this the child fails to 'conserve' duration, and makes certain charac-

teristic mistakes, which will be detailed below.
3.   Operatory stage (around the age of 12). The child is able to
     co-ordinate series of events with reference to an abstract
     notion of 'duration', which is conserved consistently. The
     child that has reached this stage is able to make use of
     'reversible' operations (see p.          below). These revers-
     ible operations form the basis of the notion of time em-
     ployed in scientific calculation, physics, etc.

     The chronological 'ages' corresponding to mental stages
     must not be interpreted too rigidly, since children vary
     widely in their developmental time-table, and the stages
     themselves overlap and merge into one another. But Piaget
     consistently maintains their distinctiveness, and the fact
     that they follow one another in a fixed order corresponding
     to an endogenously determined genetic process of intellec-
     tual maturation.

With respect to time, Piaget's 'stages' can be identified via the
following experimental procedure. The child is presented with a
pack of cards depicting two flasks, of different shapes, one
straight-sided and one pear-shaped. When arranged as in
Figure 12.1a the cards show water draining out of the pear-
shaped flask into the straight-sided one.

During stage 1 the child has only an 'intuitive' grasp of time.
Time, so far as the stage 1 child is concerned, is entirely bound
up with observable changes and processes in the outside world,
and cannot be abstracted from them. Given a shuffled pack of
the cards showing the filling up of flask II and the emptying out
of flask I, the child is unable to put them into any kind of order,
i.e. is capable of neither lining up the set of cards showing each
flask individually, still less of putting the series showing flask I
into its correct relationship with the set showing flask II. This
stage is surpassed once the child discovers that the cards for
each flask separately can be made to represent a process. At this
stage (stage 2a) the child is able to group the phases of a process
within that process as a whole. A process-classification, one
might say, has been achieved, ordering the cards showing a
flask filling or emptying. According to Piagetian theory, this
cognitive achievement is not the result of learning or experience,
though naturally the child must be furnished with the necessary
observable models of processes taking place, real flasks full of
water, and so on, but is the outcome of an endogenously con-

**Figure 12.1 Piaget's experiment**

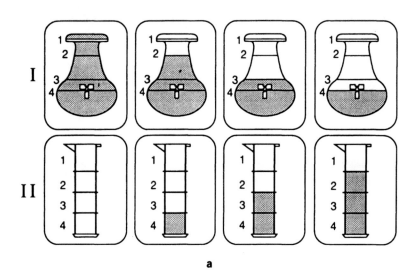

a

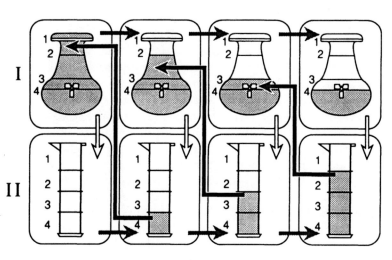

b

trolled process of mental growth. At this early stage the child, though aware of the nature of a series of phases adding up to make a process, has no notion of the durational aspect of this or any other process in isolation from the process under consideration.

The next stage arrives (stage 2b) when the child realizes that for any member of the series $I\backslash 1 \rightarrow I\backslash 2 \rightarrow I\backslash 3 \rightarrow I\backslash 4, \ldots$ there corresponds one member, and one only, of the set $II\backslash 1 \rightarrow II\backslash 2 \rightarrow II\backslash 3 \rightarrow II\backslash 4$. At stage 2b the child is able to perform 'co-seriation', i.e. can grasp the fact that there is a regular relationship of some kind between the emptying of flask I and the filling up of flask II. But the child's understanding of this is still qualitative rather than quantitative. The quantitative relationship between the velocity with which the water is displaced from flask I and is replaced into flask II cannot yet be comprehended. The child does not yet 'conserve' duration. For instance, the child assumes that a drop of 20 cm in the water level in the pear-shaped flask occupies the same duration as a rise of 20 cm in the water level in the tall, straight-sided flask. The child at stage 3 is unable to see that only in the latter flask (II) will a fixed relationship be preserved between duration and changes in the water level, while in the curvaceous flask the relationship between changes in the water level and time will be variable.

In other words, Piaget's experimental design casts the straight-sided flask in the role of an old-fashioned water-clock (though Piaget never remarks on this fact), and the mental aptitude being tested is: (1) the child's ability to infer the clock-like properties of the straight-sided flask, fed by a tap which runs at a constant rate, and marked off into equal divisions on its sides; and (2) to make correct inferences about the significance of changes in the water level in the curvaceous flask, given that the child has at his or her disposal the straight-sided flask to use as a clock. The child up to stage 3 is incapable of performing the necessary deductions or 'operations', and is hence categorized as 'pre-operatory'.

Piaget states that a fully operational grasp of time depends on the acquisition of a mental skill he calls 'reversibility'. Suppose we wish to grasp the fact that the irregularly spaced marks on the curvaceous flask correspond to displacements of water occupying identical durations to the displacements which take place between the regularly spaced marks on the straight flask. We cannot do this by simply following events as they happen in real time. If we do this, all we know is that $I\backslash 1$ corresponds to $II\backslash 4$

(empty), I\2 corresponds to II\3, I\3 corresponds to II\2 and I\4 corresponds to II\1. But we have as yet no grounds for saying that the displacement I\1 → I\2 equals I\2 → I\3, and that this displacement is equal in turn to I\3 → I\4, because the level markers on flask I are irregularly spaced. But the marks on flask II *are* regularly spaced, so it is obvious that the displacements II\4 → II\3 equal II\3 → II\2 and both equal II\2 → II\1. In order to establish the identity of the displacements I\1 → I\2 = I\2 → I\3 = I\3 → I\4 it is necessary to reason backwards, *undoing* a process that has already elapsed in real time. Thus:

*If* II\4 → II\3 = I\1 → I\2
*and*
II\4 → II\3 = II\3 → II\2
*and*
II\3 → II\2 = I\2 → I\3
*then* I\1 → I\2 = I\2 → I\3, which was what needed to be established.

I\1 → I\2 must be equal to I\2 → I\3, despite the irregularity of the marks because by 'thinking backwards' over the displacements taking place concurrently in flask II the identity of the displacements (i.e. the durations) is established. I have tried to indicate this idea in Figure 12.1b. The forwards-running, horizontal arrows correspond to the stage 2a idea of time embodied in separate, unique series. The vertical arrows correspond to the stage 2b pre-operatory idea of co-seriation. The diagonal, backwards-leaning arrows correspond to the idea of 'reversible operations.'

In Piagetian theory, the acquisition of reversible operations which enable the child to use the straight-sided flask as a water-clock to calibrate the displacements in the curvaceous flask, are linked with the simultaneous acquisition of a whole battery of operational mental skills involving causal relationships, arithmetical and logical relations, etc., which are essential forms of abstraction needed to solve computational tasks of the kind encountered in the technical activity of the numerate elite in advanced societies. The reversibility needed to analyze the phases of a process in terms of abstract 'duration' rather than in terms of 'work done', i.e. concrete physical changes occurring in real time rather than in abstract, manipulable, time, is cognate to the mental skill needed to see that the order in which a commutative arithmetic operation is carried out has no influence on the eventual sum.

(a) $7 + 4 = 11$ (b) $4 + 7 = 11$ (c) $5 + 3 + 2 + 1 = 11$

The pre-operatory child regards (a), (b) and (c) as three different additions because in the second sum the numbers to be added are presented in a different order, and in the third they are different numbers. The operatory child is capable of constructing an abstract set of all possible partitions of the integers between 1 and 11 into two, three or more subsets, and is hence able to see that (a) and (b) are the same partition, and that (c) is the same partition further subdivided. Operatory thought, in other words, is the ability to range freely within an analytical domain, here arithmetic, but the same applies to the making of durational judgements, unconstrained by the phenomenal order of things, objects, processes, etc. The operatory child thinks with abstract models (reversible operations), while the pre-operatory child makes use of concrete models (concrete operations).

There is no doubt that Piaget is seeking to delineate cognitive universals of time, and it is implied, though not stated, that all children eventually attain to the operatory stage. However, Piaget's work has been read in a very anti-universalist way by Hallpike in his work *The Foundations of Primitive Thought* (1979). Hallpike represents another variant of cultural relativism, not one that contrasts cultures as operating incommensurable, culturally determined 'world-views', but a kind of relativism based on a purported cognitive-developmental hierarchy. According to Hallpike, the ability to abstract 'time' as a computable aspect of *all* processes, in terms of duration, succession and simultaneity, is an aptitude not possessed by members of pre-technological societies. 'Primitive' thought remains wedded to an intuitive, concrete, conception of time, which is still in every case geared to actual processes in nature and society. Primitive conceptions of time are pre-operatory because they are linked to real processes and these processes do not reverse themselves. Time is not understood as an abstract dimensional continuum, e.g. as what can be represented by the symbol 't' in physical equations and which can be integrated with spatial displacement so as to express a joint product, velocity, in the equation $V = s/t$ (velocity equals displacement in space per unit of elapsed duration). In primitive thought the technical concept of velocity is replaced by the pre-technical concept of *speed*, which is a property objects possess in their own right, as redness is a property of apples, ferocity a property of lions, and so on. 'Quickness' and 'slowness' are concrete and qualitative characteristics of specific objects and processes; 'velocity' is an abstract conceptual tool for relating the behaviour of objects and processes to spatio-temporal co-ordinates defined independently of any particular entities.

This absence of a general schema of duration, linked to an abstract notion of space via the intermediary concept of velocity, inhibits computation requiring reversible operations. From one point of view time is too much bound up with the real world, in that it cannot be grasped in isolation from specific real-world processes materializing in real time, and from another point of view it is too isolated to be conceptually useful, in that there is no articulation between time and space, time and causality, time and number, geometry, and logic generally. Pre-operatory time, therefore, cannot be incorporated into abstract analytical/ explanatory models, of the kind so essential in scientific and technical thought. According to Hallpike, time concepts in pre-technological societies are typically, though not universally, process-linked, concrete and non-homogeneous.

Bloch (1989: 117) responded to Hallpike simply by arguing that Hallpike had mistaken 'collective representations' – particularly, presumably, the counter-intuitive collective representations which are promulgated in ritual – with underlying cognitive processes. But although this is undoubtedly true, it is not the whole story, because some of Hallpike's evidence for his assertions, comes, as we shall see, from non-ritual contexts, and even from Piaget-inspired cross-cultural psychological experimentation, and moreover, a close study of Piaget's text reveals fairly clearly that Piaget sees the practical implementation of 'operatory' thought in contexts (involving calculation, the construction of scientific explanatory models, and the like) which would be difficult to find beyond the confines of advanced technological societies.

# Chapter 13

## Critique of the Piagetian Approach to Time Cognition

One of the most important features of Piaget's ideas on cognitive growth is his recognition that earlier stages in intellectual development do not simply vanish once they are superseded by later ones, but continue to exist, their scope limited by the later additions but still active within restricted domains. Preoperatory intelligence survives, encased in operatory intelligence, as the sapling lives on within the mature oak. Piaget and Hallpike tend to believe, however, that the advent of an operatory grasp of time has pervasive rather than localized effects on time conceptualization, and that the normal intellectual attitude to time in the case of educated members of technologically advanced societies is operatory in nature and can be more or less identified with the variable T in physical equations. This is the part of the developmentalist case which I believe needs careful scrutiny.

In this chapter I shall put the case that it is only in certain circumstances that time is conceptualized as an abstract dimensional continuum, and that for the most part social and practical life is carried on using a battery of time-handling concepts which are not markedly different from those utilized in pretechnological societies. Moreover, operatory time, as defined by Piaget and Hallpike, though characteristic of certain technical/computational contexts in advanced societies, is not identifiable with physical/mathematical time as understood by physicists and philosophers of science. The current scientific conception of time is not the culmination of some endogenously generated process of mental growth and/or the outcome of familiarity with technological processes. Physical time is not just a continuum, but a particular kind of continuum, i.e. linearly-ordered, dense, continuous and of the order-type of the real numbers (Lucas 1973: 35ff). Piaget writes:

All this (i.e. his experimental analysis of the development of time concepts among children) . . . points to the common nature of temporal operations in all spheres, and to the close relationship between psychological and physical time: both are co-ordinations of motions with different velocities, and both involve the same 'groupings'. This is only to be expected since both are derived from practical or sensory-motor time, which, in turn is based on objective relations and on personal actions. As the external universe is gradually differentiated from the inner universe, so objects and actions become differentiated as well, but remain closely interrelated. (1970: 277)

Piaget maintains that cognitive time is both akin to physico-mathematical time, and is also emergent in sensori-motor, or subjective, personal time. This is I think far too ambitious. Cognitive time is not unitary, but remarkably diverse and context-sensitive. How people handle time depends on their frame of reference, and this varies not just according to the gross parameters of culture, age and education, but also according to the task at hand, the needs of particular situation and a particular intention.

Fraisse (1964) has noted that Piaget's approach to time, emphasizing the relatively late development of the child's ability to engage in abstract analysis of temporal relationships in physical systems (such as the arrangements of flasks described above) fails to do justice to the child's very rapid acquisition of the ability to handle time in social relationships, i.e. to understand the organizational framework of the day, the meanings of time-reckoning expressions of the non-metric type, and their function, in conjunction with the tense and aspectual verb system in natural languages, in the communication of complicated kinds of socially salient information.

Piaget's experimental studies document, not the emergence of the concept of time in the child, but the emergence of a particular mental skill, the kind that is needed in order to do calculations. I find it implausible that the necessary ability is morphogenetically pre-programmed in the biology of mental development; on the contrary, throughout the experimental dialogues recorded in Piaget's book, of which I shall examine a representative specimen in a moment, I hear only the very audible grinding of pedagogical gears.

The pedagogical milieu which supplies the implicit backdrop to Piaget's researches, and which is incidentally the primary reason for their being of little cross-cultural applicability, is the formation of the numerate technical elite in advanced industrial societies. The extent to which the pedagogical milieu of the Maison des Enfants in Geneva imposes itself in forming the background assumptions is strikingly brought out in this aside, from Piaget's text: 'To the adult, who is used to measurement, and steeped in the ideas of classical mechanics, distance and time are primitive concepts, from which velocity must be derived: $V = S/T$' (1970: 29).

Obviously, to call this merely ethnocentric is too weak, since not all adults, not even all members of the elite group in our society, could be described 'as steeped in the ideas of classical mechanics'. Moreover, this statement is factually dubious on at least two counts. Adults in our society share with children the concept of 'speed', which has nothing to do with distance or time. Moreover, investigations show that even the members of the numerate elite who ought to be 'steeped in classical mechanics' actually hold quite conflicting beliefs on the subject of dynamics. A study of American students majoring in physics (McCloskey 1983) produced the striking finding that more than a quarter (27 per cent) believed that a ball dropped by a running man would fall to earth on a spot directly underneath the position in space occupied by the runner's hand at the moment he let go of the ball, i.e. the ball would fall straight down, or even curve backwards, according to some. Among students not actually majoring in physics the proportion who were found to hold this belief rises to an astonishing 87 per cent. In other words, after more than 300 years of exposure to classical mechanics, the majority of members of technologically advanced societies hold exactly the same views about mechanics as they would have held had Galileo and Newton never existed. Of course, the physics majors in the sample will have to mend their ways, and abandon their reliance on pre-Galilean 'impetus theory' if they want to pass their final exams. But one wonders whether such views, though suppressed for the purposes of passing exams, are really banished from the set of background assumptions underlying cognition in less formal contexts.

For these reasons it is not possible to draw a firm dividing line between 'primitive' and 'modern' societies with respect to concepts of time. The most that one can say is that in certain societies technical advances have been made in the development of computational procedures requiring the introduction of a notion of homogeneous duration of the kind used in technical contexts. But these technical contexts are strictly limited and the concept of time used in one technical context may differ sharply from the concept of time used in another. Meanwhile, the more general purposes of social co-ordination continue to be served by a body of symbolic knowledge dealing with the entirely non-homogeneous, process-linked, time-reckoning concepts used in daily life. In this respect there is no difference in the general level reached by different societies, though there are of course very great differences in the contents of the temporal schemata in use in different cultural contexts. Examination of the time handling expressions in common use in our own language reveal the very widespread use of process-related time indicators of a non-metric type. We talk about events and organize ourselves in relation to them by making use of a socially embedded temporal schema. At the short end of the spectrum we have expressions like 'in a jiffy/a flash/two ticks/half a mo', and at the long end 'for ages/donkey's years/time out of mind/ ever and a day', all of which are quite adequate in context, but none of which has metrical significance. In fact, to say, 'I've been waiting here for ages' is much more informative, in context, than to say, 'I've been waiting here for 11 minutes and 36 seconds', since the intended message is about the relationship between the expected waiting time and the time actually spent waiting, not about the duration of the wait itself. Expressions which have to do with conventional expectations about the scheduling of activities are so much more prevalent than ones reporting actual durations, that statements overtly embodying the latter kind of information are routinely commandeered to communicate the former. Someone who says, 'I've been waiting here for hours' having waited a total of 45 minutes is neither lying nor misusing the English language. 'Five minutes' can mean anything between two minutes and twenty, depending on the circumstances; guessing the actual duration intended requires a deep knowledge of the pragmatics of English and the workings of the everyday world. And of course, everybody understands what is meant by references to a long day, a film which goes on for ever, an enchanting visit which is over in an instant.

Not only is the technical vocabulary of homogenized time, seconds, minutes, hours, years, continually made use of in ways which apply the standard, not of the clock, but of accepted social practice, but the clock itself succumbs to the social context. The clock has two roles to play, first of all to measure time, its Piagetian use, and second, to serve as the armature for a collectively recognized schedule, its symbolic use. In one conceptual frame the sixty minutes between the hours of 3 and 4 p.m. are the same as the sixty minutes between 8 and 9 a.m., but symbolically, in terms of what Zerubavel (1981) has called the 'socio-temporal order', these two durations of sixty minutes are entirely incommensurable. Homogeneous duration, outside the technical or laboratory context, is a myth.

Practical time is non-homogeneous because any given stretch of duration is cognitively salient only in conjunction with socially relevant processes, governed by a scheme of expectations. It is true that in our society we place great reliance on clocks and calendars in order to co-ordinate both work and leisure activities. Clocks, as technological innovations, facilitated certain important historical transformations in the productive basis of industrial society (Le Goff 1980; Thompson 1967; Attali 1982). But the throng of watch-dependent denizens of Megalopolis never use their time-keeping devices to measure, or otherwise manipulate, abstract duration. No 'operatory intelligence' – no intelligence of any kind, perhaps – is needed in order to heed the commands of the little slave-drivers we wear attached to our wrists. No 'co-ordinations of motions with different velocities' fill the buses and trains with commuters during the morning and evening rush hours, and decants them at other hours into their workplaces, homes and places of entertainment. These mass movements are not produced by individuals' co-ordinating their activities on their own behalf, but simply by individuals following a socially established schedule. This schedule can be modified in marginal respects, by flexi-time arrangements, or by such *ad hoc* procedures as leave-taking, absenteeism or working late at the office. But these individually determined rearrangements always take place and acquire their significance against a background of established expectations as to the symbolic character of the hours of the day. The hours between 6 p.m. and 7 a.m. are not 'working hours'. Work undertaken during non-working hours is not at all the same, for all that it may involve the same *activities*, as work undertaken in working hours. The time-divisions marked on the clock-as-schedule, as opposed to the clock as measuring-device, are points of inflection within a symbolically structured day. A man is seated at his office desk, feeling jaded, hungry and impatient.

He glances at his watch – 4.41 p.m. He is not measuring time: he has no need to calculate that he must remain confined for a further 49 minutes. All he wants is to check the symbolic meaning of the hour against his own subjective state. No planning decision of rescheduling of activities hinges on finding out that there are 49 work minutes left; what the man wants to do is to locate himself within the pre-structured working day, each part of which has its particular feeling-tone. At 4.41 it is legitimate to anticipate the end of the day, at 3.25 it is not.

The problem of the contextual sensitivity of knowledge is not raised by Piaget, and is skirted also by Hallpike. By contextual sensitivity I mean that how much a person 'knows' about the world depends not only on what he has internalized and what, so to speak, is in his permanent possession, but also on the context within which this knowledge is to be elicited, and by what means. The following quotation from Girard is used by Hallpike as evidence of the pre-operatory nature of primitive time conceptualization:

> The impossibility of conceptualising the future unfolding of the different phases of a seasonal phenomenon displays itself in a particularly surprising way when we try to discover from a group of men how, in the course of the agricultural year, they will carry out the necessary work in the cultivation of yams, to which they devote the major part of their efforts. On this particular evening it was impossible for us to obtain any information on the order of tasks with which they would occupy themselves for the weeks and months to come for the successful cultivation of this plant. . . . They do not represent to themselves, in their totality the agricultural tasks to be carried out in the course of a year; the appropriate moment for beginning each of them is not determined by counting time; it is the appearance of a seasonal phenomenon of similar periodicity which is taken as the reference point. It is for this reason that the garden magician . . . who decides the appropriate moment for undertaking different tasks does not rely on the counting of years, months, or days; he derives his knowledge from an acute and attentive observation of the various signs that nature affords him. (Girard 1968–9: 173–4; Hallpike 1979: 351)

First of all, one notes the fact that non- 'primitive' farmers do not plant their crops or tend them according to a schedule 'determined by the counting of time', because the variability of weather conditions from year to year hardly permits it. Farmers in technologically advanced countries are equally obliged to take note of the 'different signs that nature affords [them]'. Secondarily, the horticulturalists interviewed by Girard lacked, apparently, the ability to give a coherent verbal account of the cycle of yam cultivation, whereas Hallpike assumes that any farmer in our own society would be able to do so. Some would, no doubt, but others might not be able to, not for lack of farming knowledge but through an insufficiency of expository skill. A great deal, one suspects, would depend on how a farmer acquired his knowledge of farming; systematically, by passing through agricultural college or piecemeal, from parents, relatives, and by practical experience. What is absolutely clear from this passage is that the possession of a certain body of technical lore (related to the timing of horticultural operations) is quite distinct from the ability to expound this lore in an organized way. Girard's informants all knew, more or less, what the garden magician knew concerning the seasonal signs to be followed in timing garden work, but none of them, up to and including the garden magician himself, was able to furnish a clear account of just *what* they knew. This knowledge could only be elicited in a specific context, i.e. actual gardening operations.

A basic premise of Piaget's method is that it is feasible, under experimental conditions, to identify cognitive abilities in isolation from any specific context of application, to drive a wedge between 'thinking ability' and the everyday contexts in which thinking is applied practically. For instance, Piaget notes that children tend to believe that larger people are older than smaller ones, that an oak tree, which is tall, 'must' be older than a pear tree, which is short, and so on. This he attributes to a basic deficiency in the thought processes of the pre-operatory child, i.e. an inability to dissociate time and space from processes that involve both. Piaget says that children reason that growth equals displacement in space over time, therefore, more growth equals more displacement in space, hence more time, therefore tall trees, or people, are older than shorter ones.

The alternative interpretation would be that what children lack is not reasoning ability but information. How is a child supposed to know how old a tree or a person is? On the other hand, in the context of the child's social world, relative age is often very pertinent information, particularly where adults and other children are concerned. In the absence of actual knowledge, children are often obliged to guess the relative age of their associates, and misjudgements can have serious consequences.

Because age and height are strongly if not absolutely correlated in the child's social world, a heuristic assumption is made that in the absence of conflicting information, taller equals older. And this works well until an experimenter entraps the child into unwary statements on the subject of trees, objects whose relative ages are unlikely to have been a major concern to the child hitherto. Children also think that male adults are older than female adults. Once again, this has nothing to do with faulty concepts of time and space, and everything to do with the child's all-too-sophisticated grasp of the dynamics of the world of social conventions and gender symbols. 'Fathers are older than mothers' is a sound heuristic assumption, in accord with statistical realities, and moreover, the child is aware from a very early age of the symbolic association of masculine roles with relative age, maturity and intra-familial authority, feminine roles with relative youth, immaturity and dependence.

The experimental designs which are used to monitor the emergence of operatory intelligence always carry with them contextual attributes which interact in various ways with the extra-experimental experience of the subject undergoing the test. It is never easy, or perhaps possible at all, to ascertain whether the experimental results reflect underlying cognitive capacities, or an arbitrary reaction produced by a mismatch between the contextual background of the experimenter and the experimented upon. An outstanding instance in which contextual factors are held to have biased the results of a Piaget-type experiment is the 'aberrant' conservation of quantity by Tiv children (Pryce-Williams 1961; Hallpike 1979: 272ff). Tiv children aged 7 to 8 showed total conservation of quantity, that is, the ability to judge that the amount of liquid in a tall, thin container remained identical when it was transferred to a short, fat one. This is above the European standard for that age, and Pryce-Williams argues that Tiv are particularly good at this kind of conservation because they are all excessively familiar with a game, the African Hole Game, in which small pebbles are transferred between holes of different shapes and sizes. So they are well aware that such changes in the shape of the container leave the quantity transferred unchanged.

Hallpike gives considerable prominence to the results obtained by another cross-cultural Piagetian experiementer, Bovet, who tested Algerian peasants in the same general way (Bovet 1975; Hallpike 1979: 270ff). Bovet also found Algerian children and

adults to be very good conservers of quantity, but for reasons both
he and Hallpike find inadequate from the standpoint of Piagetian
theory. The Algerian subjects when presented with water in tall vs.
fat flasks, and with long thin rolls of plasticine vs. round balls,
completely ignored the changes of shape and said that as it was the
same water/plasticine in both cases, it must be the same quantity,
since it was the same stuff. When challenged by the experimenter,
who pointed out the changes in shape to them, they retracted their
previous statements and said that the quantity had become smaller
or larger.

Bovet and Hallpike call this 'pseudo-conservation', of a kind
different, we are led to infer, from the 'genuine' conservation
which would have been produced by European subjects under
equivalent circumstances. This is a remarkable instance of faith
in the efficacy of theories over the results of experiments. Having avoided, in an unforeseen way, the trap set by Piaget to
catch the pre-operatory child, the Algerians must be beguiled
into making the mistakes they 'ought' to make, and are forcibly
propelled into it. But how long would European children persist
in their conserving ways if they were confronted by the experimenter in similarly critical vein? At this point the experiments have little to do with any 'bedrock' cognitive processes
and everything to do with the dynamics of the experimenter/
subject relationship.

One of Bovet's experiments is directly concerned with time
estimation, and it brings out very well the way in which the
implicit context of application of a certain line of reasoning
determines the response to the test situation, not some generalized cognitive resource. Two model cars are set to race one
another following parallel courses round a circular track. They
both leave the starting line and recross the same line to finish at
the same moment. Bovet's Algerians tended to say 'incorrectly'
that both cars travelled at an identical speed, ignoring the fact
that the car on the outer track had further to go and hence had to
travel faster in order to arrive at the finish line at the same
moment as the car on the shorter track. But what it seems to me
the subjects are really saying is simply that the race, as a race, is
a dead heat. If a track athlete gets boxed in and has to run very
wide, consequently losing the race to another runner who has
run a shorter distance and marginally slower, this is of no
account in the awarding of gold medals. In the race-context, as
opposed to the intended context of the experiment, the Algerian

respondents are perfectly justified in what they say. What we encounter here is not a difference in mentalities, but in the cultural/symbolic context within which identical experimental materials are interpreted.

What emerges from Bovet's work is the immense difficulty his subjects had in understanding the nature of the problems presented to them. Once having done so, they often had little difficulty providing the answers, which were perforce more or less handed to them on a plate in the course of the laborious initial explanations. That these should have been so necessary in Algeria, while they are apparently much less necessary when the same experiments are carried out in Geneva, is all the evidence one needs in order to support the conclusion that it is the pedagogical milieu which is the real influence determining the outcome of Piagetian testing procedures, rather than a biological process determining the morphogenesis of general intelligence.

These remarks on Bovet show that between genetic intelligence and experimental or observational results there is always a dense screen of unstated presuppositions. We can explore this theme further by considering two instances of apparently 'aberrant' temporal reasoning, which are not, I believe, as aberrant as they look. One of these instances is extracted from Piaget's work on temporal reasoning among children. The other comes from my monograph on the Umeda, where a young adult produces an apparently comparable kind of statement.

First, a dialogue with Lin (aged six), one of Piaget's subjects at the Maison des Enfants:

| | |
|---|---|
| *Experimenter:* | How long does it take you to get home from school |
| *Lin:* | Ten minutes. |
| *Experimenter:* | And if you were to run, would you be getting home more quickly or more slowly? |
| *Lin:* | More quickly. |
| *Experimenter:* | So would it take you longer or not? |
| *Lin:* | Longer. |
| *Experimenter:* | How much? |
| *Lin:* | It would take ten minutes. |

Lin obviously has some way to go before he has an operational grasp of time. But perhaps he has even further to go before he attains a pragmatic understanding of the communicative intentions behind the kind of questions he has just been asked. On the surface, he has signally failed to answer them correctly, or even, it would seem, coherently. His last two answers are so extravagently wayward that they invite a second look. Why does Lin commit himself to saying that if he ran home from school, it would take him the same amount of time (ten minutes) as if he walked (contradiction 1), and then that it would actually take him *longer* to get home if he went more quickly (contradiction 2)? We cannot explain these responses by invoking an explanation in terms of inadequate conservation: what we appear to be faced with are contradictions in logic; or we must suppose he is answering at random.

But let us note one extremely important fact, which is not stressed in the original account: namely, that the experimenter has invited Lin to consider a hypothetical case – what would be the case in a 'possible world' in which Lin runs home from school. This is a course of action he would doubtless not dream of taking in this (actual) world, since in this (actual) world all six-year-old boys dawdle on the way home from school. In other words, Lin and the experimenter are discussing a counterfactual conditional, what would be the case in another world than this one, one in which Lin is obliged to run home from school.

Herein lies the key to what Lin says. Lin is being quite reasonable in his replies, given that they relate to another world, which he can imagine, in which it would be necessary for him to run in order to get home in ten minutes. The experimenter, meanwhile, thinks (incorrectly) that Lin and he are all the while talking about this (actual) world. Thus, Lin and he are agreed that in this (actual) world-context, it takes Lin ten minutes to get home, at his normal pace. Also, Lin and he are agreed that if Lin runs, he will get home more quickly – at a quicker *pace*, that is to say, since running is a quicker means of locomotion than walking. But at this point the frames of reference of Lin and the experimenter start to diverge. The experimenter is still thinking in terms of the (actual) world in which the distance between school and home is such that it takes Lin ten minutes to get home at the normal pace, and a closely related, geometrically identical counterfactual world in which this journey time is reduced because Lin speeds up (he runs). Lin has defined the counterfactual world he is talking about differently. He is thinking of a counterfactual world with different geometry, in which, *even if he runs*, it takes him ten minutes to get home. Lin has incorporated the ten-minute journey home from school into the counterfactual world which (he thinks) both he and the experimenter are discussing. In the counterfactual world which he (Lin), but not the experimenter, has in mind, Lin is perfectly correct in asserting that he would get home quicker (at a quicker pace) than in the actual one, because he would be running, not walking. But the journey would 'typically' take longer, because it would be a longer journey, further to go, and typically taking more time, because small boys do not always hurry on the way home. But this 'longer' journey would still take 'ten minutes' because that would be the journey time Lin was aiming to keep to.

It is the experimenter, not Lin, who is the naive one. The experimenter has failed to notice the shift in implicit world-context introduced by the hypothetical 'if'. Lin picks up on this and elaborates an entirely coherent counterfactual world. The dialogue reveals little about 'co-ordinations of motions and velocities' and everything about the deficiencies of the Piagetian experimental procedure. Of these, the most damaging is that it is impossible to control for the complex presuppositional texture of natural language, which can vary arbitrarily, and which, as in this instances, may have far greater importance in determining the child's responses than his hypothetical degree of cognitive maturity.

This analysis will also enable me to correct a misleading impression I myself have been guilty of conveying in a passage from *Metamorphosis of the Cassowaries*. There, I report some remarks of an Umeda informant, which have been quoted by Hallpike, and which clearly bear analogies to the kinds of statements made by Piaget's 'pre-operational' children, though Hallpike forbears to say so specifically:

> when walking between two villages with a youth, I remarked to him on the rather leisurely pace we were keeping, suggesting that we might not arrive before dark. He (knowing perfectly well there was no danger of this, as it proved) assured me that if we were to walk fast, the sun would go down correspondingly quickly, whereas if we stuck to our leisurely pace, the sun would do likewise. In short, lunar or other astronomical indices of time were not considered to be more accurately or rigidly determined than any other events, a yardstick against which they could be measured, but simply on a par with human activities, the seasonal cycle, biological processes, the weather, etc., all of which hang together in an unanalysed way, but none of which was seen as the prime mover of all the rest. (Gell 1975: 163)

While I stand by my original comments, I no longer think my informant's statement regarding the movements of the sun are evidence of their being true in quite the way I supposed. What my informant was really saying was that *if* (counterfactually, and transparently so to him, but not to me) there were a possible world in which it was necessary to hurry in order to get from village A to village B, which would be in all relevant worlds a fixed distance apart, *that would be* a world in which the sun moved much more quickly through the sky than it does here. Perfectly logical on his part: what he was trying to do was to straighten out in my mind certain properties of this actual world – a problem with which anthropologists' informants must wrestle eternally and often in vain – by pointing to the properties possessed by a non-actual world.

It would obviously be beyond the scope of this book to consider all the implications of Piagetian theory for anthropology (Mimica 1989; Toren 1990). But it is clear that it is not possible to extract from Piaget's work a working theory of cognitive universals of time. More recently, Bloch himself has arrived at an identical appreciation of the situation, when he writes:

> Piaget's solution, that cognitive structures should be seen as the result of individual construction, runs into the difficulty that if Piaget had looked more closely at the nature of anthropological data, at its complexity, its highly cultural specific character, one cannot believe that he could have felt confident that the kind of theories he was suggesting could ever have explained . . . [cognition in natural settings]. Quite simply, there seems to be an unbridgeable gap between the general and simple mechanisms which he proposes and the highly complex product which it would have to have produced. . . . [w]e cannot see how cultural variation can occur in such a degree as it does, since the mechanisms he gives us are not specifically cultural nor is the environment he takes into account in any way specific. (Bloch 1989: 116)

With this one can only concur. But in this his later text, as in his original text (1977) on cognitive universals of time, Bloch does not rely on Piaget in isolation, but Piaget in conjunction with psycholinguistics. The final common pathway for strong forms of cognitive universalism is towards the study of natural languages. There is no doubt that human beings are biologically predisposed to become speakers of a natural language. There is no doubt, either, that all natural languages permit speakers to encode intelligible messages about the temporal relationships between events. Therefore it is a natural move, in the construction of the anti-relativist case on temporal cognition, to appeal to the evidence of comparative linguistics, as Bloch does. It is this evidence from language that I must consider next.

# Chapter 14

## Linguistic Arguments for the Cognitive Universality of Time

One important point raised by Bloch against temporal cultural relativism was his claim that the world's natural languages all, without exception, handle time in broadly the same way:

> Evidence for such a conclusion . . . comes from . . . the mass of recent studies of syntax and semantics of different languages that have been carried out by American linguists. Disagreements and polemics in this field are many, but at least consensus seems to be emerging on one point, and this is that the fundamental logic employed in the syntax of all languages is, Whorf notwithstanding, the same. The implications of this for notions of time are clear. The logic of language implies a notion of temporality and sequence and so if all syntax is based on the same logic, all speakers must at a fundamental level apprehend time the same way . . . (1977: 283)

Bloch is correct in saying that the consensus of linguistic and psycholinguistic opinion is to reject the strong form of linguistic relativism espoused by Whorf (Carroll 1956), whose views I shall briefly outline below. But Bloch is very unspecific about the nature of the substantive language universals which manifest the underlying temporal cognitive uniformity of humankind. It could be that languages are just as different from one another as Whorf maintained, but that Whorf's hypothesis fails because language does not directly affect, or reflect, cognition in the way Whorf supposed. And not only Whorf, because it is apparent from this passage that Bloch implicitly agrees with Whorf that language directly reflects cognition, and that he only differs from Whorf in denying that languages are fundamentally different from one another in their temporal 'logic'. We have to determine whether linguistic cultural relativity fails because languages are all based on an identical grammatical pattern, or because grammatical devices and cognition are relatively independent from one another. It may prove that the reasons behind the elaboration of grammatical forms are to do with the functional requirements of discursive speech and writing, not that language mediates underlying cognitive processes.

In this chapter, I shall outline, as briefly as possible, the way in which time and temporal relationships are handled in natural languages. I will then proceed to consider two relevant areas of linguistic debate. First, I shall consider linguistic cultural relativity *per se*, and second, returning to the Piagetian themes of Chapters 12–13, I shall discuss the 'acquisition of time-talk' by small children as a source of independent evidence on the cognitive development of the notion of time.

All natural languages have time-adverbials, aspects and modalities, and the vast majority of them have tenses. These are the four basic components of the time-handling mechanics of natural languages; but although they can be analytically distinguished, in practice they interact continually, so that selecting a certain adverbial (like 'tomorrow') often determines the selection of a particular tense for the verb of the sentence or clause in which 'tomorrow' occurs (usually future). The syntactical rules governing the interactions of adverbials, tenses, aspects and modalities is the main subject matter of the technical literature on this branch of linguistics.

## 14.1 Time Adverbials

These are expressions which are incorporated into sentences in order to indicate the time-frame of the main verb or the verb of the clause in which they are found. They are called adverbials because they are either genuine adverbs (e.g. I will go to Birmingham *immediately*), or they function in the same way (I will go to Birmingham *tomorrow, next Wednesday*, etc.). Not all languages have the same set of adverbials: English has a huge set; Umeda a very much more restricted set. Nor are they defined in the same way in different languages: in Hindi *kal* means 'yesterday' and 'tomorrow', and only the tense of the verb or the context of the utterance will enable one to say which is the correct English translation. Adverbials can be created at will, in the form of adverbial phrases, introduced by 'when', 'as soon as', etc.: 'I will go to Aberdeen, as soon as' it stops snowing'.

Besides these 'explicit' adverbials, it may be said that all utterances contain implicit, unrealized, adverbials as part of their underlying 'semantic representations' ('semantic representations' are the mental representations which embody the communicative intentions of the speaker and/or the mental representations formed by the listener once having interpreted the sentence). These 'implicit' adverbials are the adverbials which *would be* appropriate to the semantic representation, which, by definition, is never devoid of *any* temporal frame, however indefinite. Thus the 'implicit adverbial' of 'the cat sat on the mat' is 'at some time before the present' because of the past tense of the main verb, 'sat'. Implicit, unrealized adverbials can perhaps be called 'Kantian adverbials', on the grounds that it is a necessary truth that any phenomenon (and hence any semantic representation of a phenomenon) is temporally located.

## 14.2 Verb Tenses

Tenses are bound inflections of the verb, or auxiliary verb constructions, which indicate at which moment, or over which interval of time, the action, process or state-of-affairs indicated by the verb obtains. It has become widely accepted, though not universally so, that the most convenient way of analyzing tense in natural languages is to make use of (variants of) the 'three-time' system introduced by Reichenbach (1947). He was the first to distinguish between (1) ST or speech time, the moment at which an utterance takes place, (2) ET or event time, the moment at which the event referred to takes place, and (3) RT or reference time, which is the 'temporal point of view', which is taken on the event, before it, after it or simultaneously with it. An example in which ST, ET and RT are all different is:

Before he went into battle, Sir Percival *had confessed* his sins. ET ( = the confession) / RT ( = going into battle) / ST ( = the later time at which these events are narrated).

The pluperfect tense of 'had confessed' contrasts with the simple past of 'went into battle', indicating that the confession was prior to the moment of the battle, which is in turn prior to the moment at which the narration is taking place. Speech time, event time and reference time can thus be distinguished, but are not by any means always distinguished. In many simple statements of fact they all coincide, as in the proposition (implicitly true for all times) 'crows are black', or the fleetingly true, present-focused report on current events, 'here comes Mr Brown', where ET = ST = RT. Or two of the three may coincide but not the other: thus the sentence:

John has swum the Channel (ET ——— RT = ST)

reports a (present) fact about John, i.e. that at one time he swam the Channel. Reference time and speech time coincide, to the exclusion of event time (the date of the Channel swim John made). Whereas:

John swam the Channel last year (ET, RT ——— ST)

reports an event in the past from the perspective of that event's time of occurrence (last year). Here reference time and event time coincide to the exclusion of speech time. It would be ungrammatical to say:

John has swum the Channel last year*

because the effect of the adverbial phrase (last year) is to back-date the time-frame of the sentence as a whole to last year, which is inconsistent with the keying of the reference time to speech time (i.e. to the present) by means of the perfect tense form (has + past participle swum). This is a typical instance of the interaction between adverbials and tenses, which was mentioned a moment ago.

Most tense constructions are deictic, that is to say, they are related to S, the moment-of-utterance, and they communicate the pastness, presentness or futurity of an event with respect to some transient 'now'. They thus resemble spatial expressions like 'here' and 'there', which depend for their meaning on the speaker's spatial position, which can change. Tenses sometimes actually derive from spatial expressions, e.g. the use of the verb 'go' as a regular auxiliary for expressing future actions which may have nothing to do with moving anything, anywhere (e.g. 'I'm going to think hard about this').

Tenses which are deictically bound to S, either including it or excluding it, are 'absolute' tenses (Comrie 1985). But there are also relative tenses in which a relation between E an R is established, but not any particular relation between either of these and S. Usually these occur in subordinate clauses, where the tense of the main verb establishes the absolute time reference of the sentence as a whole (ibid: 60ff). But at this point the analysis of tense constructions merges with the analysis of aspect, the most recondite, but at the same time the most genuinely 'universal' of the grammatical devices found in natural languages for handling temporal relations. There are, as we shall see, languages which do not have tenses, but there are no languages without aspect distinctions.

## 14.3  Aspect

This refers to the temporal 'shape' or contour of events, processes or states. Does the verb indicate an 'event' which comes to a climax, and results in an obvious change in the way things are (John broke the pencil)? Or does the verb only indicate something ongoing, incomplete or progressive (John thought hard)? 'Breaking' is point-like, 'thinking' is line-like; these verbs have different 'contours' in time. The problem about aspect, from the linguist's point of view, is that some of the time communication of the differences in 'temporal contours' between point-like 'events' and line-like 'states' is a function of different semantic categories of verbs (non-stative vs. stative verbs), while at other times the distinction is a function of different inflections or markings of the verb independently of its 'inherent' aspectual characteristics.

This can be brought out by making a comparison between Russian, a language with a very prominent system of grammaticalized aspect, vs. English, which also has aspect as a grammatical category, but to a lesser degree. In Russian, the verb *lecit* (imperfective, incomplete action) means 'to *treat* a disease' and the same verb, inflected for perfective aspect (completion of the action), *vylecit*, means 'to *cure* a disease'. Russian achieves through the use of the aspectual inflection of one single verb what English achieves through the use of two verbs belonging to different semantic categories, statives vs. non-statives.

However, in English, it is possible to give naturally stative verbs like 'treat' a non-stative gloss, by using them in the English perfective aspect, as in:

The doctor has treated the patient,

which implies that the treatment, successful or not, is at least complete. And conversely, the non-stative verb 'cure' can be converted into a verb indicating an ongoing, as-yet incomplete process

While the doctor is curing my leg, I will stay off work.

Despite these complexities, it is not too hard to establish a general feel for aspect both as an inherent feature of the semantics of verbs and as a grammatical category. The essential distinction so far as 'inherent' aspect is concerned is the one between stative and non-stative verbs. Statives are verbs like like, know, want, feel, which are not 'actions' and which characteristically do not appear in the present progressive aspect:

I am liking ice-cream*

because 'to like' is *inherently* progressive or enduring. Non-statives are verbs of action, like break, start, die, which refer to climactic or 'punctual' events. In between obvious statives and obvious non-statives there is a grey area of (basically non-stative) 'activity' verbs, like run, swim, learn, which depend more on the context as to whether they are interpreted as stative or non-stative, and will be marked for aspect accordingly.

I am learning French (progressive aspect, French not yet
   learnt)
vs.
I have learnt French (perfective aspect, learning of French
   presently accomplished).

Languages differ enormously in the extent to which aspect is grammaticalized. In English, aspect is marked in a rather regular and obligatory manner in all tenses, as opposed to French, in which only the past imperfective is regularly marked grammatically. English makes two aspect distinctions, (1) progressive-imperfective aspect (I was walking, I am walking, I will be walking) vs. (2) perfective-completive aspect (I walked, I have walked, I will have walked). English has other aspects as well, such as the use of the neutral present to indicate a habitual action:

I walk to work, these days.

And other languages have aspect markers for reiterated actions, unusually prolonged actions or unusually brief actions, beginning actions, ending actions, and many more.

Why do languages make aspectual distinctions with such regularity? In some sense, aspect, much more than tense, classifies out a fundamental generic property of events and states of affairs, i.e. whether we are interested in them as productive of a result, a change, or whether we are interested in them as a 'background condition' against which events of a more punctual nature take place. But it is also important to realize that aspect marking comes about not as a means of 'classifying out' the world as an end in itself, but because unless these distinctions are maintained, it is hard to construct a coherent discourse. Just to take one example, consider the discursive use of the English past imperfective:

> While Henry was looking the other way, Nelly picked his pocket.

Without the imperfective, it would be far harder to convey the sense in which the focal event, the event which carries on the story-line (Nelly picking Henry's pocket), is contained or enfolded in another event, Henry looking away, which began before the focal event, persisted during it and only ended after it was completed. In abstract terms 'Henry looking away' is just as much a punctual event as 'Nelly picking Henry's pocket'. But in discourse terms, Henry looking away forms the temporal background, within which we position ourselves, in order to observe Nelly at her nefarious activities. It is therefore not out of a love for classifying 'temporal objects' for their own sweet selves, that languages mark for aspect, but because there are functional, discursive reasons which make this kind of marking communicatively useful.

### 14.4  Modality

Verb modality is the grammatical marking the epistemological status of the proposition asserted in the sentence, i.e. whether the sentence asserts something which is known for a fact, or which is reported by hearsay, or is a probable inference, or an imaginary (counterfactual) possibility, or merely an expression of what ideally 'ought' to be the case. Modality, unlike aspect, has nothing to do with time intrinsically, but in natural languages there is a strong tendency for tense and modality to be tied together. This tense-modality linkage arises because assertions about the present, assertions of historical fact or assertions of 'timeless' truths ('crows are black') are modally certain (realis) while statements about the future, when they have an RT and an ET which are both future, are of necessity hypothetical (irrealis). Hence many future forms of the verb are modals, which indicate futurity by indicating modal less-than-certainty. In English, for instance, the future auxiliary 'shall' is derived from a modal verb indicating duty:

'I shall go to Birmingham' ( = it is my duty to go to Birmingham)

and the auxiliary 'will' from the modal verb of 'willing':

'He will come here' ( = it is his will that he comes here).

The modal auxiliaries 'shall' and 'will' have lost their transparent role as independent deontic or voluntative verbs, and now function as frame-of-reference shifters, moving RT into the future, but there is still a tincture of modality about them, and they can be used as modals with reference to present or recent-past events, as in making a guess:

(a loud crash in heard) That will be Henry falling downstairs, I dare say . . .

Meanwhile, not all future constructions are modals. Many futures are based on verbs of motion, as in

I'm going to be an astronaut

(pronounced 'gonna') – though the likelihood is that children learning 'go'-futures are not aware of the idea of physical movement from place to place when using 'go' auxiliaries, any more than they are aware of any connection between 'will' as a future auxiliary and 'willing' something to come to pass. But despite

the existence of many complicating factors, it may be offered as
a rule of thumb that there is a particularly strong interaction
between future tenses and 'irrealis' modal constructions, as
there is between past tenses and one type of aspect, i.e. perfective aspect, in that for an action to be a completed whole, it must
be completed in time, i.e. past. Presentness, on the other hand,
in intrinsically connected with 'realis' modality and often with
imperfective modality. Saying 'it will rain tomorrow' implies the
modal uncertaintly inherent in all acts of prediction, while
saying 'it is raining' implies no such unreality/uncertainty.

Having very briefly introduced the relevant parts of linguistic
theory (for more comprehensive surveys, see Lyons 1977; Comrie 1976, 1985) I shall turn to the bearing of linguistic research on
the topic of cognitive temporal relativity. This subject was
opened up by Whorf, in a number of essays on Amerindian
languages written in the 1930s and 1940s and collected together
by Carroll (1956). One of these essays focuses specifically on
time in the language of the Hopi of Arizona, and is thus particularly germane to the argument. Whorf makes a global contrast
between what he calls 'Standard Average European' (SAE)
languages and Hopi. SAE languages characteristically substan-
tify time, so that it is treated as an extended, divisible, space-like
substance. Hopi, by contrast, does without the category of time
at all: 'the Hopi language is seen to contain no words, grammatical forms, constructions or expressions which refer directly
to what we call "time"' (Carroll 1956: 57). Whorf's basic grounds
for making this sweeping statement was the absence, or what he
took to be the absence, of constructions in Hopi equivalent to
SAE tenses. Instead, Hopi had what would nowadays be called
modalities, giving the speaker's propositional attitude towards
the content of his assertion. He distinguished three Hopi modalities ('assertions'):

1. Reportive (the unmarked form of the verb, used to report on
   events which have happened).
2. Expective (-ni: used to convey the modal attitude of expecting
   an event to happen).
3. Gnomic (-ngwu: used to convey the modal attitude of gnomic
   truth, i.e. P is true at all times and all places).

Whorf's claim was that these modalities had no intrinsic tense meanings, and therefore that 'time' was not built into the design of Hopi grammar at all.

The first thing to say is that quite apart from the defensibility of the 'Whorf hypothesis' in general, Whorf's specific claims about Hopi, for which he never provided much evidence, are very unsound. Malotki (1983) has published a lengthy monograph showing (1) that Hopi characteristically and systematically uses spatial metaphors to indicate temporal facts, the very feature which Whorf indicated as being characteristically SAE; and (2) that Hopi has a two-tense system (unmarked non-future vs. future -ni) and a very elaborate aspect system which allows for consistent distinction within the non-future between perfective-aspect/past-time and imperfective aspect/present-time interpretations. Not only is Whorf completely wrong about Hopi linguistic 'timelessness', but it could as well be said that of the two languages English is the more timeless, in that, as we have seen, English future is a modality, English present is an aspect, and while English past is primarily a tense for factual assertions about the past, like Hopi non-future, English past does duty as an 'irrealis' modality in sentences like:

I wish I *knew* how to play the piano.

As Church (1976: 58; Malotki 1983: 672) says: 'if English had been an American Indian language, it could have been used as an example of a language in which time relations are not distinguished. But few of us would believe that English speakers fail to make such time distinctions. It is clear that the grammatical structure of a language tells us little about our way of thinking about the world.'

Hopi is not a timeless or a tenseless language. They may be no 'timeless' languages, but there certainly are tenseless ones. Burmese and Dyirbal, an Australian language, are cited by Comrie (1985: 50–3) as instances of this type of language, in which the only categories marked on the verb are modalities, basically realis vs. irrealis. But nothing really changes, communicatively or cognitively, as a result of the failure of a language to convey tense by inflection of the verb or auxiliary verb constructions. The same result is achieved by adverbials, by the 'implicit' tense flowing from the aspectual contrast perfective/imperfective, and by the context – the context of utterance (the statement in relation to the real-world situation in which it is produced) and

the context of discourse (the statement in relation to neighbouring statements in the flow of discourse, narration, text, etc.). A
great many more languages, which are not tenseless, have two-
tense systems like Hopi non-future ( = past + present) vs.
future, or alternatively, past vs. non-past (= present + future).

Does the grammatical structure of language really have
nothing to do with anything outside itself? Does it have nothing to
do with culture, on the one hand, or cognition on the other? Let
me briefly consider another variant of the Whorf hypothesis,
what one might call the diachronic Whorf hypothesis, which
would be to claim that the diachronic evolution of language over
time may reflect changes in patterns of thinking, general ways
of construing the world and its meanings, as these change in
history. Here I can invoke a very appropriate example, namely,
the evolution of the future tense in Romance languages, i.e. the
family of European languages (French, Spanish, etc.), which
developed from the Latin spoken in late Roman times and
during the Dark Ages (Fleischman 1982).

Latin had a well-marked future paradigm for verbs (e.g. *cantabo*) with strictly temporal (rather than modal) meaning. Modern
Romance languages also have a distinct future paradigm (*chanterai, cantaro, cantaré*, etc.). But there is no direct line of descent
between modern Romance futures and *cantabo*. What has happened is that during the development of Romance between *c.*
500 AD and *c.* 1000 AD *cantabo* fell into disuse and was replaced
by an auxiliary verb construction for expressing futurity *cantare
habeo* (to-sing I-have). This periphrastic future construction then
became agglutinated to the verb stem to give rise to the modern
inflectional Romance futures. The infixed -r- of modern Romance is the remains of the Latin infinitive (*cantare*, to sing) and
the case endings are the remains of '*habeo*', worn smooth by
time.

Fleischman's absorbing study (1982) of the evolution of Romance futures traces this and allied developments. One problem she discusses is what, precisely, prompted the decline of
*cantabo* and the rise of *cantare habeo* during the second half of the
1st millennium AD. Why should the unambiguous Latin future
be replaced by an ambiguous periphrastic construction – essentially a deontic modal – with 'implied' future time reference?
One argument she considers is a cultural one, advanced in its
most developed form by Coseriu (1958: 97–8), who considered
that 'the determining factor in the remodelling of the Latin

future to have been the impact on the Roman Empire of Chris-
tianity' (Fleischman 1982: 47ff). Coseriu argues that the abstract,
purely temporal, Latin future could not accommodate the
changed ethical orientation of Christian Europe. The 'old' future
was external to the agentive self, the 'new' future was internalized, charged with personal responsibility (for salvation) and
moral obligation. Hence it was not by chance that a periphrastic
construction indicating deontic modalitiy of obligation (to-sing
I-have, i.e. I have to sing) took over from the impersonal Latin
future paradigm. Moreover, the 'future' meaning of *habeo* constructions is first documented in the writings of the Church
Fathers, the fountainheads of the new 'ethical orientation'. St
Augustine seems to be conveying precisely this new sense of
time as something 'subjective' rather than 'objective' in the
famous passage in the *Confessions* (XI: 20) in which he says that
time exists only in the mind, the past is memory, the present is
perception and the future is expectation.

Other writers cited by Fleischman (1982: 45) give a slightly
different version of a similar argument, when they hypothesize
that the decline of *cantabo* and the rise of *cantare habeo* reflects the
rise of popular culture (attendant on the decline of 'Classical'
civilization), which is inherently antipathetic towards abstrac-
tions and prefers the concrete, personal idea of 'having' the
future, as a modal field of 'present' possibilities and opportunities, rather than contemplating it objectively, and from the
abstract point of view, as not-yet-elapsed time, not ontologically
distinct from elapsed and elapsing time. The popular-culture
view and the ethical-orientation view are clearly not inherently
in conflict; both trends could have been occurring simultaneously and both would have promoted the rise of the *habeo*
construction.

These cultural interpretations of the remodelling of the Latin
verb paradigm in the shipwreck of Classical civilization and the
contemporaneous rise of Christendom are much more compelling than Whorf's palpably fantastical elaborations on the
cultural/cognitive implications of Hopi. But they do also imply a
kind of 'cultural relativity' between diachronic phases in the
continuous development of European thought and language.
Language had to change to accommodate a new personal ontol-
ogy, a new conception of history and agency, a new rhetoric of
motives and life-goals. I do not think that it is necessary to
discount this kind of argument altogether, so long as it is

restricted to what is known as the 'weak' version of the Whorf
hypothesis, to wit, the hypothesis that different languages, by
virtue of their conventions, facilitate different patterns of
thought, different rhetorical strategies, different standardized
arguments and images. But even so, there are historical problems with the argument. The claim that the development of
Romance languages from popular regional dialects resulted in
the rejection of the 'too abstract' *cantabo* paradigm, founders on
the difficulty that Latin itself was once a 'popular' dialect, and
that the original 'tribal' Latin speakers said *cantabo*, but did not
have, presumably, an 'abstract' view of life. This, if it ever
existed, was the product of the (much later) 'Classical' Roman
civilization. It seems that Indo-European (and other) languages
regularly swing between having 'synthetic' (inflected, abstract)
tense paradigms and 'analytic' (auxiliary-verb, concrete) tense
paradigms. *Cantabo* itself was once an auxiliary verb construction in proto-Indo-European ( cant-a + *bhwo, the verb 'to be').
And the modern *chanterai* paradigm, rendered synthetic by the
agglutination of *cantare habeo*, is often displaced, now, by the
'go'-future ( *je vais chanter*) which is analytic, but based on a verb
of motion, not deontic modality. Fleischman notes that the
Spanish 'go'-future ( *yo voy a dormir*) seems to have entered yet
another cycle of agglutination in the popular speech of Hispano-
American, where *yo vadormir* is to be heard. The next 'future'
inflection of the verb stem may be a prefix, va- rather than a
suffixed element with -r-. If these swings between synthetic and
analytic tense paradigms are such a regular feature of diachronic
linguistic change, can particular instances of change, such as
the *cantabo* → *cantare habeo* sequence, be attributed to specific
historical/cultural circumstances? It would appear from Fleischman's account that the primary factors involved in the history of
Romance future constructions have been internal to language
itself, notably the profound change between Latin, a language
in which the verb usually came last, after the object (OV) to
modern Romance languages all of which have the word-order
subject–verb–object (SVO).

   None the less, it appears to me that even though it is true that
the cyclic alternation between analytic and synthetic futures in
Romance was determined, not by specific ideological factors,
but was just one facet of a global transformation of Latin (OV)
into Romance (SVO) – which in essence is Fleischman's argument – it still remains arguable that the particular selection of a

deontic-modal periphrasis as the basis for the 'analytic' pre-Romance future paradigm, from the range of available late-Latin periphrastic constructions with 'future' implications, is a significant, and strictly cultural, fact. By this, I do not mean to imply linguistic/cognitive relativism, such that users of *cantare habeo* 'could not think about the future abstractly' because of the design of their language. But I do not think it is absurd to think that language incorporates a sedimented rhetoric, the congealed residue of a tradition of conventional arguments, which were once active thoughts, achieved against the resistance of language (as I have to struggle with language now, in order to say what I want to say, and not something else) but which become, by-and-by, discursive clichés and eventually automatisms of 'grammar'. Language and discourse are continually poised between convention and discovery. What is wrong with Whorfism, is not that language imposes a barrier, facilitating the expression of certain ideas and inhibiting the expression of others (it surely does) – but to imagine, as a consequence of this admissible fact, that thought is 'determined' by language. On the contrary, thinking (discovery of new ideas) typically goes against the grain of language, tortures it, deforms it (see the writings of philosophers and sages, filled with paradoxes and neologisms). These denaturings of language in the service of the creation of new meanings, or the more 'expressive' communication of old meanings, provide the psychological underpinnings of language change as a global, impersonal evolution. Yesterday's trope is today's grammar, and as repositories of tropes, languages are culturally relative entities. But, by the same token, languages, as the raw materials for destructive restructuring, are what sets cognition free to pursue its unfettered path through history.

# Chapter 15

# The Development of Time-talk

The next issue concerning temporal cognitive universals which I wish to discuss is the question of the emergence of time-handling constructions during language acquisition, among infants exposed to different languages. This material sheds some interesting light on what may be considered the most 'elementary' features of time cognition, in so far as cognitive processes are reflected in language use.

The previous overview of the natural language 'grammar of time' has perhaps provided sufficient indication of the rather complex nature of this branch of grammar, and perhaps also of the formidable problems which the child has to grapple with in order to become a competent user of natural language. The essential question from the psycho-linguistic standpoint is not simply to observe the appearance of particular grammatical construction in child speech at different stages of development, but to ascertain exactly what a child might intend when using them, i.e. what the underlying 'semantic representation' might be. Suppose a child uses a verb in a particular tense form which seems non-standard in the situation. That child might (1) be using the form perfectly correctly, but to describe a situation which he has misperceived, i.e. the grammar is right, but the semantic representation is awry by adult standards; or (2) the child might have the entirely appropriate semantic representation, but be insufficiently in command of the grammar of his language to communicate the representation he has of the situation correctly, or (1) and (2) might both apply simultaneously. It is very hard to know exactly what children mean when they say things, because both meanings and utterances may vary independently from the adult norm.

However, a number of experimental studies have been conducted which attempt to control for these factors, and naturalistic observations, with adequate specification of the context of child utterances, can also be employed to reduce the inevitable uncertainty. The upshot of the limited amount of work which has been done on the acquisition of tense and aspect does, however, consistently indicate that children employ tense constructions in a non-standard way to begin with.

Bronckart and Sinclair (1973) studied the choices as to tense made by French children in providing descriptions of actions performed by an experimenter. What they discovered was that younger children (around 3:7) regularly used the French present tense to describe actions which took a relatively long time and were not climactic (a truck slowly pushes a car towards a garage) and regularly used the French 'past' (the auxiliary *avoir* + the past participle) to indicate actions of a rapid or 'punctual' nature (a car hits a marble which rolls rapidly into a pocket). What they concluded was that children at this young age are insufficiently aware of 'pastness' to use the French past tense as a genuine past, and that instead, they used it to encode the aspectual category non-durative, rapid or climactic events (which are given the 'past' tense because they are over quickly). More enduring, non-climactic events, which are no less 'past' according to adult notions of appropriate tense, are coded as 'present' because this tense is associated with the aspectual category of progressivity, not chronological presentness. In other words, in early childhood true tense does not develop, despite the appearance of past tense forms in utterances. Because the child's perspective is still predominantly egocentric, time as a linear extension has yet to take shape. Instead, the same overt linguistic forms are used to code aspectual distinctions within egocentric spatio-temporal co-ordinates. Older children gradually become more consistent in using the past tense for all their descriptions of their experimenters' actions, without regard to the durativeness or otherwise of the particular action involved. From the age of six onwards, pseudo-tensed utterances, which actually code aspect, not tense, are replaced by genuinely tensed utterances, with a mobile RT. This experiment is presented as supportive of Piaget's general theory of cognitive growth. Why these findings should be considered particularly supportive of Piaget is not altogether clear. From one standpoint aspect is a less 'egocentric' way of classing events than tense. Aspectual features of events are 'objective' in that they are not dependent on the child's own spatio-temporal co-ordinates.

Tense features of events, on the other hand, do depend on these co-ordinates. Tenses are articulated to subjective time, the momentary awareness of presentness as opposed to the subjective irrecoverability of pastness and the inaccessibility of futurity. If mere egocentricity was the defining feature of child cognition, tenses ought to appear before aspects. Evidently, it is the lack of the 'self-consciousness' which is needed in order to identify egocentric spatio-temporal co-ordinates (which are required for assigning tenses to utterances) which makes aspect the more accessible feature to code for, from the child's point of view.

Meanwhile, it seems well established that aspect rather than tense marking was taking place among Bronckart and Sinclair's younger subjects. But at this point it is necessary to ask whether their results for young French speakers provide a basis for cross-cultural (cross-language) generalizations about ages and stages in cognitive development. It does not seem so. Aspect may be prior to tense in France, but children learning English seem to grasp tense at an age at which French children are still mainly coding for aspect, using tense forms. The language to which a child is exposed exercises an independent effect on the order in which mastery of different types of grammatical distinctions is achieved.

This result was established in an experiment reported by Smith (1980: 272). In her study of American children, using an experimental set-up similar to Bronckart and Sinclair's, she found that fewer than 7 per cent of responses employed the present tense, even with children as young as 4:7, but there was variability as between perfective aspect and imperfective aspect which appeared to depend on the kind of action they were attempting to describe. As they became older, Smith's children became consistent users of the English aspectual system, as well as the tense system. It is possible that at ages below 4:7 there might have been more use of the present/past distinction to convey aspect. She herself quotes an utterance by an English child as young as 1:8 recorded by Halliday (1975), which replicates the Bronckart and Sinclair pattern (the child is spontaneously attempting to narrate an incident which occurred during a recent visit to the zoo):

Try eat lid . . . goat . . . man said no . . . goat try eat lid . . . man said no.

Here the unavailing efforts of the goat to eat the lid (imperfective) are in the present tense, but the the 'punctual' event of the man saying 'no' is, remarkably enough, in the correct irregular past form of the verb 'say'. Smith cites this passage to show that English-speaking children have a notion of pastness from the outset. That may be true, but this utterance does not prove it, since it seems equally open to an aspect-based interpretation.

Smith cites work on English and other languages which show that by the age of four past tenses are consistently used to indicate temporal pastness, not just perfective aspect. This raises the problem of identifying the intrinsic features of English which might predispose children to learn to use past tenses relatively early, by contrast to the intrinsic features of French, which tend to delay this development. The conclusion Smith reaches is that because the marking of perfective vs. imperfective aspect in all tenses in English is systematic and obligatory, children do not use tense forms to express aspects. In French, on the other hand, aspect is only intermittently marked, all tenses being aspectually neutral apart from the past imperfect, which is used in narratives but not in the kinds of simple descriptions Bronckart and Sinclair were eliciting. Moreover, in French the present tense is more multipurpose than its English equivalent. It is aspectually neutral between the present progressive and the aspectually unmarked simple present. In order to convey progressivity in the French present tense it is necessary to use an adverbial such as 'actuellement' or and adverbial phrase '. . . est en train de'. It is also much more natural to employ the 'historical present' in French than it is in English, i.e. to recount a story in the present rather than the past tense, in the manner of Damon Runyon (' . . . so this guy, he hits me, and I go down . . .'). The French 'past' tense (avoir/être + past participle) does duty both for the English present with perfective aspect (John has swum the Channel) and the English past tense with perfective aspect (John swam the Channel). French does have a another past tense (passé simple – John *nagea* la manche) but it is obsolete, and certainly not used by young children.

Because aspect-marking is complicated and variable, French children initially employ tenses to code aspects as a stop-gap measure, so to speak, because the aspectual differences between the stimuli presented to them by the experimenters were obvious and salient . It is thus the complexity of the French

language, not the autonomous rhythms of cognitive development, which is responsible for Bronckart and Sinclair's results.
English children, on the other hand, show earlier control over
tense marking (which cannot, as it can in French, be hijacked for
aspect-marking purposes), and they wrestle with aspect as best
they may, learning to distinguish perfective and imperfective
within tense frames which are consistent and unchanging.

Similarly, in another study of tense acquisition in young children, by Antonucci and Miller (1976) (based on observation in
naturalistic contexts, not experimental ones), the differences in
the order in which constructions were acquired seems to have
more to do with the language being learnt than any autonomous
process of mental growth. Here the language in question was
Italian – rather similar in structure to French, one might have
thought. Past tense forms of the verb appear very early among
Italian children, by the end of the second year, in fact. But
Italian children evidently learn the past tense (in the guise of the
past participle of the verb) initially as an adjective, devoid of the
auxiliary, but agreeing in number and gender with the noun
object of the sentence. This is very aberrant, because the adult
grammar specifies agreement between the past participle and
the subject, not the object, of transitive verbs. Then, during
their third year, they learn to use the normal Italian past tense,
with an auxiliary, and then the (inflected) Italian imperfect. This
contrasts with French children, who do not seem to use the past
imperfect at the same age to anything like the same extent. What
appears to happen with Italian is that children at this age invent
a rule, which is that verbs which have intrinsically 'punctual'
inherent aspect (i.e. which denote actions having definite results) are given past tense forms with auxiliary + past participle,
and verbs with non-punctual inherent aspect (i.e. which denote
ongoing or continuous actions) are given pasts in the inflected
imperfect form. So there are two distinct classes of verbs, with
non-interchangeable past tenses, punctual 'action' verbs with
perfective pasts, stative or activity verbs with the imperfective
pasts. Antonucci and Miller's results support Bronckart and
Sinclair's to the extent that the distinction between 'action' verbs
with perfective pasts vs. 'ongoing state/activity' verbs with
imperfective pasts shows precocious sensitivity to aspectual
distinctions leading to the formation of abberrant 'rules' in
child-Italian. But the Italian children differ from the French in
consistently marking pastness for both aspect categories from a

much earlier age. They may be oversensitive to aspect, but they are certainly sensitive to tense as well, in that from the third year accounts of past happenings are consistently conveyed in one or other of the past tenses, not in the present tense.

However, Antonucci and Miller themselves, taking the Piagetian line, do not believe that Italian children around the age of four are marking pastness as such when they make use of the past imperfect. They offer the interesting suggestion that this tense, which occurs only when children are inventing stories, actually marks irrealis modality – 'let's pretend . . .'. This appears to be an unduly narrow interpretation, and it is not explained why punctual verbs in the perfective past tense are not marked for irrealis in the same way when they occur in fantasies, as they are equally prone to do. And it is also relevant that Italian, unlike French or English, uses the past imperfective form as the tense for the narration of events, to give a sense of immediacy and flow, comparable to the use of the narrative historical present in French

> *L'assasino apriva* [imperf.] *la porta, entrava* [imperf.] *nella stanza e strangolava* [imperf.] *la sua vittima.* (The murderer opened the door, went into the room and strangled his victim. (Antonucci and Miller 1976: 169)

Consequently, early use of the past imperfect by Italian children probably reflects the prominent place of this tense in Italian narrative style. But the suggestion has merit, none the less, in that it may well be true that pastness and a modalization may be fused together in early use of past tenses in child language generally. Past tense can be used in (adult) English with irrealis modal implications, as noted in the previous chapter.

Italian, French and English are reasonably closely related languages, yet it is apparent, even from this narrow selection among the thousands of languages distributed around the globe, that there are wide divergences in the specific sequencing of the learning of tense and aspect constructions. It seems reasonably certain that young children do have a basic understanding of 'pastness' as distinct from perfective aspect, though this fact may be obscured by the simultaneous need to code for aspect without recourse to adverbials or other circumlocutory devices. Speakers of 'tenseless' languages, no doubt, are precocious users of adverbials and modals compared to their

European counterparts, although I have no data on the acquisition of tenseless languages to support this deduction.

It is apparent that divergences in the detailed structure of French, English and Italian are the source of considerable difficulties in attempting to extract a pattern from the data on language acquisition and in particular the acquisition of tense. These languages are old, complicated ones, each a palimpsest of layer upon layer of diachronic changes, old constructions, old tenses and aspect markers, partly effaced with newer ones, coexisting in rich disorder. Are there any simpler languages, in whose structure it might be possible to glimpse a 'primordial' tense/aspect/modality system free of historical encrustations and other complicating factors?

According to Bickerton (1981) and Givon (1982), such languages are indeed to be found. They are the languages called Creoles. Creoles, according to Bickerton, have come into being in communities which have been linguistically disrupted, usually through the impact of colonialism and the importation of large numbers of culturally and linguistically diverse labourers and/or slaves into socially chaotic plantation economies. The ethnically mixed coolies, displaced tribesmen, etc. initially develop a heterogeneous array of grammatically unstable pidgins, but continue to speak their native languages among themselves. But at a certain point, because of the collapse of traditional forms of family life and ethnic exclusiveness, there comes into being a generation of young children whose primary linguistic experience is of the range of grammatically unstable pidgins spoken by the adult generation. These children are in an exceptional situation, because they have no consistent linguistic input at all; they hear varieties of pidgin and varieties of non-pidgin languages, but are presented with no single, dominant, linguistic standard. They have, according to Bickerton and Givon, to 'invent' a language; not exactly from scratch, because they have the pidgin vocabulary to work with, but the main work of stabilizing the grammar of the input pidgin has yet to be accomplished. It is a remarkable fact that the Creole languages which the children 'invent' (i.e. the end-product of their stabilization of the local pidgin, so that it becomes an effective first language which can be transmitted in the ordinary way to the following generation) show remarkable structural convergence, even though these Creoles have arisen in geographically dispersed locations, and on the basis of different 'substrate' (pre-pidgin) languages.

Bickerton has written a very interesting book in which he claims that the grammar of Creoles provides us with a window onto the innate linguistic 'bio-program' of the human species; Creole grammar is hard-wired, so to speak. In his hands, this hypothesis is made to seem remarkably reasonable, though of necessity somewhat speculative. Givon takes the more cautious view that the grammatical parallels between historically unrelated Creoles are more usefully explained with reference to universals of a functional-communicative nature, rather than innate biological factors to do with the brain.

Despite these differences of interpretation, to which I shall return later, Bickerton (1981) and Givon (1982) give identical descriptions of the tense/aspect/mode system of Creole languages. The Creole verb can appear unmarked (∅), in which case it conveys past actions or present states, or it can be preceded by three markers: (1) an aspect marker ('stay' or some equivalent) which conveys non-punctual, continuous aspect, iteration, habituality, and so forth; (2) an irrealis modal marker ('go' or some equivalent) indicating, futurity, conditionality or the imperative, and finally (3) an anterior/perfect tense marker ('bin' or some equivalent), which indicates perfectivity in stative verbs and perfectivity of the action in relation to some past RT, in the case of non-stative verbs (pluperfect tense). When used in combinations, the markers always appear in the same order, with the aspect marker immediately preceding the verb, the modal preceding the aspect marker, and the anterior tense marker preceding the modal.

Bickerton and Givon both imply that functional equivalents to all four forms of the Creole verb, i.e. ∅-V, stay-V, go-V and bin-V are language universals. No languages can exist which do not make these distinctions, although they may make many other distinctions, and grammaticalize many more tenses, modes or aspects than Creoles do. I am in no position to assess the correctness of this claim. Bickerton does not discuss non-Creole languages, which depart radically from the pattern just described, but Givon (1982: 141–6) does consider one such case in some detail, the New Guinea language Chuave. This is a language which appears to violate the claim that all languages must have an equivalent to the 'anterior' marker 'bin'. Chuave sentences are created by stringing together clauses, only the last of which is asserted and tensed, either as non-future (present or past) or future (irrealis, conditional). There is no trace of a past

tense with a past RT. In other words, there is no provision in
Chuave for the manoeuvre we make in English, when we say:

By the time John went to school, he had learned to read,

or in (Umeda) Tok Pisin, approximating a Creole:

Olosem taim John i-go long skul, em i bin save long rit,

in which the action of the main clause, John learning to read,
precedes in time the action of the subsidiary clause, John going
to school. In Chuave, Givon states: 'If an event preceded in
time, it cannot be mentioned after an asserted clause that followed it in real time within the same chain' (1982: 145). The
upshot of his discussion is that the functional load carried by the
Creole anterior/perfect/pluperfect marker 'bin' is transferred to a
completely different mechanism. Instead of modifying the verb,
Chuave imposes strong constraints on order-of-mention of actions in the chain of clauses: if actions occur early on in the
chain, they provide background information, identify the topic
of the sentence and the presuppositions needed to interpret the
final clause, which is the one that asserts something and that
carries the narrative one stage further. One can imagine this as a
kind of moving RT which sweeps through the sentence, from
beginning to end, arranging actions in temporal sequence,
clause by clause, until the final, assertion-clause establishes the
definitive RT of the sentence as a whole. Givon notes that as a
matter of statistical fact, in any language, verbs in sentences
containing more than one verb overwhelmingly occur in an
order-of-mention, which corresponds to the order in which actions take place, and so Chuave only makes a rule of what is
otherwise a general but not obligatory practice. He also says that
this rule is found in other New Guinea Highlands languages,
and in Tibeto-Burman, which may shed light on the reported
tenselessnes of Burmese, mentioned earlier. His argument is
elegant and persuasive, though what exactly remains of the
purported 'universal' significance of Creole grammar, in the
forms in which it actually exists in Creole languages, is rather
hard to say. The greater the weight placed on 'functional'
equivalences between languages which show profound mor-
phosyntactic differences, the less scope there is for deriving
conclusions about cognitive processes from the characteristics of

any language, or family of languages, in particular.

I shall return to the subject of functional interpretations of tense/aspect/mode (TAM) systems later. Meanwhile, there is another branch of the study of Creoles which is more Bickerton's speciality than Givon's, and that is the investigation of the interesting idea that the 'stripped down' TAM system of Creole can be identified with the system used by children learning their mother tongue, before they have learned the adult system in its full structural diversity. If the scenario outlined earlier for the genesis of Creoles is correct – and Creole languages do indeed bear the traces of having been 'invented' by children – relatively unconstrained by input from adults, then it might be expected that the 'experimental' languages devised by children as way-stages on the path towards the acquisition of adult speech, might possess 'Creole' features. Such is certainly the contention made by Bickerton (1981).

Thus, for example, he notes the remarkable fact that English children, before they acquire any other tense or aspect form whatsoever, begin to use '-ing' to distinguish the present progressive aspect of action verbs from the unmarked present. They indicate an ongoing action with the -ing form, and everything else, past, present or future, with the base form, the verb stem. They do this even by the end of the second year, while French or Italian children only make comparable aspectual distinctions very much later. And what is still more remarkable, English children never 'overgeneralize' '-ing' by attaching it to stative verbs, i.e. verbs whose inherent aspect is progressive rather than punctual, such as 'like'. They never say, 'I am liking ice-cream*, even though they are in an ongoing state of liking that wonderful substance. They overgeneralize elsewhere in the language, producing no end of incorrect plurals, 'sheeps', 'mouses' and 'foots', and incorrect past tenses, 'eated' for 'ate', 'flied' for 'flew', and so on. But they never overgeneralize by adding -ing to stative verbs, which is surely curious. Bickerton claims that this is because they are innately aware of the fact that stative verbs have inherent progressive aspect, and that hence to add -ing to them would be redundant.

Is sensitivity to the state/process distinction innate? The main argument against supposing this is that whatever the uncanny abilities of English children to distinguish stative from non-stative verbs, this ability is not manifested everywhere, not in France, not in Italy, not perhaps in very many places at all.

Bickerton believes, none the less, that 'errorless learning' of
the state/process distinction by English children is pre-
programmed, 'not because of its universality', which may be as
low as Brown [1973: 326] suggests, but because it plays a crucial
role in Creole grammars (Bickerton 1981: 160). This is surely a
dangerous line to take, unless it is uncontroversially true that
only if a construction is found in Creole can it be deemed innate,
and that other languages reveal the workings of the innate
language programme only in so far as they resemble Creoles,
without in any way damaging the innateness hypothesis if they
do not. Creole does not just reveal the workings of the 'bio-
programme', but also sets the standard for what is 'programmed' vs. what is contingent. There is evidently a danger of
circularity here.

Another possible explanation for 'errorless learning' of the
state/process distinction is that English children actually learn
action verbs in the present progressive form. This is the form
used by adults when demonstrating an action to a child, which
they are obliged to do by the rules of English. Thus, the child is
shown what it is to ride on something, to the accompaniment of
the utterance 'riding . . . riding . . .' so that progressive aspect
marking is inherently part of the demonstration/learning context
for action verbs. Stative verbs are learnt in different contexts and
are not 'demonstrated' in the same way; so the fundamental
difference may be in the pragmatics of learning situations rather
than in any programmed semantic opposition between states
vs. processes.

In similar vein, Bickerton accepts Bronckart and Sinclair's
finding that children initially use the French past tense in order
to mark punctuality (of aspect) rather than pastness (of tense)
but instead of putting a Piagetian gloss on this finding, as they
do, he interprets it as a linguistic phenomenon, not a cognitive
one. It is not that these children lack a decentred notion of
'pastness'; it is rather that the programme that controls language
acquisition is primarily geared to making aspectual distinctions
between states and processes, and only latterly to distinguishing past tense from present tense. Because this finding is
consistent with the Creole model it is accepted, but nothing is
made of the fact that English children of the same age are well
able to use past tenses which cannot be interpreted as pseudo-
aspects, nor as the equivalent of the Creole 'anterior' past,
which has a past ET which is anterior to the RT which is in turn

anterior to the ST. The English child past (of action verbs) has an
ET and an RT which are both equally anterior to ST, i.e. they are
simple pasts, and would be realized in Creole via the Ø form of
the verb. The Creole 'anterior' past is most equivalent to the
English, French or Italian pluperfects, which are late developments, not at all common in the speech of (European) children
in the under-five age-group. The grammar of 'bin' in Creole has
no counterpart in the speech of European children. Indeed, I
wonder very much whether it plays any part in the speech of
Creole children in the under-five group either, and if so, it is
impossible to argue that the grammar of 'bin' was invented by
children or reflects the 'childhood of language'. For confirma-
tion one only has to turn to Bickerton's (1975: ch.2) analysis of
'bin', 'don' and 'a' in Guyanese Creole, which is decidedly
complicated. This fragment of Creole grammar could surely
only have been invented by adults.

However, this is not the place to discuss innateness in any
detail. It would be more profitable to conclude by raising more
general considerations about time cognition and language. Why
do natural languages have tenses, modes and aspects at all?
Even if one agreed with Bickerton that human beings were
programmed to create languages with just these characteristics,
that question would still have to be answered, because it would
have to be shown how an 'evolutionary' advantage accrued to
creatures speaking this type of language, as opposed to other
languages of dissimilar type.

Tense mode and aspect have to do, most of all, with organizing information in discourse. Tenses and aspects are particularly
important in narrations, in recounting and explaining sequences
of actions and responses, usually those of animate beings. Modalities are particularly important in making plans for the future,
in distinguishing reliable from unreliable statements, and in
using language performatively and prescriptively. The sentence
level semantics of particular utterances which are coded for
tense, modality and aspect are subordinated to the requirements
of particular generic kinds of discourses, story performances,
planning discussions, the exercise of authority through speech,
the activity of teaching, or whatever. What children learn is not
'the grammar of the language' but grammatical constructions in
relation to a variety of pragmatic discursive frames, which develop and multiply with their growing capacity to participate in
a wider variety of types of social interaction. The significance of

Creole grammar is that it provides a useful model for a pragmatic-discursive core system, not universal in terms of grammatical forms, or underlying cognitive capacities, but reflecting essential functional constraints on language as a discursive tool, in a relatively transparent way. This seems to be Givon's approach. Following Bickerton's lead, he posits three functional universals:

1. Being able to communicate the temporal order of events.
2. Being able to communicate whether something is known via the senses or is imaginary.
3. Being able to indicate whether an events (or state) protracts itself or whether it occurs once, or repeatedly.

These communicative requirements are underwritten by the cognitive capacity to make the relevant distinctions – for instance, between real and imaginary events. In Creole, function (1) is carried by the general rule that order of mention in discourse corresponds to the order of events in reality. The time-frame of a narrative moves forwards from clause to clause, from sentence to sentence, *except* when the anterior marker 'bin' is used to 'look back' behind the narrative ongoing past/present, into some anterior condition. The function (2) is carried by the modal marker 'go' for futurity, hypotheticality, etc., and function (3) is carried by the aspect marker 'stay' for continuity of action or state.

Because Creole provides for just these functional requirements, without the many additional features possessed by other languages, Givon argues, plausibly it seems to me, that Creole reveals a primordial discursive mechanism. This mechanism is not hard-wired in the brain, but directly reflects, he says 'the features most important to code in the communicative system of humans, as the most pertinent generic observations to be made about events: Their sequence, their factuality, their duration. It is also likely that there may be practical, survival-related reasons for singling out these features in the coded communicative system' (1982: 156; author's emphasis omitted). But the functional-pragmatic approach to tense and allied phenomena takes us away from a strictly developmental perspective, since the dominant forces shaping speech pragmatically are the demands of adult existence, and the integrity of the communicative practices of adult society.

Here I bring to a conclusion this brief discussion of time in relation to natural languages. Though one may tentatively identify natural-language 'universals' in the time-handling mechanics of language, it is clear to me that these do not correspond to cognitive universals in the strict sense (or in the sense required by Bloch (1977)), but only to pragmatic-functional universals relating to discourse, rather than conceptual understanding in the broad sense. In other words, one cannot attempt to construct a model of the psychic foundations of time cognition (psychological temporal universals) on the basis of natural-language grammars. In order to do that, time has to be considered more abstractly, as a feature of experience as such, not as a just feature of discourse.

But, as everybody knows, it is hard to think about time in the abstract without getting immediately into severe intellectual difficulties. So far, the general upshot of this critique of relativist and anti-relativist approaches to the anthropology of time has been to emphasize practice and function, over against abstraction and pseudo-metaphysics. But one cannot let matters rest there, because practice and function rest on cognitive foundations, which have remained unexplored. And one cannot advance a theory about *noesis* (the process of cognition) without having simultaneously a theory about *neoma* (that which is there to be cognized). Thus far, indeed, the category 'time' itself has remained unexamined, and it has only been shown that, whatever time is, it is not a sociologically determined category, not a hard-wired natural-language universal, or endogenously determined concept, or whatever. The moment has come to outline a positive doctrine of time as a prelude to a more rational time-anthropology. How do human beings think about time, and what is there for them to think? How does time actually become salient for us? How does it come about that there is a past, a present and a future? Are these features of the universe, or do they somehow arise from our special point of vantage on the universe as sentient organisms? It is to questions of this order that I shall turn next.

# Part II

## Time-maps and Cognition

# Chapter 16

# Time in Philosophy: the A-series vs. the B-series

One of the main objectives I have been pursuing up to now has been to dissuade anthropologists from unwarranted metaphysical speculation. This metaphysical strain in symbolic anthropology I have identified as a malign inheritance from Durkheim (among others). I have maintained that it is never really the case that ethnographic investigations throw up results which would require, for their interpretation, the revision of philosophical ideas of a positive character which one might otherwise be inclined to accept. But one of the reasons why anthropologists are unsufficiently critical when it comes to writing about time is because they have no very clear philosophical ideas on this topic anyway. They are puzzled and mystified by the whole subject. And they have no workable model of time cognition as a mental process. So one essential service which a book on the anthropology of time can perform is to remove this generalized sense of puzzlement that the ghostly notion of *time* evokes, both by presenting a coherent philosophical account of time, and by elaborating a general model of time cognition. This is a difficult task for a non-philosopher to accomplish, but certainly no less difficult than the task that would confront a philosopher who attempted to present his/her philosophical views in a manner accessible to anthropologists, rather than the customary audience of other philosophers. Consequently, nothing daunted, I propose at this stage to outline one particular view of the philosophy of time, the one I have found most useful, first, in dispelling the mysteriousness of time, and second, as a basis for a general model of time cognition, which will be elaborated later in this book.

Of course, there is no universal consensus among philosophers about how time should best be understood. Views range between an extreme subjectivism, impenetrable mysticism, on the one hand, to relentless, dehumanized objectivism and physicalism on the other. But, having sampled as much of the available literature as I felt able to, I reached a very firm conclusion. Most work on time in philosophy belongs to the philosophy of science, particularly physics, and deals with problems (relativity, time-travel, etc.), which have no bearing on what one might call 'human' time. The best-known works by philosophers specifically concerned with human existence – Husserl and his successors, Heidegger, Sartre, Merleau-Ponty, etc. – had much to say that was relevant, and Husserl, in particular, provided a model of internal time-consciousness which will be expounded in detail later, but their works are far from self-explanatory. They are all exceptionally difficult writers. But I did discover one philosophical author who appeared to me to square the circle between lucid irrelevance and relevant incomprehensibility. The author in question is D. H. Mellor, whose short book *Real Time* (1981) I found by far the most useful general guide to the subject in hand. Mellor is an analytical philosopher who belongs to the dominant Anglo-American school. I make no bones about saying that my views on time derive from him, and thus indirectly from the thinkers from whom he has derived his ideas, back to McTaggart, Russell, Broad, etc. It is worth adding that, although I espouse Mellor's analytical views on time, that does not imply that I am actively hostile to the humanistic-phenomenological writers I have just mentioned, Husserl, Sartre, etc. On the contrary, I believe that it becomes much easier to read phenomenological texts with some degree of genuine comprehension once one can approach them from the stable metaphysical standpoint provided by analytical philosophers like Mellor. In particular, the study of internal time-consciousness (Bloch's cognitively universal time) has to be founded on phenomenological psychology, and I shall later present a model of time-consciousness constructed in precisely that fashion. But in order to be in a position to do this, one has to get basic time-metaphysics clear in one's head. And only the analytical approach, favoured by Mellor, enables one to do this.

Time has been a subject of philosophical reflection from the very beginning. Kant's views on the subject have already been alluded to (in Chapter 1), but I do not intend to discuss the long and complicated history of the subject, and shall confine myself to the recent period. This century has seen, on the one hand, the rise of a space-like view of time (under the influence of relativistic physics) and, on the other hand, the rejection of this spatialized time by another group of philosophers, many of them influenced by James and Bergson, who emphasize the dynamic, subjective, stream-of-experience aspect of time. Between these two extremes, physicalism and phenomenology, there are, of course, many subtle shades of opinion. Fortunately, it is relatively easy to detect, amid the turmoil of conflicting voices, two dominant opposed tendencies, which will be labelled the A-series view and the B-series view.

We owe these convenient labels directly to the contemporary philosopher R. Gale (1967, 1968) and indirectly to the turn-of-the-century Cambridge idealist, McTaggart, who, in the course of an attempt to show that time is 'unreal' – an attempt which is generally considered to have failed – introduced the distinction that has greatly simplified the task of classifying metaphysical standpoints on the 'time' question. McTaggart's contribution was that he distinguished two quite different kinds of time and labelled them 'A' and 'B'. McTaggart's argument against the reality of time runs as follows.

(1) We categorize events according to their being at any one time past, present or future events. All events are one of these, but not unchangingly, since any event which has occurred, has been a future event up to the time of its occurrence, a present event as it occurs, and a past event thereafter. This differentiation among events according to criteria of pastness, presentness, and futurity McTaggart calls the A-series.

(2) We also categorize events temporally according to whether they occur before or after one another. Events do not change with respect to this criterion in the way that they do with respect to the criterion of pastness, presentness and futurity. This before/after series McTaggart calls the B-series.

(3) These two series, the A-series (past/present/future) and the B-series (before/after) are the two kinds of time. McTaggart goes on to say that the A-series is essential to the idea of change, since it is hard to see how change can be accommodated by the B-series which is just a row of events strung together, like the beads on a necklace. The A-series incorporates the idea of transition or 'passage' – things being arranged in one way and then becoming arranged in some other way. Since change is that

aspect of the universe that the notion of time seems specifically designed to handle, it must be that A-series time, changing time, is *basic*, while B-series time must be derived from A-series time, and is therefore not basic.

(4) But this gives rise to a problem. How can the A-series properties of events be 'real', as four-leggedness is a property of horses, when any one event (a recent past event, for instance) is simultaneously 'future' in relation to more distantly past events, present in relation to events synchronous with itself, and very-much-past in relation to events still in the future. If pastness, presentness and futurity are 'real' characteristics of events, how can one event have these incompatible characteristics simultaneously, as if a horse had four legs, and two legs, and no legs, all at once.

(5) This difficulty seems to be surmountable if it is stipulated that only at a given moment in time does an event possess a given degree of pastness, presentness or futurity. At one time (4 July) event *e* was still future, at another time (5 July) it was present, and at another time still (6 July) it became past. But on none of these days did event *e* possess incompatible attributes of present-pastness, or pastness-futurity. Event *e* had just one of these attributes at a time, and not the others.

This answer, while satisfactory in that it clears up the problem raised in (4) above, does so by distinguishing 'moments in time' at which event *e* has non-conflicting A-series attributes, by *dates*, or by some equivalent of dates. Dates belong to the B-series because date-attributes of events are not attributes which change like pastness/presentness/futurity. The moment in time indicated by the date-expression 12 January 1995 does not alter as the century rolls on, nor will it by the time we have reached the twenty-fifth century. Any event which will happen on 12 January 1995 already has that property, not that we know much about any such events.

It would appear that the only way to make pastness/ presentness/futurity attributes stick to events without producing contradictions is to introduce a back-up in the form of a B-series of dates *at which* events have these A-series attributes.

(6) But if the assertion in (3) above is true, the B-series is derived from the A-series. But we seem to be in need of a B-series in order to establish the A-series on a sound logical footing. So there must be a second A-series from which this B-series is derived, i.e. the one we have just invoked in order to

prop up the first A-series. But in order to prop up this second A-series we need a second B-series too. And a third A-series from which the second B-series is derived, and a . . . and so on down a vicious logical regression. McTaggart concludes that time must be unreal because no real characteristic of the world could give rise to insoluble logical paradoxes.

Even if one has no very strong feelings about whether or not time is to be accorded the privilege of being called 'real', this argument has a certain fascination. It is the steps leading up to the conclusion which engage the attention, rather than the conclusion itself, which most people would find implausible however strong the arguments marshalled in its favour. Philosophers have devoted a good deal of effort to diagnosing what they take to be the logical ailments present in McTaggart's reasoning, though a few (Dummett 1978) have pronounced it perfectly sound. The dissenting majority, however, are anything but united among themselves. The argument, to succeed, depends to the correctness of two claims, first, that there must be both an A-series and a B-series; and second, that these cannot coexist without paradox ensuing. Critics can deny either or both of these claims.

The commonest response has been to deny the first of these claims, i.e. that there are two series rather than one, and that they have to coexist side by side. Either this is because the A-series does not need the B-series, or because the B-series does not need the A-series. The paradox arises because the genuine member of the pair is being contaminated by the false one. At this point the really important question becomes: which is it to be? Does the A-series have the credentials to be considered real (basic, universal) time, or should it be the B-series? Is time based on the passage of events out of the future, into the present, and out again into the recesses of the past, or is time an unchanging relation of before-ness/after-ness holding between dateable events, as in the B-series? Gale (1967) was the first to show how philosophers of time can be neatly divided into the A-series crowd vs. the B-series crowd, according to the varying answers that they give to this crucial question, the touchstone of time-philosophical opinions. Gale himself is an A-series man, Mellor a 'moderate' B-series supporter. I am a moderate B-series supporter, too. But this is of little importance for the present. What needs to be done now is to take a closer look at the A-series and the B-series themselves.

This is particularly necessary in that one of the main points I wish to establish in this chapter is that the A-series/B-series distinction is not only of parochial philosophical interest, but can be seen to have ramifications extending throughout the human sciences, including under that heading economics, sociology, psychology, geography, etc. as well as anthropology. Very roughly, A-series temporal considerations apply in the human sciences because agents are always embedded in a context of situation about whose nature and evolution they entertain moment-to-moment beliefs, whereas B-series temporal considerations also apply because agents build up temporal 'maps' of their world and its penumbra of possible worlds whose B-series characteristics reflect the genuinely B-series layout of the universe itself. Much of my subsequent discussion will be devoted to attempts at making this point clearer, so it is essential to get the A-series and the B-series straightened out to begin with.

Philosophers can be divided, as I remarked, into the A-series crowd and the B-series crowd. In order to gain some insight into the different mental 'set' which typifies members of one or the other party, it may be helpful to provide two short quotations, characteristic of each, for immediate and stark comparison. I shall use rather antiquated texts, since present-day philosophers are inclined to put their views forward in rather more cautious language than of old, and none of them perhaps would wish to associate themselves wholeheartedly with the rather extreme positions of Weyl and Mead, my sources. But for their exemplary value, they will do very well. It is simpler to take the B-series first, so here is a classic B-series statement from the philosopher-physicist, Weyl:

> The objective world simply is: it does not happen. Only to the gaze of my consciousness, crawling up the life-line of my body, does a section of the world come to light as a fleeting image in space which is continuously changing in time. (Weyl 1949: 116)

Weyl has in mind here the famous Minkowski diagram, which shows the life-line of any individual thing, such as a body or a star, as a linear streak of events embedded in four-dimensional space-time, like currants in a slab of fruit-cake, forever *there*, and linked to the rest of the universe by a web of converging and diverging causal relationships. Four-dimensional space-time, thus construed, is a stable field, rather than a process of becoming, and we have the idea that events 'happen' only because we 'encounter' them in a particular causal order, not because time itself actually progresses from future to present to past.

Now consider, by contrast, this classic A-series statement from G. H. Mead:

> Reality exists in a present. The present implies a past and a future, and to both of these we deny existence.
>
>   Time arises through the ordering of passage of unique events, . . . The causal conditioning passage and the appearance of unique events . . . gives rise to the past and the future as they arise in the present. All of the past is in the present as the conditioning nature of passage, and all of the future arises out of the present as the unique events that transpire. The long and the short of it is that the past (the meaningful structure of the past) is as hypothetical as the future. (Mead 1925: 33)

Whereas Weyl suggests to us a congealed time, more or less coextensive with space, Mead conceives of time as a wafer-thin screen of unique events in a continuously changing and moving present. It is presentness alone which confers reality on anything, but the present bears within itself the residual effects of the whole of the past, and prefigures the whole of the future. Time, and indeed the whole cosmos, is coterminous with this present-in-process. This is the extreme A-series view of time.

# Chapter 17

# The B-series

The contrasts between the A-theory and the B-theory can be set out as in Table 17.1.

Not all A-theorists adhere to everything on the A-series side of the table, or vice versa for B-theorists, but this suffices to give a general idea of the two-party division. Now I shall sketch in the 'moderate' version of the B-series position taken by Mellor, and in the process give his solution to the McTaggart paradox. Mellor is a 'moderate' to the extent that although he thinks that 'real' time is B-series time, he accepts that all our actions in the real world arise from choices we make on the basis of 'tensed' (A-series) beliefs, which we cannot do without. This position depends on accepting certain parts of the McTaggart argument, and rejecting certain others, as follows.

1. McTaggart was right to have distinguished the A-series and the B-series in the first place.
2. McTaggart was incorrect in thinking that the B-series was based on, or derived from, the A-series.
3. McTaggart was also wrong in thinking that pastness, presentness and futurity are needed in order to account for change.
4. McTaggart was quite right in thinking that labelling events as past, present and future does not result in a consistent or coherent temporal system.

I shall take point (1) to be uncontroversial, and shall proceed to indicate briefly the reasoning behind (2), (3) and (4). Why should the B-series be considered less 'basic' than the A-series (point 2)? Because, according to A-theorists, an event only has the date it has because it was at one time future, occurred on a given date, and thereafter was past. But it can be objected to this

**Table 17.1** The A-Series vs. the B-series

| A-theory | B-theory |
|---|---|
| Time = Future → present → past. | Time = Before vs. after. |
| Basic ideas: 'passage', 'becoming'. | Basic ideas: 'being' 'four-dimensional space-time'. |
| Time is dynamic. | Time is not dynamic. |
| Truth time-dependent. | Truth not dependent on time. |
| Pastness, presentness and futurity *sui generis* characteristics of events. | Pastness, presentness and futurity are not real characteristics of events but arise from our relation to them as conscious subjects. |
| There are basic (ontological) differences between past, present, and future events. | There are no basic (ontological) differences between past, present, and future events. |
| Human subjective time consciousness (of passage of time) provides appropriate schema for understanding time. Subjective temporality reflects 'becoming' as an objective phenomenon of the universe. | Human subjective time consciousness inadequately reflects the 'real' nature of time. 'Becoming' is not an objective phenomenon. |
| Change results from 'becoming'. | Change is concomitant variation between the qualities of a thing and the date at which these qualities are manifested by that thing. |

that an event has the date it has quite independently of whether it is past, present or future. All events, including future events, have their dates, which are unqualified temporal attributes of events. The date of an event does not change with the passage of time (i.e. the specification of *today's* date). If an event occurs at all, it must do so at a definite date, which can be placed in relation to the dates of every other event, past, present or future. Naturally, we do not have any means of knowing the dates of future events, or whether they will occur sometime, or will never occur at any time. But the limitations on our capacity to make predictions does not make future events dateless, any more than our inability comprehensively to reconstruct the facts regarding past events – whether they occurred at all, and if so, when – means that any past events are without dates either.

The B-series is not based on, or derived from, the A-series because there is no reciprocal effect between some event's *changing* A-series status and its *permanent* temporal attributes in the B-series. The passage of weeks and months brings the events of a future date closer to us, but it is not because of this passing of time that events have specific dates. Events just have dates anyway, as an essential attribute of event-hood, but it is no essential attribute of event-hood to be located at some point in the future, present or past. These are fleeting attributes which events gain and lose from day to day.

One can make an analogy between the A-series attributes of events, and the visual attributes of spatial objects. A rectangular card, lying before me on my desk, has, in outline, the appearance of a trapezoid. I can, if I wish, make it appear as a variety of other trapezoidal and rectangular shapes by moving it about, or by moving about myself. But these various shapes are not characteristics of the card itself, but of its appearance when viewed from different angles. It would be wrong to reply to the question 'what shape is this card?' by stating that it is trapezoidal, or a variety of rectangular shapes. The card has one, and only one, shape (assuming it is not bent), i.e. the shape you would get by measuring its dimensions and the angles formed by its edges. B-series supporters believe that the dates of events are the temporal equivalent of the 'real' spatial attributes you could identify by measuring the card, and the illusory spatial attributes of trapezoidality, variability, etc., which the card 'seems' to have, but does not really have, correspond to the A-series temporal attributes of events, which are also illusory.

Is that all there really is to time, then, the fact that events have dates? Not quite all, perhaps, but a great deal of what needs to be said on the subject does in fact boil down to just this. It is certainly very hard to make any progress with the subject without introducing the concept of a date, (which is the first lesson of the McTaggart paradox), but to reduce time to dates is an unpopular move in the eyes of many. I am sure that my anthropological colleagues will be most dissatisfied with the turn the argument seems to be taking. How can one possibly claim that time is a matter of placing events in dated series, when most human beings, outside calendar-using, literate societies such as our own, hardly seem to have the concept of a 'date'?

I do not mean to argue that everybody makes use of a system of calendars and dates which is the same as the one we use; in fact, what I am saying has no cultural implications at all. The facts are that people are aware of temporal relationships between events, and behave accordingly in the conduct of their affairs. That they are capable of this shows that they have a schema for relating events to one another in time. The *indices* provided for events in terms of whatever culturally transmitted schema is in operation are their 'dates'. These indices may relate to a metrical scheme, such as a calendar of some kind, or they may not. From a logical point of view, this does not matter, though from the point of view of anthropological understanding it matters a great deal.

The fact that events have dates, non-changing B-series temporal attributes, is the basis of the solution of the metaphysical problems of time; but it is only the initial starting-point of the practical 'problem of time' so far as human conduct in a temporal world is concerned. We care about events because they affect our vital interests. Having a date is an intrinsic property of events. It follows that we cannot care about events and not care about their dates of occurrence. If I care to shoot a pig at all, I care to shoot a pig on a definite date, whether or not I have any means of predicting that date, or expressing my prediction in terms of a calendrical or other time-measuring scheme. Date-specificity is built into the notion of 'event' or state-of-affairs, including all the events or states of affairs that an agent might wish to bring about by purposive action. It is quite true that I feel quite differently about a pig-killing event which I foresee occurring next week than I do about a pig-killing event which I anticipate in the next ten seconds. But next week's pig-kill maintains the invariant temporal attribute of occurring at a certain date at all times between now and next week when it does (with luck) transpire. Otherwise I would not recognize this event as the one I had anticipated with such eagerness a week ago. I cannot recognize it as such in virtue of any of its A-series characteristics, because during the intervening period it has had, and lost, innumerable such characteristics, all of them in conflict with one another.

The question of 'temporal perspective', which is real enough, can be considered separately. All I want to establish for the present is that in so far as agents are interested in events at all, they are interested in their dates. The availability of cultural artefacts for expressing these dates has no bearing on this. It may well be that, as in Umeda, the accepted means of expressing the date of an approaching event is often to use a 'now'-based deictic expression, e.g. 'the day after the day after tomorrow, we kill a pig'. Said on D-minus-three, this is equivalent to 'the day after tomorrow, we kill a pig' said on D-minus-two, and to 'tomorrow, we kill a pig' said on D-minus-one, and to 'today, we kill a pig' said on the day of the pig-kill. Linguistically, the speaker uses the changing A-series attributes of the pig-kill to identify it, but there is only one pig-kill which can satisfy all these changing temporal specifications, applicable on different days, and that is one that occurs on the appropriate date.

The time-boundness of an event is a factor dependent solely on its date; its specification, using the calculus of a natural language, may demand the employment of expressions which depend for their meaning on the context in which they are uttered, as well as on the temporal context of the event specified. We have to make a distinction between the (real) temporal facts, and the cognitive and communicative resources of the human agent. The underlying temporal substratum is B-series in character, but this substratum is only an unattainable limit. The B-series temporal facts are as they are, always were and always will be, but this is not in itself a useful thing to know. Our problem is knowing how to further our interests by getting a handle on the B-series facts, while having to make do with inescapably A-series-ish cognitive resources.

How this is done I will attempt to reconstruct in Chapter 24. But I must now return to McTaggart's paradox, and the third of the five points listed above. Even granted that datedness is the fundamental temporal property of events, can the B-series handle *change*? McTaggart thought that the passage from future to present to past had to figure in any account of the phenomenon of change. The B-series supporters deny this; if B-series time is real, and change is also real, then change has to be accommodated in B-series time. Just why McTaggart, and others who share his opinion, should believe that A-series time is more suitable than B-series time for this purpose is not hard to gauge; A-series time 'changes' on its own behalf, and other things can change along with it. B-series time just sits there, static and unmoving, and events strung out in B-series time do not change as B-series time changes, because B-series time does not change.

In order to rebut the view that B-series time cannot accommodate change it is necessary to say a little more about 'events'. Events are changes in things. Things change, events are the changes that happen to things, bringing about new states of affairs, but events themselves do not change.

Events come in two varieties: pseudo-events and real (causal) events. An example of a real event is a kettle boiling, as the result of the application of heat. A pseudo-event is one that does not have any causal preconditions or consequences. An example of such an event is the change in the truth-value of the proposition, 'today is Monday', which will suddenly become true at midnight tonight (Sunday). No causal links bind together the proposition 'today is Monday' and physical objects in the world, such as the clock, which is the local arbiter of when Sunday ceases and Monday begins. Propositions are not the kind of entities to which causal linkages can be attributed at all, so a change in the truth value of a proposition is not a change in that proposition, not an 'event' in which it participates. The temporal characteristics of events and pseudo-events are rather different; pseudo-events can take place instantaneously (there is no halfway-house between Sunday and Monday) whereas real events take time to take place. Events are temporally extended, some parts of an event will be nearer the beginning of that event and other parts of an event will be nearer its termination. This is the basic distinction between events and 'things': things are extended in space but not in time, i.e. they do not have temporal parts.

This is a rather contentious part of Mellor's doctrine, since other B-theory supporters hold that things, like events, also have temporal parts (Taylor 1955). The advantage gained by denying this is that if things do not have temporal parts, the temptation to ascribe certain parts of a thing to the past, others to the present and the future, cannot arise.

If things have no temporal parts, they have no temporal characteristics at all. But surely, it will be objected, things have the temporal property of existing at some times and not existing at others? The Crystal Palace existed between 1851 and 1935, but not previously or subsequently. But it is more precise to say that the Crystal Palace participated in a series of events which took place on dates between 1851 and 1935, and not in any events which occurred outside this temporal interval, rather than say the building itself belonged to any date.

This way of speaking about things seems paradoxical, since we normally do associate dates with many of the objects we encounter in everyday life. I can refer here to the discussion of *chirunga*, Magna Carta, etc. (see Chapter 3 above). Buildings, documents, relics, etc. can function as signs, directing our minds to conjure up images of the past epochs in which they were created. So can any object function as a sign, a sign for its origins, its use, its owner, and so on. But the fact that a thing can signify the events associated with its own creation does not mean that the thing itself has temporal attributes: only the events in which it participated can be said to have these. Things do not have dates, but they do go through stages in their careers as things, being new, old, etc.

The causal properties of things often vary according to the stage in their thing-careers they have reached, so it is not merely from historical interest that we often need to know what stage in their careers they have reached. For instance, cars in later stages of their careers do not behave as they did when new. According to the logic of the passage quoted earlier from G. H. Mead, I could advertise my 'V' registration Ford Fiesta as a 1991 car, on the grounds that my car is real, and everything real is of present date. But I would still be considered guilty of misrepresentation, since it is a well-known fact to all secondhand car buyers that 'V' plates indicate a car, however immaculate its condition, which dates from 1979, not 1991, i.e. the events associated with its construction took place in that year. On the other hand, my car is not a fragment of 1979 which has somehow made it as far as 1991. My car is all here: it is not a slice of a temporally extended car which is partly a 1979 car, partly a (slightly older) 1980 car, partly a 1981 car (beginning to show signs of use), partly a 1982 car, and so on up to the present. Things do not have an internal temporal structure of beforeness/afterness or pastness/present-ness/futurity.

According to Mellor, change is a concomitant variation in the properties possessed by a thing at different stages of its thing-career, and the dates at which these stages are reached. Thus if a thing has property P at one stage of its career at T1, and has lost this property at another stage of its career at T2, then a change has occurred. This suffices as a definition of change which does not rely on the A-series transition between past, present and future, nor does it require that things have temporal parts.

The points we have been considering (2 and 3) are ones on which the B-series supporters disagree with McTaggart. But the fourth and final point is one on which they agree with him, viz. that specifying events according to the past/present/future criteria gives rise to logical contradictions. Why? Because the same event, the same link in a single chain of cause and effect, is at one time future, another time present, another time past. This sounds like a quite acceptable set of properties for an event to have, like a cup of tea being at one time hot, at a later time lukewarm, and at a still later time, cold. But it is not really like this, because at any one moment an event singled out as 'present' is a future event from the standpoint of past 'presents' and a past event from the standpoint of future 'presents'. A cup of tea is not simultaneously hot and lukewarm and cold from different points of view. According to B-theory supporters events can have only one genuine temporal characteristic, and that is occurrence at a certain date (or over a certain interval of dates). A-series specifications of events are not temporal properties of events, because events cannot have incompatible properties: 'The A-series is a myth' (Mellor 1981: 93 ff).

Mellor argues that all A-series efforts to rebut the charge that A-series specifications of events are mutually contradictory amount to the argument that it is not contradictory to say of an event that it is future (on one day, i.e. today), then to say later on (tomorrow) that it is present, and then to say later still (the day after tomorrow) that it is past. The event has changing characteristics of futurity, presentness and pastness, but not all at once. Past events were future events once, but are no longer, future events will be past, but are not past yet, and so on. Mellor contends that this move helps to conceal the difficulty but does not actually remove it. It amounts to a duplication of tenses:

| 'Present' | = | Present in the present |
| | | Future in the past |
| | | Past in the future |
| | | |
| 'Past' | = | Past in the present |
| | | Present in the past |
| | | Past in the future |

| 'Future' | = | Future in the present |
|----------|---|----------------------|
|          |   | Future in the past   |
|          |   | Present in the future |

But suppose we grab hold of some event in the future. There are going to be events which are future in relation not only to the present, but also to the future relative to the event we have singled out, i.e. future in the future. When the event we have singled out actually comes about, those still later events are still going to be future events. This contradicts the idea that 'future = present in the future', because the future has arrived, and those events still are not present. Even more damagingly, there are going to be future events rather closer to the present than event in the future we have singled out, while it is still a relatively distant future event. They are future, but not by quite so much. When the event we have singled out comes about (becomes present) these events will already be past events. These future events are going to be past in the present. 'Past in the present' is an A-series characteristic of past events, not future ones, according to the list given above. So obviously something is wrong. Saying of future events that they are present in the future does not absolve the class of future events, as a whole, of the charge of having contradictory A-series properties, i.e. with being simultaneously past and present and future with respect to itself. Not all future events are going to be present in the future, because at any given moment of future time, some of them will have become past events, some of them will still be future events and only a tiny fraction of them will be present events. An event can be, without contradiction, present in the present, past in the future, and future in the past; but inevitably it is thereby future in the future, past in the past, present in the past, and present in the future.

So the reduplication of tenses does not help. Nor is it any good trying to extend the argument by adding yet another layer of tenses. Thus an A-series defender might say, 'Well, who would have thought that an event could be past in the past and simultaneously future in the future?' The event was only past in the past when it was past at some future time, at some future time (an event being past in the past is not incompatible with the event being past at some future time at some future time). And similarly, an event is future at some future time only when it is future at some past time at some past time. But although this makes the duplicated tenses consistent, it only results in the generation of a whole new set of temporal properties of a three-stage kind, which cannot all be held compatibly by one event, i.e. an event will be past at some past at some past and also future at some future at some future. Thus an endless regression is instituted, in which each successive layer of complex tenses removes the contradictions inherent in the one beneath it in the series, but gives rise itself to fresh contradictions, which can only be resolved by adding another layer, and another, *ad infinitum*.

This argument is a more technical counterpart of McTaggart's, given earlier, and is considered valid by B-theory supporters. The upshot is that A-series characteristics of events do not reflect the real temporal properties events possess. B-series time is 'real', i.e. it reflects the temporal relationships between events as they really are, out there. A-series time cannot do this, because it cannot represent temporal relationships between events in an unambiguous, non-contradictory way. Events either are or are not before or after other events (this applies in relativistic physics, too, though I will not go into details). But events are not unambiguously past, present or future.

Meanwhile there is absolutely no doubt that a great deal of our thinking with regard to events and the temporal relationships between them does make use of the A-series set of discriminations. We think differently of events if we think them to be future, as opposed to present or past. If the A-series is not 'real', why is it so much a feature of our normal experience? It is to this question that we must now turn our attention.

# Chapter 18

## The A-series

B-series supporters hold that A-series statements, such as 'the day after tomorrow, we kill a pig' are not true in the light of any A-series facts about future (vs. present or past) pig-kills, because there are no such facts. They are true, if at all, because of the B-series facts. These are that the event in question occurs at the specified date, a date which this event had at all times prior to its occurrence, contemporaneously and subsequently. Truths, including truths about when events happen, are timeless. Any A-series statement is rendered true or false not by the 'coming into being' of the facts to which it refers, but by virtue of the time-indifferent truth that the events referred to are/are not the case at a specific date.

But in order to make this point clearer, it is necessary to introduce some new definitions. Since I have agreed with the party that believe that only B-series time is genuine, I shall for the moment reserve the term 'time' for B-series time, and A-series time will be downgraded to 'tense', since past, present and future are the three basic tenses. It should be borne in mind that the linguistic phenomenon known as 'tense' does not necessarily correspond to A-series time, although in fact it often has a lot to do with it. (see Chapter 14 above). The central B-series thesis can thus be restated as: any *tensed* statement has *tenseless* truth conditions. That is, the facts which have to be the case, for a tensed statement to be true, are not tensed facts but tenseless ones, viz. that X-is-so at D, where D is a date. Temporal facts are all tenseless, i.e. true at all moments of time if they are true at all, false at all moments of time if false.

But the remark 'The day after tomorrow, we kill a pig' is clearly not true at all moments of time if it is true at all. It is true at some times and not at others. It is true if uttered two days before a pig-kill, uttered at other times it is a false prediction or a deliberate lie. So we have to make a distinction between the tenseless facts which bring it about that a tensed statement is true or false, and the statement itself, as an artefact of the human mind representing a real or feigned belief, which has the property of being true on some occasions and not on others.

Philosophers are accustomed to calling remarks, utterances, statements, unverbalized internal judgements, opinions, beliefs, etc. 'tokens'. They are called tokens because the same remark could be made, the same belief or opinion entertained, on more than one occasion by more than one individual. Different utterances of the same statement are different tokens of the same 'type' utterance. The type/token distinction has already been introduced in relation to event-types and event-tokens (see Chapter 4).

Suppose, on day 1, an Umeda says, 'The day after tomorrow, we kill a pig', and on the following day, day 2, another Umeda says, 'The day after tomorrow, we kill a pig.' In one sense these two utterances are 'the same', i.e. they have the same form of words. But they do not have the same truth-conditions. The first and second Umedas must either be referring to two quite separate pig-killing events, or alternatively one is in the right about the timing of the pig-kill, and the other is in the wrong. This is far from being the case for all the remark-tokens these Umedas might produce. If one Umeda had said, 'There are always plenty of cassowaries down by the Mesa river', another token of this remark-type would be just as true, if it is true at all, coming from the lips of a different Umeda on another occasion, or indeed from the lips of Julius Caesar in 43 BC.

Only certain remark-types possess the property of having true tokens on certain occasions/at certain spatial co-ordinates/when uttered by certain individuals, etc. Others have true tokens independently of the context of their utterance. One remark-type which belongs to the former category is, 'My name is Alfred Gell.' Uttered by me or by any namesake of mine, tokens of this remark-type are true, uttered by other individuals they constitute an imposture. This kind of remark-type is known to logicians as an *indexical*; tokens of indexicals are true if, and only if, the conditions for their production are met, conditions which are embodied in the tokens themselves. There are no conditions on the production of tokens of 'pigs are greedy animals' – everybody has an equal right to produce such tokens, and who does so, in practice, has no bearing on the truth or falsity of what is asserted. Tokens of 'my name is Alfred Gell' are true or false depending on who utters them. 'The day after tomorrow, we kill a pig' is also a token of an indexical, a token which will be true if it is uttered under the right circumstances, i.e. when the B-series facts about the date of a pig-kill warrant it.

What applies to utterances overtly made by speakers also applies to private beliefs. Some of my beliefs are such as to be true or false all the time, including some of my beliefs about the temporal relationships between events, but many of my beliefs are such as to be true some of the time and false at other times. My belief that today is Sunday (currently a correct one) will cease to be true if I continue to entertain it beyond midnight tonight. I will then have to update it, and this will contribute to my feeling that time is passing. Mental tokens of indexical beliefs are, however, somewhat different from uttered tokens of indexicals.

Utterances are events, and as such, have dates. Beliefs are not events, not things you do but things you have. I think of beliefs as *inscriptions*, things one has written down inside one's head as part of a big listing entitled 'things I believe', which can be added to, subtracted from, or altered at will. The real events associated with beliefs are acquiring them, referring to them, modifying them and shedding them. The pseudo-events associated with beliefs are occasions of belief-inscriptions changing their truth value as circumstances alter. My belief-inscription that 'my name is Alfred Gell' is the mental equivalent of the physical inscription I am obliged to wear at conferences, in the form of a little nameplate, reading 'Alfred Gell'. I can refer to this permanent mental inscription whenever I need to remind myself of who I am, just as my fellow conference-goers can remind themselves of who I am by looking at my nameplate. If anybody were demented enough to steal my nameplate and mischievously attempt to impersonate me, then a pseudo-event would occur, and the truth value of my nameplate would change from true to false.

Similarly, mental tokens of tensed (A-series) beliefs are permanent inscriptions (or semi-permanent inscriptions, since beliefs can be revised or forgotten) to which the holders of beliefs may refer when the need arises. Whether or not the belief-inscription is actually referred to is a matter unconnected with its truth value at any given moment. It may never cross my mind, in the small hours, to ask myself what day it is, but that does not prevent me from holding the false belief that today is still Sunday if I have failed to notice that midnight has come and gone.

Tensed tokens of utterances, if sincerely spoken, are evidence for the presence of tensed beliefs on the part of the utterer. The speaker has a belief which is true if he holds it at the appropriate time (a time specifiable only by the tenseless facts of the B-series). If 'the day after tomorrow, we kill a pig' is a true belief token, by the next day, the holder will have to update his belief to 'tomorrow, we kill a pig', not because the facts about the pig-kill have changed in any way, but precisely because they have *not* changed. If the facts about the event have changed – there is illness in the camp, and the pig-kill is postponed by a day – he can persist in his belief in a pig-kill the day after tomorrow, only recognizing that his belief of yesterday in a pig-kill the day after (yesterday's) tomorrow was a false one.

It is the desirability of holding only true tensed beliefs which necessitates the continual modification of the tensed beliefs, that we have. But true tensed beliefs are always difficult to come by, more difficult in fact than true tenseless beliefs. This can give rise to misunderstandings between anthropologists and their informants, because anthropologists are inclined to interpret easy-to-come-by true tenseless utterances made by their informants as true tensed utterances based on true tensed beliefs. This is the explanation for a prominent component of anthropological oral folklore – the 'ever receding ceremony syndrome' – why the syndrome does not get into print very often will be apparent once I have explained it.

'How many moons will pass before you conduct the Great Ceremony?' the anthropologist asks, early on in his stint of fieldwork. The answer comes back, 'Six moons pass before the Great Ceremony: one moon for fishing, one for hunting, one for making gardens, one for gathering nuts, one for visiting relatives, and then the Great Ceremony occurs.' The anthropologist relaxes, happy in the knowledge that the Great Ceremony will occur while he is still in the field. A couple of months go by, but nothing much seems to be happening. Eventually, the anthropologist asks again: 'How many moons will pass before the Great Ceremony?', and is dismayed to receive an identical answer to what the informant, most annoyingly, seems to consider the identical question to the one he was asked months before. And the process is repeated, month by month, until the anthropologist is despairingly convinced that he will never see the Great Ceremony, of whose very existence he begins to entertain strong doubts. Then, just as perflexingly, he is one day informed that everybody has gone to gather nuts for the Great Ceremony, which will happen in due course. Four months later it really does come off, and the anthropologist is happily able to witness it, but in the process he has acquired rather jaundiced and essentially false notions of the indigenous 'concept of time'.

But the informant who, when originally asked, said that the Great Ceremony would occur after six months, instead of after fifteen months or however long it is, was speaking perfectly truthfully and in perfect cognizance of the available temporal facts. Yes, we intend to hold the Great Ceremony (a tenseless token of an abiding intention), And when? After we have prepared for it for six months (a tenseless token corresponding to the B-series facts about the temporal organization of the ritual event). It is at all times true that the Great Ceremony requires six months' preparation, just as it is always true that it requires three and a half minutes to boil an egg. The informant is wholeheartedly co-operating with the anthropologist in providing useful and permanently true knowledge about the B-series temporal relationships between events associated with the ceremony. Most likely, this is as much as he knows, since exactly how things stand with regard to the local consensus on when to hold the ceremony and what stage preparations for it may have reached, is hardly easier for him to determine than it is for the anthropologist. He is naturally impatient when the anthropologist asks the same question again and again, and seems moreover to be annoyed by the fact that he is getting the same answers again and again, which, given that it *is* the same question, he should surely expect. What the anthropologist wants, of course, are not tenseless tokens, however true, but tokens of tensed beliefs, preferably true ones, as to 'where we are now' in relation to the Great Ceremony. But it is because tensed tokens have this alarming propensity to suddenly change from being tokens of true beliefs into being tokens of false beliefs, it is much harder to arrange for the provision of valid tokens of this kind.

The anthropologist's need to entertain true tensed beliefs arises from the fact that he needs such beliefs in order to plan, and hence act, in a timely manner. Although the truth-conditions for his tensed belief that the Great Ceremony will occur on a certain future day are decided by the tenseless

B-series facts, the date of the ceremony *per se* is not what interests him. His interest is the practical one of fitting his various activities together so that he will be in a good position to take anthropological advantage of the ceremony when it comes about. This interest is not one that is shared by his informant, since he will participate in the Great Ceremony whenever it comes about, and has no worries about grant money running out, etc. This is one reason why he thinks his answers to the anthropologist's questions are perfectly good ones, while the anthropologist himself does not. The other reason is that the informant wants to give only truthful answers, and so interprets the anthropologist's questions as requests for such truthful information as he has at his disposal, which mainly takes the form of tenseless beliefs, since we always have much better reasons for trusting our tenseless belief-inscriptions than our tensed ones.

But I have not yet said why we have to have tensed beliefs at all, given that there are really only tenseless facts. The short answer to this is because of perception. Perception is nowadays regarded as an active process of forming judgements or perceptual hypotheses by the percipient about what there must be in the outside world which would explain the physical excitations of various kinds relayed from the percipient's sense organs. Naturally, this is a complicated, multi-stage process, which it would be laborious and unnecessary to describe (cf. Marr 1983, for a recent account of vision). The output from perception is added to the corpus of belief-inscriptions, as 'perceptual beliefs' which have the general form 'Right now, I judge that I am perceiving an X', where X is a crow, a cup of tea, the opening bars of Beethoven's Fifth, or whatever it is. To perceive something is, by definition, to believe that one perceives it, i.e. to judge that one's hypothesis that one is perceiving that thing is confirmed. But tokens of perceptual beliefs are all tensed tokens, since the perceptual belief 'Right now, I judge that I am perceiving a crow' is true only when that particular perceptual hypothesis is being confirmed by the appropriate physical excitations, and not at other times. If the crow one perceives takes to the air and flies away, then goodbye to that particular perceptual belief.

Now one could be wrong in believing that one had perceived a crow in terms of the real-world facts, if, for instance, one's physical excitations had actually been caused by an escaped mynah bird from a zoo, which looked sufficiently like a crow to be mistaken for one. But the perceptual belief that one judges that one has seen a crow is true whether or not the crow is correctly or mistakenly identified. My perceptual judgements may be way out, but not my tensed beliefs that so I judge. Perception gives rise to a stream of automatically correct but only transiently true beliefs to the effect that now one judges that one perceives this, then that, then the other, and so on. These beliefs are indexicals, like beliefs that it is now Sunday, Monday, Tuesday, etc.

This account of perception allows Mellor to dispose of one of the main planks in the A-theory supporter's platform. One reason for holding that A-theory time is 'real' is that A-theory time fits the facts of our subjective experience better, or seems to. The quote from Weyl, given earlier, puts the problem in plain view. It is all very well for physicists to speak of conscious-ness crawling up life-lines in four-dimensional space-time; but they are not in the business of explaining the world as it seems to *us*. And nobody would recognize a likeness of our workaday world in the portrait painted by Weyl. The evident weirdness of the results of attempts to visualize the unvisualizable – and four-dimensional space-time cannot in fact be visualized – has been a major factor in creating a climate of opinion in favour of distinguishing 'physical' time (B-series time) from 'human' time, i.e. time as subjectively grasped by conscious subjects (A-series time). Actually, no such distinction can be maintained; B-series time is not any less 'human' than A-series time. But there is certainly a much greater appearance of naturalism in A-series time, which fits the facts of our experience in that we do experi-ence our world as 'present', a concept not easy to attach any meaning to in the B-series scheme of things. Mellor argues that the presentness of experience is to be explained not by any difference between present facts and any other kind of facts, but by the necessary coincidence between the carrying-out of per-ceptual judgements and the entertaining of tensed beliefs to such effect.

The subjective phenomenon of temporal passage, which is recognizably the most potent factor giving *prima facie* plausibility to A-series-based time metaphysics, is explained in B-series terms as the consequence of the fact that (1) perceptual judge-ments give rise to tensed belief tokens, and (2) that tensed belief-tokens have to be continually updated in order to keep the whole collection of such belief tokens as current as possible. The passage of time is not a phenomenon of the layout of the universe, it is a by-product of the process of belief-updating taking place among percipient beings, such as ourselves. We are 'anchored in the present' by virtue of the necessary coincidence in time between the perceptual judgements giving rise to our beliefs that such-and-such is the case, and the production of the corresponding belief tokens. We cannot have any perceptions which are not 'present' (though not 'of the present', since through powerful telescopes we can see events that took place at dates very much earlier than today's date). Having perceptions is the only causal factor capable of informing us of the need to alter our tensed beliefs, as well as being the factor responsible for the formation of such beliefs in the first place. The mere occurrence of events at some point in the B-series does not, in itself, give rise to any of our tensed beliefs, though the occurrence of these events is the sole arbiter of whether our beliefs are true or not. It is only by perceptual mediation, through a causal chain leading from the external world, via the sensory modalities, to the formation of tensed perceptual beliefs – no sooner entertained than superseded – that the B-series world impinges on the A-series subject. And the subject has every reason to feel that time is passing, because of the work-load involved in continually updating beliefs. This work-load is a series of 'real' (time- and energy-consuming) events, which is part of the cybernetic functioning of the organism. We feel time as a quasi-substantive dynamic force pulsing through the world because we have to *work* to stay abreast of it; but this work we put into changing ourselves, ditching old belief-inscriptions and installing new ones. Time is not the least dynamic; it is we, on the contrary, who are.

The pressure to keep abreast of time (because whatever else time does, it certainly does not carry us along with it) comes from our overwhelming need to act in a timely manner, in order to realize our desires. Action must be timely because most actions need specific circumstances in order to succeed. We entertain relatively easy-to-come-by tenseless beliefs about the appropriate circumstances for engaging in different kinds of action, but we have to work hard to acquire true tensed beliefs to the effect that these appropriate circumstances are actually present. I may know that I must plant in springtime, but has springtime arrived? (I scan the dubious sky for signs that might point one way or the other.) My tenseless belief guides my action in that I at all times believe that planting should be done at a certain time; but this does not suffice to tell me that 'now' is that time. Mellor is careful to point out that it is not the objective B-series facts that provide the spur for action, but the mere fact that beliefs are entertained, true or not. It is the farmer's belief that springtime is truly here, and that frosts will not damage the growing shoots, which causes him set to and plant his fields.

# Chapter 19

# B-theory Economics vs. A-theory Economics

We have seen that philosophers are divided among themselves on the question of whether to grant priority to the A-series or the B-series. Supporters of the B-series are 'B-theorists', who give a B-theoretical account of time metaphysics; supporters of the A-series are 'A-theorists', who give an A-theoretical account of time metaphysics. Although I side with the B-theory, I cannot pretend that the philosophical argument is over. Where philosophers divide, even on issues which do not seem very pertinent to non-philosophical concerns, it often turns out that there is an underlying fault-line in the geology of knowledge, which can extend far into domains otherwise claimed by the special sciences, including both natural sciences such as physics, and social sciences such as anthropology, sociology, geography, etc. I believe that the A-theory/B-theory confrontation is a case in point, which raises questions of fundamental methodological significance in the social sciences. Take economics, for example.

Figure 19.1 is modified from Shackle's *A Scheme of Economic Theory* (1965), in which the author, the most prominent economist to make a special study of time, classifies economic theories according to the kind of 'time' on which they are based. My figure differs from the original in omitting a few names and in including Shackle himself, at the extreme end of the 'expectational time' axis, for reasons that will be given in due course. I also include Sraffa in what I assume to be the appropriate place, as a B-theorist along with Böhm-Bawerke. This should alert readers to the fact that just because economists share certain metaphysical attitudes to time does not necessarily mean that they have identical attitudes towards every other aspect of economics. My figure also differs from his in identifying 'expectational time' with A-series time, and 'mechanical time' with B-series time.

**Figure 19.1    Expectational vs. mechanical time**

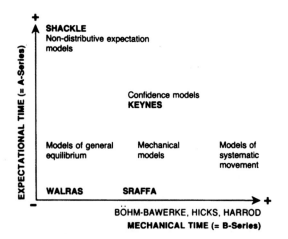

One does not need to be thoroughly conversant with all the details of the theories of Walras, Hicks, Harrod, Keynes, etc. in order to grasp the idea that, in economic theory, there is a three-way contrast between:

(1) Theories that describe 'timeless' equilibrium states. Equilibrium models of the Walrasian kind do not try to represent changes in the relationships between the variables in the model over time. Such changes are treated as disturbances in the *ceteris paribus* assumptions surrounding the model as an 'ideally isolated system', not as features of reality to be described by the model itself.

(2) 'Models of systematic change' include an enormous variety of economic models which describe systematic change through time, such as the 'economic growth' models of Hicks and Harrod. These models, which underlie much policy thinking in modern economics, treat the economy as a network of quantitative relationships between indices (investment, prices, productivity, growth, etc.), which vary concomitantly with one another over time. 'Growth' models come at the extreme end of the mechanical time axis because they describe processes of systematic (non-reversible) change. But cyclical 'replacement' models in the political economy tradition revitalized recently by the work of Sraffa and his school (Sraffa 1960; cf. Kreigel 1970; Harcourt 1972) are also B-theoretical in that they do not deal

with psychological or 'fiduciary' elements in economic life. I have called these 'mechanical models', not least because they look very like 'mechanical models' in the anthropological tradition of Lévi-Straussian structuralism, a point that has been emphasized by Gregory (1982).

(3) A third category of economic model, one that is much less common, is 'expectational' models. B-series models describe the economy in terms of causal linkages between economic forces, which show up as concomitant variations in the values of indices such as net investment, saving, productivity, etc. 'Expectational' models see such indices as stimuli, which act on members of the business community, causing them to act as they do. Keynesian 'confidence models' are A-theoretical in that they introduce 'fiduciary' elements into the explanation of changes in the values of economic indices, which are the aggregate outcome of 'choices' made by members of the business community in the light of their transient A-series tensed beliefs about the current economic predicament. Keynes himself is only a half-hearted A-theorist, in that his theory of the relationships between major economic indices (investment, employment, money supply) remains firmly grounded in equilibrium assumptions shared equally by B-theoreticians; where he deviated was in suggesting that the government ought to intervene so as to cause these indices to assume a configuration which would inspire businessmen to act in the general interest. A 'pure' A-theoretical economist has to eschew the use of macroeconomic models altogether, since these are by nature B-theoretic constructions. Shackle does this, as we shall see.

It is interesting, from the point of view of anthropology, to pursue this digression into economics a little further. I want to present two economic models in greater detail, Böhm-Bawerk's and Shackle's own, so as to substantiate, first of all, my claim that social science theories can be contrasted as B-theoretical vs. A-theoretical. Second, the two models are interesting in themselves, and could be adapted for anthropological use in contexts outside the strictly economic ones for which they were devised. Finally, the two models I shall consider are both examples of 'mythological charters' for the entrepreneurial class, or rather, two entrepreneurial classes, one that existed in Austria before the First World War, another that exists in Britain at the present day. In other words, the A-series/B-series opposition can have 'ideological' significance: the B-theory generates myths that support the interests of the ruling oligarchies in agrarian societies, and equally the ruling oligarchies in centralized socialist systems; the A-theory generates myths that support the interests of the individualist entrepreneurial class which controls, or at least aspires to control, non-centralized capitalist economies such the British one.

Let me take the B-theory first, in the person of Böhm-Bawerk, founder of the 'Austrian' school of capital theorists. Böhm-Bawerk, under the remarkably resonant slogan 'Capital is Time', put forward a theory of the economy which comes closest of all to the pure B-theory 'Block Universe' concept of cosmic time, which, intriguingly enough, was being developed in Austria, at the very same time, by Lorenz and Minkowski.

Böhm-Bawerk wrote in the social context of late nineteenth-century Austria, a society whose elite still mainly drew their incomes from land and agricultural production. Böhm-Bawerk himself belonged to this class and served as Finance Minister under the Emperor. For this reason it may have come rather naturally to him see the economy along lines suggested by production in rural settings such as large farms, plantations, wine production concerns, cheeseries, and the like. Productive capital, according to Böhm-Bawerk equals *delay*. It is true, especially from the landlord's perspective, that the 'production' of crops largely consists of waiting for them to grow. They do not grow by human agency, they come up of their own accord, and all that we can do is create the circumstances in which nature can get to work. This is still more the case with commercial forestry, another important Austrian industry.

Böhm-Bawerk's central idea was that productive capital was equal to the sum total of goods-in-production from the inception of the production process to its conclusion, once the goods have been sent to market and consumed. Thus, suppose that in Ruritania 1000 bottles of brandy are consumed daily, all of which come from a single concern. Standards are high (brandy is the elite drink), and not a drop is sold until it is ten years old. This means that the brandy concern must manufacture an average of 1000 bottles of unmatured brandy each day, and must store each day's production for a further 3650 days. In order to support this rate of consumption, the brandy concern must keep a stock of 3,650,000 bottles of brandy in its warehouses. On Böhm-Bawerk's analysis the proprietor of the brandy concern gets a return on his capital which recompenses him for each act of abstention from consumption, with respect to each of these 3,000,000 + bottles of brandy, over a period of ten years. The capitalist is paid a wage, not to take risks, but to wait out the period of production, at the end of which he can perform an act of consumption which is equivalent to all the acts of abstention from consumption he performed earlier. The proprietor of the Ruritanian brandy concern, a notable benefactor of society, in abstaining from consuming 3,650,000 bottles of brandy, is suitably rewarded in the end. The capitalist also has to bear the labour costs incurred in the production-process. Wage payments, deducted from the income drived from sales, are interpreted as abstentions from consumption as well. Far from exploiting the workers, the capitalist 'supports' their consumption needs out of income he might otherwise spend on himself.

One can imagine the economy as a whole as being, in general, like the brandy concern. Capital is the stock of goods-in-production spread out over time, and the average period of production (all goods) is the measure of the overall capital wealth of society. The factors of production (land and the labour needed to divert the forces of nature in a productive direction) are added in to the value of the capital stock incrementally, day by day, the paying of wages to labourers a form of saving by capitalists, the labourer being paid immediately for the work of advancing the goods towards the finish-line in the production process, while the employer must wait until the goods have actually crossed the finish-line before he can recoup the deferred consumption he has incurred by paying his labourers rather than spending his money elsewhere.

It is not difficult to sense the appeal of this picture of the economy, which, so to speak, summons the social order into being as the adjunct of the essentially natural temporal patterning of the production process. Nature decrees that it takes ten years to produce acceptable brandy, a year to produce a crop of wheat (or a loaf of bread), and $x$ number of months to build a house or make a suit. These natural lags or intervals between the completion of successive stages of a causal process bring into being the capitalist and the worker; the former investing in the consumption of the latter, so as to reserve for himself the right to own the product in the fullness of time. The economy rests on the 'natural' foundation of the causal texture of the production process, spread out in time and independent of human volition.

One notices the absence, in this theoretical scheme, of any element of uncertainty: the proprietor of the brandy concern is not taking a gamble that his brandy will taste better after ten years than it does after one year, nature ensures that it will. He does not have to make entrepreneurial decisions either; his contribution to the production process lies exclusively in adjusting his consumption so as to avoid consuming all the bottles of brandy in his possession, and so as to have funds to pay his labourers. He can spend his days pursuing whatever activity pleases him, so long as it does not threaten to eat into his capital; official duties, patronage of the arts and sciences, piety, anything that does not cost too much. He is essentially apart from the production process which his abstemiousness allows to take place. His crucial role is causal non-intervention in a natural causal process. The capitalist is a world-transcending ascetic; like Brahma, he supports the world by keeping out of it.

This truncated account of Böhm-Bawerk's capital theory should make clear why his views found a good deal of favour among members of the leisured class in Austria at the turn of the century. Leisure is good, is actually productive, so long as it is not capital-intensive. The leisured class stand guard over the capital wealth of the country, ensuring that it continues to be put to productive use. Credible or not as myth, Böhm-Bawerk's writings serve as an excellent example of economic theorizing in the B-theoretical mode. Production is a spread of dated events linked by a network of causal relationships. The economist simply maps out this network of events in congealed, B-series time, which is entirely independent of conscious choice, deliberation, uncertainty, risk, etc., and advises against any ill-considered attempts to intervene in the natural order of things. The picture is one of a Laplacean universe of total determinism, each event happening because it must, and as it was predetermined it should, given its causal context. Time is seen as the stable framework within which these predetermined events occur in inexorable order, static, objective and unchanging. This Shackle calls 'mechanical' time, but it is also recognizably B-series time in the manner of Weyl, whose detached consciousness crawling up the lifeline of his body can surely be compared to Böhm-Bawerk's detached, non-interfering, entrepreneur.

The great majority of models in both the natural and social sciences are B-series models, like the one we have just examined, showing relationships between a spread of events linked by causal relationships. But we have noted in the discussion contained in Chapters 17–18, the *causes* of actions by sentient beings such as ourselves are transient A-series or 'tensed' beliefs: there is therefore a logically impeccable case for introducing A-series considerations into the explanation of human action. In economics, B-series models are in competition with A-series models, which explicitly take into account 'subjective' or 'fiduciary' elements, i.e. the independent causal role played by the 'expectations' or moment-to-moment belief-states of businessmen seeking the timely moment to profit by circumstances which may not recur. Shackle has developed this branch of economics to the fullest extent, and I shall now give an account of his theory. The source I use is his *Time in Economics* (1958) and papers from a volume on Shackle (Carter ed. 1957).

The first thing one notices in reading *Time in Economics* is that the economy, as one is accustomed to find it described in textbooks, has more or less vanished. All that is left is the lone businessman, locked into the 'solitary moment' of time, irremediably ignorant of the true facts of his situation, and compelled to *decide*.

How do we decide? There are, of course, many theories about decision-making. There are descriptive theories, such as the one elaborated by Schutz ('Deciding among projects of action', Schutz 1967: vol. I) and there are also prescriptive theories, such as the game-theory model of Van Neumann, which has also been imported into anthropology (Barth 1959). The theory of decision-making is closely related to the theory of probability, since we assume that in an uncertain world decisions will reflect agents' beliefs as to where the balance of probable advantage lies. Decisions made under conditions of absolute certainty as to the outcome are from this point of view not really decisions; not in the sense that people can justify high pay to management as a reward for making the 'right' decisions.

There are two schools of thought on the subject of probability. One school of thought considers that 'probability' is a characteristic that events just have intrinsically, as part of the layout of the universe, and that we can come to know this probability rating by classifying events into types, sampling them and counting the number of instances of outcome A vs. outcome B under what we consider similar circumstances. The other school of thought considers that probability is not anything to do with events themselves, but is a measure of our *degree of belief* in a particular outcome. It is not hard to guess which of these theories of probability belongs with the A-theory and which with the B-theory. Theories of decision-making which are based on the first type of probability theory take the form of attributing processes of inductive inference to the agent. Faced with the need to produce a decision, he runs over in his mind the occasions on which similar decision situations have arisen before. He then recalls the decisions made, and their outcomes, comparing the ratio of successful outcomes which occurred following different possible lines of action. He then selects the line of action which, in the past, most frequently led to a successful outcome. This is decision theory based on the idea of distributive probability (i.e. arising from frequency distributions of outcomes). Sociologists and anthropologists may be inclined to agree with Shackle that this theory of decision-making is descriptively inadequate, even if it is prescriptively sound. The grounds on which Shackle rejects this approach are, however, not the ones that would occur to a sociologist (viz. that people are not that rational, and decide on the basis of habit, tradition, etc. rather than on the basis of an objective assessment of all possible lines of action). Shackle's grounds for rejecting distributive probability as the basis for decision-making are that decision-making situations never recur, and consequently cannot be statistically sampled. Each presents a unique configuration, a sample of one.

Shackle argues that any decision, truly to count as such, is a new venture, a step in the dark. The businessman avails himself of his experience while making up his mind, but his eventual decision is a creative act of choice. He has no access to the dark web of causality within which he, and his actions, are embedded, and which will eventually determine the outcome, good or bad. Were this so it would hardly be incumbent on him to decide, for he would simply have to aquiesce in a given situation. But decisions are not subjectively experienced as acts of aquiescence in the face of the inexorable working-out of a predictable pattern of causally linked events. Rather than aquiescing in a pre-given world, the decision-maker, according to Shackle, brings a new world into being, a world about which nothing can be said with any certainty until the consequences of this act of creation have become apparent.

Subsequently, of course, things may not turn out as the businessman had hoped or expected, but the outcome of the decision is irrelevant to the analysis of the processes which lead up to the decision being made in the first instance. Economic life consists of a flow of decisions taken in advance of the possibility of knowing anything factual about the outcomes of these decisions; the decisions and their outcomes are logically independent.

In focusing on the 'expectation' of gain as the subjective motive behind economic behaviour, rather than the certainty of gain predicted by models cast in the B-series idiom of mechanical causality, Shackle represents a Keynesian point of view. Besides being an economist, Keynes was also a philosopher and a mathematician; an important pioneer of the view of probability theory mentioned above, which interprets the probability rating of events as a measure of the strength of our belief in their occurrence. This 'subjective' view of probability, as a function of incomplete knowledge on the part of sentient beings, rather than of randomness in the working-out of events themselves, carries over into Keynes' economic thinking. Just as gambling odds are not retrospectively determined by the actual outcomes of the horse races for which these odds are quoted, so the reactions of the city are not determined by the actual economic processes and contingencies to which the city is reacting. The business climate is determined by the current state of 'sentiment' among the business class, sentiments which can be at variance with reality and which can be manipulated by appropriate governmental actions. Shackle describes Keynes' *General Theory* as 'kaleidoscopic', in that it envisages periods of stable, if tenuous, equilibrium punctuated by episodes in which the consensus suddenly collapses, so that even indices which had been regarded as 'normal' suddenly appear ominous, liquidity preference increases sharply, and a wholesale failure of economic morale ensues. Shackle reflects the psychological side of Keynesianism, though reducing it from the level of crowd psychology to the level of individual psychology. Shackle's lone businessman is permanently in a state of radical uncertainty, which Keynes attributes to the City at times of panic.

What Shackle says is that if one wishes to understand economic behaviour, then one must recognize that businessmen take those decisions that afford them the greatest degree of *anticipatory joy*, compared to other decisions they might take in the circumstances. Unless one is going to be really radical (like Bourdieu 1977) and deny that decision-making is based on making choices among alternatives, then this point seems to me impeccable. Thus, the causal factor which makes a company director invest heavily in a new project is not the causal events associated with that investment, the eventual profit or loss on the deal as it will appear on subsequent balance-sheets, but the psychological fact that, at the time, that was the decision which afforded its maker the greatest delight. B-series models in economics are logically flawed if they interpret the causes of decisions made in the course of economic life as stemming from the consequences of those decisions, for this is to reverse the order of causality. Profit is the 'in-order-to motive' (Schutz 1967) for engaging in economic activity, not the 'because motive'. Action has to be understood in the light not of its real-world antecedents and consequences, but in the light of the fantasy-system which inspires it. These fantasies take the form of indexical beliefs, transient hypotheses about what the state-of-affairs is 'now', and what will be subjectively experienced in future 'nows' once the deed is done. Shackle provides an elegant analysis, more complex than any to be found in the sociological literature, of the processes which underlie the formation of token-indexical beliefs motivating actions.

When deliberating his choice (e.g. between two possible investments) the businessman constructs two mental graphs, one for each of the competing possibilities (Figure 19.2). On the horizontal plane, the x-axis corresponds to expectations of profit and loss, while the y-axis corresponds to the *degree of potential surprise* attendant on the achievement of a certain measure of profit or loss in the venture. Shackle assumes that around zero in the profit and loss scale potential surprise is at a minimum, i.e. it occasions relatively little surprise if a venture is neither very profitable nor very loss-making, but that away from this central region, potential surprise values curve upwards, so that very profitable or very loss-making outcomes would occasion progressively greater degrees of surprise, were they to result. What the businessman is looking for are not 'theoretical' possibilities of securing very high profits, but the prospect of possible profits which would not occasion very great degrees of surprise were they actually to eventuate, and moreover, opportunities for making profits which can be exploited without incurring the possibility of any but very surprising (and hence discountable) losses.

So we need an indicator, $\phi$, which will express the extent to

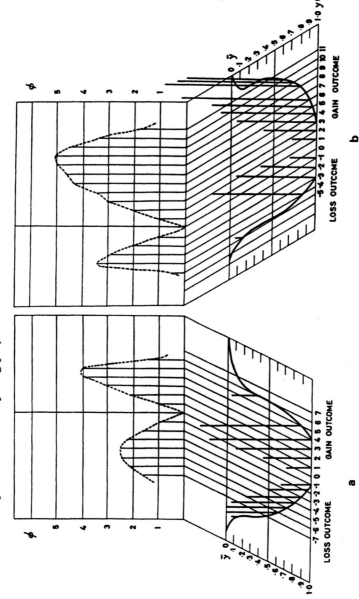

Figure 19.2 Potential surprise for two competing projects

which an outcome of given profitability scores high marks for salience as a fantasied profit or loss, but is progressively discounted if it simultaneously scores very high on the scale of potential surprise. $\phi$-values = profit/loss expectancy $x$ potential surprise.

A businessman will not long consider a project, even one potentially attended with vast profits, if he would feel excessively surprised should these profits ever accrue. He is only interested in ventures which, in his opinion, would occasion mainly not-too-surprising profits and only very surprising losses. The results of multiplying profit and loss expectancies ($x$) by potential surprise values ($y$) to produce $\phi$-values are shown in Figure 19.2 projected as curves on the $\phi$-surface (the vertical plane). On each of the two $\phi$-surfaces are two curves, one on each side of the no profit/no loss trough in the middle of the surprise graph. These curves rise to peaks at two points, one on each side, which are local maxima for combinations of expectations of loss/profit divided by potential surprise. These curves are low in the middle of the graph because expectations of profit and loss are low in this central region; to either side they rise because in this intermediate region profit/loss expectations are higher but not yet discounted by high values of potential surprise, rising to two points of inflection ('focus outcomes') before falling again towards zero as high profit/loss expectancies are discounted against increasing degrees of potential surprise. For each of the two possible courses of action diagrammed above, the focus outcomes occur at the points measured on the scale of profit/loss expectancies (the x-axis), which for project A have the values 4.0 (profit)/2.5 (loss) and for project B the values 5.0 (profit) and 3.5 (loss).

The question now is, how is a businessman to decide between two sets of focus-outcomes, one for project A and one for project B? Will he do one or the other (assuming he cannot do both), or will he refrain from doing either? There is no way of mechanically calculating the answer to this using economic theory alone, just as economic theory cannot predict when a student will cease to buy additional cans of Coca-Cola and will start laying out his money on textbooks instead. What determines the marginal utility of Coca-Cola vs. textbooks is a matter of 'taste'; all that economic theory can do is predict the rational behaviour of a student of given tastes. Similarly, it is a matter of taste, so far as the businessman is concerned, which decides which combinations of focus outcomes are sufficiently attractive to provide the spur to actual investment in some project. Shackle represents this by constructing a 'gambler indifference map', in which the set of focus losses which exactly balance focus gains are represented as an indifference curve, modelled on indifference curves in conventional microeconomics, which show the combinations of relative prices between Coca-Cola and textbooks which would leave the student undecided as to whether to plump for the marginal utility of an extra textbook vs. an extra can of Coca-Cola. Figure 19.3 is such a gambler indifference map showing indifference curves for focus gains vs. focus losses for two businessmen, Mr Gold and Mr Green. Assuming (unrealistically) that both these businessmen have the same curves of potential surprise, and hence perceive the same focus outcomes for project A against project B, we can see that Mr Gold will choose project B because its focus outcomes fall on the 'do it' side of his gambler indifference curve, while project A falls on the 'don't do it' side of his curve because he is basically not interested in small gains at near 50/50 odds. Mr Green, on the other hand, will opt for project B because his indifference curve slopes sharply downward for focus losses approaching 4. He will accept a losing gamble (3.5 loss vs. 3 profit) so long as he can be certain of suffering only limited losses.

However, there is a technical problem with 'non-distributive expectations' which can lead us back from the existential dramas of A-theory economics to the more bread-and-butter world of B-theory social science, which will be our primary concern for some while yet. Kenneth Arrow (1951), in a critique of this and other brands of decision-theory, raised the question of what would happen to potential surprise if it were applied to coin-tossing. Suppose there is a venture which depends on the toss of a coin. Since the businessman must know that the likelihood of a coin coming down heads or tails is equal, the potential surprise occasioned by its landing heads is zero and landing tails is also zero. But it is essential to Shackle's theory that each decision moment be unique, if businessmen are really locked into the 'solitary moment' and do not in fact rely on inductive inferences from multiple series of 'trials' of a particular course of action when deciding whether to engage in that course of action again. But faced with a series of decisions based on the toss of a coin, the businessman would not continue to be equally unsurprised if, on the tenth occasion, the coin came down heads,

**Figure 19.3   Gambler's indifference map**

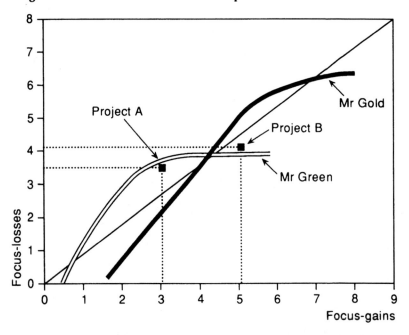

having also come down heads on all nine previous occasions. By
the tenth occasion he would be very surprised indeed if the coin
came down heads yet again, even though from the perspective
of a 'solitary moment', heads is just as likely as tails. So the
potential surprise curve, in this case, would reflect a series of
trials, becoming progressively more skewed in favour of one
outcome (tails) and against another (heads).

That is to say, our potential surprise curves reflect previous
experience and inductive generalizations therefrom (i.e. non-
indexical beliefs about the general layout of the universe)
rather than moment-to-moment transient A-series beliefs. The
businessman may be operating under conditions of uncertainty,
navigating using a map of the reliability of which he cannot be
sure, but he is not navigating without a map at all, which is
what the notion of non-distributive expectations seems to suggest.
And the businessman's map consists of his B-series models
of the nature of the causal relationships between the events in
which he is interested. These models aim at 'timeless' truth: if a
businessman believes that high inflation rates are a good sign
for purchasing gold shares, he believes that to be true at all

times, not just at times of high inflation. That belief is part of his cognitive map of economic realities, not part of his moment-to-moment beliefs about the state of affairs obtaining in his 'solitary moment'. So the upshot is that an A-theoretical choice-model, such as Shackle's, is radically incomplete as it stands, since it does not trace the process whereby B-theoretical beliefs of a general, time-indifferent kind are converted into A-theoretical beliefs about the situation 'now' obtaining, in the light of which beliefs action is eventually taken. In Chapter 24 below, I shall put forward some ideas which help to fill this gap in pure A-theory accounts of decision-making. My suggestion is that we have 'cognitive maps' of time, which are to be distinguished from our moment-to-moment beliefs about what the situation is 'now'. These cognitive maps are mental constructions of the B-series temporal layout of the 'real' (B-series) world. They are founded on our experience of this world. We must therefore now turn to the description of the objective B-series temporal world itself, and the branches of time-sociology which seek to account theoretically for features of this objective reality.

# Chapter 20

# Chrono-geography

Just as the writings of economists can be categorized as showing a B-series orientation (Böhm-Bawerk) or an A-series orientation (Shackle), so the same can be said of the writings of sociologists. Some sociological writing is concerned with 'subjective' time (Schutz 1967; Bourdieu 1977; cf. Chapters 27–29, below), but a great deal more has a B-series orientation, and is concerned with the observable patterning of events in 'objective' B-series time. This 'B-series time sociology' deals with social events as they occur in 'physical' or clock time, but just because time is here treated in a manner akin to the space-like time of the physicists' 'block universe' does not mean that it is a simple measure of duration. B-series time is causal time, the time within which objects (including people) assume the configurations which give rise to causal events. Human agents are interested, above all, in the world as a web of causality, on whose particular configuration depends the realization of their projects. Causality has many aspects, but it is never without its geometric component. Therefore, it is hardly physicalist 'reductionism' to approach the study of social time from a B-series point of view.

In the 1930s Sorokin and Berger (1939) pioneered the empirical investigation of the temporal distribution of activities over the 24-hour cycle. Since that time, these 'time-budget' studies have proliferated (Szalai et al. 1972, in a particularly comprehensive compilation). Time-budget studies have many practical uses, not many of which have much to do with the sociology of time as such. But in the 1970s a group of social geographers began to explore in more detail the implications of the regular patterning of social activities in time. Thus it has come about that in recent years the theoretical analysis of time-budget data has become a speciality of social geographers rather than sociologists (Carlstein, Parkes and Thrift 1978; Parkes and Thrift 1980: Carlstein

1982). This is reasonable enough, given the B-series approach which underlies this kind of research. 'Social time' *qua* spread of events in the fourth dimension obviously belongs to geography as of right, given that social geography otherwise largely consists of accounting for the distribution of activities in the other three (spatial) dimensions. But the impetus behind the upsurge in geographical interest in the fourth dimension derives primarily from the highly innovative work of a distinguished Swedish geographer, Hägerstrand, founder of the 'Lund school' of time-geographers. One of Hägerstrand's school is Carlstein, the time geographer who probably has most to say to anthropologists.

The time-geographic approach can be summed up as the study of time-budget and similar kinds of data in the light of 'timing' constraints impinging on individual behaviour. The time-geographic model-building process is grounded in an analysis of the theoretical possibilities of 'choreographing' social activities, given the fact that activities have to be carried out in specific places, at specific times, by specific actors, in conjunction with specific others.

Hägerstrand's basic model, from which an enormous class of empirical and analytic models can be derived, is exceptionally simple, and consists of little more than the construction of two- or three-dimensional maps, in which one dimension is allowed to represent time rather than space. However, once one begins to represent time in this hard-edged, geometric way, certain themes and topics in the sociology of time become much more amenable to coherent discussion. In effect, Hägerstrand is concerned with the representation of society as a concrete, physically real process in physicist's 'block universe'-type time. But one should not be misled into supposing that this apparent physicalism is the methodological outgrowth of a determinist theoretical stance. Hägerstrand is not concerned to demonstrate that what is so (empirically) must be so (rationally). On the contrary, time-geography is concerned to discover what is 'possible' in the light of permutable structural models of the choreography of social life in real space-time.

The space-time patterning of social events is constrained by a variety of factors. Human beings cannot be physically in two places at one time, cannot undertake causally incompatible activities at the same time, cannot move instantaneously from place to place, and so on. For the sake of brevity, these constraints can be summed up under three headings: (1) 'capability' constraints (such as the ones just mentioned); (2) 'coupling' constraints, i.e. the constraint governing social activities which involve more than one person, that they must be co-present, or in communication; and (3) 'authority' constraints, i.e. individuals are constrained to act only in ways that are socially permitted.

Hägerstrand treats 'authority' constraints as different in nature from 'physical' capability constraints and coupling constraints. This is actually rather a tricky distinction, since it is not easy to decide when a constraint on allocating time to a given activity is institutional-normative vs. physical-causal or both at the same time. Thus, the reason why I cannot plan on cashing a cheque at a bank on Sunday is the institutional constraint which determines that banks, as a social rule, are closed on Sunday; but it is also physically impossible for me to enter the bank on that day (capability constraint) or conduct business there even if I could get in, in the absence of the necessary bank staff (a 'coupling' constraint, in Hägerstrand's terminology). I think that it is reasonable to think that 'constraints' are all fundamentally physical-causal, in that what is at issue is always, in the final analysis, the possibility/impossibility of bringing about 'real' causal events. Thus, take the institutional constraint which prevents me from taking a straight-line path across the quadrangle of Trinity College, Cambridge (something only Fellows can do, as it involves walking on the grass). It is not the existence of the rule that deters me from usurping the Fellows' spatio-temporal privileges, but my awareness of what would follow causally from infringing the rule – I should be shouted at, and perhaps man-handled, by the college porters. The framework of institutional (normative, regulatory) constraints on activity allocations represent socially codified expectations about potentially real events and cause-and-effect relationships between these events. This is no less the case if the expectations in question are based on false information about the way the world works. For example, constraints on action may exist because people believe that certain courses of action will be attended by subsequent punishment in Hell. It may physically speaking be untrue that the flames of Hell will burn the performer of some prohibited action because there are no such flames, but it is still the case that if the action is refrained from on account of the agent's belief in the existence of Hell-fire, he is dissuaded from it for 'physical' reasons, just as he would feel physically dissuaded from rescuing his possessions from a burning building.

We may take it, then, that physical constraints and institutional constraints are really the same kind of thing; i.e. constraints on the bringing about of certain desired states-of-affairs, which are regarded as physical possibilities even if they are not so in reality. However, the most important point is that in establishing these fundamental constraints, Hägerstrand is not merely interested in making empirical generalizations, in the manner of conventional time-budget studies. His approach is structural, deductive, permutational: he is concerned with defining the consequences of different patterns of physical and institutional constraints on the 'possibilities' for realizing events in social systems, defined as bundles of space/time 'paths' pursued by particular individuals ('life-lines').

Hägerstrand's time-geographic model shows the population as a network of individual 'paths' in time and space. Paths are always inclined upwards relative to the plane, to reflect the fact that movement in space is time-consuming. Vertical lines indicate stationary objects or temporarily stationary people or things. Spatial relationships are projected on the horizontal plane, temporal relationships, interactions, etc. on the vertical plane (Figure 20.1).

Using this kind of cartographic convention, it is possible to indicate social occasions involving interactions between many individual paths as 'bundles', and spatial locations such as houses, schools or factories, as 'stations' between which paths move and criss-cross one another. Of course, it would be fiendishly complicated to map real-world situations of any great complexity using this method. But using stripped-down models, it is possible to express the organizational essence of real-life problems in a revealing way.

One important institutional constraint is the 'home base' constraint, i.e. the daily round is organized on the assumption that there is a home base which must be returned to every night, where essential domestic functions are performed (eating, sleeping, etc.). From this home base a certain segment of space-time is accessible, whose size is a function of the means of transport at the disposal of the individuals whose daily paths are being modelled. The shape of this segment of accessible space-time will be lenticular, though it is known by time-geographers as the 'daily prism'. Perhaps, in view of its confining nature, it should really be called the 'daily prison'. It is this segment of accessible space-time which determines the scope of

**Figure 20.1   Hägerstrand time-map**

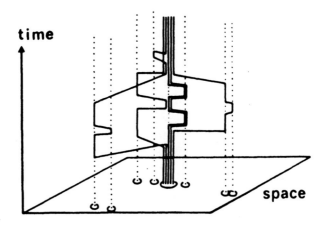

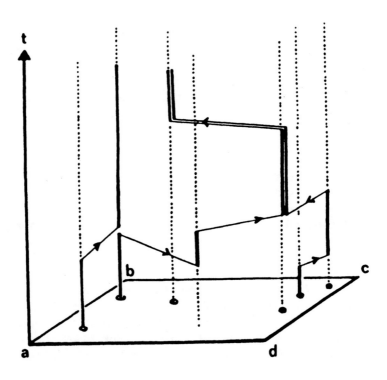

feasible projects for social individuals, and in the light of which the opportunity-costs attendant on particular geometric configurations of socially significant 'stations' (home, work, recreational facilities, libraries, etc.) can be computed.

For instance, we do not normally think of the disadvantages of women in the labour-market as being a problem of geometry. However, Palm and Pred (1978; cf. Parkes and Thrift 1980: 269) have provided an illuminating discussion of this problem from the time-geographical standpoint. Unmarried mothers, obliged both to work outside the home and care for children are often faced with organizational dilemmas which can be graphically expressed, as in Figure 20.2, which shows the daily prism of 'Jane', one of Palm and Pred's case examples.

Jane's problem is that she has to choose between two possible types of employment, W1, less well-paid and not such as to allow her to capitalize on her qualifications, and W2, a much better job, but located on the other side of town from the only available nursery which will look after her child. Both jobs, and the nursery, are located within Jane's total daily prism, but whereas it is geometrically possible for her to combine the time demands of her own childcare responsibilities, the opening-hours of the nursery and the hours required for employment at W1, it is geometrically impossible for her to reconcile her competing time-demands if she accepts the better job at W2. For Jane, the *de facto* geometry of home, nursery and workplace represents a series of subjectively borne opportunity-costs, which can be objectively computed in the light of the model.

> We can now see that the space-time environment discriminates against this individual because it does not allow her to realise intended projects, from the day-to-day problem of where to shop to the lifetime problem of building a career. Many surveys have shown that women seem to take positions of lower status and responsibility than their abilities would suggest are open to them, above all because of their role as mothers (Tivers 1977). The time-geographic approach pinpoints the space-time environment as one of the major culprits in generating the problem. (Parkes and Thrift 1980: 270)

Of course, one might question the statement that the 'space-time environment', rather than the gender-specific role-definitions current in our society, are the 'real culprit' in this case. In fact, neither can be regarded as primarily responsible, because they are not really distinct. Certain spatio-temporal

**Figure 20.2   Jane's prism**

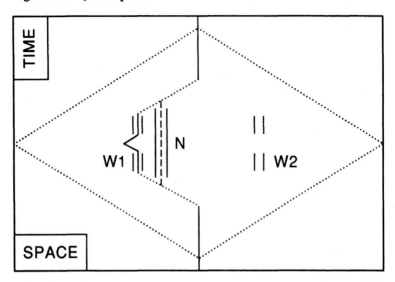

expectations, derived from the real world and its layout, are
built into the social definition of motherhood, as of every other
role. To perform a role is, among other things, to be confined in
space and time in a particular way. The intention behind this
kind of research is to change roles by changing the environment
– making childcare facilities more accessible so as to upgrade the
employment possibilities of women with childcare responsibilities. This requires, however, not just a physical change in the
environment (co-ordinating employment and childcare facilities
in space and time) but conceptual changes in socially recognized
priorities; diverting resources to this particular objective rather
than other possible ones. And this in turn implies a revaluation
of the legitimate role-expectations of women in Jane's position.
So it is not really a question of whether one is to take a line
which says, 'these problems are basically physical and can be
solved by making physical changes' vs. 'these problems are
ideological and can only be solved by changing people's ideas'.
Without changes in ideas, the physical changes will never happen; but changes in ideas in the absence of physical changes in
the space-time environment would not help anybody.

The lesson I think one can draw from this is that the time-
geographers, while formulating their problems in overtly phys-
icalistic terms, are implicitly dealing with social ideas, just as

much they would be if their discussions were cast in the conceptual language of roles, expectations, ideologies, etc. in the conventional sociological manner. That is to say, any socially consequential set of ideas about role-relationships, legitimate access to labour, land, water, residential accommodation and other resources can be represented in the form of a model of its physical (spatio-temporal) implications. There is a mapping between ideological forms and the geometrical layout of the real world. It is not convenient to express every aspect of social life in this physicalist idiom, but none the less, very many important ideas can be represented in this way. The time-geographers' constructions are, in other words, an analytical language for exploring social systems, not simply a descriptive language for representing objects and events distributed in space and time. It is a language in which it is possible to construct permutable structural models which represent both the spatio-temporal relationships in the environment which are the geographers' primary concern, and also the implicit dimension of social ideas which are embodied in these relationships.

The feature of time-geographic theory which I wish to examine in a little more detail is the account they give of time allocation to competing activities on a population-wide basis. This analysis raises two issues fundamental to time-sociology (and anthropology), namely, (1) the relationship between the 'division of labour' and time; and (2) the question of 'time' as a *resource* which is distributed socially, like other resources.

In the 'unreflective attitude of everyday life' (Schutz 1967) the age/sex/status categories underlying the social division of labour are accepted as 'natural', but critical analysis and comparative research reveal that they are far from being immutable. It would be perfectly possible to arrange matters so that airliners were piloted by specially trained eleven-year old girls, if we wanted it that way. But the division of labour itself, as a feature of the organization of labour and society, *is* a natural fact, even if the assignment of particular tasks to particular categories of persons is not. Thus, we could give the task of piloting airliners to little girls, but they would still have to be specialists, performing this task at the expense of other possible ones (such as playing with dolls). What we could not do would be to assign the task of piloting jets to all the population on a proportional basis – i.e. if the average member of the population utilizes 0.5 of an airline pilot-hour per year, we could not have it that everybody spent exactly half an hour piloting jets each year.

In fact, biological considerations aside, the division of labour is not, in essence, a question of 'specialization' in aptitudes, techniques, knowledge, etc. at all, but has to do with space-time relationships. There is a 'division of labour' even in the case of two men carrying a log; one man is temporarily specializing in carrying the front end of a log, the other man the rear end. Unless the two men and the log assume a certain configuration in time and space (the two men performing complementary roles), the log will not get moved from A to B and their interests will suffer. The fundamental division of labour, therefore, is the division of labour in time and space. The social distribution of role-complementarities in the organization of work is a secondary consequence of the inescapable constraints governing the work process as a sequence of causally-linked events unfolding in time and space. The division of labour is consistent with technical specialization, but primarily arises from the fact that it is spatio-temporally impossible for one individual to perform, within a finite period, all the activities that might contribute to his or her welfare.

Since the era of Marx and Durkheim, it has been universally accepted that the division of labour in production, reproduction and consumption is the fundamental nexus around which social systems grow. If, in addition, it is conceded that in essence the division of labour is a 'geometrical' problem, we can envisage a branch of social theory which concerns itself with exploring the relationship between time, space and activities under varying kinds of demographic, ecological, technical and social constraints. This is the ultimate objective of time-geography in the Hägerstrand tradition, and Carlstein's treatise (1982) shows very well the theoretical and empirical advances which can result from looking at the data in this way.

Aggregate time-supply is defined as the total population of some regional system multiplied by 24 hours (or some other period). Time demand is defined as a set of activities, distributed in time and space, which seek for bearers in the population over that period. Time-geographic theory examines the space-time 'packing problem' involved in distributing human time resources so as to satisfy time-demand in the system (Carlstein 1982: 302ff).

Total population multiplied by a time-period is only a crude measure of time-resources, since these models have to take into account socially institutionalized role definitions and biological constraints. Thus time supply is further broken down into time-supply per social category of actors (males, females, infants, children, adolescents, adults, the elderly, etc.) or, if need be, by such criteria as caste, educational attainments, special skills or ritual qualifications, etc. In Figure 20.3 these sub-categorizations result in the vertical partitioning of population time-supply.

Turning to time demand, the model seeks to represent the fact that activities do not just require to be performed at 'some' time in a given period, but at times that are dictated by capability constraints, coupling constraints and institutional constraints of many kinds. Thus, teachers are obliged to restrict their teaching to the hours when their pupils are present, and the pupils much of their learning to the same hours. Activities such as teaching/learning, which require the regular, simultaneous participation of relatively large numbers of people in a restricted spatial frame, tend to be organized according to a predictable schedule. Other activities which require less co-ordination, such as shopping or leisure activities, are fitted in where gaps occur. Certain biologically necessary activities, such as sleeping and eating, tend also to be scheduled in a predictable way. These activities are scheduled to occur at times of day set apart as unavailable for purposes of social co-ordination: people are predictably absent from their offices between 6 p.m. and 9 a.m., and during the lunch hour, but this serves to increase the degree of predictability that they will be there at other times.

Just as the population time-supply is partitioned vertically into bands representing different social categories within the population, the population time demand graph is partitioned into horizontal bands representing the socially established scheduling of particular activities. Figure 20.3b shows the banding of time demand for sleep, and school attendance by teachers and pupils. It will be seen that while school attendance involves the whole population in the 5–16 age-bracket, it only involves a small proportion of the population in older age-brackets.

Finally, Figure 20.4 summarizes the supply-demand picture as a whole. Time demand (a) fluctuates according to scheduling constraints, at different points in the time-period (the day, perhaps). Time demand is shown as equal in volume to time supply (b), but is unequally distributed. The next figure (c) shows 'impossible' time supply (i.e. the time demands lying

**Figure 20.3   (a) vertical and (b) horizontal partitioning of the time-supply**

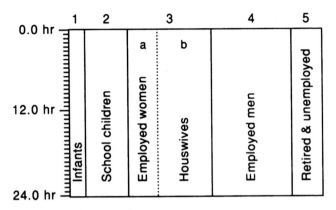

Number of individuals

**a**   Vertical partitioning of the total population time-supply

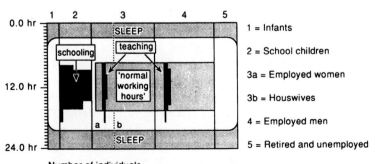

Number of individuals

1 = Infants

2 = School children

3a = Employed women

3b = Houswives

4 = Employed men

5 = Retired and unemployed

**b**   Horizontal partitioning of the total population time-supply

**Figure 20.4  Time-supply and time-demand**

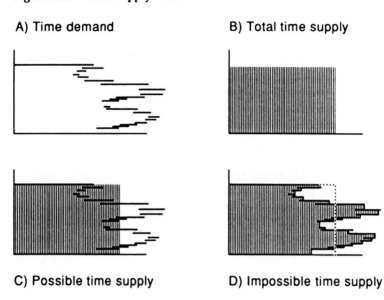

A) Time demand

B) Total time supply

C) Possible time supply

D) Impossible time supply

*Source*: Parkes and Thrift (1980: 257)

outside the limit of time supply). These time demands cannot be fulfilled, because time, unlike money, cannot be held in stock, for alternative use when demand is greatest. An hour must be devoted to some activity when and as it occurs, once that hour has passed, it is irretrievable. Unspent money, on the other hand, can be retained for subsequent use (barring the effects of inflation). Figure 20.4 shows 'possible time-supply' and the 'excess demand' in the system. Rational modifications of the time-supply/time-demand system must presumably be aimed at substituting of projects which involve excess time-demand with alternative projects which utilize time-resources for which demand is deficient, i.e. substituting 'cheap' time for 'expensive' time, measured in terms of opportunity costs.

Just as collective opportunity costs are incurred (as 'gaps' in the packing of activities in space-time) in any empirical distribution of time resources to the realization of projects taken in the aggregate, so each individual in the population incurs individual opportunity costs in opting for one particular path through the daily prism, as opposed to other possible ones.

The time-cost of an activity is the time this activity takes away from the performance of alternative activities. Thus the total time at the disposal of the individual is less than the total time the individual could spend in activities which would contribute to his welfare (i.e. time is absolutely scarce in relation to its potential uses); and second, scheduling constraints mean that the performance of activity A at T1 make unfeasible the performance of alternative activities B, C, D, which, like A, have to be performed at T1 or not at all. Time allocation, in the individual case, is finding solutions to the problem of optimizing the individual's temporal path through an activity-space so as to minimize total individually incurred temporal opportunity costs.

But, as Carlstein correctly observes (1982: 323ff), there never is a one-person time/activity system. Models of individual time scarcity and choice are inherently unrealistic, because the constraints on optimizing a path derive primarily from the effects of the actions of other individuals in the system, whose actions are reciprocally governed by the actions of the first individual, and so on, up to the population level.

One can make models (on Hägerstrandian time-cartographic lines) of isolated two- or three-person sub-systems. By imagining this progression from the one-person case to the population-as-a-whole case we can arrive at a notion of 'social time' as an enormous equilibrium system in which the activity mix and activity timings adopted by each individual are adjusted to neighbouring individuals, occupying cells in a matrix which includes all the individuals in the system. This matrix would be the time-allocational equivalent of the well-known Leontieff matrix in macroeconomics, which displays the economy (particular industries, sectors, etc.) as cells in a matrix between which finance, goods and services flow.

We can also approach this problem from the other end, starting with the aggregate frequencies of activities, derived from time-budget surveys. Hägerstrand's model was initially developed from Swedish data. These data (simplified) give the following breakdown of activities and the time devoted to them in a 24-hour cycle:

| *Activity* | *Hours per day* |
| --- | --- |
| Sleep | 8.5 |
| Personal care (eating, etc.) | 1.5 |

| | |
|---|---|
| Travel and leisure | 5.5 |
| Cooking, housework | 1.25 |
| Schooling | 0.75 |
| Employment | 4.5 |
| Looking after children | 2.0 |
| TOTAL | 24.0 |

Hägerstrand makes a distinction among the activities listed above, between those that are 'delegable' (the last four on the list) and those that are non-delegable, i.e. have to be performed by individuals on their own behalf (the first three). Time-demand for non-delegable activities is 'inelastic' (Szalai et. al. 1972) as it is for non-substitutable commodities in conventional economic theory, whereas individual time-demand for delegable activities is relatively elastic because time-input by any given individual into a delegable activity can be substituted for, if need be, by some other person's additional time input into that activity.

Ignoring scheduling constraints, we can see at once that multiplying the 24-hour list of time-demands by the number of individuals in the population fails to reflect the distribution of activities at all faithfully, except in the case of the most indelegable of all activities, sleeping, which is biologically necessary and also time by 24-hour circadian rhythms of natural origin. But it is far from true that the average school-going child spends 0.75 hour in school per day, or the average working person 4.5 hours at their place of work even though these are the average aggregate figures of time-demand for these activities for the population as a whole. So delegation is taking place. School-going is 'delegated' to children, employment is 'delegated' to adults, especially male breadwinners, and cooking, housework and looking after children is 'delegated' to married women.

Given that individual allocations of time to activities over a 24-hour cycle conform not at all to population aggregate time-demand for activities over the cycle, we can next look at the position for a 'typical' family of six, consisting of one infant, two school-age children, their parents, and one elderly retired grandfather, who lives with them. A family of six members has a total time-supply of 144 hours (= 6 × 24). We can see without difficulty that the 'average' family is non-self-sufficient so far as satisfying time-demand is concerned. Thus:

| Sleep | 8.5 × 6 = | 51.0 |
|---|---|---|
| Eating, etc. | 1.5 × 6 = | 9.0 |
| Travel, etc. | 5.5 × 6 = | 33.0 |
| Cooking, etc. | 1.5 × 6 = | 7.5 |
| Schooling | 0.75 × 6 = | 4.5 |
| Employment | 4.5 × 6 = | 27.0 |
| Childcare | 2.0 × 6 = | 12.0 |
| | TOTAL | 144.0 |

The demand for 'employment' is now greater than can be met from the family's resources, since if all three adults work an 8-hour day, the total time in employment would not be more than 24 hours for all of them combined, which is less than the 27 hours required. The imbalance is even greater if we are to assume that the old grandfather does not work, and that the mother undertakes a large proportion of the 12 hours of childcare demanded. Not even the most hard-pressed paterfamilias works a 27-hour day.

Multiplying the number of 'typical' families in the system will not mend matters, since all of them will show the same imbalances and unfulfillable time demands as this one. More radical, population-wide, rather than family-wide delegation of activities has to be envisaged. There must be institutionalized activity-complementarities such that school-age children undertake the whole of the schooling time-demand, in exchange for undertaking none of the employment demand, others are freed from childcare to devote themselves to employment, while others again mop up excess demand for childcare, and so on, according to institutional constraints governing the sexual division of labour and the lifecycle division of labour.

The equilibrium outcome of this confrontation between the forces of aggregate social time-demand and individuals' patterns of activity in space and time is the social division of labour.

We can make important structural distinctions between societies with what Durkheim (1960) called 'mechanical solidarity' and those showing 'organic solidarity' on the basis of the degree of structural conformity between time allocations as the micro- (domestic) level of analysis and time allocations at the macro- (population) level of analysis. Under mechanical solidarity, or the more refined concept of 'the domestic mode of production' introduced by Sahlins (1972), there is a high degree of convergence between the time allocated to activities at the level of the self-sufficient household, and the time-allocations of the population as a whole. There is very little 'trading' in time between households. But in the case of societies such as Sweden, the source for the data used above, the degree of convergence is much less, corresponding to the fact that there no longer exists any 'basic unit', like a self-sufficient household, in such societies, and that individuals' allocations differ sharply from one another, even if they fall into broadly the same age/sex categories.

# Chapter 21

# The Economics of Temporal Opportunity Costs

Some economists (notably Becker 1965; cf. Linder 1970; Soule 1955) have discussed 'time' as a form of raw material which is allocated to competing ends on 'economizing' principles. Let me give the gist of Becker's theory. This author discusses time allocation in relation to the economics of the household in advanced capitalist economies. The household is seen as a microscopic firm, receiving inputs in the form of goods, services and time, and producing outputs in the form of consumption-events, which also require time. Households thus combine market goods and time to 'produce' more basic commodities, called Z, which give rise to utility. Thus, family members 'process' a resource (e.g. a production of *Hamlet* at a local theatre) by contributing their time (getting to the theatre, watching the play and returning) so as to turn this resource into another commodity, called 'the seeing of a play', which has utility.

Time in this scheme of things is a resource which has other possible uses besides becoming an ingredient of Z, such as being devoted to paid employment. Time can be devoted to increasing the input of resources of other kinds (X) into the household, or it can be used in the household production process itself, as an ingredient of Z, which gives rise to the utility function (U) in the Figure 21.1.

Becker states that the problem facing a household is the maximization of U subject to two apparently independent kinds of constraints. The first of these is the scarcity of resources; the goods used in household 'production' must not exceed in value the family income, which has two components, V, income which is not obtained via the expenditure of time, and is not sensitive to additional investments of time, and W (wages) which is treated as a dependent variable of Tw, time spent at

**Figure 21.1  The Becker model**

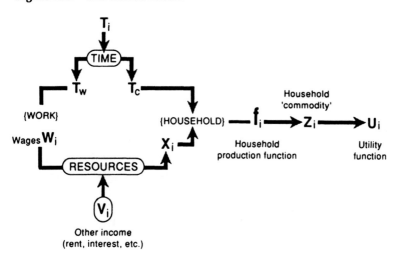

work. *W* will increase with additional investments of time. The discussion in Becker (and Linder 1970; cf. p. 209 below) applies to economies with nearly full employment and very tight labour markets. Not all economies are like this, needless to add.

The second set of constraints are time constraints affecting the production of Z within the household. Time utilizable for the production of Z is 'consumption time' *Tc*; (*Tc* = total time *T* minus *Tw*). Becker's argument consists of the exploration of the consequences of the fact that these two sets of constraints (resources and time) are not, in fact, independent of one another at all, in that time can be turned into consumption goods *X*, by means of increasing time at work, but only at the expense of marginally raising the 'costs of production' of Z in the household, because the relative time-cost of consumption will be increased.

The treatment of consumption-time as a cost incurred in consuming is a curious but not outrageous idea. That consumption has indirect costs, apart from the direct cost of the consumed item to the consumer, is well supported by the fact that the average American household controls capital equipment ancillary to consumption (house, car, furniture, domestic gadgets, cameras, boats, sporting gear, etc.) vastly exceeding in value the average value of the capital goods at the disposal of the wage-earner at his workplace, as an adjunct to productive enterprise.

American industry may be capital-intensive, but the 'factories' producing Z are even more capital-intensive.

Increasing the wage-income of a household (W) without increasing the time-cost of working for them Tw, i.e. a rise in real wages, decreases the time 'cost' of working, and increases proportionately the time 'cost' of consumption. Thus rising real wages make the household a less efficient producer of Z than before by decreasing the household production-function (f) and lowers the resulting value of Z. To keep U at the same level as before, Tw must be increased, increasing W still further, to compensate for the fact that the conversion of W into U has become marginally less efficient. Thus, where the conventional labour/leisure indifference curve (found in all elementary microeconomics texts) predicts that rising real wages will result in the substitution of labour by leisure, since equivalent levels of psychic satisfaction can now be achieved by working for fewer hours, the Becker model makes the opposite prediction, namely, that rises in real wages will intensify the worker's desire to extend working time at the expense of leisure time. That he often cannot do so, even where there exists unsatisfied demand for additional labour in the economy, results more from government intervention and labour unions than from the wage-earners' own volition:

> The incentive to economise on time as its relative cost increases goes a long way towards explaining certain broad aspects of behaviour which have puzzled and often disturbed observers of contemporary life. Since hours worked have declined secularly in most advanced countries, and (so-called) leisure has presumably increased, a natural expectation has been that 'free' time would become more abundant and be used more 'leisurely' and 'luxuriously'. Yet, if anything, time is used more carefully than a century ago. If there were a secular increase in the productivity of working time relative to consumption time . . . there would be an increased incentive to economise on its use because of its greater expense (our theory emphatically cautions against calling such time 'free'). Not surprisingly, it is now kept track of and used more carefully than in the past. (Becker 1965: 513)

Despite the fact that working time, given increased real wages, becomes progressively a better bargain than consumption time, consumption time cannot be compressed indefinitely since increased real wages necessitate more consumption activity, and more time for this activity, even though this time is 'expensive'. At a certain point it is necessary to work less in order to make more efficient use of the goods made available for consumption, so as to convert them into Z. But consumption time has to be used sparingly, and agonizing decisions have to be made.

According to Linder (1970), consumption bottlenecks, created by the excessive time-cost of consumption, set natural limits to economic growth. In ultra-affluent economies the signs of consumption bottlenecks are clearly present: Parkes and Thrift (1980) note the emergence, particularly in California, of a new breed of 'Leisure Counsellors', whose expertise is precisely the efficient use of leisure (i.e. consumption) time, given the super-abundance of resources for consumption in relation to the time needed to consume them. Perhaps the recent rise in 'green' anti-consumption sentiment stems from a recognition that consumption is becoming inefficient as a means of realizing utility because of the high perceived opportunity costs of any given consumptive use of time *vis-à-vis* its alternative uses.

Within the household 'firm' there will be a division of labour: those whose opportunity costs are least prohibitive will specialize in consumption, leaving those whose earning power is greater more time to devote themselves to fulfilling that function exclusively. And the pattern of consumption decisions will be dictated by these pressures as well. Goods will be chosen, not because of their intrinsic desirability, but because they are items whose consumption represents least in terms of 'earnings forgone' (i.e. they can be consumed quickly and at maximum expense). Photography, for instance, is a form of consumption behaviour which absorbs a relatively large amount of money in relation to the time it takes anyone to take, and subsequently look at, a snapshot. Chess, by contrast, is a very inefficient form of consumption in that it absorbs a great deal of time and costs very little money. Russia is a poor country where many people play chess; America is a rich country whose inhabitants criss-cross the face of the globe, in a great hurry and at great expense to themselves, taking photographs.

Becker, and also Linder, in a book whose title *The Harried Leisure Class* (1970) admirably sums up its contents, refer to the consumption/time dilemma in the context of prosperous, expanding economies. But what about economies which are low in productivity, providing most people with scant opportunity for either employment or consumption, and hence low opportunity

costs for any kind of investment of time? Linder devotes some
space to these economies as well, calling them 'time surplus'
economies, as opposed to 'time famine' economies like the
United States or Sweden. Most anthropologists will be familiar
with the table showing the time budgets of Arnheim land aborigines (Mountford 1960), which Sahlins used to such good effect
in his 'The Original Affluent Society' (1972):

| Activity | Time allocated (hours) | |
|---|---|---|
|  | Women | Men |
| Sleeping/lying | 9.0 | 12.0 |
| Sitting/talking | 8.3 | 5.0 |
| Prepare/repair instruments | — | 1.0 |
| Prepare/cook kangaroo | — | 0.3 |
| Collecting food | 4.3 | — |
| Prepare/cook food | 2.0 | — |
| Singing/dancing | — | 1.3 |
| Hunting | — | 4.0 |

Sahlins cited this leisurely daily round of the Arnheim land
hunter-gatherers in order to demonstrate that it was not 'want'
which induced mankind to advance beyond this stage in social
evolution. This basic thesis may be accepted, though the data
from Arnheim land have recently been supplemented by more
thorough studies, which tend to show both sexes working
rather more intensively, especially at certain seasons of the year
(Altman 1984). It is also worth noting that Carlstein (1982), on
the basis of much more data than were available to Sahlins,
suggests that there is no very clear relatioship between 'intensi-
fication' in the use of resources (land, agricultural capital, time)
in more complex eco-technological regimes, and the amount of
time *directly* devoted to food production. For example, in ultra-
intensive Indonesia, women spend twice as much time cooking
food as they spend growing it (White 1976; Carlstein 1982:
381–2). The filling out of time which accompanies the intensi-
fication of production takes many different forms, of which
expansion in agricultural work time is only one. The more complicated social structure, which is necessary to sustain a complex
system of production, exchange and consumption, is itself a
source of heavy time demands (trips to and from market,
marketing itself, negotiating to buy or sell labour, negotiations

to secure political protection, complex household routines, ritual duties, education, etc.).

There is a reasonably clear distinction between societies which do not make very intensive use of time and which seem to have low opportunity costs, vs. those societies that make intensive use of time and in which people are very conscious of opportunity costs. But I do not think it is correct to refer to low opportunity cost regimes as 'time surplus' systems. Linder's criterion for 'surplus' time is time in which nothing is being produced and nothing being consumed. But I feel that it is better to follow Becker and deny that there is such a thing as 'free' time at all. Something is always being 'produced', even if it is only 'conversation' or 'sleep', or other 'household commodities' belonging to his category Z.

Sitting around a fire talking to other people is certainly a very resource-conserving kind of activity, but it does involve the mobilization of resources all the same, i.e. firewood, 'company' and time. People are never doing nothing at all, even if they seem to be. If people are always producing and consuming something, and using up time in the process, no time is free. Truly surplus time could be abstracted from the individuals life-line so as to leave no trace, like a sequence cut out from a film by an impatient editor; but clearly all time is consequential, however minimally.

There are, of course, stretches of time which we would *like* to have 'edited out' of our biographies. We say things like 'Henry spent the afternoon killing time', which suggests that the afternoon in question was surplus to Henry's requirements. But what this really means is that Henry had to wait out the afternoon, engaging in irksome, obligatory, underfinanced consumption, when in another world, he could have been engaged in activities more to his taste. The notion that Henry's tedious afternoon is 'surplus' cannot be given any meaning in the light of the quantity of time in that afternoon as opposed to any other one, since this quantity would have remained just the same had Henry spent the afternoon in his mistress's arms, or robbing a bank. It is not the 'objective' facts which make time surplus or deficient; 'surplus' time is simply time which we have to spend doing X when we would rather be doing Y.

In other words, time surplus/shortage is a function of perceived opportunity costs, not of objective quantitative relationships between 'real' resources like land, labour, energy, specie, etc. These are *things*, and only things are capable of being in any objective sense plentiful or in short supply. Time and space are not things but dimensions, measures. We can talk about relationships between things (and the events which things participate in) in terms of space-time quantities, but time and space themselves are not doled out in variable quantities, depending on circumstances, as are other economic resources. They are measures of other resources, but are not resources in themselves. I disagree with Soule (1955, quoted in Parkes and Thrift 1980: 144) when he argues that time should be regarded as a scarce resource in the economy 'co-ordinate with labour, land, and capital'. This author suggests that popular opinion is wrong in supposing that the wage-earner sells his labour to his employer; what he sells, according to Soule, is his time. I do not think so. What the employer buys (or rather hires) is not the employee's time, not his 'labour', but *him*, a solid, chunky object, having the disposition, under the right circumstances, to set in motion trains of causal interactions in the physical world which are to the employer's advantage. On Soule's analysis, if a farmer buys a cow, he buys the cow's time, not the milk, meat or calves the cow produces/consists of. This is plainly absurd: but I do not see that there is any fundamental difference between a farmer buying rights over a cow, and an employer buying temporary rights over an employee-object.

It is necessary to distinguish between the time-based opportunity cost measures which are used to evaluate one activity *vis-à-vis* an alternative activity, from the 'real' entities which can participate in economic transactions, which do not include 'raw' time as a factor of production.

There is no 'raw' time because time is always associated with an activity, that is to say with causal processes involving things. When Becker speaks of 'time' as an input into the 'little factory' which produces Z, he does not mean empty time but time filled with a certain form of activity. Time as such cannot be switched between earning or consumption, what is switched is causal interaction of the human being *qua* thing, into one form of activity rather than another, an investment measurable in temporal units, but not an investment of time itself. Time by itself, and without the participation of things, is not a resource which can be economized on or diverted from one use to another, as though it were some ethereal natural resource like sunlight. Not being an economizable entity, it has no value.

The time-reifying language of the type of theory just described is perhaps rather misleading in that time is not a physical resource which can be in abundant or short supply, bought/sold, etc. like ordinary resources. But despite this I do not wish to impugn models like Becker's, or time-geographical constructions in the Hägerstrand/Carlstein manner, on the grounds that this kind of theory treats time as a 'resource' for model-building purposes. At the level of models, one can legitimately treat time as a resource, because this is a convenient way of talking about *opportunity costs*. This, I consider, is the really crucial theoretical concept which should forge the much-needed link between economic theory, time-geographic theory and anthropology/sociology.

Let me return to the implications of the Arnheim land time-budget shown above. It will be recalled that Sahlins saw here signs of 'primitive affluence', i.e. people live up to their expectations without working unduly hard – hunter-gatherers live off the 'unearned income' of their often very productive environments, which is fine so long as there is plenty of 'environment' to go round. But not everybody sees signs of 'affluence' here. Just (1980) has suggested that rather than being 'affluent', hunter-gatherers like these are 'unemployed' – after all, many of the unemployed in our society do very much as the Arnheim-landers do, i.e. invest a lot time in low-cost consumption, hanging about, conversation, football, etc. According to this theory, the Arnheim-landers have such a leisurely lifestyle because they are poor, not because they are affluent. Their economy is capital-starved, unproductive. They have surplus time because they have no other resources to combine time with so as to produce commodities, whose consumption would further increase total time-demand.

Where does the truth lie between affluence and unemployment? If we are to define affluence, as I think we should, along the lines suggested by Becker and Linder, as relatively low opportunity costs measured in terms of resources ($X$) and relatively high opportunity costs measured in terms of time ($Tw + Tc$) the Arnheim-landers are not 'affluent'. Even if one concedes that Arnheim-landers have access to abundant real resources, in the form of rich environments ($X$) the technical exploitation of these environments is not time-demanding, so the opportunity cost of non-productive time is low, and moreover, the product of these environments comes in a form (food) which is not 'costly to consume' in the opportunity cost sense, because cooking and eating are obligatory activities under any economic regime whatsoever. Arnheim-landers have low temporal opportunity costs whichever way one looks at the problem, and if one builds high temporal opportunity costs into the definition of affluence, they are not affluent.

On the other hand, I do not think they could be called 'unemployed' either. An individual can only be 'unemployed' in relation to an employment opportunity which under some definition of 'possible worlds' that individual is qualified to fulfil. I do not, at present, hold a job in a steelworks – but that does not make me an 'unemployed steel-worker'. A skilled but redundant steel-worker who makes a living as a double-glazing contractor can be reasonably regarded as an unemployed steel-worker, even though he is not technically 'unemployed' at all, in the eyes of the Department of Employment. 'Unemployment' is not something that can be defined in cut-and-dried terms, despite the existence of official statistics. Everything depends on a socially defined set of 'rational expectations' as to who can legitimately aspire to a particular type of employment. Unemployment in this or any other economy is defined as the difference between employment conditions in a notional 'ideal' economy in which everybody has the job to which they can legitimately aspire, and the actual distribution of jobs in the population. Children are not counted as 'unemployed' in our society, not because there are not many kinds of work which children can undertake, and used to undertake in the past, but because we have decided that children 'ought' not to be made to work. Among the poorer classes in many Third World countries, children not gainfully occupied are socially regarded as unemployed, even though the authorities in such countries do not recognize the *de facto* position on 'child unemployment' in preparing their official statistics, since these are already horrifying enough.

On this kind of criterion, the Arnheim-landers are clearly not unemployed in their own terms, since they are fully capable of finding opportunities to pursue all the productive activities they themselves regard as legitimately belonging to them. But they are unemployed according to official statistics. Aboriginal people in Australia now largely subsist on unemployment benefits, which they have come to regard as just another of the exploitable resources available to them, in addition to hunting/

gathering resources (cf. Endicott 1979 on the equivalent attitude among Malaysian Aboriginals). Being 'unemployed' is their employment.

It seems to me that we can distinguish four possibilities, rather than two, according to which the Arnheim-landers are neither affluent, nor are they unemployed. To be affluent, a society has to have high temporal opportunity costs, and low 'resource' opportunity costs (i.e. high real wages, etc.). 'Affluent' western economies fall into this bracket. Next we can consider societies which have high temporal opportunity costs *and* high resource opportunity costs. Such societies would manifest long but ill-rewarded working hours, and high opportunity costs on consumption because consumption eats into working time. Many traditional craft producers (e.g. weavers) and non-unionized factory-hands in underdeveloped countries have precisely this regime, as did large sections of the nineteenth-century urban proletariat. Next there are to be considered societies showing low temporal opportunity costs and high resource opportunity costs. The long-term unemployed in the United Kingdom belong to this category. The UK unemployed have low temporal opportunity costs, but are strapped for cash, i.e. have high resource opportunity costs. Finally, we have regimes with low temporal opportunity costs and low resource opportunity costs: this is where the Arnheim-landers belong.

The notion of unemployment, like the notion of affluence, is intrinsically connected to the opportunity costs involved in substituting one set of activities distributed in space and time for another, alternative set. A man is an 'unemployed steel-worker' if, and only if, he could in some possible world deemed *feasible*, if not actual, be employed in a steel-works. Because this alternative world is feasible, but not actual, the unemployed steel-worker incurs the opportunity costs attendant on the non-realization of this alternative 'possible world'. But the key concept here is 'feasibility'. We do not think that Om Parkash, a bottle-washer in a grimy *dhaba* on the outskirts of Kanpur, has incurred serious opportunity costs by not becoming President of IBM. Neither does he. But exactly how close does one have to get to being President of IBM before these opportunity costs begin to arise? A senior executive of IBM who is offered a managing directorship in a smaller, rival company has to consider these opportunity costs seriously if he thinks it is feasible that, if he stayed with his original company, he could do even better. There can be no 'objective' solution to career decisions of this kind, which are particularly susceptible to analysis by the Shackle A-theory decision model (see Chapter 19 above), because they are characteristically unique, once-in-a-lifetime choices. Indeed, there are no strictly 'objective' opportunity costs, since such costs are determined by the relationship between this world and other 'possible worlds' which have no objective existence. Opportunity costs are computed in relation to what will be called, in the next chapter, a 'B-series time-map' of the relevant domain, not in relation to the 'objective' B-series itself.

# Chapter 22

# Opportunity Costs and the Fatefulness of Human Existence

Opportunity costs arise from the fact that the representations, or conceptual models we make of the 'real' world, represent the world as being *capable of being otherwise* than we believe it to be, actually. The world is as it is, but we think it could be otherwise, and it may be otherwise than we think. Although there are no 'real' opportunity costs, because the real world is not in an alternativeness relationship with itself, from the standpoint of our cognitive representations of the world, opportunity costs are very real indeed.

The value of an object in this actual world is a function of the advantages and disadvantages incurred by *not* substituting, for this object, the alternative objects which could be substituted for it in a feasible alternative world. Similarly, the value of an event, the advantages and disadvantages which accrue from having that event come about, are a function of the feasible substitutes for that event in alternative possible worlds, i.e. alternative 'what if' scenarios. The definitions of what constitutes a 'feasible' alternative world to the actual one are hermeneutic, depending on socially determined ideas not objective facts. We have no physical access to alternative possible worlds, since if we contrive to make them physically real, they are no longer alternative possible worlds, but the actual world itself. None the less, our evaluations of both objects and events in the actual world depend crucially on our notion of what constitute the alternatives to these objects and events, in the penumbra of non-actual worlds surrounding this one. The alternativeness relation where activities are concerned is their temporal opportunity cost: activities which have high opportunity costs are ones which have highly advantageous, highly feasible alternatives in terms of the map *of the field of possible worlds* imposed by a given culturally standardized construction of reality.

Time-geography studies the spatio-temporal geometry of these possible worlds, in B-series time. Only one world is physically real, but using time-geographical analytical methods we can gain insight into the subjective evaluation of the geometry of the space-time environment. This subjective evaluation arises from the perceived opportunity costs attendant upon the geometry assuming one configuration rather than another. Thus, the space-time environment of Jane, the unmarried mother (p. 196), is evaluated by her in the light of the feasible but non-actual world(s) in which it would be geometrically possible for her to have a much better job.

In so far as time is *fateful* it is so in the light of the perceived opportunity costs of events in time pursuing one course rather than another. What determines, to a great extent, the course of events in this or any other possible world is the space-time geometry of the environment. Geometrical considerations are uppermost in time-allocation decisions; any theory of the sociology or anthropology of time must begin with the primitive fact that in order to actualize a state-of-affairs 'things' must be made to assume an appropriate geometrical configuration. Time is salient, in the conduct of human affairs, primarily in connection with the organization and co-ordination of persons and things in the real world, in order to encourage causal forces to bring about some desired result. But although we are obliged to act in the real world, and real-world events are the ultimate arbiters of the efficacy and timeliness of our actions, the source of projects of action, and hence action itself, are the beliefs we hold about the world, not the world itself. These beliefs, or representations, are the maps we use in order to navigate in time.

The progress of a social individual through life may easily be conceptualized as a series of escalating opportunity costs. Nothing much hinges, or seems to hinge, on the acts a child performs out of his or her own independent agency. In so far as they control their own destinies, children act in a field of open possibilities. But with every year that passes, as actions become more consequential, so also do their opportunity costs. The positive relation between the consequentiality of actions and their increased 'cost' in terms of alternatives forgone is intrinsic and inescapable. From every act made by an agent, there ensues an additional restraint upon action which arises from the blocking-off of one more branching series of possibilities, once open, now foreclosed. Nor can the agent evade, by inaction or delay, the diminution of scope for action which is the necessary counterpart to action itself. The funnelling-in of the field of 'open' possibilities as age advances is inexorable. Open possibilities vanish of their own accord, and transient opportunities must be grasped, costly though they may be in terms of *other* opportunities. Age, like childhood, is without opportunities, but differs from childhood in that it is lived out in the shadow of the (by now almost infinite) opportunity costs of actions taken long ago. Risks were accepted in the knowledge that they represented losing gambles at best, but those were the most favourable terms on offer, the ones with the lowest apparent opportunity costs. Now the dark web of causality stands revealed. Opportunity costs which were once merely hypothetical now have confirmed magnitudes, because they can be calibrated against the accepted record of fate's vicissitudes. But even so a residual doubt remains. Maybe we can now be sure about how things have actually turned out, given that long ago we saw our best opportunities as lying in certain directions, and acted accordingly, thereby foreclosing on certain alternative possibilities, which were once open to us. But do we have any real grounds for supposing that our latter-day estimations of what 'would have happened' had we made alternative selections among our once-feasible options are well founded? If we presume that a world once existed in which we could have 'chosen differently' and suffered different consequences, that world would have had to have been different in other ways as well, for otherwise we would not have chosen differently, but just as we did, unless our actions were randomly dictated. Once we start to judge actions and outcomes in the actual world against the imaginary standard of alternative scenarios stemming from once open but subsequently closed possibilities, we enter an area of radical uncertainty. There is really no means of knowing what the consequences of an untaken action might have been. Even though opportunity costs become ever greater and ever more computable, they never cease to be, in the final analysis, subjective.

But in order to elaborate a theory of social time which grasps, not just the organizational surface, but the subjective fatefulness of human existence, it is necessary to return once more to the problem of time-cognition, that is to say, to A-series time. We need a theory of time-cognition which is founded on the notion of the calculation of opportunity costs through retrospection and prospection, the cognitive processes through which we situate ourselves in time and in the light of which actions in time are inwardly determined. No theory of this kind exists in anthropology, nor in the conventional psychology of time. But philosophers have come much closer to understanding time in this way, especially phenomenological philosophers in the tradition of Husserl. Therefore, it is to Husserl's model of internal time-consciousness that I shall turn next.

# Chapter 23

## Husserl's Model of Internal Time-consciousness

In this chapter I turn to the subjective character of time. Subjective time is at once the most familiar and the most puzzling aspect of temporality. Through every waking moment we sense the passage of time, and our daily lives are lived within a set of temporal 'horizons' which shift continually, like the landscape viewed from the windows of a moving train, while always retaining their underlying continuity and uniformity of structure. The time we experience immediately – as opposed to the time we 'construct' as part of a cultural schema or scientific theory about how the world works – is A-series time.

We can profitably commence a discussion of A-series time sociology by outlining the philosophical theory which has exercised the most obvious influence on recent A-series time sociologists, in particular Schutz and Bourdieu. The theory in question would not have been categorized as 'philosophy' by its originator Husserl, the pioneer of phenomenology, but as 'psychology' (i.e. phenomenological psychology). Husserl's ambition was to construct an epistemology and philosophy of science 'without presuppositions' (notably, the 'naive realist' presuppositions of positivist empiricism) and, as a prelude to constructing this 'phenomenological philosophy', he undertook a very careful series of investigations into cognitive processes of all kinds (perception, ideation, etc.) including a notable account of the 'psychology of internal time-consciousness' (Husserl 1966) certain of whose main themes I shall summarize at this juncture. Husserl's account of time-consciousness has exercised a major influence on subsequent developments in continental philosophy. Major portions of the works of Heidegger, Sartre and Merleau-Ponty can be traced to the stimulus provided by this particular text of Husserl's, but these developments cannot be discussed here. Husserl's theory deserves to be considered in detail, because it remains the most careful and intricate account of subjective time available to us, even after all these years.

Husserl begins by considering the views held on the subject of time-consciousness held by his teacher, the introspective psychologist and proto-phenomenologist, Brentano. Brentano was interested in the problem of the continuity of the subjective/perceptual 'present' given the conventional idea that the present is a knife-edge between the future and the past. This is the problem which led William James to formulate his theory of the 'specious present' in terms which bear many points of similarity to the account given by both Brentano and Husserl (James 1963). Brentano asked how we are able to hear a continuous tone, an A played on the oboe and lasting 5 seconds, as a continuous duration. By the time we are into the fourth second's-worth, the first second's-worth is no longer present and no longer audible; but perceptually speaking it is still a component of the tone we are hearing in the present. Brentano supposes that we hear only the now-present tone, but that we enrich this hearing with 'associations' derived from earlier hearing-experiences in the sequence. We make, he says, a 'primordial association' between the tone we are currently hearing and what we are able to reproduce in fantasy of what we have just heard. In other words, Brentano has a model based on short-term memory: 'hearing a continuous tone' consists of forming associations between auditory input and inputs replayed from short-term memory. The recent past is 'fed forward' (to use the terminology of cybernetics) and matched against present input: if there is a match, then there is perception of a temporally continuous 'time-object' (a tone that endures).

Husserl's views are cognate with those of his predecessor, but he introduces some additional distinctions, which are needed in order to overcome the difficulty posed by the fact that we can distinguish clearly between 'remembering' the experience of hearing an A played on the oboe, as a time-consuming event which took place in the past, and the kind of feed-forward from the recent past which is involved in generating the impression of continuity in the present. Brentano's solution to the continuity problem will not work if the 'primordial association' between the first second's-worth of the A-tone and the fourth requires us to relive the first second's worth as a fantasied 'present moment' concurrently with experiencing the fourth second's-worth of the tone in the real present; because this means that there is a multiplicity of 'now' moments (associated with one another, but distinct) rather than just one 'now', which extends into the past and is open towards the future. The effect is a fragmentation of 'nows' like individual frames of a cine-film, with associative relationships between them. Husserl overcomes this problem by distinguishing between 'retentions' of experiences and 'reproductions' of experiences. 'Retentions' (contrasting with both perceptions and memories) are what we have of temporally removed parts of experiences from the standpoint of the 'now' moment; 'reproductions' are action-replays of past experiences of events carried out from the standpoint of a remembered or reconstructed 'now' in the past.

Husserl treats 'retention' and its future-oriented counterpart 'protention' not as fantasied memories or anticipations of other 'nows' associated with the present 'now', but as horizons of a temporally extended present. In other words, he abandons the idea of a knife-edge present, a limit – itself without duration – between past duration and future duration. The 'limit' remains as the 'now'-moment, but the 'now' and the 'present' can be distinguished. The present has its own thickness and temporal spread. Listening to the final second's worth of the 5-second A-tone, I do not 'remember' (reproduce) the first second's-worth; I am aware only of a single tone, which prolongs itself within a single present moment which includes the whole of the tone, but within which this tone is subjected to a continuous series of 'modifications' brought about by a series of shifts of temporal perspective as the present unfolds and transforms itself.

Husserl's distinction between retention and reproduction makes it possible to conceptualize the way in which temporal experience coheres from the standpoint of the present: 'retentional awareness' is the perspective view we have of past phases of an experience from the vantage point of a 'now' moment which slips forwards, and in relation to which past phases of our experience of the present are pushed inexorably back. Reproduction of some recollected event, by contrast, involves the temporary abandonment of the current 'now' as the focal point around which retentional perspectives cohere, in favour of a fantasied 'now' in the past which we take up in order to replay events mentally.

Retentions, unlike reproductions, are all part of current consciousness of the present, but they are subject to distortion or
diminution as they are pushed back towards the fringes of our
current awareness of our surroundings. We also have 'perspective' views of future phases of current events as they emerge out
of the proximate future, and Husserl likewise suggests that we
should distinguish between what are seen as continuations of
the present and future events, which we reproduce from the
standpoint of a fantasied future present. The perspective views
we have of the proximate future Husserl names 'protentions'.
Retentions and protentions are forms of the basic Husserlian
category of 'intentions', by which is meant, not 'inclinations to
do something' as in standard English, but all relations linking
*noesis* (processes of cognition) and *noema* (that which is cognized). Intentional relations between *noesis* and *noema* arise in
the process of perceiving something, remembering something,
believing in something, imagining something, and so on; in
modern philosophy, intentionalities are often called 'propositional attitudes' (Hintikka 1969).

In order to expound his ideas, Husserl makes use of a diagram, of which Figure 23.1 is a version. The horizontal line
$A \rightarrow B \rightarrow C \rightarrow D$ corresponds to the succession of now moments
strung out between the past and the future. Suppose we are at
B: our perceptual beliefs are token-indexically true (i.e. up-to-
date) at B. The temporal landscape at B consists of the now-
present perceptual experience of the state of affairs at B plus
retentions of A, (as A' – sinking down into the past). A' is a
'modification' of the original A, what A looks like from B, i.e.
attenuated or diminished, but still present. Perhaps one can
think of the 'modification' of A as it sinks down into the past
$(A \rightarrow A' \rightarrow A'' \rightarrow A''' \ldots)$ as a gradual *loss of verisimilitude* affecting
the perceptual judgements entertained at A as these are super-
seded by the perceptual judgements entertained at B, C, D, etc.
Our token-indexical perceptual beliefs do not become inappli-
cable simply by virtue of the passage of time, but only gradually,
because the world does not change all at once and in all respects. We can no longer, at B, say that the state of affairs at A is
'now' the case, because of the change of the temporal index; but
many of the features of A have counterparts at B. The fading out
of the background of the proximate past as successively weaker
retentions $(A' \rightarrow A'' \rightarrow A''' \ldots)$ corresponds to the increasing
divergence in contents between beliefs entertainable as token-

**Figure 23.1   Husserl's model of internal time-consciousness**

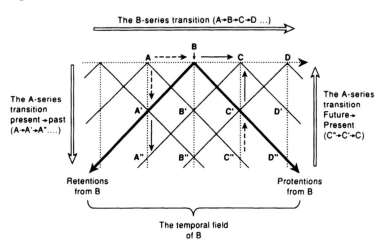

The B-series transition (A→B→C→D ...)

The A-series transition present →past (A→A'→A"....)

The A-series transition Future→ Present (C"→C'→C)

Retentions from B

Protentions from B

The temporal field of B

indexically true at A and increasingly distant points in the succession of 'now' moments (A'/B, A"/C, A'''/D, etc.). But out-of-date token-indexical beliefs are still salient because it is only in the light of these divergences between out-of-date beliefs and current beliefs that we can grasp the direction in which the events surrounding us are taking, thereby enabling us to form protentions towards the future phases of the current state of affairs.

Retentions can thus be construed as the background of out-of-date beliefs against which more up-to-date beliefs are projected, and significant trends and changes are calibrated. As beliefs become more seriously out of date, they diminish in salience and are lost to view. We thus perceive the present not as a knife-edge 'now' but as a temporally extended field within which trends emerge out of the patterns we discern in the successive updatings of perceptual beliefs relating to the proximate past, the next most proximate past, and the next, and so on. This trends is projected into the future in the form of protentions, i.e. anticipations of the pattern of updating of current perceptual beliefs which will be necessitated in the proximate future, the next most proximate future, and the next, in a manner symmetric with the past, but in inverse temporal order.

Husserl does not describe things in this way (i.e. in terms of perceptual beliefs, an idiom I have borrowed from Mellor) speaking only of retentions as 'modifications' of perceptions.

We can follow him in thinking of these modifications as analogous to perspectival diminutions and attenuations because this is a powerful visual metaphor, though it has to be borne in mind that temporal perspective and visual perspective have entirely different origins.

Let us return to Husserl's own explanation of his model. At B, A is retained as A' (A' is A seen through a certain thickness of time) and C is protended as C', the favoured candidate as successor to B. Time passes, and C' comes about as C (presumably not quite as anticipated, but approximately so). B is now retained in consciousness as B', related to (current) C as A' was to B when B was current. But how is A related to C? From the standpoint of C, A is no longer retained as A', because this is to put A' and B' on a par with one another, and fails to reflect the fact that when B (currently B') was current, A was even then only a retention (A'). Consequently, from the standpoint of C, A has to be retained as a retention of A', which is itself a retention of A: i.e. as A". This can be expressed more clearly, perhaps, by using brackets. Thus: A → (A)B → ((A)B)C → (((A)B)C)D → etc. where brackets, mean 'retention', double brackets 'retention of a retention', triple brackets 'retention of a retention of a retention', and so on.

Husserl says that as A sinks to A' at B, A" at C A''' at D, and so on, A becomes a retention, then a retention of a retention, then a retention of a retention of a retention, and so on, until reaching the stage of final attenuation and sinking beneath the temporal horizon. The effect of this argument is to abolish the hard-and-fast distinction, still apparent in Brentano's argument, between the dynamic present and the fixed and unchanging past. Past, present and future are all of a piece, and all equally dynamic in the Husserl model (embodying an important cognitive truth) because any modification, anywhere in the system, sets up correlative modifications everywhere else in the system. Thus the modification in the present which converts C into C' automatically entrains corresponding modifications everywhere (B' → B", A" → A''', D' → D, etc.). 'The whole past sinks in a mass, taking all its arranged contents with it' (Findlay 1975: 11). But the past does not just 'sink' as the present progresses; it changes its significance, is evaluated in different ways, and sets up different patterns of protentions, according to the way in which the present evolves. This dynamic past, and the future which continually alters in its complexion, cannot be accommodated in B-series time, because from the strict B-series point of view both the past and the future are unalterable. But in providing his model of retentions, protentions, modifications, etc. Husserl is not describing an arcane physical process which occurs to events as they loom out of the future, actualize themselves in the present and sink into the past, but is describing the changing spectrum of intentionalities linking the experiencing subject and the present-focused world which he experiences. 'Modification' is not a change in A itself, but a change in our view of A as the result of subsequent accretions of experience. It is only in consciousness that the past is modifiable, not in reality and not according to the logic of 'real' time: but that this modification takes place is undeniable.

Husserl summarizes his view of internal time-consciousness in the following passage:

Each actual 'now' of consciousness is subject to the law of modification. It changes into the retention of a retention, and does so continuesly. There accordingly arises a regular continuum of retentions such that every later point is the retention of every earlier one. Each retention is already a continuum. A tone begins and goes on steadily: its now-phase turns into a was-phase, and our impressional consciousness flows over into an ever new retentional consciousness. Going down the stream, we encounter a continuous series of retentions harking back to the starting-point . . . to each of such retentions a continuum of retentional modifications is added, and this continuum is itself a point in the actuality which is being retentionally projected . . . each retention is intrinsically a continuous modification, which so to speak carries its heritage of its past within itself. It is not merely the case that, going downstream, each earlier retention is replaced by a new one. Each later retention is not merely a continuous modification stemming from an original impression: it is also a continuous modification of all previous modifications of the same starting-point. (1928: 390, cited in Findlay 1975:10)

If I have understood Husserl correctly, I think that one can treat the horizontal axis of the diagram as representing the B-series sequence of dated events or states-of-affairs (A → B → C → D . . .) and the vertical axes as the A-series 'changes' in events as they acquire and lose tense-characteristics of futurity/ presentness/pastness (A → A' → A" → A'" . . .). From the B-series perspective, events do not change; they *are* changes: but from the A-series perspective events do undergo a kind of change, just as our view of a landscape changes as we move about in it, and observe it from different angles.

Future events likewise do not really change as a result of the fact that, from our point of view, they are becoming less indefinite, more imminent, and can be anticipated with increasing degrees of precision as they approach. But we have a strong compulsion to view them in such a light. Husserl's model treats this via a continuum of continua of protentional modifications. Protentions are continuations of the present in the light of the kind of temporal whole the present seems to belong to: 'To be aware of a developing whole incompletely, and as it develops, is yet always to be aware of it as a whole: what is not yet written in, is written in as yet to be written in' (Findlay 1975: 9).

Protentions are not anticipations of other present moments-in-being, but projections of the subsequent evolution of this one. As such, protentions may be disappointed or decisively fulfilled as the present evolves. It makes a great difference to the evaluation of an event or state of affairs if it were protended in a way highly at variance or not at all at variance to the way in which it actually occurs. Thus, if C' (future) protended from B is very different from C as it actually occurs, that will make a difference to the way in which C' (past) is retained subsequently at D. The way an event was anticipated as a future event (or not anticipated) makes a difference to the way in which that event is integrated into the past.

# Chapter 24

## The Temporal-perceptual Cycle

The next step in the construction of a general account of time cognition must be to place Husserl's protentional-retentional model in the context of an appropriate psychological theory of perception. It is not difficult to do this. Husserl's model is already half-way to being a psychological theory of the required kind, and it may indeed have indirectly influenced the construction of the generalized theory of perception I am about to outline, which is derived from the work of the noted cognitive psychologist, Ulric Neisser (1976). Although there has been much activity in the field of cognitive psychology since 1976, when Neisser published his account of the 'perceptual cycle', on which the ensuing account of time-perception is based, I am reasonably confident that Neisser's model still has a considerable degree of consensual support among cognitive psychologists, in broad terms, if not in all its details. It is certainly perfectly sufficient for the purposes of the present discussion, and it has the advantage of a high degree of formal compatibility with the Husserlian concept of subjective time, introduced just now.

Cognitive psychologists like Neisser emphasize the 'active' side to perception. To perceive is to match a perceptual input with a stored schema. This idea is easier to get across in the case of under-used perceptual channels (like touch) than it is with our most used senses (like sight). If one is blindfolded, then handed a small object with a request to identify it, mere passive registration would usually be insufficient to perform this task. To find out that the small object was, say, a potato-peeler would require some degree of active manipulation, otherwise it would hardly be distinguishable from an apple-corer, or even an ordinary, small kitchen-knife. This 'active' interrogation of the perceived object, so as to match it against a schema, Neisser calls 'sampling'. The outcome of active sampling, and the success, partial success or failure of attempts to match the sampled information with a stored schema, gives rise to another active feature of cognition, namely the modification of the stock of schemata in the light of subsequent experience. This active view of perception contrasts with the passive notion of perception as the registration of input for which the percipient is wholly irresponsible. Summarizing his view, Neisser writes:

> Perception is indeed a constructive process, but what is constructed is not a mental image appearing in consciousness, where it is admired by an inner man. At each moment the perceiver is constructing anticipations of certain kinds of information, that enable him to accept it as it becomes available. Often he must actively explore the optic [or haptic, auditory, etc.] array by moving his eyes or his head or his body. These explorations are directed by anticipatory schemata, which are plans for perceptual actions. . . . The outcome of the explorations – the information picked up – modifies the original [anticipatory] schema. Thus modified it directs further exploration and becomes ready for more information. (Neisser 1976: 20–1)

According to Neisser, perception is a cyclical process having three distinguishable phases: (1) input of information from the world outside, on the basis of exploratory movements or 'sampling'; (2) the application of an appropriate schema, from the stock of schemata available to the perceiver, to construe this information; and (3) the initiation (on the basis of the output of phase (2) of renewed exploratory movements or perceptual 'anticipations'. This feature of 'three-ness' invites immediate comparison with Husserl's threefold distinction among intentionalities towards the past (retentions), towards the present (percepts) and towards the future (protentions). It seems reasonable to observe that there is a parallelism between schemata and retentions, exploratory movements and protentions, and between constructs of the present environment and 'percepts'. That is to say, perception of the fleeting present is a phase in a more comprehensive process through which retentions of the past are fed forwards as anticipations of the future.

On the surface, Husserl's protentional-retentional model and Neisser's concept of the perceptual cycle seem to be designed to deal with distinct and unconnected intellectual questions. Husserl's model is a model of time-perception or 'internal time consciousness' – if not of A-series time itself; while Neisser's model is a model of perception, which the author does not present as having anything intrinsically to do with the psychology of time. Yet, if Husserl's 'protentions' coincide with Neisser's 'anticipations', Husserl's retentions coincide with Neisser's 'schemata', and if the general Husserlian framework of cognition as 'intentionality' essentially coincides with the psychologist's notion of perception as an 'activity' rather than as a passive registration of the external world, then there is reason enough to suspect that the two models are substantially identical.

This formal convergence has an important and obvious implication, namely, that perception is intrinsically time-perception, and conversely, time-perception, or internal time-consciousness, is just perception itself, not a special type of perception undertaken by special-purpose, time-perceiving senses. That is to say, time is not something we encounter as a feature of contingent reality, as if it lay outside us, waiting to be perceived along with tables and chairs and the rest of the perceptible contents of the universe. Instead, subjective time arises as an inescapable feature of the perceptual process itself, which enters into the perception of anything whatsoever. Time as an abstract dimension has no perceptible form, and in this sense there is no such thing as time-perception. There is only perception of the world in general, in all its aspects, which, whether it changes or not, is perceived via a cognitive process consisting of the endogenous 'perceptual cycle', or the 'retentional modifications' of Husserl, i.e. via a cognitive process which consists of changes or cumulative differences occurring over time.

A-series time, the kind of time that is modelled in Husserl's A-series diagram, is not in the final analysis a kind of 'time' at all, but a particular process which goes on in time and which is intrinsically temporal, namely, perception or more generally cognition, the active exploratory activity of the mind which goes on in time and through which time impinges on us subjectively.

The phases of the perceptual cycle of Neisser can be roughly identified with three traditionally recognized 'faculties' of the mind; the faculty of memory (of the immediate past), the faculty of perception (of the immediate present) and the faculty of imagination or foresight (of the immediate future). But in the perceptual cycle model these three faculties are revealed, not as independent, but as phases or moments of a single cyclical process. The difference is that whereas on the older faculty psychologies 'perception' was restricted to the passive

registration of inputs, in the cyclical model perception has acquired a new, expanded sense as encompassing the operations
of memory (the source of schemata to which inputs are matched
and in the light of which they are interpreted) and also foresight
(which directs the exploratory movements which produce perceptual inputs).

Neisser's perceptual cycle is a descendant of the 'cybernetic'
psychological models of Miller, Pribram and Galanter (1960) in
the theory of behaviour. The modification of schemata corresponds to the cybernetic notion of feedback (i.e. the updating of a
schema is the operation of feedback from perceptual exploration
onto the repertoire of perceptual schemata maintained by the
organism) while the operation of 'anticipation' corresponds to
the cybernetic notion of feed-forward (perceptual exploration is
directed by the feed-forward of previously laid down schemata).
We may propose, therefore, that the A-series notion of the 'past'
as something continuously undergoing modification, as in Husserl's model, is the temporal cognitive outcome of the cybernetic
process of feedback which continuously renews the stock of
schemata which constitutes the internal representation of reality
maintained by the subject. Conversely, the A-series notion of
the 'future' corresponds to the processes of feed-forward whereby the contents of internal representations (schemata) become
the basis for anticipation, exploration and engagement with the
world. Past and future have no absolute ontological basis, but
are aspects of the cognitive functioning of the organism, obliged
to contend with a world (i.e. the ontologically real world spread
out in B-series time) which transcends the accessible domain of
subjectivity, by forming internal representations of it, which are
continually modified and updated.

If we equate Husserl's central idea of 'modification' with the
analogous idea employed by Neisser (cybernetic feedback), then
we are in a position to offer a constructive criticism of Husserl's
model as it stands. Because it is clear that there is nothing in
Husserl's model which corresponds to the idea of 'feed-forward'
yet implicitly the whole model rests on it. If we look once more
at the Husserl diagram (Figure 23.1), we see a network of protentions probing into the future. But what are the origins of the
stipulated states-of-affairs thus protended as the imminent future of a given present? Protended states-of-affairs can have no
other basis than that they are extrapolated (modified) versions
of the past. In other words, 'protentions' are intentionalities

directed towards feed-forward versions of the past, but this feeding-forwards of retentions as protentions is not explicitly represented in Husserl's model, giving rise to the illusion that protentions are towards some ontologically real 'future', not towards a merely 'stipulated' future, which is derived from modified, fed-forward retentions of the past. Husserl's diagram can be recast to incorporate feed-forward, at which point it becomes essentially identical to the Neisser perceptual-cycle model (Figure 24.1).

Having established the idea that time-perception is coextensive with perception *per se*, and more generally, that time-cognition is coextensive with cognition as a process, the next step in the argument must be to articulate the relationship between A-series processual/perceptual/cognitive 'time' and B-series time, i.e. ontologically real time, time which is not an aspect of cognitive functioning, but a feature of the layout of the objectively real world. Here it is useful to introduce an analogy with spatial perception/cognition. There is an obvious similarity between 'subjective' space (i.e. space as viewed from a set of egocentric co-ordinates with objects displayed in perspective, diminishing and fading away into the distance) and A-series time, which depends on the 'perspective' of the momentary 'now'-moment. But, as was noted above (Chapter 17), just because solid rectangular objects 'look' like irregular trapezoids, etc. when seen in perspective, that does not mean that we believe them to possess any attributes in themselves, which depend on our particular perspectival vantage point when viewing them from our own spatial co-ordinates. They are as they are (i.e. rectangular) however they may appear, momentarily, to us. Their 'real' spatial attributes are the ones which would be recorded, not in a perspective view, but in a designer's set of plans, in which right-angles would consistently be represented as right-angles, and so on. Similarly, to represent the spatial 'truth' about a landscape requires a map or its equivalent, not a topographical sketch, however realistically executed, or a photograph, taken from some specific vantage point within the landscape to be represented. The distinction between the 'plan' of an object, or the 'map' of a place, and a 'view' or 'image' of an object or a place dictated by a particular set of 'perspective' co-ordinates corresponds to the logical distinction between 'non-indexical' and 'indexical' utterances, propositions, truths, etc. That is, if we consider a perspective drawing of an object as

**Figure 24.1   Husserl's model as a perceptual cycle**

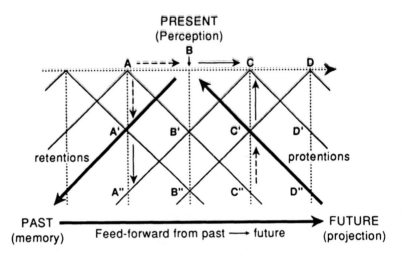

a kind of 'utterance' (which it is) then it is an utterance which is 'true' only if it is uttered at certain spatial co-ordinates, i.e. the ones which dictate precisely the diminutions, foreshortenings and changes in angular relations shown in that perspective view, and not in all the other possible ones. But a plan or a map is non-indexically true, if it is true at all, i.e. it has truth conditions which are the same whatever the perspective from which the object represented is viewed, by a viewer who entertains this plan, or this map, as a 'true representation' of the object.

'Tensed' propositions or beliefs are analogous to perspective views in having indexical truth-conditions, Thus, to say, 'I am going to Birmingham today' is true if said on days when a trip to Birmingham occurs, and not on any other days, while the tenseless statement, 'Alfred goes to Birmingham on the 14 May 1999', if it is true now, was no less true in 1066, and as it will be in 2001. The distinction between indexical, 'tensed' or 'perspectival' utterances, beliefs, representations, etc. vs. untensed, non-indexical, or 'map' beliefs, representations, etc. has already been introduced in the discussion (Chapters 17–18) of Mellor's defence of the reality of B-series time. In the course of that discussion, mention was made of the fact that sentient individuals hold two kind of 'beliefs' about the world, which Mellor describes in terms of a transient flow of 'tensed' perceptual indexical beliefs deriving from the process of perception, on the one hand, and a stock of non-indexical, tenseless beliefs on the other. The problem, as Mellor notes, is to act always in a 'timely' manner, on the basis of indexically true beliefs about what is the right thing to do *now*, in the face of the twin difficulties that (1) tensed beliefs are continually becoming false, automatically, because we no longer occupy the co-ordinates which alone guaranteed their fleeting truth, and (2) that tenseless beliefs, even if true, are by definition not such as to apply to particular co-ordinates, and cannot therefore provide the spur to timely action. There is only one solution to these difficulties, and that is to establish a system for converting indexically true beliefs of fleeting truth into non-indexical beliefs which are potentially applicable to all co-ordinates, and conversely for converting non-indexical beliefs into a set of indexically true, equivalent beliefs, which correspond, in content, to any given non-indexical belief, interpreted for particular sets of indexical co-ordinates.

I have published separately an article (Gell 1985b) dealing with this question in relation to the problem of navigating in space. When we make use of a map (which is a set of non-indexical spatial beliefs) we allow the map to generate a series of mental images which correspond, not to the map itself, but to certain perspectival views of the world, street-level scenes, as it were, which, if they correspond at all to what we can actually see of our current surroundings, permit us to identify our current position in map-space. Maps have to be turned into images in order to become useful, because the world never appears to us as it appears in a map. But on the other hand, no matter how exhaustive a set of indexical images we may have stored up, showing our spatial surroundings from all possible perspectives, none of these images is of any use navigationally unless they can be located on a map. The process of spatial navigation consists of turning maps (including 'mental maps', i.e. non-indexical spatial beliefs) into images, and conversely, locating images (indexical spatial beliefs) on maps.

The same kinds of consideration apply to events in B-series time as apply to places in map-space. Turning to Figure 24.2 we can make the following distinctions. The temporal B-series, pursuing the navigational analogy, can be identified as the 'territory' – the real layout of events in time – of which we, as sentient individuals, have to form representations, which take the form of maps. The B-series temporal territory is, however, inaccessible. We have no capacity to know events as they are laid out in

B-series time, but we are obliged to construct representations of this layout in order to 'navigate' in time, that is, in order to know how to act in a timely manner, so as to minimize our opportunity costs (see Chapter 22 above). The internal representation we construct of the B-series temporal territory consists of a B-series 'time-map', or a corpus of non-indexical temporal belief inscriptions. But this internal representation or cognitive map of B-series time does not correspond to perceptual time. Perceptual time, the time which, unlike the time of the B-series temporal territory, is accessible to consciousness, is an on-going A-series flux of images, undergoing the protential/perceptual/retentional sequence of modifications described by Husserl. Figure 24.2 shows the temporal-perceptual cycle as a two-way series of conversions through which incoming perceptual information is mapped onto the internal time-map, by locating on that map the co-ordinates which generate the image (or schema) which corresponds best to perceptual input, and reciprocally, the map is made to generate anticipations, or protentions, of the proximate future which are fed forward to guide perceptual exploration and, if necessary, action, with respect to the real temporal territory. Thus, within the A-series enclave – the lighted circle of our intuition – indexical images, generated from non-indexical cognitive maps, are matched against incoming information from perceptual exploration and physical manipulation of the environment, leading to the formation of perceptual beliefs (indexical 'fixes'). These token indexical fixes are then fed back into the corpus of internalized 'map' beliefs, which may be updated if necessary.

The perceptual cycle underlying cognition in general, and time-cognition in particular, is now represented as follows:

1. Inputs to perception, causally conditioned by the interaction between the form of the B-series temporal territory and the endogenously produced perceptual-exploratory movements of the percipient are matched against fed-forward 'images' derived from underlying B-series map-beliefs. The outcome of this matching process are token-indexical perceptual beliefs specifying the 'present' state of affairs.
2. The image which is 'confirmed' as 'true-at-present' is then referred back to the underlying cognitive map, and the co-ordinates which generate that particular image are identified (i.e. 'if image A is true at present, then I, the percipient, am at

co-ordinates x, y, on the map'). These co-ordinates may be the expected ones, in which case the map is valid, or they may be unexpected ones, in which case the map may be modified, old map-beliefs being discarded and new ones substituted for them (feedback).

3. On the basis of the most recently determined co-ordinates, the cycle recommences via the generation of a further series of images from the map of proximate 'future' perceptual inputs, which will be matched agaist the actual input resulting from the appropriate exploratory movements, etc.

In general terms, temporal cognition can therefore be conceptualized as a triangular relationship between perception (input), memory (schema, recall) and anticipation (foresight, projection). Perception appertains to the present, memory to the past, anticipation to the future. The basic cycle runs from perception (present) to memory (past) to anticipation (future), and so on, in an endless round. It is the continuous activity which we ourselves engage in, generating images, matching them with perceptual input and locating them at co-ordinates on our internalized maps of the world, which persuades us that future, present and past are rushing by with an uncontrollable dynamism of their own. The continual updating of our perceptual belief gives rise to our inward sense of 'time' as a dynamic process rather than a simple dimensional characteristic of the real world which we inhabit. In time's passage, however, we only encounter the flux of our own spiritual powers, which we reify and project onto the cosmos, which simply *is*, and knows nothing of past, present and future.

Perceptual images are mapped onto the corpus of B-series belief-inscriptions, which form the basis of mental maps of time. These internal representations of B-series time, besides providing the co-ordinates onto which perceptual images are mapped, also generate templates, in the form of anticipations of the proximate future, which are involved in the active process of perception itself. It is only in as much as incoming information can be construed as corresponding to something already *stipulated* (i.e. generated from the corpus of belief-inscriptions) that perceptual identifications are possible, and perceptual beliefs arise. We thus have two kinds of image: those that are of the proximate past and are identified with co-ordinates on the map, and those that are of the proximate future, and are generated from this map. Internal time-consciousness consists of the flux through which images of the proximate future (protentions in Husserl's terms) are confirmed (via a process of 'sampling' of incoming perceptual information) as images of the proximate past (retentions) which are added to the corpus of perceptual beliefs.

The general model presented in Figure 24.2 shows the Husserlian model of internal time-consciousness *encapsulated* in its B-series context, rather than standing on its own as originally presented (see Figure 23.1 ). The A-series, the world of images, the world of subjective time-awareness, is an enclave within the 'real' B-series world, the world that is logically prior, but perceptually inaccessible. The A-series is the temporal world we experience directly. But it is not the temporal 'territory', the real world itself, laid out flat in B-series four-dimensional time, of which we form representations, also B-series in character, which are our mental maps of time. In the B-series temporal territory, there are only the events that happen, and moreover must happen by logical (but not causal) necessity, since if the proposition, couched in the B-series idiom of dates, that 'event e happens at date D, is true now, it always was true and always will be true, and could never be other than true at any time whatsoever. The temporal territory is the layout of events in the four-dimensional universe: what makes the things we believe about events in time timelessly true or false, but to which we have no access directly. We have no direct access to the temporal territory because all our mental life, all our experiences, beliefs, expectations, etc. are themselves datable events, confined to their localized time-frames, like all other datable events. Even though some of these temporal beliefs may, logically speaking, be true at all times, the believing of these beliefs (arriving at them, confirming them, changing them or whatever) are events in time. Whether our temporal beliefs in the logically 'timeless' mode are 'timelessly true' we shall never know one way or the other. What we *can* know, on the other hand, is that images formed from perceptual information are *consistent* with images generated from our maps of the B-series temporal territory. The A-series enclave is sandwiched between the 'real' B-series temporal territory, and the B-series representations we maintain in the form of internal simulacra or 'models' of the real world. On these internal B-series models we base our interpretative schemes for construing perceptual inputs, and the anticipatory

**Figure 24.2  A general model of time cognition**

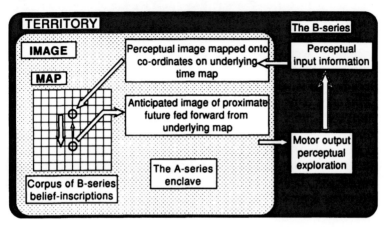

'projections' which underlie our activities in the real world.

But at this point we must introduce the theme of the multiplicity of 'possible worlds'. There is a fundamental asymmetry between the 'real' B-series temporal territory, and the representations we maintain of this territory in the form of mental time-maps. The temporal 'map' preserves the B-series temporal logic of the 'real' world, but not the relationship between the real world and the subject. We have *total access*, as subjects, to our maps of time; but we have no access, as subjects, to the four-dimensional manifold of which these are the maps. There is no experience, which a human being is capable of having, which corresponds to a view of the 'real' four-dimensional space-time manifold comprehended *sub specie æternitatis*. This is the essence of time as a human, rather than merely physical phenomenon. All our vital interests, in health, wealth, progeny, salvation, depend on the disposition of 'real' events in 'real' time, but we have no recourse to these events taking place in real time because, physically speaking, each one of us is only another smear of events, not belonging to another category at all from the events in which we are so interested. Our happiness depends on mastering time and transcending it, but time is us: as Borges (1970) says, 'time is the river which carries me away, but I am that river; time is the tiger that devours me, but I am that tiger'. Our access to time is confined to the A-series flux, through which we interact with 'real' time, via the mediation of temporal maps which provide us with a surrogate for real time.

These reconstructions of B-series time are not the real thing (the map is distinct from the territory), but we are obliged to rely on them.

Because time-maps are not the real thing, they are capable of including events and states of affairs which are in alternativeness relationships with one another, whereas the temporal territory is as it is, always was and always will be. This is the basic difference between 'human time', i.e. time as cognised by us, and 'real' time. The temporal world to which we have access directly lies on the hither side of the dividing line between the temporal territory and the A-series enclave; 'human' as opposed to 'physical' time is an encapsulated world of images and maps, constructs, beliefs, etc. This encapsulated temporality has a different logical texture from the temporal territory which it seeks, more or less faithfully, to reflect. In particular, human time is *modalized*, (describable, that is to say, only according to a logic which admits of alternative 'possible' truth-values for propositions) whereas there seems no reason, to me at any rate, to admit to the category of 'real' events and states of affairs in the B-series manifold, events and states of affairs which are only possibly or 'potentially' the case.

I distinguish sharply, therefore, between the domain of human (i.e. cognitive) time and the domain of physical time: even when human beings construct B-series time-maps (internal models of the temporal territory, in the light of which they construe their experience and formulate plans of action) these models are constructed according to a logical pattern, which is not at all the same as the presumptive logical patterning of the relationships between events and states of affairs in the physical substrate. The temporal territory is a unique, deterministic, closed system. Our internal representations of this territory, in the form of maps, are multiple, indeterminate and logically open-textured. They are this way because of the imperfect nature of knowledge, the inaccessibility of spatio-temporally remote regions of the four-dimensional manifold, and the fact that many interpretations can be placed even on the information we have at our disposal. The internal models which guide perception and behaviour are multitudinous, variable, changeable and provisional: the real world is none of these things. The real world is pervaded by causal relationships, and in as much as we are embedded as physical beings in this physical matrix, we are part of this causal texture ourselves. But our relationship, as subjects, to the mental models we ourselves maintain is not one of causality in any simple sense. What we have towards our internal representations are not causal linkages, but 'propositional attitudes' (belief, disbelief, conditional belief, etc.). To believe a belief is not to do anything causal to that belief or have that belief do anything causal to oneself: it is only to have a certain attitude towards that belief, i.e. to hold it to be true in itself and to have true consequences. Everything begins and ends in the 'real' world, but that is not 'our' world. 'Our' world is a shifting play of images, and maps that locate and generate these images.

# Chapter 25

# The Modalization and Counterfactuality of Time-maps

A time-map is not a unique representation of a fixed complement of states of affairs which are realized at particular temporal and spatial indices. It represents, not a single world, but a network of possible worlds, linked by a lattice of interconnections which branches and merges – the 'Garden of Forking Paths' of which Borges has written so evocatively. The underlying logic of temporal cognition is the logic of this network of possible worlds, and the process of temporal cognition consists of charting the paths which lead from one possible world to another. A branch of modal logic (temporal logic) deals with the formal properties of networks of temporally indexed possible worlds. If we want to gain an idea of temporal cognitive universals, it is to this branch of logical enquiry that we must turn.

The first point to make in introducing temporal logic as a possible basis for temporal cognitive universals is that from the point of view of standard logic, it is redundant.

Since the publication of B. Wilson's collection on *Rationality* (1971) anthropologists have been accustomed to the idea that rules of ordinary logic are necessary for any communication system operated by human beings for the purpose of exchanging intelligible messages to one another, and are not special products of western culture. Human beings are not necessarily aware of these rules, but they apply them for practical reasons all the time. In so far as human beings think reasonably, this is how they must reasonably think:

> 'p implies p' 'not (p and not p)' 'p and (p implies q) implies q' [axioms in standard logic] express more than axioms in a particular system of rules or rules in a particular game. They express, rather, requirements for something's being a system of logical reasoning at all. (Hollis, in Wilson 1971: 232)

But just because of this, there is no reason suppose that 'temporal logic' is part of the foundations on which all intelligible thought must rest, in the manner of Hollis. Here is a typical syllogism in standard logic:

All P's are Q's
V is a P
therefore, V is a Q.

And here is a piece of temporal reasoning:

All people born on 12 June are Geminis
Alfred Gell was born on 12 June
Alfred Gell is a Gemini.

Simply because the ostensible subject matter of an instance of logical reasoning is a temporal fact does not mean in the least that 'temporal logic', as we are about to encounter it, is in any way involved. Ordinary logic is time-indifferent; temporal operators make no appearance as part of the logical *apparatus* (all, some, assertion, negation, true, false, etc.), and temporal indices only appear as part of the faceless P's and Q's which serve as 'variables' in the system. Ordinarily, temporal considerations are not permitted to intrude into the standard system of propositional calculus, and if the undoubted adequacy of this system for formally representing truth and inference is anything to go by, the implication would be that time does not have any specific 'logic' which would set it apart as a cognitive universal; i.e. men might think as they like about time and leave the fundamental categories of logic unaltered, since these are by definition time-indifferent, which would mean that we would be frustrated in seeking a 'logical' basis for time as a cognitive universal.

There is, however, a possible let-out. If it should prove that temporal logic is not structurally different from detemporalized logic, then the validity and universality of detemporalized logic would itself be grounds for accepting a temporal 'reading' of logic as an adequate representation of the way we are obliged to think about temporal relations. And this, as I understand it, is essentially what modern logicians, following the pioneering investigations of Prior (1966, 1968), have achieved, in demonstrating the structural affinities between temporal logic and certain

generally accepted systems of modal logic, which were originally
developed entirely without temporal considerations in view.

Modal logic is the branch of logic which extends the propositional calculus by including operators for necessity (□) and
possibility (◇), as well as the usual array of propositional variables (p, q, ) and operators for conjunction (●), disjunction (v),
implication (→), equivalence (↔) negation (~), plus the universal
and existential quantifiers (all, none). Temporal logic can be
understood in its simplest terms as what happens to modal logic
when temporal (called 'Megarian') interpretations are given to
the modal operators □ and ◇. This is done by linking 'possible'
to the existential quantifier (some, at least one) and 'necessary'
to the universal quantifier (all) and thinking of necessary truth
as that which is true at all times, and contingent truths as true at
at least one time. Compare these two interpretations of the
modal operators:

□ p means that p is the case in all possible worlds
◇ p means that p is the case in at least one possible world

□ p means that p is the case at all times (dates)
◇ p means that p is the case at at least one time (date)

While the second set of interpretations, the Megarian ones, are
without doubt inferior to the first (modal) ones, none the less
they do link 'necessity' vs. 'possibility to 'all' vs. 'some' in the
same general way. Add to this the Aristotelian idea that any
event is possible prior to its occurrence, actual as it occurs, and
necessary thereafter, and the foundation is laid for a treatment
of modalities in which possibility/necessity is a function of dated
states of affairs (temporal worlds) viewed as *enchained possible
worlds*. If we take the further step of restricting 'possible worlds'
to imagined world-states of this actual world (the world we
believe in, the world shown in our cognitive maps) rather than
the limitless possible worlds, not necessarily believed in, or
believable in, of logicians' fictions, then we can conceive of a
modal/temporal logic operating in a possible-worlds context
sufficiently like the world as we actually believe it to be, to serve
as a realistic simulacrum of the logical mechanism actually employed by individuals while subsuming their experience under
universal logico-temporal categories.

But how does temporal logic actually work? The strategy of

temporal logic is to refashion the axioms of various systems of modal logic using Megarian operators. One very concise exposition of temporal logic in this manner is Rescher's *Chronological Logic* (1968), which is the temporal-logical analogue of the modal-logical system S.5 formulated by Lewis, which is now considered the most appropriate formulation of the logic of truth and necessity (Rescher and Urquhart 1971; Hintikka 1969; for a brilliant and engaging introduction to S.5, see Bradley and Bradley 1979). Rescher introduces the idea of 'chronological realization' as a more precise way of stating whether 'p' is the case at a given time or set of times. Thus, R means 'it is realized' and Rtp means 'it is realized at time t that p', where t stands for a date in a chronological system (i.e. not a deictic, token-indexical time-expression like 'today', 'tomorrow', 'three days hence', etc.). Rescher's axioms for chronological logic are as follows:

Axiom T1 Rt (~) p → ~Rt (p) (negation)
Axiom T2 [Rt (p) • Rt (q)] → Rt (p • q) (conjunction)
Axiom T3 (for All t) Rt (p) → p (necessity)
Axiom T4.1 [(for All t) Rt (p) → Rt (p) (possibility)
Axiom T5.1 (i) Rt '[Rt (p)] → Rt (p)
Axiom T5.1 (ii) Rt '[Rt (p)] → Rt' + t (p)
(Rescher 1968)

We do not need to follow out the working of this system of temporal logic in any detail. The first two axioms relate directly to ordinary logical notions about conjunction and negation (i.e. are identical in content to the logical axioms considered by Hollis and others to be essential to any intelligible system of reasoning). The third axiom is the temporal-logical definition of necessity. The last two axioms (T5.1 (i) and (ii), which are alternatives, are only relevant if the fourth axiom is retained, and it is on this fourth axiom that our attention needs to be focused. Rescher's axiom 4.1 corresponds to the crucial defining axiom of the S.5 modal logical system of Lewis, the original codifier of modal logics.

What I am about to argue is that this axiom is too powerful for the kind of temporal logic which underlies ordinary cognition. This axiom distinguishes prescriptive, metaphysical, temporal logic from the kind of temporal logic which descriptively can be held to characterize our natural thought-processes. It represents the logic of the temporal territory, as it *must* (logically speaking) be: but it does not represent the kind of logic which governs our cognitive maps of time. It is the logical axiom which would hold if our mental maps of time showed us a world which was perfectly known, perfectly accessible to us: but our mental maps do not show us such a world, only a plurality of mutually alternative worlds, some of which we may encounter, some of which we never will, but we do not know which.

The modal axiom to which T4.1 corresponds is the Axiom A 10 of Lewis's modal system S.5, which is $\Diamond p \rightarrow \Box \Diamond p$. What A 10 says is that if p is possible, it is necessary that p is possible. Given Megarian interpretations of $\Box$ and $\Diamond$, this is the same as saying: if p is the case at at least one time, then it is at all times the case that p is the case at at least one time. Let us see how this corresponds to Rescher's axiom T 4.1. This states that the realization of p at t, being realized at all times, is the same as the realization of p at t. Or, loosely, but I hope comprehensibly, if some event is going to be realized at t, it would be true to say at *any* time, that that event was going to be realized at t.

This way of formulating temporal logic puts an outer shell of necessity around a soft body of possibility. In Rescher's system, states of affairs which are possible, i.e. realized at some time, are admitted only under the tutelage of necessity: axiom T 4.1 ensures that every statement which refers to an event in some possible temporal world is equivalent to a more comprehensive statement which refers to that event in all possible temporal worlds.

The effect of an axiom like T 4.1 is to secure the hegemony of chronological logic, so that it becomes strictly equivalent to non-temporal modal logic, in particular to S.5, the most powerful system of modal logic. But the consequence of this gain in logical power is that temporal logic loses the kind of cognitive verisimilitude we are seeking. Each temporal world in this system is a mirror-image over every other one, in that whatever is true or false in any one of them, is true or false in all the others, the only difference being a shift in temporal co-ordinates. There is, however, an alternative axiomatization of modal logic, Lewis's system S.4, in which A 10 is deleted and is replaced by the weaker axiom A 9, which is $\Diamond p \rightarrow \Diamond \Diamond p$ ('if it is possible that p, then it is possible that p is possible'). That is, in S.4 one does not argue, as one does in S.5 from the existence of a certain possibility to the necessity of that possibility (i.e. $\Diamond p \rightarrow \Box \Diamond p$).

With Megarian operators this comes out as 'if it is at some time the case (in some temporal world) that p, then it is at some time (in some temporal world) the case that p is the case at some time' (but not in all temporal worlds, only in *some* of them).

The modal logical idea of necessity is founded on the idea that what is necessary is necessary in all possible worlds ($\Box p \rightarrow \Box\Box p$) and that what is possible is necessarily possible in some world or worlds ($\Diamond p \rightarrow \Box\Diamond p$). This formalization is the preferred system for system *alethic* logical contexts (Lyons 1977), contexts in which ultimate metaphysical doctrines about truth and necessity are under consideration. Because a possibility which is not ever, in fact, going to be realized, is not from the standpoint of a theory of ultimate truth really a 'possibility' at all. It is not even a might have been, because never, at any stage, was it really going to be the case. But S.5 is not the system of choice in *epistemic* contexts, i.e. contexts in which not ultimate truth, but the *de facto* characteristics of human knowledge and belief systems, are the focus of concern. Because here we are obliged to think of possibilities as genuinely existing at certain times, in relation to certain possible worlds (worlds which we believe to be possible, anyway, even if they are not so in reality) but as not existing in relation to other possible worlds, at other times, in other circumstances (worlds in which that particular possibility has been foreclosed on, and has lost the feasibility it once may have possessed).

S.5 is the modal system of 'timeless' truth: S.4 gives rise to a path structure of enchained possible worlds. In S.4 it is allowable to express the idea that if we take a route through possibility A, then possibility S arises; while if we take a route through possibility B, then possibility R arises, and not vice versa, although we may also think that possibility S and possibility R both make for the possibility of Z. In S.5, this cannot work, because what is possible in any one world is necessarily possible, i.e. equally a possibility in the light of all the worlds in the system and hence is 'modally accessible' from all possible worlds. Figure 25.1 contrasts the modal-accessibility relation between worlds in S.5 vs. S.4.

We are now in a position to follow certain arguments which have been put forward by Lucas (1973) who provides a discussion of temporal logic (and tense logic) which can readily be interpreted cognitively. Lucas presents his account of tense logic in the context of the following definitions of necessity and possibility, which reflect the idea of temporal pathways between enchained possible worlds. A world is reachable (modally accessible) from another world if the second world is 'feasible' in respect to the first.

$\Box p$ = 'p true in all worlds which are feasible in relation to a given world'.

$\Box \sim p$ = 'p is true in no world which is feasible in relation to a given world'.

$\Diamond p$ = 'p is true in at least one world which is feasible in relation to a given world'.

$\Diamond \sim p$ = 'p is not true in at least one world which is feasible in relation to a given world'.

$\Box$ and $\Diamond$ are interdefinable ($\Box p = \sim \Diamond \sim p$, $\Diamond p = \sim \Box \sim p$).

Modal tense logic, constructed using these definitions, will show which worlds are modally 'open' (feasible contingents, neither necessary nor impossible) and which are modally 'closed' (either the case in all possible worlds or the case in none of them). In temporal logic with S.5 axioms the relationship between relative possible worlds is an equivalence relation; if $\Diamond p$ then $\Box \Diamond p$ 'if p is possible, then for all possible worlds, p is possible'. But in tense logic with S.4 axioms where $\Diamond p$ only implies $\Diamond \Diamond p$ for the system as a whole, then there is no contradiction between p being a possibility in relation to world A and not being a possibility in relation to world B. The relation between worlds in S.4 is not an equivalence one, but a transitive, asymmetric one. This enables one to capture the idea of possibilities being open at some times and foreclosed on at others, and accords well with the idea of temporal cognitive maps as a relational networks between mutually interacting worlds/states of affairs, focused on the sociological subject and articulated in terms of his projects and his beliefs about how the world works, or may possibly work.

However, Lucas goes on to say, S.4 suffers from the defect that in representing temporal worlds as a network of asymmetrically related relative possible worlds, S.4 does not secure a linear enchainment of worlds, but only an oriented network (as in

Figure 25.1) and that this conflicts with our standard notion of time as linear (non-branching, non-merging). If, under S.4 rules, we construct a network diagram of relative possible worlds, the relations between nodes (worlds) in the network are transitive and non-symmetric, so the arrows have to point in one direction.

Suppose we interpret the solid arrows on Figure 25.2 as meaning 'is a feasible future world of W O' and the dashed arrows as 'is a feasible past world of W O', W O being a zero, or index, world. Reading figure 25.2 according to the solid arrows gives a plausible picture of a branching, 'open' future, in which the truth of ($\Diamond$p • $\Diamond$q) in W O, can give rise to a path leading to a world in which (p • q) is true (W O 1.2), one in which (p• ~q) is true (W O. 1.1) and to one in which ~ (p • q) is true (W 0.2.2). This kind of branching future, in which some of the possibilities which are open in a given 'present' will be abolished if events take a certain course in the future, is the natural way of thinking about the future adopted by sentient, decision-making agents.

It is not, however, a natural way of thinking about possibilities for logicians or philosophers, who are inclined to believe that a possibility which is not going to be realized is not a possibility, whether or not this fact is known, or knowable, by any sentient being. To use a classical instance, if there is a shell on the bottom of the sea, which is not, in fact, ever going to be seen by anybody (and there must be plenty of such shells), it is not logically speaking a possibility that such a shell be seen, even if it is quite feasible in terms of the state of the art of diving technology for someone to go and have a look at it. This follows directly from A10 (if it is contingently not the case that p, it is necessarily contingently not the case that p, where 'p' is the seeing of the shell by someone). The S.4 future, logically unattractive from the alethic point of view, is much more attractive from the epistemic point of view, since it allows us to take into account the persistent seeability of never actually to be seen sea-shells. It mirrors the cognitive process whereby we project, on the basis of possibilities which seem to be open to us in the present, a multiplicity of incompatible futures, between which we must choose.

But what happens when we read Figure 25.2 according to the dashed arrows? Can we contemplate a branching, incompatible array of pasts? Could there be one past in which (p • q) was the case, and another past in which (p • ~q) was the case, and still

**Figure 25.1   Modal accessibility relations in S.5, S.4 and S.4.3 modal systems**

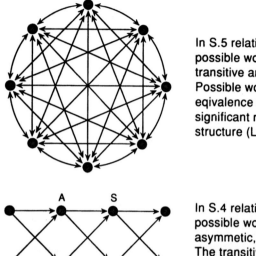

In S.5 relations between possible worlds are reflexive, transitive and symmetric. Possible worlds form an eqivalence class without significant relational structure (Lucas:266)

In S.4 relations between possible worlds are reflexive asymmetic, and transitive. The transitivity of the S.4 relational structure mirrors the before/after relation between worlds, but the past, present, and future are not unique.

In S.4.3 the only permissible arrangement is the linear one.

another in which ~(p • q) was the case? Lucas accepts the verisimilitude of the branching future, but says that an S.4 past would contradict a basic assumption that the past should be linear and unique.

Here, I think, Lucas is adopting a particular philosophical stance, one which is no doubt highly defensible, but not one which need play any part in our specification of temporal cognitive universals. What he is really seeking is a metaphysically justifiable conception of *tense*, rather than time, i.e. basic ontological discrimination between past, present and future states of affairs, which is the A-theoreticians' primary philosophical objective. I am not convinced that this particular objective can be

**Figure 25.2  The branching future and/or past**

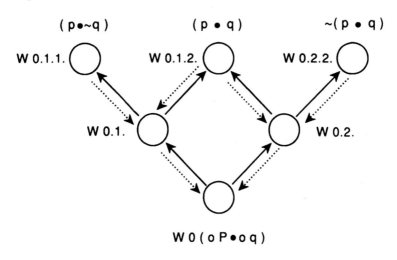

W 0 ( o P • o q )

attained, since, as I have made clear, I think of tense (the A-series past–present–future transition) as an epiphenomenon of our organismic point of vantage on the world, not as a real feature of the B-series temporal territory. But what I am attempting to do here is to specify the kind of minimal logical attributes of *B-series time-maps*, the internalized representations of the temporal territory which guide our practical cognition and activity. I am not trying to describe the logic of the B-series itself, but only the logic of our internal representations of it. Consequently, what is from Lucas's point of view a disadvantage of S.4 temporal logic – failure to represent the difference between the linear past and the branching future, is from my point of view an advantage, since it is of the essence of the idea of a 'map' – including a time-map – that it remains unaffected by the co-ordinates of the map-user. Lucas's temporal model with its linear past and branching future has indexicality built into it, and consequently lacks this property.

Let us look at Lucas's arguments on this point, however. We can entertain, he says, the idea that starting from different points of origin (say W 0.1.1 or W 0.2.2), separate lines of development might have ensued, both of which culminate in W 0, but this cannot alter the fact that only one of these lines of development could actually occur. We need, therefore, a means of keeping the enchained possible worlds of S.4 within linear bounds, so that the only past possible worlds which are feasible relative to a given world, are the worlds which actually did lead up to the world in question. Dummett and Lemmon (1959) added a further axiom to S.4, which, translated into temporal-logical terms, ensures that relative possible worlds are enchained only linearly, and not in branching or lattice configurations. This axiom is equivalent to the modal axiom:

$$\Diamond p \bullet \Diamond q \rightarrow \Diamond (\Diamond p \bullet \Diamond q) \text{ v } \Diamond (p \bullet \Diamond q) \text{ v } \Diamond (p \bullet q).$$

The addition of this axiom to S.4 renders the branching sequence between W 0 and W 0.1.1 (p • ~q) and W 0.2.2 ~ (p • q) infeasible, because it ensures that if ($\Diamond$p • $\Diamond$q) is the case, any world in which p is the case or possible the case is a world in which q is the case or possibly the case, and vice versa. Or, turning 'possibly' into 'in some past world', if p and q are the case in the past of W 0, or if only p was true in some past world of W 0, q was true in some world which was possible relative to the world in which p was true, and did become true later, or alternatively, if q was true in some past world of W 0, and not p, p was true in some world possible relative to that world, and likewise did become true later. We can write the axiom out as:

Past p • Past q → Past (p • q) v Past (Past p • q) v Past (p • Past q).

The system S.4 plus the Dummett–Lemmon axiom ensuring the linear enchainment of possible worlds is known as the system S4.3, and is intermediate between S.4 and S.5. Lucas takes the view that it is the correct axiomatization for the past, but sees no reason to introduce it for the future, since the S.4 future makes sense as a plurality of now-feasible, incompatible futures which will come about, or not, according to the actions we decide to engage in, and their outcomes. Lucas draws a comparison to a man's genealogical tree. The past, he says, is like a man's ascendants (he has one father, his father had one father, etc.), while the future is like a man's descendants (he has many sons, his sons have many sons, and so on). The point where the past ends and the future begins is the present, which is preceded by a unique series of pasts and is followed by a branching tree of alternative futures.

Why should the past be unique, though? And if the past is unique, should not the future be so as well? The 'genealogy' analogy should not mislead us: this world may only have one unique enchainment of antecedent father-worlds, but it is not going to have a diverging array of son-worlds, just one unique enchainment, even though, as of now (the son-world having yet to be born) the identity of the son-world is undetermined, and numerous possibilities exist. Father-worlds and son-worlds on Lucas's genealogical-tree analogy have different statuses, father-worlds being unique, determinate, competitor-less, son-worlds multiple, merely potential, unrealized. But if one took the analogy literally, it would imply that one antecedent world could really give rise to many subsequent ones, which cannot be the case.

Meanwhile, Lucas's arguments for the uniqueness of the past are alethic ones. His main argument boils down to the assertion that the Dummett–Lemmon axiom is needed for the past because past states of affairs have either been the case, or they haven't, and there is no room in the past for events which once might have taken place (at some past time, prior to the appropriate moment for their realization) but did not, in fact, do so. This appears to me to be a wholly valid alethic argument about the past, but I see no reason to think that it is not alethically valid for the future as well. Future events, which seem possible to us, but which are not actually going to take place, are not 'real' possibilities in the alethic sense: they would be excluded, as necessarily not the case from the compendium of possible worlds. Epistemically, things are different: certainly we can contemplate as epistemic possibilities a plurality of possible futures: but epistemically we can also contemplate a plurality of possible pasts, and possible presents too, for that matter. We may be sure that the past consists of a unique series of antecedent worlds, but we do not know which these worlds are, any more than we know which worlds are going to be realized in future. Nor do we really know which of a number of 'possible' present worlds, the present world truly is.

Rather than following Lucas's tactic of associating S.4.3 with the past and S.4 with the future, I suggest the following. The logic of the B-series temporal territory, and the *alethic* frame of reference generally, is S.5. Purely from the standpoint of truth and necessity, the universe consists of the totality states of affairs which actually are going to be realized at determinate space-time co-ordinates. Truth and falsehood, in this frame of reference, are timeless, as ordinary logic insists. But we do not have access to the B-series temporal territory. All we have are images, images which are formed by matching perceptual inputs against image-templates derived from underlying cognitive maps of the B-series. Maps have to be considered in an *epistemic* context, not an alethic one, because the map and the territory are logically quite distinct. Maps are just representations. These underlying maps indicate all possibilities deemed feasible according to a particular system of temporal belief. Since the branching and merging of modal accessibility-relations between possible worlds in the epistemic framework of underlying cognitive maps is unrestricted, the logic of time-maps is S.4. In between the S.5 temporal territory and the S.4 underlying cognitive map lies the A-series enclave. Our subjective experience of time is confined to this enclave, within which we synthesize the flow of images to which we attach the indexical labels, past, present, future.

Let us suppose that the temporal equivalent of a spatial map is something like the lattice of possible worlds, linked by modal accessibility relations, as depicted in Figure 25.3. This 'map' indicates the extent of our knowledge (belief) as to how temporal worlds ·are disposed with respect to one another: 'for all we know' a plurality of antecedent worlds can give rise to a successor-world, and any antecedent world can have more than one successor world. But not all worlds are accessible from every world in the system. Successor-worlds cannot give rise to antecedent worlds, but only vice versa, and some successor worlds are inaccessible from some antecedent worlds (if they lie outside the 'maximal envelope' of possible inter-world pathways between two worlds indicated in Figure 25.2 for world O – the origin – and world G – the goal).

Let us suppose that map-world O generates an image (like the images generated by spatial maps), which matches with perceptual input, so that we have an *indexical fix* 'now we are at world O', and we are considering ways of bringing it about that, by and by, we will be at world G, i.e. our future inputs will match images generated by world G on our time maps. In terms of the logic of the underlying time-map, there are numerous ways of getting from O to G, though there are also many paths from O which lead to destinations other than G.

We therefore must deliberate. Given that we have selected G, and not some other world, as our goal, we must choose the likeliest method of getting there. If this were a spatial map, we would be considering alternative routes between, say, Cambridge and London (via the M11 or the A10 or the A1). In making this choice of routes we would mentally rehearse images of each route (the M11 is fast but boring, the A10 prettier but often congested). One series of images would prove the more attractive, and that route would be selected. The point to note, however, is that each route is considered *separately*, as a series of images corresponding to that particular route. The map which shows 'all possible' routes between Cambridge and London is converted into images (or sequences of images) of particular journeys between these locations. In deliberating over the map, one *linearizes* it. In terms of the map, the M11 route and the A10 route simply coexist as open possibilities, along with all the other routes between Cambridge and London. Objectively, in the light of given criteria for expeditious journeying between Cambridge and London, there is an optimal route, but because we only have the map, not the journey itself, we do not know which that route is. In order to select it, we project onto the map each route in turn, calling forth a sequence of images specific to it. Each route becomes a separate entity, and the one which most coincides with the criteria for optimality is the favoured one.

The same kind of 'linearization' applies to time-maps. The 'now' moment is identified with one particular world on the underlying time-map, which is singled out – possibly erroneously – at the world whose images correspond to the state of affairs 'now' obtaining. From this origin world extend pathways into the future towards desired or feared goal worlds, and also pathways into the past, towards possible antecedent worlds.

When we contemplate future courses of action, we compare particular linear enchainments of possible worlds, and we make our decision by singling out a particular sequence as optimal, i.e. the one with the lowest opportunity cost in terms of the sum of our (often conflicting) desires and our estimates as to their likelihood of realization. Our considerations are determined by the fact that, although our maps show us many possible futures, there is, in fact, only going to be *one* future, and we had better make sure that that future is the one we want it to be. The cognitive activity of 'projecting', therefore, consists of *linearizing* time-maps, drawing out specific paths.

But something is still missing from our depiction as it stands. When we contemplate the network of possible worlds between origin (O) and goal-worlds (G) not all these worlds are regarded as equally likely, even though they may all be considered possible. We need to introduce a concept of *modal distance* between possible worlds, such that the preferred route between O and G will be the one that has the least opportunity costs, while at the same time conforming to our estimates of the intrinsic likelihood of events, only a few of which are under our direct control. The realization of some worlds on our time-maps would 'surprise' us, to use Shackle's term. We are often prepared to gamble, that is, to contemplate pathways through time which are contingent on the realization of surprising worlds, but not, usually, if the same objectives can be obtained via a pathway which leads us only though worlds which are not surprising at all. An undifferentiated S.4 network of enchained possible worlds does not represent this feature of our cognitive maps of time. In order to supply this need, an additional element of logical machinery is needed.

We can clarify this issue by inscribing the equivalent of latitude and longitude lines onto our hypothetical time-map (sorting the possible worlds into rows and columns, as in Figure 25.3). Columns consist of *synchronous* possible worlds. Rows consist of possible worlds bearing maximal *similarity* to one another.

Each column of possible worlds has a temporal index, corresponding to a date in B-series time, which I have numbered from O at the origin world, backwards and forwards. This indexing of worlds by dates needs present no problem. The set of worlds shown in the map as a column consist of a set of synchronous alternative possible worlds. The world in this column which generates images which correspond to perceptual input is indexed as the 'actual' world (now). If we move up and down the column, above and below the world indexed as 'actual' are the closest *counterfactual* worlds to the 'actual' world. They are the worlds, so to speak, which are the case if we are only slightly mistaken in making our determination as to the identity of the 'actual' world. At further removes, up and down the column, are progressively more dissimilar worlds, differing from the world indexed as actual in more serious respects. These are more surprising worlds.

In treating the 'actual' world as the focal member of a set of

**Figure 25.3 Temporal cognitive map**

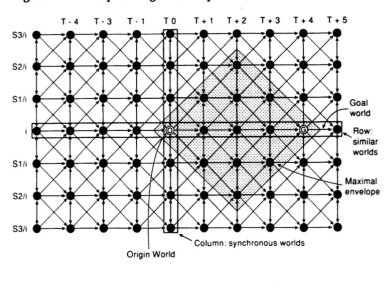

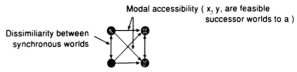

progressively more dissimilar worlds, I am exploiting a theory put forward by the philosopher David Lewis, in his remarkable book *Counterfactuals* (1973). Lewis's problem (his initial problem, anyway) is to explain why counterfactual conditionals, like:

If Henry had gone to the party, he would have talked to Gina

are true, even if Henry did not go to the party. Lewis's answer is that such counterfactual conditionals are true if the counterfactual world in which Henry and Gina go to a party and talk to one another is modally 'closer' to the real world than an alternative possible (counterfactual) world in which Henry and Gina both attend a party and fail to talk to one another. 'If Henry had gone to the party, he would not have talked to Gina' is thus a false counterfactual inference.

Lewis discusses degrees of counterfactuality in terms of a series of 'spheres' centred on a world indexed as (1) which is the 'actual' world. The world (1) is surrounded by a sphere containing the set of most closely resembling worlds to (1) – those that are counterfactual in ways which, on balance, are not very important (S1). Outside this is a second sphere containing more seriously non-resembling worlds (S2), and outside this, a sphere of even more dissimilar ones (S3), and so on. I do not need to discuss Lewis's theory of counterfactuals in any detail, but there are two points that I want to extract from his treatment of the subject.

The first is the idea that the world indexed as 'actual' is at the centre of a set of worlds which are, in varying degrees, 'like' the actual world. The world as we actually believe it to be is associated with a penumbra of more or less believable competitor-worlds, some of which we would not be too surprised to discover were not counterfactual at all (though, as of now, we believe them to be so), others which would occasion us great surprise if they proved to be the case. Different cultural belief-systems apportion worlds differently to the Lewisian spheres: Dobuans (Fortune 1935) once believed that this actual world was one in which yams walked about at night (sphere i, or if they were a bit dubious about their own cultural belief system, sphere S1); we, on the other hand, would regard ambulatory yams as a very remote possibility (S1000). Given the sphere-assignment Dobuans gave to the world in which yams walked about at night, it was reasonable for them to attempt to attract their neighbours' yams into their gardens by appropriate magical techniques, and conversely to fear the consequences of their neighbours' possibly more efficacious countermeasures. They either believed that yams really did walk about, or at least that this was a serious possibility, against which they could insure themselves by taking a Pascalian gamble.

Lewis's system of spheres provides an excellent device for representing the relativity which exists between the actual and the possible, the believed-in, the half-believed-in, and the barely-considered-possible. I have incorporated the Lewisian spheres into Figure 25.3 showing the general form of a time-map, as the system of rows (latitude, so to speak) above and below i, the row of worlds indexed as having a maximal credibility rating. Above and below i, the equator, are the highly possible S1 worlds, above and below these the less believable S2 worlds, and so on. If we take a column of synchronous worlds (say the column from T0) what we are looking at is a cross-sectional view of a system of Lewisian spheres.

I am obliged to represent the spheres this way because I have only one dimension at my disposal whereas Lewis has two. I need the other dimension to represent longitude, i.e. time. Here there arises the second point I want to extract from Lewis on counterfactuals. It might be felt that I was indulging in a bit of sleight-of-hand, in having time as longitude, and 'similarity' as latitude on the time-map, in that longitude and latitude are entirely comparable kinds of co-ordinates, whereas it might be felt that temporal index and 'similarity' are quite different. But this is not so. Perhaps this can be brought out by coining a new expression, on the lines of 'counterfactual', namely, 'counter-temporal'. Worlds are opposed on the longitudinal axis on the basis of their mutual 'counterfactuality' (they are synchronous worlds of different factual content). They are counterfactual but not countertemporal. Worlds on the same latitudinal axis, by contrast, are countertemporal (distinguished by their temporal indices) but not counterfactual (i.e. they are temporal continuations of the same kind of worlds, worlds factually constituted in the same way). Lewis himself proposes, and approves, this particular move:

> Contingent sentences have different truth values at different worlds; many sentences likewise have different truth values at different moments of time. In fact, most of our sentences depend for their truth values on a bundle of co-ordinates; world, time, place, and many more. To avoid distraction, I have tried (with imperfect success) to keep the other dimensions of variation out of sight by sticking to examples where they may be held fixed. Let us, for a change, now isolate dependence on time, tacitly holding the world and the other co-ordinates fixed. Moments of time now play the same role as possible worlds hitherto. Sentences are true at them; propositions are sets of them, and systems of spheres are sets of them. (Lewis 1973: 104)

Lewis then constructs a system of temporal logic using his counterfactual operators as temporal-logical operators. (Lewis's 'sentences' may be taken to be equivalent to my 'images from maps'.) This passage, I consider, justifies my decision to treat temporal succession of world-states of a given world (latitude) as a modal contrast/accessibility relation, on a par with modal contrast/accessibility between counterfactual worlds assigned to different spheres (longitude).

Let us return to the problem which provoked this detour into the theory of counterfactuals, which was, it will be remembered, the problem of how temporal cognitive maps provide the criteria for selecting 'optimal' pathways between origin-worlds and goal-worlds, given that all that the map showed, initially, was a multiplicity of alternative pathways; 'open possibilities' for getting from O to G. Now that we have superimposed a 'grid' onto the network of possible worlds, we can consider a 'least distance' criteria for optimizing pathways between origin and goal worlds. The optimal path between O and G is the path which leads to the *least* countertemporal world consistent with G, via the *least* counterfactual intervening worlds. But the 'least distance' criterion is not sufficient all by itself, because the attainment of G via the most modally accessible intervening worlds may have opportunity costs which we would prefer to avoid. In other words, we never have just one overriding objective which has to be attained, come what may, but more usually we have a large number of conflicting aims in mind simultaneously, and we hope to realize these aims in such a way that the attainment of any one aim does not rule out the attainment of too many of the other ones. Consequently, 'navigation in time' is not an automatic business of selecting the shortest path between O and G, but of finding a more-or-less circuitous path within the envelope of non-counterfactual and close-counterfactual worlds which are consistent with the attainment of multiple, competing goals with lowest overall opportunity costs.

# Part III

## Time and Practice

# Chapter 26

## The Natural Attitude and the Theory of Practice

Let Chapters 23–25 stand as an account of time cognition in the abstract. But there are many reasons for thinking that a mechanical-cybernetic cognitive model of the kind just sketched fails to reflect many of the most important aspects of the temporal experience of human subjects in the culturally and historically grounded world. How is it possible to proceed from the time of the decontextualized 'cognitive model', to the embedded, concrete time of the anthropological subject and agent, enmeshed in the temporal rhythms of collective life, and operating, not according to the principles of disembodied 'reason', but according to the unreflective routines of established social practices? The dangers of over-intellectualizing the anthropological conception of time are only too apprent. Indeed, the model presented is open to a fundamental objection precisely on the grounds that it represents human cognition as a species of scientific enquiry. Cognition is shown as a systematic search for the truth of the world (the truth of the B-series temporal territory) carried out via the collection of 'data' from perception, the codification of the data in the light of judgement (the application of interpretative schemata) and the formation of 'perceptual hypotheses' which motivate fresh 'exploratory movements' or data-collection forays. Does not the suspicious convergence between the 'scientific' model of cognition and the generic activity of scientists (hypothetico-deductive model-building) suggest that what is being produced, while purportedly a representation of the cognitive processes of 'minds' in general, is really no more than a transcription of the intellectual activities of the scientific model-builder, and none other? So that such intellectualist models, while pretending to describe human experience in the world, can only succeed in describing their own processes of construction, at one remove. The inherent danger of entry into such a hall of mirrors is apparent enough. But how to escape from this deceptive objectivism which threatens, on closer inspection, to become a closed system?

There are two possible ways out. They both involve a return to Husserl, but in different ways. The first of these is to propose a more radical kind of 'subjective' analysis of time than anything attempted hitherto, at least in this book. This move, which can be called transcendental subjectivism, was promoted philosophically by Husserl himself, but was carried further by Husserl's philosophical successors, notably Heidegger and Sartre. I shall deal (and that only briefly, for reasons which will soon emerge) with Heidegger.

Any interested sociologist or anthropologist, on first opening Heidegger's *Being and Time* (1962) could be forgiven for imagining that a work that is devoted to the exploration of 'being-in-the-world' (*Dasein*) must contain, among its many pages, not a few which would be directly relevant to the kinds of descriptive and interpretative problems which interest sociologists. But this is not so, nor was it part of Heidegger's intentions that it should be so. Heidegger's book is metaphysical prescription, not psychological description, and everything that constitutes normal human experience is condemned from the start as 'inauthentic'. *Being and Time* is about transcending the categories of ordinary, inauthentic, everyday understanding of the world, so as to experience an authentic 'moment of vision' (*Augenblick*). This vision (which is a revelation of 'Being', a category which Heidegger's translators think is really a paraphrase for God) is to be obtained by allowing the horizons of selfhood (*Dasein*) to obtain final recognition, stripped of all contamination by worldly concerns and illusions, as the ultimate, encompassing reality. Moreover, Heidegger thinks that the armature of authentic *Dasein* is subjective time (A-series time) – '*Das Dasein . . . ist die Zeit selbst.*' Authentic time is not public time (the time that can be measured by the clock) but the integral time of selfhood, which, unlike clock-time, is finite (being rounded by death) and also without sequence, because the past is drawn up into the present and is repeated, and the future is present because the present is always a 'preparation' (accomplished through repetitions of the past). At least, this is so when time is grasped authentically, or, as I think it is legitimate to say, religiously or spiritually, since the 'repeated past', 'prepared-for future' and 'all-encompassing present' seem to me to correspond exactly to the temporal framework of rituals or sacrifices (such as Christian communion) as understood by theologians. For the rest, there is only inauthentic time, about which Heidegger does not say anything special, and which he is perfectly willing to describe in terms which would raise no objections among the most rationalist philosophers. Heidegger does not deny ordinary, everyday time, i.e. 'social time' as an anthropologist or sociologist might define it; rather, he systematically devalues it, and sees it as the product of the 'fallen' or 'thrown' condition of ordinary humankind – '*Dasein*'s thrownness is the reason why there is time publicly' (1962: 464). Humanity 'takes refuge in reality' in order to defer the moment of authentic recognition of time, which is the moment at which the finiteness of time (death) also has to be accepted. But this escape is actually enslavement to an alien and inauthentic time. It is being 'in' time, rather than, so to speak, 'being time' by recognizing, in the visionary moment, first of all that time is encompassing, and second, that time is the self.

Heidegger's transcendental subjectivity is a consistent, though idiosyncratic development of Husserl's philosophy, which was equally transcendental in intention, though less anti-rational and anti-scientific in execution. To say that it has no bearing on social or psychological questions is to treat it with maximum respect, rather than otherwise. Alternatively, one can interpret it as the philosophical expression of romantic, reactionary ideology, consistent with Heidegger's well-documented commitment to fascism. But in any case, there is no point in prolonging the discussion of a point of view which is so emphatically disdainful of the common conceptions of time entertained by the mass of persons engaged in the ordinary business of living, which is the subject-matter primarily under discussion here. And there would be no need to discuss Husserl either, were Husserl only a transcendental philosopher. But Husserl, besides elaborating a philosophical metaphysics, also created pre-philosophy, a phenomenological psychology which examines the fused mass of presuppositions comprising the 'natural attitude' to life, and it is from Husserl's pre-philosophical analysis of 'natural' thinking, rather than from transcendental phenomenology as such, that his significance in the social sciences derives (Schutz 1967: 115). Husserl's pre-philosophy is the source of the 'phenomenological' strand in post-war social scientific thinking (e.g. Schutz 1967; Berger and Luckman 1966; Garfinkel 1967, etc.). Phenomenologically-inspired social-scientific thinking is not concerned to valorize 'authentic' understanding (Heidegger) or 'understanding within the reduced sphere of the phenomenological epoché' (Husserl) over against the kind of understanding evinced within the natural attitude. Indeed, mankind 'in the natural attitude' is the object, not just of curiosity, but also of solicitude, in pre-philosophical phenomenology, and authenticity is sought nowhere else, certainly not in any 'moment of vision'.

Granted the necessity of drawing back from the abyss of transcendental subjectivity, phenomenological sociology or anthropology still has a dilemma, in that the obvious alternative seems to be the kind of objectivism, scientism and naive realism which phenomenology was itself initially designed to combat. This, at any rate, is taken as the point of departure by Bourdieu (1977), of all anthropologists the one who owes most to Husserl, especially in his detailed investigations of the nature of social time. For Bourdieu, the dilemma in the social sciences is to make a break with 'objectivism' (primarily structuralism, neoclassical economics, techno-ecological determinism, and so on) on the one hand, and simultaneously with 'subjectivism' (which means primarily the kind of existentialist social theory, itself derived from transcendental phenomenology, developed by Sartre, and secondarily all theories which 'bestow on [the agent's] creative free will the . . . power to constitute the meaning of the situation' (ibid.: 73) – and the power to form projects intended to alter it to the agent's own advantage).

Bourdieu argues that the concept of 'practices' derived from Marx provides the means of obviating the 'false dilemma' of mechanism-cum-objectivism, and finalism-cum-subjectivism. 'The natural attitude' of Husserl moves to centre-stage, not just as a contingent array of 'typifications' of the mundane attitude to life, but as an historically constituted product which produces man historically.

Thus Bourdieu, like Sartre, combines Husserl with Marx, but it is a different Husserl, and no doubt a different Marx, too. Whereas the thematic idea in Sartre's writings is freedom, in Bourdieu's output the emphasis is placed on practices, i.e. the very specific restrictions on the subjective definition of 'the possible', which is imposed by historicity, as an intrinsic limitation on freedom. Bourdieu's preoccupation is with the inertial density of societies, not with the millenarian fantasies of the intelligentsia. The idea that history, traditions, socialization and education are absolutes where human beings are concerned, not things which can be 'bracketed away' or transcended through acts of choice dictated by purely ideal goals, is one which is characteristic of the sociological point of view, but which is only sporadically represented in philosophy.

Bourdieu's critical Marxism is exclusively sociological, rather than revolutionary. The leading idea derived from Marx is that man produces himself, or, to put it in a way which avoids the implication that this production occurs instantaneously, man is produced by history, which he produces. 'History' in this context is clearly not the record of the past, laid out flat as a series of datable events in B-series time, but the residue of the past embodied in existing men, existing structures of social relationships, and existing constellations of reality-interpreting ideas.

It is essential to note the deep affinity between the A-series concept of time, and the concept of time implicit in the Marxist historical dialectic of the production of man by history and the production of history by man. This 'history' is not the unchanging, inaccessible, B-series 'past', but a past that is dynamically interconnected to the present, and that changes as the present changes. It is not a simple accretion of new events (changes) at the temporal front-line demarcated by the 'now'; instead, the change initiated at the now-moment occurs in depth. The whole of history changes as the present changes, because of the continual interactions of historical residues in the current situation, which is centred on the 'now', but which embraces the past and the future as well.

The dynamic conception of historicity is one of Bourdieu's most important borrowings from Husserl's philosophy because it is here, precisely, that the elective affinity between the Husserlian version of the A-theory philosophy of time and Marxist sociological theory arises. We have only to review the account given of Husserl's model of internal time-consciousness given in Chapter 23 to discern a remarkable convergence between the model of dynamic interaction between the contents of consciousness within the temporal field of the ego, outlined by the phenomenological philosopher, and the model of dynamic interactions between the mediating elements in the social field (historically produced structures which structure history) envisaged by critical Marxist sociologists, Bourdieu in particular. The critical Marxist version of historicism is Husserlian phenomenological psychology writ large.

Husserl's model shows us the form of a *dynamic present which encompasses the past and the future*. The past and the future change and interact, via the network of protentions and retentions, as the present processes, setting up 'the continuum of continua', the indefinite reduplication of time-continua already envisaged by McTaggart as a necessary consequence of the A-series concept of time. However unsatisfactory from the point of view of ordinary logic (cf. Mellor's critique, Chapter 17 above), this way of looking at things does reflect the fact that subjectively speaking, for each moment of time (T1, T2 . . . Tn) there is a unique perspective on the whole of time within the temporal horizon of the subject, whereas the B-series only gives us one perspective on time, which includes all of its moments, past, present and to come.

It is only by multiplying the number of 'time' continua to reflect the accumulation of successive 'now' moments that the A-series can be realized; in the same way, it is only by invoking a dynamic concept of 'history' in which each conjuncture is identified with a unique configuration of historical forces which can resolve the conundrum implicit in the idea that man, the historical product, produces himself (via history). Because ordinary logic suggests that if man is produced by history, he cannot be the one that produces history. Sausages are produced be sausage-machines, but sausage-machines are not produced by sausages. The only agency which could be imagined as producing 'history' would be the history of preceding periods. The history of the eighteenth century produced the history of the nineteenth century, and so on. But in this case we are back at simple historical determinism, the very trap critical Marxism is concerned to avoid. But if, as suggested, we imagine that 'history' at a given conjuncture is not a simple enchainment of causal antecedents, but a unique configuration of residues of the past in the present (= retentions) and emergent elements of the future in the present (= protentions), in play within historic 'horizons' which are set by the current predicament, then the conditions are realized for a different conception of human historicity; one in which relationships are not causal but dialectical, i.e. subjectively mediated by man himself, not imposed from without but generated from within. 'History' in this sense is multiplex, dynamic and perspectival: just as 'events' in the Husserlian model of internal time consciousness *undergo* 'changes' as well as *being* changes in themselves (a notion that is meaningless except in a subject-centred universe) so also do the elements constituting human historicity; becoming a series of interactions mediated by men, under the sway of a certain historically produced kinds of consciousness.

In other words, the A-series concept of time is not only compatible with the critical Marxist conception of history, it is actually logically necessitated by it: from the B-series point of view the Marxist postulate of the relativity of the present to history, and history to the present, is entirely inadmissible. From the B-series perspective, 'what happened in history' is *not* dependent on 'what is happening now'. And if 'what will happen in future' is dependent on 'what happens now' in a causal sense, it is not *logically* dependent on the present; future events could be different from what they are actually going to be, without interference in the logical articulation of B-series time. From the A-series point of view, all this is radically transformed: the past of a given present is the past of that present, and of no other present, and ditto the future of that present. Thus, if the retention of A from B is A', A is retained as A' from no other now-moment; as a particular 'past event' it is specific to B as present. At C, B is a different 'past event' (B''), and so on. Similarly, if we consider the critical Marxist analysis of elements of ideology, we can construct an identical analysis. For example, chiefly authority, which lives on in certain societies as an historic residue, formative in producing a certain pattern of social relationships in the present, yet which (*qua* 'formative influence') is not what is taken up, reinterpreted and put to use now, in constructing new modes of power-relationships which point towards an emerging future, because the time-context in which the 'formative influences' were in play is not the time-context which exists now. The 'chiefly past' which produced the present is not the 'chiefly past' which the present is producing, and which will produce the future. Between the two there lies a gap, a gap which is filled by men as the agentive source of history; *le pli dans l'être*, as Merleau-Ponty says.

Let these remarks suffice as an explanation of the fundamental affinity between critical Marxism and A-theoretical approaches to time: it is no exaggeration of the position, in fact, simply to assert that as the A-series is to the B-series, so the

Marxist conception of history is to the Orthodox one. Moreover, one can turn to Figure 23.1 and see there a precise representation of the essential logical basis of critical Marxist historiography and sociology.

Later, I shall trace the precise outlines of Husserl's protentional/retentional model of internal time-consciousness, in Bourdieu's accounts of the way in which the peasant Kybele of Algeria are inserted into their own characteristic temporal flux. But before turning to Bourdieu's outstandingly interesting ethnographic analyses more needs to be said about the 'theory of practice' in general, and the critique of sociology which it embodies.

In *Outline of a Theory of Practice* Bourdieu places the A-theoretical model of temporality in the context of a general theory of social behaviour which is a critical-Marxist counterpart of the social psychology developed by G. H. Mead, the pragmatist philosopher and noted A-theorist (see Chapter 16 above) in *Mind, Self, and Society* (1924) and described by its inventor as 'social behaviorism'. Goff (1980) has commented on the convergence between Meadian pragmatist social psychology and Marx's concept of ideology, and if Mead can be shown to have reinvented Marx, perhaps it should not come as a surprise that latterday Marxists should reinvent Mead. The 'theory of practice' presents Husserl and Marx in the context of a behaviouristic theory of the origination of social action. This seems a paradoxical position, in that philosophically, phenomenology and behaviourism represent very opposed points of view, and noted 'phenomenological' sociologists (e.g. Schutz, Berger and Luckmann, etc.) are explicit opponents of behaviourism, if the scope of 'behaviourism' is confined to mechanical, reductionist, explanations of behaviour on the basis of reward/punishment histories.

But despite the admitted incompatibility of phenomenological philosophy (i.e. transcendental subjectivism) and behaviourism, there is no such incompatibility between pre-philosophical phenomenology and Mead's much less reductionist brand of behaviourism (as Schutz, who greatly admired Mead, recognized). Bourdieu brings this convergence to fruition.

It will be recalled that Mead distinguished two aspects of the social self; the 'I' (the spontaneous core of individuality) encapsulated within the 'me' – the internalized summation of the reactions of social others towards the agent, or, to put this in words which recall the terms used in the preceding discussion, the internalized 'history' of the agent – the residues of yesterday's man and prefigurations of tomorrow's man which constitute the man of today. The Meadian 'me' is the subjective embodiment of the objective realities of the social context, and consists of a complex series of habitual responses which secure the interests of the individual (control over events) by means of *adaptations* to external circumstances (Mead was influenced by Darwinian theory). Psychologically speaking, Mead's account of social action as socially adapted and socially adaptive 'habits' can be identified as a *'peripheralist'* theory, to employ the term used in the history of psychology to denote theories which treat behaviour (and thought) as 'responses of the organism as a whole' – as opposed to theories which stress the autonomous role of cognition in the generation of conduct ('centralist' theories). Mead and Bourdieu are both proponents of peripheralism. If we equate peripheralism with behaviourism, as it seems to me we should, then both Mead and Bourdieu are behaviourists – Mead avowedly so, Bourdieu more cryptically.

The 'me' described in *Mind, Self, and Society* is equivalent to the concept of the *habitus*, the concept central to Bourdieu's 'theory of practice':

> a system of durable, transposable dispositions, structured structures predisposed to act as structuring structures . . . 'regular' without being . . . the product of obedience to rules, adapted to their goals without presupposing a conscious aiming at ends . . . collectively orchestrated without being the product of the orchestrating action of a conductor. . . .
> [The] durably installed generative principle of regulated improvisations . . . History turned into Nature. (1977: 72, 78)

Bourdieu's concept of the *habitus* – the allusion to the key behaviouristic notion of 'habit' (Fr. *habitude*) is patently intended – provides the basis for the escape from the 'false dilemma of mechanism and finalism'. In offering his critique of sociology, Bourdieu opposes, as was noted earlier, 'objectivist' theories which take an observer's view on society – Lévi-Strauss once compared his intellectual approach to that of an entomologist studying the goings-on in an ants' nest – and 'subjectivist' theories of the Sartrean kind, which are based on the notion that human beings 'choose' to be what they are because to be human is to be free, in some absolute sense. His first move is to reject structuralist objectivism, on the grounds that this approach commits the 'fallacy of the rule' which arises as *ex post facto* descriptive generalizations are converted into causal explanations of the behaviour being described, as in the following sequence:

1. I observe certain behaviour.
2. I concoct a rule which fits this behaviour – i.e. *if* rule R existed, and *if* people obeyed it, the observed behaviour would result.
3. I assume that the rule which 'fits' the behaviour, 'guides' it: i.e. that the agents concerned have a conscious or unconscious intention to follow the rule as formulated.
4. I conclude that the observed behaviour is causally explained by the existence of the rule.

In this way descriptive generalizations, constructed from an outsider's point of view, are projected onto the subjects of anthropological discourse, who become mere puppets manipulated by a structuralist puppeteer.

On the other hand, 'decision' theories are rejected, not quite so stringently, as versions of naive humanism which fail to come to grips with the historically formed, deeply 'conventional' character of social conduct. The way out of the impasse is to break both with 'mechanism' and 'finalism', by recognizing the autonomy of 'practice' over against both 'rules' and 'projects', is via the invocation of the *habitus*.

Bourdieu's basic perception is that social agents do not behave like puppets on strings, as they tend to do in conventional structural models, nor yet are they free spirits. They are, he says, more like jazz musicians, who enter a session equipped with a body of practical techniques for playing their instruments and an agreed format for collectively improvising on a theme, but who produce music which cannot be anticipated in advance, even by themselves, and which is traduced if it is analysed *post festum*, as the 'realization' of a musical structure which existed prior to, and independently of, the actual playing of the notes.

In this way, Bourdieu dissociates himself from the mechanistic aspects of structuralist model-making, but retains the more valuable aspects of structuralist theory, i.e. the capacity to focus on systems as systems, not merely as collections of heterogeneous elements. The 'structured structures predisposed to act as structuring structures' are *systematic*, but they are not transcendent structural models or unconscious laws. Rather, they are precipitates of history immanent in the dispositional propensities of active social agents.

Again, although individuals are recognized as individuals in Bourdieu's theory (a subjectivist legacy) Bourdieu emphasizes the collective harmonization of the *habitus* of each individual agent forming part of a collectivity: the *habitus* of separate individuals coincides because they participate in the same historical process. Individuals' cognitive and motivational structures coincide with the objective requirements of 'the system' because of the dialectical (circular) relationship between the historical production of the collective *habitus*, and the reproduction of a given set of historical conditions via collective action.

It is interesting, and characteristic, that in searching for an image to convey the collective harmonization of habitus, Bourdieu lights on a venerable parable from the philosophy of time, both because the harmonization of the *habitus* is essentially a rhythmic or musical (i.e. temporal) phenomenon – as the jazz-improvisation metaphor implies – and because society is through-and-through temporal, because it is an historical process rather than a synchronic fabric of rules. Thus, in the course of a fascinating discussion, Bourdieu invokes Leibniz, comparing the objective homogenization of the group or class *habitus* to the synchronous striking of two clocks, which can be attributed to (1) mutual communication between the clocks, (2) the actions of a workman, who keeps the two clocks in time with one another, or (3) the fact that they have been made 'with such art and precision, that we can be assured of their subsequent agreement . . . *following only* [his] *own laws, each none the less agrees with the other*' (Leibniz, *Monadology*, cited in Bourdieu 1977: 80). Social agents are like (3) – Leibnizian monads or well-made clocks – already adjusted to each other's responses by an 'immanent law' (*lex insita*) laid down 'by earliest upbringing'.

Perhaps the sheer virtuosity of Bourdieu's presentation of this point should give one pause. The concept of the *lex insita* is exceptionally beguiling, but is it true to life? Are we (or are the Kabyle) really like Leibnizian 'windowless monads' – co-ordinated, that is to say, entirely without social communication, the exchange of information, the rational construction of projects of action, the following of rules of behaviour embodied in collective representations, and so on? Is it impossible to point to actual instances of these things? Even granting that the 'universe of information' is socially restricted, so that agents are free to project only a limited array of possible futures (the ones they can imagine on the basis of a specific collective and biographical past) and free to communicate only a limited array of messages (which conform to presuppositions accepted collectively) there still appears to be ample room for the exercise of reason, rational persuasion, the construction and evaluation of rival projects of action, and the conscious following of rules of behaviour on rational rather than habitual grounds.

Above all, it seems difficult to maintain consistently the 'behavioural' theory of knowledge which is essential to the position maintained by Bourdieu. The behavioural theory of knowledge identifies 'knowing' with 'doing'. 'The rat knows that there is food in the left-hand branch of the maze' is reducible, according to the behavioural theory of knowledge, to the behavioural disposition of the rat to run down the left-hand branch of the maze and eschew the right. In the light of the theory of practice, all knowledge is of this kind, i.e. a set of dispositions to respond to stereotyped situations in a stereotyped way which has been previously 'inculcated' in the agent's behavioural repertoire. I concede that there is 'knowledge' which can only be expressed in the performance of some activity (i.e. 'knowledge-how': Ryle 1949); knowing how to ride a bicycle is an instance of this kind of knowledge – but there is also the kind of knowledge that is propositional in form (knowledge that). This kind of knowledge is a possession of the subject (like the possession of a sum of money), not a 'disposition' (like the disposition to spend money on liquor rather than books). Bourdieu treats cultural knowledge as a set of dispositional propensities of socialized agents; but this view seems to me unduly one-sided.

# Chapter 27

## The Theory of Practice and the Timing of Exchanges

Let us turn, however, to the treatment given to temporality in Bourdieu's theory of practice. The theme of time (in its A-theoretical guise) occurs almost on the first page of Bourdieu's book and plays an important part in the argument thereafter. In rejecting objectivism, Bourdieu raises the issue of the structuralist's favourite institution, delayed exchange. If A gives B a ceremonial gift, on day 1, which is reciprocated on day 100 by a counter-gift, it is nothing to A or B that in the eyes of eternity (and exchange theory) that the two gifts 'exactly cancel one another out'. On the contrary, the delay, the period during which A's gift remains unreciprocated, leading to a continuous qualitative modification of the relationship between A and B, is all-important. Depending on when the counter-presentation is made, it will be a different presentation: if the delay is short, that signifies an unwillingness on B's part tacitly to co-operate with A's desire to obtain the advantages which accrue to the creditor in a creditor/debtor relation – To betray one's haste to be free of an obligation one has incurred . . . is to denounce the initial gift retrospectively as motivated by the intention of obliging one' (Bourdieu 1977: 5–6). If the delay is over-long, that may signify indifference, inspiring resentment of a different kind. The nice judgements which actually determine reciprocity in exchange are traduced by a B-series model, in flat, non-perspectival time, such as:

$$
\begin{array}{ll}
\text{D1} & \text{A} - - - - \rightarrow \text{B} \\
& \quad * \qquad\qquad * \\
& \quad * \qquad\qquad * \\
& \quad * \qquad\qquad * \\
\text{D100} & \text{A} \leftarrow - - - - \text{B}
\end{array}
$$

which shows up the objective symmetry between the transactions involved, but conceals precisely what it is that makes a gift a 'gift'. 'If the system is to work', writes Bourdieu, 'the agents must not be entirely unaware of the truth of their exchanges, which is made explicit in the anthropologist's model, while at the same time they must refuse to know and above all recognize it' (Bourdieu 1977: 6). Instead of making a B-series model of their transactions, which would expose the banality of mere reciprocity, the parties involved decide to give or not give, repay or refrain from repaying, according to feelings dictated by the retentional awareness of past gifts slipping away (A → A' → A") and protentions of impending ones (B" → B' → B). Although Bourdieu does not explicitly refer to the Husserlian model in this connection, it is clear that only the A-series perspective can capture the qualitative subtleties of delay, suspense etc., so essential to the game-like character of ceremonial exchange.

Bourdieu denies that the time of 'scientific' models is capable of illuminating the dialectics of practice: 'science has a time which is not that of practice':

> practice . . . is annihilated when the scheme [i.e. the *habitus*] is identified with the model: retrospective necessity becomes prospective necessity . . . things which have happened, and can no longer not happen, become the irresistible future of the acts which made them happen. This amounts to positing, with Diodorus, that if it is true to say of a thing that it will be, then it must one day be true to say that it is. . . . All experience of practice contradicts these paradoxes. . . . Once the possibility is admitted that the 'mechanical law' of the 'cycle of reciprocity' may not apply, the whole logic of practice is transformed . . . uncertainty, which finds its objective basis in the probabilistic logic of social laws, is sufficient not only to modify the experience of practice . . . but practice itself . . . (ibid.: 9)

Bourdieu's reintroduction of the thickness of time into the abstract anthropological concept of reciprocity is a point well taken. But it is notable that his discussion, though illuminating, is not very specific, and refers to relatively informal kinds of gift-giving, rather than to 'competitive' ceremonial exchanges of the type best documented in Melanesia, i.e. the Kula, Moka, Tee, etc. (Malinowski 1922; Leach and Leach 1983; Strathern 1971; Meggitt 1976). As I shall seek to demonstrate later, the timing of gifts and counter-gifts in the latter type of system often cannot be accounted for except in the light of overtly 'calculated' strategies which cannot be attributed to agents who 'conceal from themselves and others the truth of their practice'. But before turning to these matters, it is necessary to linger for a moment on another point, namely, Bourdieu's general contention that 'structural' models (like the one just given) are misleading, first, because they are timeless, and second, because they are deterministic, showing only one, inevitable outcome, while in real situations (especially exchanges) there are many possible outcomes.

The reference to Diodorus needs some explanation. The Greek philosophers developed a series of time-paradoxes around the fact that the logical truth and falsity of statements are 'timeless' features of that statement, yet the statements themselves may make reference to datable events. The most famous of these paradoxes is the paradox of the sea-battle, discussed by Aristotle, and essentially identical to the idea of Diodorus. Aristotle argues that statements about the future cannot be true or false (but must be indeterminate) because if I could truly say, today, that there would be a sea-battle tomorrow, then there would be nothing the admirals could do to avert the battle. They might change their minds, but the battle would go ahead anyway, simply because I had truly said it would. But it clearly *is* in the admirals' power to avert the battle if they want to, so it must be that my statements about the future are not true or false.

Bourdieu is asserting that the employment of B-series models is tantamount to the kind of fatalism which arises from assuming that if a proposition is 'timelessly' true, that is a sufficient cause of the occurrence of the events it reports. Implicitly accepting Aristotle's (fallacious) reasoning, he supposes that model-making leads to fatalism, because of the following syllogism:

$A \rightarrow B \ldots B \rightarrow A$ happened in the past . . .
The proposition (model) '$A \rightarrow B \ldots B \rightarrow A$' is tenselessly true . . .
*Therefore* $A \rightarrow B \ldots B \rightarrow A$ occurs inevitably (and will continue to occur inevitably).

In fact, this does not follow at all. If model-makers actually did reason in this way, they would of course be in the wrong, but there is nothing in the nature of model-construction *per se* that obliges them to do so. The logical truth of a true statement about events occurring at a particular time is time-independent; i.e. if it is true to say that 'a sea-battle occurs at date D' it always was and always will be true to utter this proposition concerning the events of this specific date. But this has nothing to do with (1) the causal necessitation of these events, or (2) the causal process whereby we come to be informed of these events, so as to have reasonable grounds for uttering this proposition rather than another one. Suppose that one of the admirals refuses to engage at the last moment, and sails away, thus averting the battle which had seemed imminent. The fact that, as a result, the proposition 'a sea battle occurs at date D' has the status of being timelessly false, always having had and always having subsequently that truth value, not a whit lessens the admiral's personal responsibility for the non-battle. Also timelessly true is the valid counterfactual inference 'if the admiral had not sailed away, there would have been a sea-battle' which pins the responsibility decisively one him, the admiral, not on any inevitable destiny.                                           .

More generally, it is not justifiable to think that the construction of B-series models implies universal determinism, although Lévi-Strauss, it is true, has somewhat muddied the issue in drawing a sharp distinction between so-called 'mechanical' and 'statistical' models (Lévi-Strauss 1963). Statistical models are indeterministic, yet no less 'mechanical' than any other kind of model. Models are advanced, not because their proponents believe that the event-sequences they depict must happen 'inevitably', or because they believe that whatever happens, happens by stringent necessity and cannot happen otherwise. They are advanced as more or less plausible readings of events which may possibly have happened or may possibly happen. It is perfectly feasible to incorporate into a B-series model the fact that the agents whose behaviour is being modelled are operating under conditions of uncertainty – Keynes' model of liquidity preference is an instance of such a model, if one were needed.

More generally, we can say that it is not the prerogative of A-series models to reflect the 'indeterminate' aspect of real life, as opposed to life as depicted in models. Basically, I think that here Bourdieu is confusing the issue of the *modalization* of time (i.e. the distinction between non-modal time which is a linear (non-branching) enchainment of states of affairs or 'worlds' vs. the 'modal' form of time which is a network of possible worlds, some of which are realized, and some of which are not) – with the logical distinction between A-series time and B-series time. The notion of coexistent, competing 'possible worlds' in alternativeness relationships with one another is compatible with B-series time as well as with A-series time, i.e. modalization is an intrinsic feature of the B-series time-maps described earlier (Chapter 25). Thus the form of a 'modalized' B-series model of the exchange transaction discussed earlier would be:

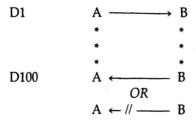

On D100 there is a modal 'worlds-alternativeness' relationship between the world in which A's gift has been reciprocated and the world in which it has not. If we wish to maintain that agents actually do construct internal representations of their temporal field as a model system in B-series time, it is not necessary to assume that they maintain only one such representation, whose outcome is viewed as fatalistically inevitable. They may construct an indefinitely large number of such representations in alternativeness-relationships to one another, and their hopes and fears stand on the realization of one rather than another of these 'possible worlds'.

Rather than interpose an impermeable barrier between timeless explanatory models and temporal practices, it seems more profitable to recognize their coexistence: in other words, the anthropologist's model of an exchange cycle may be possessed by the agent, not as a graph, but as a cognitive B-series time-map. Practices may be sedimented in this form, that is to say, as non-token indexical codified knowledge, and the temporal flux of 'practices', so much emphasized by Bourdieu, arises not so much from the logical-temporal form of the underlying set of representations, as from the always contingent process of 'locating' the current situation in the light of this codified knowledge or cognitive map.

Substance can be lent to his view by considering the strategic awareness displayed by the more successful operators, in the kinds of Melanesian competitive exchange systems alluded to

earlier. Take, for instance, the Kula, whose fundamental
mechanism – the oriented exchange of shell necklaces moving
clockwise around the 'ring' of Kula communities in Milne Bay
Province (Papua New Guinea) against the anti-clockwise movement of armshells – has been so frequently described that it
should not need specifying further. Many books have been
written on this classic competitive exchange system by foreign
anthropologists, yet it remains true that the most lucid discourse
on Kula strategy is not a scholarly model or recension of 'unreflective' or 'misrecognized' indigenous practice, but an un-
compromisingly instrumental guide to *wabuwabu* (or cheating)
dictated to Reo Fortune by Kisian of Tewara. This Dobuan
Big-Man is reported as saying:

> Suppose I, Kisian of Tewara, go [north] to the Trobriands and secure
> an armshell called Monitor Lizard. Then I go [south] to Sanaroa and
> in four different places secure four different shell necklaces, promis-
> ing each man who gives me a shell necklace, Monitor Lizard in
> return, later. I, Kisian, do not have to be very specific in my promise.
> It will be conveyed by implication and assumption for the most part.
> Later, when four men appear in my home at Tewara each expecting
> Monitor Lizard, only one will get it. The other three are not de-
> frauded permanently, however. They are furious, it is true, and their
> exchange is blocked for a year. Next year, when I, Kisian, go again to
> the Trobriands I shall represent that I have four necklaces at home
> waiting for those who will give me four armshells. I obtain more
> armshells than I did previously, and pay my debts a year late. . . . I
> have become a great man by enlarging my exchanges at the expense
> of blocking [the exchanges of others] for a year. I cannot afford to
> block their exchanges for too long, or my exchanges will never be
> trusted by anyone again. I am honest in the final issue. (Fortune 1932:
> 215)

'This account of Kula politics', comments Uberoi (1962: 93) 'is
the best we have'. My sentiments entirely, the only anthropologist to have rivalled Kisian of Tewara in this respect being
Shirley Campbell (Leach and Leach 1983: 201ff). This remarkable
text, at one level, entirely confirms everything that Bourdieu has
to say about exchange. Kisian's instructions on *wabuwabu* confirm Bourdieu's insight that, in exchange, everything in depends on using hints and insinuations and playing up to his
partners' greedy expectations, and he shows himself to be
equally cognisant of the fact that he has to be 'honest in the final

issue' if his credit as a Kula operator – his 'symbolic capital' – is to stay intact despite his corner-cutting and sharp practice. In terms of his intellectual approach, he is a true forerunner of Bourdieu himself. But here's the rub; because this degree of transcendence of the unwritten lore which governs practices, this self-conscious manipulativeness, is ruled out by Bourdieu's stipulation that practice is not founded on abstract knowledge, but on a series of unreflective intuitions which are evoked within the context of situation, and which trigger action behaviouristically, without conscious calculation even when calculation seems to be there.

But one cannot derive the strategic insights of Kisian of Tewara from habitual practices, even though, for their effective implementation, they depend on exploiting the habitual attitudes of others (i.e. the self-defeating greed of the four men of Sanaroa who are tempted to compete for Monitor Lizard when they would have been better advised to form some kind of coalition). The reason why *wabuwabu* is not a 'practical strategy', but, in truth, an intellectual's construction is that there is no reason to believe that only Kisian of Tewara, among all the operators in the Kula ring, has sufficient understanding to grasp the stratagem, nor that Kisian believes this. On the contrary, Kisian's partners will most probably be well aware of all the dangers they are running by investing their necklaces in his exchanges, rather than someone else's. And, knowing what they know, they may draw back. They will also be attempting at the same time to *wabuwabu* Kisian.

It is therefore significant that Kisian's text does not present the strategy either as an instituted 'rule', nor as a piece of proverbial wisdom, nor as an historical account of a Kula *coup* successfully accomplished, but simply as an ideal model of how the enlargement of a Kula trader's sphere of operations may, in theoretical rather than practical terms, be accomplished. If one turns to Campbell's circumstantial account of Vakuta Kula dealings (Leach and Leach 1983; cf. also Munn 1983) it is clear that the possibilities for using one shell to activate more than one exchange partnership simultaneously, though real enough, are much more restricted and carry heavier penalties than Kisian's formal model implies. For the purposes of the present discussion, that does not matter, since my aim is only to show that knowledge of Kula strategy takes a form, at least in the mind of Kisian of Tewara, and probably in others' as well, which goes

beyond the flux of initiatives and responses in the A-series, and
is embodied instead in codified knowledge of a non-practical,
non-situational kind.

Moreover, the point Kisian is making is of limitless application, not just to the Kula; i.e. the business principle that positive
cashflow in an organization depends on ensuring that debts
owed to the organization are cleared marginally faster than the
debts owed by it. Exactly the same strategy forms the basis of
success in the structurally very different type of pig-exchanges
which take place in the New Guinea Highlands. Discussing this
point in connection with the Tee exchange cycle of the Enga,
Meggitt writes:

> [Big Men acquire power and wealth] . . . by paying off those suppor-
> ters whose aid is essential to them but also retaining for themselves
> whatever resources they can abstract at the expense of weaker and
> poorer members of the group, whose claims they can safely ignore
> for a time.
>
> This is most obvious in the major inter-clan exchanges of valuables
> when little men who have fulfilled the demands of their Big Men to
> contribute to earlier distributions now find that, instead of being
> reimbursed, they are either fobbed off with promises of future repay-
> ments or (less often) simply threatened physically if they continue to
> complain. Because inter-group transactions at all levels are systemati-
> cally interconnected and because men have to participate in them to
> meet their ineluctable commitments to kin and affines, the victims of
> such exploitation can only hope, as the contribute yet again to a
> distribution organised through a big man, that eventually he will
> divert some valuables to him. Generally he does so, but only when it
> suits him. (Meggitt 1976: 190)

Meggitt goes on to indicate how an 'enduring inner network of
Big Men' united by 'self-interested and self-conscious solidarity'
achieve oligopolistic control through the manipulation of the
delay which they can impose on the repayment of contributions
to exchanges by little men. The result is 'incipient social strata'
(ibid.: 191)

There are two points which need to be underlined here. The
first of these is that Meggitt is quite clear that the delaying tactics
of Enga Big Men in the Tee are both self-consciously calculated
and subversive of the accepted moral order to which all Enga
pay lip-service, which insists that all men – especially all men
belonging to the same clan – are equal. The possibility that the

process of inter-group exchange, which traditionally provided the organizing principle for both the constitution of the territorial clan and the global relations between clans, should be subverted by an oligarchy of Big Men belonging to different clans, officially opposed but actually in alliance, officially benevolent towards their 'little men' but actually exploiting them, seems to me to point towards a kind of formal rationality in micro-politics which is inconsistent with the theory of practice, in so far as this theory insists on the impossibility of even local transcendence of conventional moral orthodoxies and conventions governing social action. The power of the Big Men depends on the fact that little men, as Meggitt says, are enmeshed in 'ineluctable commitments to kin and affines', but the manipulation of these practical commitments gives rise to a type of power which belongs to a different domain, i.e. pure political rationality. And I would argue that this local transcendence of *Gemeinschaft* morality cannot be explained within the sphere of 'practice' itself, even though it depends on the general recognition of the moral absolutes which practice imposes – just as, according to Godel's theorem, the axiomatic basis of a given logical system cannot be guaranteed within the confines of that logical system, but only by another one of greater logical power. In the same way, the political power that comes from exploiting, parasitically, the essentially non-exploitative moral bases of exchange practices, has to be referred to a different level of analysis from exchange itself.

So much for the general point about exchange and practices. The second point I want to make is more narrowly concerned with time as such. Kisian's strategy of *wabuwabu*, and the Enga Big Man's strategy of stalling on the repayment of internal debts in order to finance external partnerships with other Big Men, are essentially identical, and both have to do with the exercise of superordinate control over time. There is an intrinsic connection between local transcendence over the moral basis of exchange, and local transcendence over the rhythms of collective temporalities. In the cerebral struggle for power, which is grounded in the strictures of practice but which cannot end there, the practical categories of time, space and morality dissolve:

> Our master Caesar is in the tent
> Where the maps are spread,
> His eyes fixed upon nothing

His hand under his head.
*Like a long-legged fly upon the stream*
*His mind moves upon silence.*
                    W. B. Yeats, 'Long-legged Fly'

Yeats' image of the frictionless movement of the long-legged
fly perfectly expresses the quicksilver versatility of intelligent,
conceptual thought over against the congealed wisdom of practice, and it is this kind of thought which, it seems to me, shines
from Kisian's text (and many other texts of different origin in the
anthropological corpus) – as well as from the record of the actual
doings of New Guinea Big Men. And one component of this
frictionless thought is, I would argue, access to time as a rep-
resentable totality, or more precisely, an array of time-maps
in totalized B-series form, which permit the computation of
contingencies beyond the reach of habitual or reflex thinking.
Caesar is not looking at his map because he has his map inside
his head; moreover, it is a much better map than any carto-
grapher could provide, being in four dimensions rather than
two, and showing not just one world, but a modal array of
possible worlds (as in Fig 25.3, above). That is why Pompey –
who is just trusting to the fact that he is a good soldier and has a
large army – is doomed.

However, this inner transcendence of time is not all there is to
the relationship between time and the strategies of exchange. As
Munn (1986) has shown, in her subtle account of Gawan Kula
(Gawa is another small island forming part of the Kula ring) the
ultimate objective of the Kula operator is not the acquisition of
wealth as such, or the power which wealth confers, but the
transformation of the self into a spatio-temporally expanded
form. The inner time-transcendence of calculative reason is
oriented towards the achievement of overt time (or space-time)
transcendence in the external milieu. The Kula operator's objective is 'to climb' (-*mwen*), not just by acquiring the ability to exert
power or influence over others, but also, I think, by being able
to look down on the island world from a superior, encompassing vantage point, from which ordinary men appear as creep-
ing ants. To climb, one must be able to cause shells to move
frictionlessly towards one. As Munn notes (1983: 284ff), the
symbolism of the magical spells which 'move the minds of
others' (and their shells) depends on investing the operator
himself with limitless, frictionless mobility: 'the ritualist [i.e. the

Kula operator] slaps his body with a slippery fish thus acquiring a brilliance and mobile lightweightness (*gagaabala*) which make him so attractive the partner gives swiftly' (ibid.: 285). Successfully obtaining famous shells, the operator's name begins to travel around the Kula ring, independently of the more infrequent and restricted movements of his person. This is fame (*butu-*):

> Fame models spatio-temporal expansion of self effected by acts of influence by recasting these acts of influence (moving the mind of another) into movements of the circulation of one's name. . . . As iconic and reflexive code, fame is a *virtual form of influence*. Without fame, a man's influence would, as it were, go nowhere; successful acts would in effect remain locked within themselves in given times and places of their occurrence or be limited to immediate transactors. The circulation of names frees them, detaching them from these particularities and making them the topic of discourse through which they become available at other times and places.
>
> Since fame is the circulation of persons via their names . . . it typifies the capacity for subjective relocation and positive reconstitution of the self that is fundamental to the transaction process. . . . fame reflects the influential acts of the actor back on himself from an external source. . . . the actor knows himself as someone known by others. (Munn 1986: 117, emphasis in original)

In this way the internal transcendence of time is conjoined to the external, and a homology is established between the mind, hovering over its stock of internal representations of time, and the social persona, hovering over and transcending the spatio-temporal milieu of the Kula ring. The thickness and density of the time of exchanges, which Bourdieu has rightly emphasized, has to be understood, not just in isolation within the confined sphere of practices, but as the ground from which exchange in its ideal form detaches itself, as frictionless movement, expanded and disembodied personhood, ascending name and fame.

# Chapter 28

## A-series: B-series:: *Gemeinschaft*: *Gesellschaft*:: Them: Us

It may be considered irrelevant to invoke the time transcending activities of Kula operators against the theory of practice, since it might still be true that temporal awareness, for the average person going about his or her affairs in the social milieu of the western Pacific, or in Kybelia, would not depart from the sedimented and unreflected form dictated by the *habitus*. Competitive exchange is a very special context, and given that the very purpose of exchanges like the Kula is to allow men to aspire to becoming radically different from 'ordinary' men, it must occasion no surprise that the practices of the Kula (like *wabuwa-bu*) define themselves not in conformity with standard morality and unreflective immersion in the flux of daily life, but against them.

It is necessary, therefore, to turn to other texts by Bourdieu, which describe this ordinary, unreflective temporality. In 1963 Bourdieu published an essay on 'The Attitude of the Algerian Peasant towards Time' (Pitt-Rivers 1963: 55–72). These 'Algerian peasants' are the Kybele, and this text party reappears, with additional material, in *Outline of a Theory of Practice* (1977). In the 1963 text, we are told how the Algerian *fellah* lives according to a temporal rhythm determined by the divisions of the ritual calendar and the cycle of agricultural operations. These apparently technical activities are not perceived as such, but are constructed according to the schemata embodied in a rich accumulation of traditional attitudes; practical life is 'mythology in action'. Man lives by nature's grace, but only by violating nature with ploughs and with fire. These necessary liberties must be recompensed by sacrifices and the maintenance of ritual respect towards the earth; it is important not to be too greedy or to attempt to hurry things along:

286

> *It is useless to pursue the world,*
> *No one will ever overtake it.*

The Kabyle are immersed in nature and are part of it. They do not abstract time and set it apart from the flux of interlocking and culturally pre-ordained events which carries them along. Times are not specified chronometrically, but according to more or less vague conventions. We will meet 'at the next market'. This non-specificity is adequate (e.g. when making appointments) because, so to speak, if an event is not already inevitable as part of the working-out of the pre-ordained flow of socially expectable happenings, there is no sense in making special provisions for bringing it about – indeed, to do so is bordering on sacrilege, disrespect for the established order of things.

In Kabyle constructs of time, there is nothing which corresponds to the 'planners', which are such a prominent feature of the well-equipped modern office; shiny melamine boards marked out in calendrical intervals along the top, and divided into rows corresponding to particular executives down the side, onto which appointments, conferences, holidays, and the like can be entered with a felt pen, to be effaced and reconstructed at will. This objectified form of standardized, metricized duration is precisely what the 'lived' duration encountered among the Kabyle lacks:

> The intervals of subjective duration are not equal and uniform. The effective points of reference in the continual flux of time's passage are qualitative nuances read upon the surface of things. . . . Temporal points of reference are just so many experiences. One must avoid seeing here points of division, which would presuppose the notion of regular measured intervals, that is to say, a spatial conception of the temporal. The islands of time which are defined by these landmarks are not apprehended as segments of a continuous line, but rather as so many enclosed units. . . . The lapse of time which constitutes the present is the *whole of an action* seen in the unity of a perception including both the retained past and the anticipated future. (Bourdieu 1963: 59–60)

The week ('the market') is not a measure of time, but a temporal horizon within whose confines is to be found a familiar landscape unified by a single perspective. Following Husserl closely, Bourdieu reinterprets the standard concepts of 'present', 'past' and 'future' to accord with this perspectival time.

'The "present" of existence', he says, 'is not confined to the mere instantaneous present, because consciousness holds united in a single look aspects of the world already perceived and on the point of being perceived' (ibid.: 60). This is the 'specious present' of James expanded indefinitely beyond the putative 12 seconds attributed to it by the psychologists, to encompass weeks, months, years; a *long present* filled with dynamism and activity, yet never really displaced, because *this* present is imperceptibly transmuted into another, and another, all of which mutually enfold one another.

Turning to a consideration of the future, Bourdieu is able to exploit the fact that the French language makes a distinction between 'the future' (*le futur*) and 'the forthcoming' (*l'avenir*) which is not made very naturally in English. *L'avenir* is the 'future' of the 'long present', the '"pre-perceptive" anticipation' of the future of the present (i.e. the protended future), as opposed to *le futur*, which is future time grasped from a standpoint not located in the present, but in advance of it (i.e. the future fantasied *modo futuri exacti*, to use the terminology of Schutz (1967)). The forthcoming' is perceived in the same manner as the actual present to which it is tied by an organic unity. It is 'presented' in the course of the synthesis which establishes the present together with its temporal horizons: the 'future' lies below this horizon: it is inaccessible except as a representation, an imaginary present defined in opposition to this one, posited and simultaneously negated. Linked to this distinction between 'the forthcoming' and 'the future' is a further one between the 'possible' and the 'potential'. Possibilities are explored in the activity of 'projecting', which is free, unconstrained by 'data': 'potentialities', on the other hand, are not fantasied but are perceived, just as actualities are perceived. Potentialities are inside the world, not beyond its boundaries, as are mere possibilities (Bourdieu 1963: 61–2).

Having drawn these distinctions, Bourdieu proceeds to argue that the Kabyle are obliged by their ethos of respectful subservience to social conventions disguised as natural necessity, to occupy themselves entirely with the 'forthcoming', i.e. with potentialities encompassed within the horizons of the concrete present, rather than with 'the future' which, they say, 'belongs to God'. In this way Bourdieu is able to provide a solution to the paradox, one no doubt observable elsewhere among pre-capitalist rural societies, presented by the fact that the Kabyle simultaneously exalt foresight, and approve of hoarding, yet preach submission to time, and deny that their long-term future is in their own hands rather than God's. The distinction lies between making a virtue of looking to the forthcoming (the future of the present) by hoarding grain against the *potentiality* of a bad harvest, already inscribed and plain to see in the lore governing farming practices, and the altogether suspect practice of predicting the future (*le futur*), which is to usurp the privileged position assigned to God alone.

The 'long present' of the Kabyle (under traditional conditions) generates a system of social reproduction which maintains a steady state, constrained only in the last resort by technical and ecological factors. Agricultural surpluses are hoarded (banked) in the form of cattle, but unlike money in the bank, cattle reserves cannot accumulate beyond a finite amount, because of the limitations imposed by the shortage of pasture. Hoarding is intrinsically self-limiting because accumulation is carried out within the horizons of an already established pattern of practices, and is oriented solely towards conserving this pattern. Genuine capital accumulation results in capital funds which are liberated from the overriding necessity to perpetuate the present, and which can be invested on the basis of 'forecasts' (predictions) of future possible gains. This kind of capital accumulation is impossible for the Kabyle, because it contradicts the peasant ethos of conservatism, and threatens the compact between man and nature.

We can sum up this discussion by remarking on the fact that Bourdieu is arguing essentially that 'lived' time is A-series time, i.e. time focused around a present which is integrally a past and a future, and which hence has a natural tendency to perpetuate itself. 'Lived' time (as opposed to represented time) tends to enfold the subject in a cocoon of implicitly accepted truths about the world, because it unites the past, the actuality and the becoming of the world in a seamless texture of interconnected experiences, a flux which carries the subject along with it. At the same time, it must be emphasized that this flux is not a matter of simple causal necessity, and indeed is not an objective phenomenon at all, but is the product of subjectivity, the gap in nature into which is inserted human consciousness. The self-perpetuating character of the Kabyle world is not the result of material necessities, but of the inertia which rules in the Kabyle mind, as a result of the very activity of the Kabyle mind at work in constructing its world. For Bourdieu, therefore, the Husserlian A-series model of time-consciousness tends to suggest a principle, not of limitless novelty, but dynamic equilibrium; everything changes, but everything remains the same. Past, present and future are so intimately fused together that the distinction between them – at any rate within the 'horizon' imposed by customary attitudes – tends to disappear altogether.

Implicitly opposed to the A-series 'lived' time is another kind of time, less elaborately described, the time of objectivist social science and of rational (capitalist) accumulation and decision-making. This is the 'time' of office planner-boards and economic forecasting, the kind from which the Kabyle are excluded, and which plays no part in their practices. This objectified, regularized duration, detached from the present, is B-series time.

In other words, Bourdieu is reworking the classic sociological contrast between Toennies' *Gemeinschaft* and *Gesellschaft* (mechanical solidarity vs. organic solidarity, status vs. contract, premodern vs. modern, etc.) in terms of an opposition between 'lived' (A-series) temporality and represented or objectified (B-series) temporality. This represents an enormous advance over the Durkheim-derived tradition of temporal cultural relativity, discussed in the first part of this book (Chapters 1–8) in that it articulates contrastive regimes of social time directly to the basic discontinuity between pre-modern and modern societies, and in addition does so in a way that is philosophically justified, in that the contrast between A-series temporality and B-series temporality is logically fundamental (Chapter 16).

Can one draw this global contrast been 'us' and 'them' on the basis that whereas we operate according to a predominantly objectified or B-series concept of time, 'they' operate according to an embedded or 'lived' A-series temporal regime? At one level, Bourdieu is plainly correct in arguing along these lines. The extent to which time is represented objectively in schedule form and made subject to conscious manipulation is evidently much greater in modern, technical societies than it is among peasants, like the Kybele. Even more so among the Umedas, who have no month-names, no recurrent weekly market, and who rely for purposes of temporal co-ordination on 'indexical' day-expression like 'the day after the day after tomorrow', which have A-series, rather than B-series truth-conditions.

But it seems to me that the distinction which needs to be drawn between pre-modern and modern temporalities is not that pre-modern societies experience time only as 'lived' in the A-series, whereas we moderns turn time in a quasi-spatial B-series time-map. This cannot be so, I think, because the very process of time cognition, as I argued in Chapter 24, requires that A-series perceptions of the flux of surrounding events be mapped onto an underlying set of B-series representations during the process of interpretation. What is different between the pre-modern temporal regime and the modern one is the qualitative characteristics of representations of time, not their logical status as 'lived' A-series time or 'represented' B-series time.

Take the Umedas, for instance. The Umedas do not know that every lunar month has 29.5 days, or indeed any consistent number of days. As far as they are concerned the moon is like a tuber, growing in a garden, and tubers can grow quickly or slowly for unknown reasons to do with them. Consequently, when the Umedas notice the waxing moon, they comment on it favourably, as if the swollen moon were a contingent piece of horticultural good fortune, not an absolutely regular and predictable astronomical event. According to Bourdieu's interpretation, this shows that the Umedas experience time subjectively as 'qualitative nuances read off the surface of things' (cf. p. 287) rather than objectively as regular metricized duration. It is true that they do not understand successive lunations metrically. But it remains true that in interpreting the moon's behaviour the Umedas are employing a schema, and they know 'where they are' with respect to a given lunation, not directly, from A-series perception alone, but indirectly, by interpreting the moon they see in the light of the schema (the B-series non-indexical beliefs about the moon), which they have internalized. The difference between them and us arises from the fact that they have different beliefs about the moon from those that we hold, viz. that the moon is a vegetative organism rather than an inert astronomical body. Their time-maps of the moon are founded on a distinct set of contingent beliefs, but are not logically different from ours. Specifically, a time-map of a process of vegetative growth and decay is differently modalized, by contrast with a time-map embodying beliefs derived from astronomical knowledge. Possible worlds in which vegetative organisms grow rapidly, or only slowly, are modally highly accessible to one another. A plant may flourish, or it may not, and neither outcome affords much surprise-value. Because the Umeda's cognitive map of lunation is not a map showing an alternativeless, predictable process like ours (for us, a 'slow' lunation belongs to a very remote sphere of counterfactuality), but a modal spread of possible worlds in which lunations occur at different *tempi*, it follows that their attitude towards each lunation as it occurs is different from ours. They are more acutely concerned with the development of each lunation as it occurs, because each lunation is a distinctive actualization of lunation in general, just as each tuber is a realization of the growth of tubers in general. But this is not to say that they do not have a B-series time-map, or temporal model, of lunation in general, because, lacking this, they would be unable to say whether the moon was growing well or badly, and their favourable comments on a well-ripened moon would be meaningless.

They seem, in other words, to be, so to speak, A-series dominated, because the form taken by their B-series time-maps is such as to place extra emphasis on the temporal flux as evolving, seamless contingency, rather than as events occurring predictably in totalized, metricized duration. Their B-series representations are highly modalized, not in that they envisage any unlikely events, but in representing the temporal field as a spread of equi-probable contingencies uncalibrated by any regularized schedule, such as an astronomically-based or officially imposed calendar. In the absence of an external, public schedule, of the kind that structures time in advanced societies, they must continually make situationally specific judgements as to their precise location in relation to their temporal neighbourhood, whereas for us, this process of location in time goes without saying, because every moment of our waking lives is articulated to a schedule which is instantly accessible and which embraces everything. To this extent, Bourdieu is justified in contrasting the time of pre-modern societies to our own as A-series dominated, in that the making of temporal judgements in clock-less, calendar-less, schedule-less societies such as the Umeda is permanently problematic, and recourse cannot be made to any definitive, regularly calibrated, B-series time-map, but only to a collection of uncalibrated maps showing contingent processes (lunations, vegetative growth, seasonal weather changes, and so on) in a plurality of modal alternativeness-relations, one with another. The Umeda are A-series dominated in that they have severe limitations in representing the B-series. But this is not at all the same as saying that they do not conceptualize time in the B-series mode at all, because the making of

A-series temporal judgements (i.e. this is the right moment to plant, harvest, etc.) always depends, in the final analysis, on the possibility of interpreting indexical A-series perceptions of the temporal flux as 'images' from an underlying B-series time-map, albeit a modally uncertain and metrically uncalibrated one.

# Chapter 29

# Calendars and Consensual Co-ordination

Bourdieu's discussion of time in relation to the theory of practice is not, however, conducted in terms of the ethnography of a society such as the Umeda, who lack even the most informal calendar. The Kabyle are in a different league altogether, in that they possess an elaborate agrarian 'calendrical' scheme, including at least six named months (cf. Bourdieu 1977: 99, Figure 2) plus a number of other seasonal terms and terms indicating regular phases of the agricultural year. In providing a prolonged and exceptionally rich account of the Kabyle calendar Bourdieu's primary target is the 'synoptic illusion' to which objectivists (structuralists) fall victim, in attempting to discover logical coherence, rather than practical coherence, in bodies of cultural knowledge.

What structuralist orthodoxy wants, he says, is to discover 'a lacuna-free, contradiction-free, whole, a sort of *unwritten score*, of which all the calendars derived from informants are then regarded as impoverished *performances*' (Bourdieu 1977: 98). Not only does this unwritten score not exist as part of ethnographic actuality, it also does not have the sociological function, attributed to it by objectivists, of determining behaviour by 'regulating' it, i.e. providing a set of rules for the timing of activities to be followed by all and sundry. This calendar as musical score (the calendar as a predetermined schedule) is, according to Bourdieu, an artefact of literacy and the kind of scholarly objectives, rather than practical ones, which are uppermost in the minds of outsider ethnographers.

Bourdieu notes that the accounts given by different Kabyle, or the same Kabyle on different occasions, of the periodizations of the Kabyle year, depend on a variety of factors and may not coincide. Some say the year begins on a given date (1 September in

294

the Julian calendar); some say it begins on, or about, 15 August, when the rains begin, a day called 'the door of the year' when contracts are renewed and a sacrifice is made; still others start the year on the first day of ploughing, the important transition so far as agricultural activities are concerned.

The same indeterminacy is seen elsewhere in Kabyle ideas: let us consider only one example *'lyali'*, 'the winter of winter'. This is conventionally a period of forty days' duration, within winter, which comes to an end when the planted cereals in the fields sprout above the earth. In the middle of *lyali* lies the first day of January (*ennayer*), marking a period of renewal rites and taboos. Not only is there variability in informants' formal definitions of *lyali* in the calendrical sense (*lyali*, as a concept, only comes to the fore as people notice what is going on about them, and say 'we are entering *lyali*'), but when questioned informants may even commit themselves to the apparently illogical proposition that *'ennayer* is in the middle of winter' *and 'ennayer* is in the middle of *lyali*' but *'lyali* is not in the middle of winter'. This contradiction arises because *lyali* is the winter of winter, and winter is not the middle of the year (if the year begins in autumn, spring is the middle of the year, hence *lyali* as the winter of winter precedes the middle of winter). Bourdieu comments: 'the [informant's] practical grasp of the structure which leads him to think of *lyali* as the winter of winter overrides calculative reason' (Bourdieu 1977: 105).

The Kabyle calendar is not a fixed array of periodizations, but 'a simple scansion of passing time'. What is meant by 'scansion'? The metaphor implies that practical time-consciousness is analogous to the internalized pattern of 'ti-tum-ti-tum-ti-tum-ti-tum-ti-TUM' expectations which carry us along as we listen to rolling Shakespearean periods. These rhythmic beats keep us consciously in phase with the verse, as it unfolds, but does not constitute a fixed schema which has any significance apart from the meaning of verse itself. It would be a poor verse which was simply the filling-in of a metrical pattern: but Bourdieu's implied claim is that in constituting the ethnographic fiction of the calendar-as-schedule, that is what objectivism seeks to realize. The Kabyle year is 'scanned' in periodizations: 'the white nights of *lyali*', 'the black nights of *lyali*', 'the green days', 'the yellow days' . . ., and punctual time-indicators: 'the door of the year', 'the old woman', 'the death of the land', and so forth, which are recognized as they loom up, occur and are done with, in the flux

of practical existence, as a series of passing 'guide-marks' as to
the progress of the year, but which never undergo *totalization*, to
form a coherent schematization of homogeneous duration (i.e.
B-series time):

> Just as genealogy substitutes a space of unequivocal, homogeneous
> relationships, established once and for all, for a spatially and tempor-
> ally discontinuous set of islands of kinship . . . and just as a map
> replaces the discontinuous, patchy space of practical paths by the
> homogeneous space of geometry, so a calendar substitutes a linear,
> homogeneous, continuous time for practical time, which is made up
> of incommensurable islands of duration, each with its own rhythm,
> the time that flies by or drags, depending on what one is *doing*, i.e. on
> the *functions* conferred on it by the activity in progress. By distribut-
> ing *guide-marks* (ceremonies and tasks) along a continuous line, one
> turns them into *dividing marks* united in a relation of simple succes-
> sion, thereby creating, *ex nihilo* the question of the intervals and
> correspondences between points which are no longer topologically
> but metrically equivalent. . . .
> The establishment of a single series [via the 'false totalization' of
> the 'synoptic illusion'] creates *ex nihilo* a whole host of relations (of
> simultaneity, succession, or symmetry, for example) between terms
> and guide-marks of different levels, which, being produced and used
> in different situations, are never brought face to face in practice and
> are thus compatible practically even when logically contradictory
> [e.g. as in the *lyali* example mentioned above]. The synoptic diagram
> takes all the temporal oppositions which can be collected and as-
> sembled, and distributes them in accordance with the laws of suc-
> cession (i.e. (1) 'y follows x' excludes 'x follows y'; (2) 'if y follows
> x and z follows y, z follows x'; (3) 'either y follows x or x follows y').
> This makes it possible to apprehend at a glance, *uno intuitu et tota
> simul*, as Descartes said, *monothetically*, as Husserl put it, meanings
> which are produced and used polythetically, that is to say, not only
> one after another, but one by one, step by step. (Bourdieu 1977: 103,
> 106–7)

I think everybody would accept that the observations from
which Bourdieu proceeds are entirely valid. Versions of the local
'calendar' produced by informants in non-literate societies are
vague and inconsistent, and such calendrical schemes as exist
are applied in practice in idiosyncratic ways. Moreover, the
technical aspects of literacy, and the profound changes basic
attitudes which literacy produces, means that anthropologists,
in transforming informants' statements into codified ethno-

graphic accounts, must ask questions 'which are not questions for practice' and which have no answers (e.g. how can 12, 13 or 20 'moons' be accommodated in a solar year; cf. p. 000 below). Without disputing these points, however, one can legitimately object to some of the inferences Bourdieu draws, and in particular to the anti-cognitivist, behaviourist position this writer favours.

Let us return for a moment to this matter of *lyali*. Bourdieu's inconsistent informant is supposed not to have a 'durational' idea of time on the grounds that he sees no contradiction in holding simultaneously that: *'ennayer is in the middle of winter' and 'ennayer is in the middle of lyali' but 'lyali is not in the middle of winter'*. However, consider the equivalent problem in relation to the location of 'the midlands' in England. 'The Midlands are the middle of England' – agreed – 'Northampton is in the middle of England' – agreed (Northampton is furthest from any coast of any major city in England) – so, is 'Northampton in the middle of the Midlands'? – not at all: Northampton is on the south-east periphery of the area designated 'the Midlands' in my dialect of English, well to the east and south of Leicester and Nottingham, i.e. the 'East Midlands', whereas the 'centre' of the Midlands is surely Birmingham, in the West Midlands. This apparent contradictoriness in present throught the lexical set denoting regions in the United Kingdom. Sheffield is in 'the north of England', but is closer to London than it is to the closest border with Scotland. Glasgow and Edinburgh are both in 'central Scotland', but Edinburgh is on the east coast of Scotland, Glasgow is on the west coast of Scotland, and both are twice as far from the north coast of Scotland as they are from Scotland's border with England. And so on.

All these are instances of the logic of 'fuzzy sets' – the logic which allows one to say that a Shetland pony belongs to the set of 'small' objects (because it is a small horse), and a tarantula to the class of large objects (because it is a large spider), and still be able to say, without contradiction, (1) that large objects are bigger than small objects, and (2) that Shetland ponies are not smaller than tarantulas or tarantulas bigger than Shetland ponies. The Midlands are in the 'middle of England' in terms of the regional set: the south/east/west/midlands/north, but Northampton is in the middle of the map of England, which is not quite the same thing. Similarly 'midnight' is 'the middle of the night' (equidistant between dusk and dawn). But one would not say 'I was woken up in the middle of the night by the telephone ringing' and mean thereby 'at midnight' rather than 'in the middle of the period during which I am accustomed to sleep', which typically begins only an hour or so before midnight.

It does not seem to me, therefore, that the kind of evidence of inconsistency adduced by Bourdieu is indicative of a non-durational notion of time: what is shown is simply the complex presuppositional texture of language, which makes distinctions within domains not specifiable absolutely, but only pragmatically. If this is all the Bourdieu wishes to maintain (which some readers of his text might think the case), then I could hardly object. But the point about 'fuzzy' logics is that they are logical, and only apparently 'fuzzy'. What Bourdieu wishes to show, however, is that the Kabyle are capable of doing without the 'laws of succession' (i.e. the essential logical foundations of B-series time) on the grounds that, under certain circumstances, they appear to commit themselves to propositions which, when taken to their logical conclusions, would contradict these 'laws'. (Which the Kabyle never do, because, as Bourdieu says, to do so is to raise questions 'which are not questions for practice'.) This seems far too strong. One can admit that the Kabyle operate with a multitude of different kinds of temporal schemes, appropriate to specific contexts of discourse or action, without abandoning the notion that the Kabyle recognize the logical principle that if event x occurs 'before' event y, in a certain scheme, and event z 'after' event y, x occurs 'before' event z. They are logically compelled to do this. The notion of 'X-before-Y' carries with it, quite ineluctibly, the deductive consequences stated: (*'if* X-before-Y *and* Y-before-Z, *then* X-before-Z') because the notion of 'beforeness' invoked in the first term (X-before-Y) has no meaning unless these consequences follow. Unless the 'laws of succession' hold, nothing can be asserted in X-before-Y, and if nothing is asserted in X-before-Y, there is nothing that this assertion can conceivably contradict.

In other words, if Bourdieu is to maintain that Kabyle articulations of time are multiple, contradictory, context-specific, etc., it is necessary for him simultaneously to hold that standard temporal-logical conditions apply, otherwise these contradictions disappear. One can agree that these contradictions carry with them no practical penalties, indeed they make salient temporal articulations easier to codify than they would be otherwise. But that is not to say that they are non-existent, simply because they are not incompatible with the functions of organized knowledge. These contradictions appear only as a result of analysis. True; but the 'logic' of the system (the shifting of gears which occurs as one moves from one practical frame of reference to another) also only appears as a result of analysis. A 'false totalization' which attempted to reconstruct the Kabyle calendar in a manner consistent with consistent chronometry would, indeed, traduce this system, but unless 'totalization' of some kind is attempted, and the logical discontinuities this totalization produces are identified in the context of an abstract model, the true characteristics of such systems remain forever obscure. The subtleties of consensual co-ordination arise, not out of an illogical attitude towards the meanings of such fundamental concepts as 'before' and 'after' (which are absolutely indispensable to the construction of any kind of temporal articulation) but from the complexities of the pragmatic criteria which, under differing contextual controls, determine the application of temporal schemes of a B-series kind to the A-series flux made apparent to perception.

The logic of these B-series schemes is, in my opinion, unaffected by considerations of the kind entertained by Bourdieu. This author wishes, for reasons already discussed, to emphasize the A-theoretical side of things at the expense of the B-theoretical one, and his argument to the effect that 'the calendar' as a construct in B-series time is an artefact of analysis is designed to further this ultimate goal. The B-series exists for 'science', for bourgeois intellectuals, but not for *gemeinschaftlich* people like the Kabyle.

For reasons which I have already attempted to make clear, I do not wholly agree with this analysis. Bourdieu is entirely justified in demonstrating that the Kabyle calendar (with its insufficient number of months and its dependence on the contingent progress of agricultural operations) is not the 'local equivalent' to the Gregorian calendar, and does not constitute a chronometrical scheme 'imposed' on the scheduling of Kabyle life from without, but a device for 'recognizing' the onset of agrarian periodizations as they loom up, locally, and never mind celestial events. None the less, it is totalized, because it is only in relation to the calendrical scheme as a whole that the contingent passage of recognized periodicities has any meaning. The calendar is primarily agrarian rather than celestial, and because of this, it is not calibrated in quantitively equal periods.

But that does not make it cease to function, logically, as a calendar, just as an Umeda lunar 'month' is still a 'month', even though the Umedas accept the possibility (which we do not) that some moons grow swiftly, others slowly.

In order to understand the workings of 'primitive' (aberrant) calendars, it is necessary to do more than place the emphasis exclusively on practice, as Bourdieu does. It is also necessary to consider the characteristics of cultural knowledge; the forms of the representations in which abstract knowledge is held, and the logic of the procedures through which this knowledge is applied in practical situations. Bourdieu does not give any description of the formation of judgements about 'what time of year it is now' in the Kabyle year, only noting that these judgements are based on proverbial wisdom, and tend to vary from informant to informant. Fortunately, a detailed ethnographic study of precisely this problem in connection with the Mursi of Ethiopia has been published by Turton and Ruggles (1978).

The Mursi, a tribe of herders and horticulturalists occupying the valley and escarpment of the Omo river in southern Ethiopia, have a calendar of twelve numbered *bergu* (moons) associated with particular activities, plus a thirteenth 'unnamed' *bergu* associated with no activity but timed to coincide with the flooding of the Omo river, the key event in Mursi ecology at the beginning/end of the year. The activities are:

*Bergu* 1: Omo river subsides; move to riverside gardens
*Bergu* 2: Clearing riverside gardens
*Bergu* 3: Planting sorghum in riverside gardens
*Bergu* 4: Planting sorghum and maize, weeding
*Bergu* 5: Harvesting sorghum, weeding, bird-scaring
*Bergu* 6: Harvesting, firing bush gardens
*Bergu* 7: Store Omo crop, prepare bush gardens
*Bergu* 8: Heavy rain, plant bush gardens
*Bergu* 9: Weeding young plants
*Bergu* 10: Weeding, bird-scaring
*Bergu* 11: Bush harvest, honey collecting, duelling
*Bergu* 12: Store bush crop, drinking, duelling

For the most part, the Mursi are content to assume that the current *bergu* is the one associated with the particular activity he/she is pursuing at the moment. However, Mursi who do not have pretensions to be experts on the calendar are quite content

to admit that they personally may not be correct in their identi-
fication of the current *bergu*. On the other hand, they are usually
disinclined to cede authority in such matters to their immediate
village associates, relying instead on the (unavailable) testimony
of distant or even dead calendrical experts as the following
dialogue brings out:

Anthropologist:   What number is the *bergu* now?
Mursi:   Don't ask me.
A:   Don't you know, then?
M:   Not me. I just listen to what people say about the
*bergu*.
A:   Well, what do people say at the moment then?
M:   Some say it's 5 and some say it's 6.
A:   Which do you think it is?
M:   I told you, I just listen to what they say, I'm not an
expert on the *bergu*.
A:   Who is, then?
M:   Well, there's . . . [*pause for thought*] there's that Gongwi
man who died the other day . . . what's his name . . .
Chuah: he was a real expert on the *bergu*. If he were
alive now he would be able to tell you.
A:   Is there anybody who *is* alive now who could tell me?
M:   Well, there's . . . Girimalori [*a man living 65 miles
distant*].

(Turton and Ruggles 1978: 588)

But this widespread refusal of Mursi to commit themselves to
rigid views on the current number of the *bergu* is not merely
evidence of a 'practical' or A-series-dominated attitude to time,
but is in fact essential to the functioning of the system. This
arises from the fact that as a schedule, the Mursi calendar is
linked, however variably from year to year, to meteorological
conditions and thus to the solar year, (of 365.25 days) but as a
time-keeping device it is constructed out of lunar months, of
which there are more than twelve, but less than thirteen, in a
solar year. (On average, as solar year is 11 days longer than any
12 successive lunar periods of between 29 and 30 days each.) So
if there *were* an established Mursi consensus identifying the
moon, and it were to hold for a prolonged period, the solar/
seasonal year and the association between *bergu* and seasonal
activities would before long become out of step. No calendrical

expert would commit the elementary blunder of leaving out a moon, yet this is precisely what must happen periodically if the system is not to get out of kilter. The system works because the public can afford to be fickle, not so much about what the current *bergu* number is, but about what they thought the last *bergu* number was. Here the activity-less Omo-flooding month comes in. The fact that the Omo flooded last *bergu*, or two, three or more *bergu* ago provides a definite reference point in the light of which the beliefs held about what *bergu* it was just prior to the Omo floods can be silently reassessed. Take *bergu* 11 and 12, for instance:

| 11 | 12 | 13 |
|----|----|-----|
| Honey collecting | Drinking, duelling | No activity |

———————————— [the Omo floods] →

If we reconstruct the picture during the second quarter of lunation 12, it is likely that Mursi opinion on the *bergu* number will be divided into two parties, the 'leaders', who hold that it is *bergu* 12, and the 'followers', who, perhaps, are still collecting honey and who hold that it is *bergu* 11. Others, like Turton's informant, may claim to be undecided. Once the Omo definitively floods, as it does at this point, there is no reason to resist the consensus that the ensuing lunation is *bergu* 13. The honey-collectors will drink and duel during this *bergu*, while those who were drinking and duelling already will continue to do so. The very fact that the 13th *bergu* is associated with no activity in particular, especially not with any productive activity, makes it possible to reconcile the arbitrary insertion of this *bergu* into the otherwise relatively fixed scheme of *bergu* activities. This *bergu* identifies, *ex post facto*, the ending of the old year and the beginning of the new. Once the year gets into its stride, however, it would appear that this consensus breaks down again, since no records or tallies are kept of the passage of lunations. There is room once again for disagreement between the followers who say it is *bergu* 6 and their opponents who say it is already *bergu* 7.

To provide an additional way of fuelling these apparently interminable debates, the Mursi have invented some rather sophisticated-seeming astronomical cross-checks on the progress of the solar year. From cliffs overlooking the Omo valley, observations are made to determine the approach of the winter solstice 'when the sun goes into his house'. Although the Mursi are technically quite capable of identifying the solstice, Turton and Ruggles warn that this should not lead us into overestimating the degree of systematization of the Mursi calendar. There is no hard-and-fast rule specifying the *bergu* of the winter solstice. Sometimes it is *bergu* 5, sometimes *bergu* 6; but the sun's behaviour in this respect is contingent. If the sun goes into his house in *bergu* 5, i.e. in the *bergu* that any particular Mursi takes to be *bergu* 5, then that is held to be an ominous sign of a poor rainy season, come *bergu* 8. On the other hand, another Mursi, who is of the opinion that the current *bergu* is not 5 at all, but 6, will not be led to draw the same inferences.

In other words, the sun is observed, like the weather, to provide clues as to which *bergu* it is, mainly, no doubt, to confirm prejudices already arrived at, but is not the source of final arbitration or evidence which is in any way stronger than other evidence provided by the weather, the progress of the agricultural year, or attempts to count lunations. It is all a matter of village opinion, there being no single knock-down argument other than the annual arrival of the Omo floods, which would identify the *bergu* once and for all. Each may interpret the available clues as he wishes. The authors rightly compare Mursi time reckoning to divination, a similarly tentative procedure, and one equally swayed by currents of public opinion.

But why, in that case, do the Mursi have a lunar calendar at all? It is not as if there were any technical reasons for confining particular activities to particular lunar periods, since it is the cycle of changes in seasonal conditions, not the passage of months, which determines whether a particular activity is feasible at any particular moment. Organizationally speaking, the apparatus of named *bergu* is functionless. Yet it appears that the Mursi have an abiding interest in knowing which *bergu* it is, even though this knowledge is uncertain. The suggestion that calendar-keeping is like divination, i.e. is a form of occult knowledge, is illuminating here. Divination does not change the world, in the manner of active occult interventions such as garden-fertility magic or witchcraft. Instead, it gives passive access to a world which has enacted itself, and will enact itself, beyond our direct experience and without our intervention (Gell 1975). Divination confers power by conferring knowledge. If calendrical knowledge is like divinatory revelation, then it too is a means of obtaining vicarious transcendence. Calendrical

knowledge of the kind that the Mursi construct collectively out
of the ongoing *bergu* debate, differs from divinatory revelation
only in that it seeks mundane transcendence rather than super-
naturally guaranteed transcendence. And this mundane transcendence has a practical aspect to it, because by assessing the
degree of convergence between the progress of the ideal annual
cycle – the one encapsulated in *bergu* lore – and the actually
experienced unfolding of the productive cycle in any given year,
the Mursi are provided with systematic feedback as to their
current predicament. The calendar does not dictate practice –
only the seasonal conditions do that – but the calendar tells the
Mursi how well they are doing in relation to the totality of
productive tasks which have to be accomplished throughout the
year. By monitoring advances and lags, they know when extra
efforts may be required, or when they can afford to relax; and
they know when to anticipate the lowering of standard expectations, or the onset of conditions of unusual prosperity. And on
the basis of this feedback they are, no doubt, able to make
strategic decisions (for instance, about investing stock in marriages and rituals) more advantageously. Feedback from the
*bergu* debate is fed forward into rational decision-making.

The Mursi calendar, in spite of divinatory character (indeed,
because of its divinatory character), is much more than a 'simple
scansion of passing time'. It is a system for the continuous
production of socially useful knowledge. But like all social systems for the production and deployment of knowledge, is has a
tendency to gravitate towards 'experts'. In a sense, the efficacy
of the calendrical system arises from the fact that everyone feeds
information into the ongoing calendrical debate, but this multitudinous input seeks a final common pathway, i.e. output via a
spokesman for the consensus. The role of the calendrical expert
is the outcome, not of any longing to create hierarchy and
submit to it, but of the inclusive and democratic basis on which
the *bergu* debate rests. Unless this debate can (at least notionally)
cohere in the utterance of a single, authoritative voice, there is
only a hubbub of conflicting claims, and the production of
knowledge is blocked. Authority is therefore invoked, even
when it is not present and its pronouncements are unavailable,
as in the conversation reproduced above. More commonly,
authority is present and institutionalized, though, as we shall
see, often systematically ambiguous.

At this point there arises a question about which Bourdieu is surprisingly silent, namely, the nature of the conjunction between calendars, knowledge and power. Bourdieu does not deal with this subject – though he is exceptionally illuminating about power in other contexts – because he has determined in advance that calendars are not knowledge systems, but simply 'landmarks' which are recognized as they loom up out of the A-series, pass and are left behind. Because he argues that only scholars, whose scholarly interests have nothing to do with the constraints governing practical life, theorize about calendars, he cannot account for the fact that calendrical knowledge, in totalized, represented (i.e. B-series) form is an exceptionally important species of 'symbolic capital' in very many societies, though not perhaps among the Kabyle. It is to the nexus between calendrical knowledge and power that I must now turn.

# Chapter 30

## Calendars and Power

Burman's discussion of the calendar on Simbo (Solomon Islands) provides an excellent example of the significant political role played by calendrical authorities in numerous pre-modern societies (Burman 1981). On this island the calendar had become relatively disjunct from the production of subsistence foods (largely in the hands of women) and was instead geared to the passage of lunations and the growth and harvesting of two seasonal crops of different varieties of *canarium* nuts, one ripening from May onwards (the cold/dry/male season) the other available only from October (the wet/hot/female season). The cultivation of these nuts was of the utmost importance to the Simbo Islanders (especially the men) because they could be exchanged, on the neighbouring island of Rembo, for shell rings and pigs, of which the islanders of Simbo lacked a local supply.

The man who occupied the central position in the ritual feasts financed by the overseas dealings in nuts was the *bangara*, the calendar keeper and Big Man. This position was hereditary within the clan which occupied the most favourable terrain for nut cultivation on Simbo (though one may assume that it was competed for within this territorial group). Such a man, wealthy in pigs, shell-rings and nuts, controlled the calendar itself, the *pepapopu*, or tally of moons. This device had been revealed to the original mythic *bangara* by a god, and aroused such a degree of jealousy that the original tally-keeper had been slain by his rivals. Later the tally-keeper's ghost communicated his secret to a committee of magicians, who established the institution in its traditional form. The tally comprised a set of six half-shells of coconut, strung on a string like the beads of an abacus, so that they could be pushed to one side, and also turned over. The tally could thus assume twelve configurations, depending on which sides the nuts were on the string, and which way up they were (all the nuts were turned over at the transition between the two canarium seasons mentioned earlier). At each new moon, the tally shells were moved appropriately, and thus the months were counted. This was an esoteric operation. Only the *bangara* himself (and presumably some close associates) knew the state of the tally, or the significance of the twelve configurations.

Burman's main point is the important one that there was a direct transfer between the *bangara*'s occult calendrical knowledge and his imputed power, not just to announce the onset of the seasons, but also to control them. He was the master of events, in that his clan possessed as part of its *sacra*, five ancient shell-rings, controlling, respectively, the south-east trades, the wet season north-westerlies, the cessation of drought, earthquakes and the 'foundations of the land'. He controlled, says Burman, 'the very motion of time' (1981: 289).

However – a point Burman notices, but does not develop – the *bangara*'s eminent position was not of the 'automatic' kind which stems from the instituted capacity to assert ritual responsibility for real-world events which would happen anyway, with or without magical interventions. On the contrary the *bangara* was regularly confronted with a delicate calendrical dilemma, which the lore connected with the tallies could not have elucidated. He would have been responsible for the insertion of intercalary months at intervals of between two and three years, since the tally, as described, could only have numbered lunations up to twelve. The fact that the insertion of intercalary months must, by all accounts, have been done informally, probably explains the secrecy surrounding the tally-keeping procedure. The tally focalized the problem of ensuring the conjunction of lunar months and a solar year, but could not resolve it. If the *bangara* had allowed the tally to lose track of the solar year (which is by no means so clearly marked at low latitudes as at high ones) serious consequences would have ensued; events (such as feasts and expeditions) would have been mistimed, and the authority of the *pepapopu*, and the *bangara* with it, would have been devalued. The *bangara* must therefore have had to keep a close and independent watch on the whole range of productive activities (and especially on the progress of the two canarium crops). The calendrical process motivated a 'structured perception' of natural and social processes which was, surely, both to the advantage of the *bangara* in directing collective action – he had executive control over nut production, exchange and the timing of feasts – and also contributed to the sense that in carrying out his executive functions, he had supernatural assistance. The very lack of automaticity in the co-ordination of lunar and solar calendars ensured that socially significant information was generated and codified within the restricted circle of calendrical experts – headed by the *bangara* – whose power depended, not on unquestioned traditions of authority and subservience, but on the intellectual discipline demanded by the year-tracking procedure, and the practical advantages accruing to those with access to codified knowledge.

The complete role-convergence between the calendar-keeper and Big Man witnessed on Simbo is admittedly unusual. It is more normal to find that calendrical expertise is more widely disseminated among the tribal elite of men of wealth, elders, noted magicians, etc. In the Trobriands, for instance, knowledge of the lunar calendar was just one aspect of the expertise of the *tonowi*, or garden magicians, whose eminent social position mainly rested on their semi-hereditary knowledge of spells and garden medicines (Malinowski 1935). The Trobriand calendar is interesting from a slightly different point of view, however, in that it enables us to detect the emergence of another nexus between calendars and power; but not, in this instance, the 'personal' power of the individual Big Man-cum-expert, but the collective power exercised by a dominant political district over subordinate ones. This observation, which I have developed from an insight provided by Damon (1981), arises from the fact that the Trobriands are divided into four 'calendrical districts': (1) Kiriwina, the north-east of the main island, the dominant district (cf. Irwin 1983); (2) Kuboma, the less favoured part of north-central Kiriwina; (3) Kitava, the small island to the east of the main island; and (4) Vakuta, the island adjoining the south of the main island. All four calendrical districts operate the same lunar clandar of ten named months following the month of *milamala* (the month of the Trobriand New Year festival) plus an indeterminate number of months immediately preceeding (*milamala*. But they do not operate the calendar in phase; the *milamala* festivals are staggered by one month from district to district, in the order Kitava → Kuboma → Kiriwina → Vakuta, and the lunar calendar is also staggered accordingly, i.e. when it is lunation 1 in Kiriwina, it is lunation 2 in Kuboma and lunation 3 in Kitava and lunation 12 in Vakuta, and by the time it is lunation 5 in Kiriwina it is 6 in Kuboma, 7 in Kitava, 4 in Vakuta, and so on.

In an article published in 1950, Leach showed that the effect of
the staggering of the calendar from district to district was to
produce a consistent twelve-month lunar calendar, even though
there were only nine or possibly ten month-names in regular
use, as follows:

| Kitava | Kuboma | Kiriwina | Vakuta |
|---|---|---|---|
| 1 | 12 | [11] | (10) |
| 2 | 1 | 12 | [11] |
| 3 | 2 | 1 | 12 |
| 4 | 3 | 2 | 1 |
| 5 | 4 | 3 | 2 |
| 6 | 5 | 4 | 3 |
| 7 | 6 | 5 | 4 |
| 8 | 7 | 6 | 5 |
| 9 | 8 | 7 | 6 |
| (10) | 9 | 8 | 7 |
| [11] | (10) | 9 | 8 |
| 12 | [11] | (10) | 9 |

The bold-face numerals correspond to the nine month-names
which were clearly in regular use by *tonowi*, and by the more
knowledgeable men, (10) is *ilaybisila*, a month following *utoka-
kana* (9) named by a few experts only, and [11] is the month
immediately preceding *kuluwasasa* (12), which was, according to
Leach, left unnamed. Malinowski once asserted that this month
was called 'Yakoki' but this seems to have been the result of a
mix-up with *yakosi* (month 2). The import of this system is clear
enough; there are nine or ten recognized lunations, plus a vague
patch in between months 9 and 12. At the same time, although
one or two of the four calendrical districts might be experiencing
the vague patch between 9 and 12, the two or three other
calendrical districts would be experiencing the 'structured' part
of the calendrical sequence, between 1 and 9, so that there was
always the possibility of cross-referencing 'vague' local time
against 'determinate' time in some other district.

But how was the entire (lunar) system kept co-ordinated with
the solar year? There were two independent (and possible competing) systems. The most significant of these, in the eyes of
Malinowski's Kiriwinian informants, was the appearance of the
palolo worm *(milamala)* on the surface of the sea off Vakuta, far
to the south (the palolo was not fished off north Kiriwina).

According to Kiriwina theory, the arrival of the Vakuta *milamala* festival – which unlike the Kiriwinian one of the same name, actually featured the ceremonial eating of *milamala* (palolo) worms fixed the Kiriwina months as *yakosi* (2). Alternatively, there were certain men in the village of Wawaela, on the coast of central Kiriwina, and area of no gardening or political importance, who made observations of the rising of the star altair over Kitava (which lay out to sea directly opposite Wawela) which would identify the month as the lunation between 9 January and 8 February, which was fixed as Wawaela (Kuboma) *gevilavi* (6), corresponding to Kiriwina 5, Vakuta 4, etc. The stellar checks made by the Wawaela men were completely discounted by Malinowski, but were considered much more important by the administrator-anthropologist Leo Austen (1939) for reasons which will emerge shortly.

Leach's main point is that intercalation in Kiriwina took place by prolonging *milamala*, which was a season, rather than just one month, so that its end coincided with the onset of Vakutan *milamala*, whenever that took place. There could be two months of *milamala*, but the intercalation of the extra month was not determined by sophisticated judgements about the relative progress of the solar year vs. the lunar months, but quite automatically, because any delays in holding Vakutan *milamala* were the responsibility of the palolo worms, not the excogitations of any calendrical experts. Unfortunately, there is a fly in the ointment here, in that palolo worms have intercalation problems of their own, since they, just like Trobrianders, have problems co-ordinating their reproductive cycle (which is triggered by a lunation) and their dependence on sea-temperatures, which are determined by the solar year. So in fact, palolo worms do not rise to the surface to reproduce in just one lunation, but in two successive lunations around November–December, usually in greater numbers in one lunation than the other, depending on conditions. Consequently, it seems to me that the Vakutans could have had some discretion in timing *milamala*, and/or have been in doubt as to whether the rising of the palolo worms was the 'main' or 'secondary' one. Consequently, there was probably less automaticity in the Trobriand system than Leach suggests, and greater demands were placed on the *tonowi* in determining the month than he allows for.

But I want to pursue the argument in a different direction. Leach maintains that the staggering of the calendars by district

is there in order to produce a consistent twelve-month calendar
out of raw material consisting of only nine or ten named
months. But the same result could have been achieved by means
of a twelve-month calendar – only two more names would have
had to have been instituted, not an intellectually difficult feat.
This calendar could have been made applicable to all districts,
and timed by the palolo worms or by the stellar observations of
the Wawaela men, which clearly did take place. But it seems to
me that the purpose of the calendrical staggering is not to
facilitate year-tracking and intercalation, though it may have
assisted in this, but to do exactly what it appears to do, i.e. impose
a kind of time-slippage between separate political districts.

I would argue that this time-slippage was to the political
advantage of Kiriwina district. In effect, the staggering of the
calendar meant that post-harvest harvest exchanges of yams
and other foodstuffs, which took place during the *milamala*
season, would converge on Kiriwina, the 'central place' in Trobriand political geography (Irwin 1983). A travelling 'wave' of
harvest exchanges would be initiated on Kitava, then move
through the politically subordinated districts of Sinaketa-
Kuboma, to culminate in Kiriwina, and the harvest donations
which filled the yam-houses of the Tabalu chief of Omarakana.
The Kiriwina *milamala* would then continue over possibly more
than one month, until it was brought to an end by the Vakuta
*milamala*. Vakuta, however, was not within the system of affinal
food-exchanges centring in the Kiriwinian Tabalu elite, so the
'exchange wave' did not travel south once it had reached Omarakana, but effectively terminated there. Thus, during the period
during which the Kiriwina *milamala* was taking place, there were
always maximum amounts of giftable yams and other items
circulating in the system (the residue of the previous *milamala*
festivals in Kitava and Kuboma-Sinaketa) which would then be
able to gravitate towards Omarakana itself. That they would do
so was guaranteed by the alliance strategy of the Tabalu elite,
who first of all sent out Tabalu women to make strategic marriages in the subordinated districts, and also settled 'outposts'
there themselves, as subordinate foci of Tabalu privilege and
power. Thus, although the Omarakana chief did not exert any
recognized political authority outside his own district, he was
able (in conjunction with the rest of the Tabalu elite) to impose his power through his centripetal position in the field of
exchanges. Accordingly, it seems correct to interpret the stag-

gering of district calendars as both a reflection of the superior position of the Tabalu chief, and also as one of the mechanisms which sustained this superiority, by ensuring that his harvest gifts would always be the largest, coming as they did at the culmination of a cycle which drew resources from each district in turn, but which terminated in the yam-houses of Omarakana, and went no further. With this development, we move from the personal transcendence of the Simbo *bangara* over the calendar, to the instituted dominance of a restricted social group (the Tabalu) who have managed to impose a rhythm on collective life which operates to their specific advantage. But this story has a twist to it.

It will be recalled that Leo Austen, the administrator of the Trobriand Islands in the 1930s, placed great emphasis on the activities of the Wawela star-gazers. Wawela is a no-account place and it is most unlikely that the Kiriwina *tonowi* would have taken any notice of their calendrical advice, though it is possible that the people of Kitava and Kuboma-Sinaketa, their immediate neighbours, did promote them as the 'real' experts on the calendar, as opposed to the high-and-mighty Kiriwina people and the distant Vakutans. But Austen took them seriously for another reason, in that they seemed to him to offer the best hope of 'reforming' the Trobriand calendar, which in his opinion did not work well at all. Austen thought – in the typical fashion of colonial District Officers – that the Kiriwinians were much too dilatory about commencing gardening operations, and consequently produced less food than they might have. And this was because their calendar had 'broken down', resulting in prolonged, wasteful, *milamala* seasons. Intercalation during the non-work time of year, rather than during the work season, seemed to him just an excuse for 'slacking'.

So he instituted, by administrative fiat, a new 'native' calendar, based on twelve lunar months plus intercalation determined by astronomical observations taken in January–February (using the traditional Wawela observations of Altair). The intercalation occurred at that time of year, when garden work was at its height, rather than during *milamala*. This industriousness-promoting calendar was superseded, soon enough, by the general introduction of the Gregorian one, so it is not possible to ascertain whether Austen's neo-traditional calendar ever operated effectively. But this episode, besides providing an ironic ending to the story of Kiriwinian calendrical dominance, also serves to show how the intertwining of calendars and power is not confined to the domain of the primitive, but equally extends to the processes of colonial subjugation. Not for nothing did the ancient Chinese bureaucrats say, when they had incorporated some new region into the empire, that its inhabitants had 're-ceived the calendar' (Pelliot 1929: 208).

# Chapter 31

## Conclusions

This discussion of the anthropology of time has now reached its anticipated end, though needless to say it might have been greatly prolonged, and much more might have been said on many subjects which I have mentioned only in passing, or not at all. I have said little, for instance, about history, traditions, memories. I have concentrated instead on the action frame of reference and the shallow time of everyday life. This may result from a personal characteristic of mine, i.e. a present-focused, hunter-gathererish mind-set, coupled with a certain indifference towards the past and the future. And I have certainly not attempted anything like comprehensive coverage of the literature on time, even the limited anthropological literature of the subject. I apologize for these omissions, pleading mental exhaustion. But it is still necessary to pull the threads together and to essay some general 'conclusions'.

Throughout this book, one of my primary aims has been to dispel the aura of mystery and paradox surrounding time. There is no need to be in awe of time, which is no more mysterious than any other facet of our experience of the world. In particular, I hope I have said enough to dissuade anyone from embarking on the study of the time-anthropology (especially in exotic ethnographic contexts) as a pathway to some kind of release from the familiar, ordinary world. Not that the practice of ethnography is lacking in its epiphanies, during which the world suddenly appears reordered and revalued. But these moments of rapture do not arise from disturbances in the logic which governs ordinary experience, including temporal experience, but from our reveries of the real, the rational, the practical, which are full of surprises. The aim is not, therefore, to transcend the logic of the everyday, familiar world, but simply to be in a position to see what is there to be seen.

There is no fairyland where people experience time in a way that is markedly unlike the way in which we do ourselves, where there is no past, present and future, where time stands still, or chases its own tail, or swings back and forth like a pendulum. All these possibilities have been seriously touted in the literature on the anthropology of time, reviewed in the first part of this work, but they are all travesties, engendered in the process of scholarly reflection (Chapters 1–7). There are only other clocks, other schedules to keep abreast of, other frustrating delays, happy anticipations, unexpected turns of events and long stretches of grinding monotony. There is nothing new under the sun, in the sense, at least, that there is nothing out there to affect our estimation of the logical possibilities inherent in the world with which we are already familiar; on the other hand, most of what there is 'out there' is simply unknown, never observed, never described, never thought about, never set down on paper. That ought to be sufficient.

Time-anthropology, as I understand it, consists of the development of means of representing, dispassionately and critically, the manifold ways in which time becomes salient in human affairs. One of the main ideas underlying the argument of this work has been that there is no contradiction between allowing that time can be studied in many different cultural and ethnographic contexts, and can be understood with the aid of many different analytical frameworks, while simultaneously maintaining that time is always one and the same, a familiar dimensional property of our experienced surroundings. The whole thrust of this book has been to insist on a distinction between time and the processes which happen in time. I have opposed the trend of thought which distinguishes different species and varieties of time on the basis of different types of processes happening in time.

In my opinion there is no theoretical difference between 'physical', 'biological', 'social' or 'psychological' time; though one can easily distinguish physical, biological, social and psychological events, and interpret them as moments in physical, biological, social or psychological processes. But the whole point of an abstract category such as 'time' is precisely that it provides the means for the relative unification of otherwise diverse categories of processes. Time – which is intrinsically unitary and unifying – allows for the co-ordination of diverse processes; biological processes with social ones, psychological or subjective processes with objective, clock-timed ones, and so forth. And it is here that the interest lies. For instance, the fact that different tasks produce different subjective estimates of elapsed duration is only scientifically interesting (or interesting at all) because the expansions and contractions of time so produced are illusions, and known to be so by those who experience them (Chapter 11). Temporal subjectivity cannot be expressed in other than contrastive terms, i.e. by contrast to real-world processes, which are known to be regularly periodic. But precisely this contrast is lost if a distinction is drawn between 'psychological' time, which is good for subjective processes but not objective ones, and 'physical' time, for which the reverse holds. Then one could say that illusions of elongated and contracted durations were not illusions at all, but the truth. In that case, however, there is nothing to see, nothing to say, nothing to be at all surprised at, except the multiplication of time dimensions.

To impose notional frontiers between the temporality of different types of process is not only logically unwarranted, but is also scientifically self-defeating, because it is along such abstract dimensions as time and space that the formative analogical scheme-transfers which underlie scientific advance tend to take shape. Thus, in natural sciences such as physics, very large objects are comprehended by constructing analogies with very much smaller ones, and conversely, very small objects are comprehended by constructing analogies with very much larger ones, and the same goes for very temporally extended and very temporally compressed events and processes. Only the essential contentless-ness of space-time allows for the possibility of a relatively unified scientific concept of the cosmos, and for the intellectual manoeuvring through the gamut of possible time-scales which is essential to arriving at this cosmological model. The same applies, though on a diminished scale, to the social sciences, which are equally dependent on the relative unification of models constructed over different domains, and on analogical transfers between different 'orders' of temporality. The momentum of history 'of long duration' is built into the design, the time-tabling, of weeks, days, hours even; and conversely, the events of a day are by no means unaffected by the fact that similar days have enacted themselves for the last 500 years, and are expected to do so for the next 500 as well.

Only a minimalist approach to 'time as such' is consistent with the fundamental project of subsuming the diversity of 'what there is' under general explanatory categories. It is for this reason that I am unconvinced by Bergsonian temporal dualism despite the fact that Bergson's ideas on time, particularly his concept of duration have been promoted in Ingold's (1986) distinguished treatise on the role of the concept of evolution in anthropological thought. Following Bergson, Ingold regards it as essential to distinguish between 'abstract' time (which belongs to physics) and 'real' time, which belongs to 'being', i.e. time which is cumulative, which corresponds to the flow of consciousness and the irreversible progressive movement of evolutionary advance (conceived vitalistically, in the Bergson manner, rather than mechanically, in the manner of the more intellectually cautious biologists). All this is in the service of Ingold's primary thesis, which is to impose a sharp distinction between the evolution of consciousness, and the evolved life of consciously social agents, and evolution as a mechanical process affecting the species.

It obviously lies outside the framework of the present discussion to evaluate Ingold's thesis about the fundamental distinction between subjectivist social science and objectivist natural science, except to say that I am sceptical of the distinction he intends to draw. But I do feel it necessary to point out that no biological discoveries of any note have ever been stimulated by Bergson's evolutionary theory, and that on the contrary, the turn of the century vogue for 'vitalism' produced some of the most egregious scientific twaddle to emanate from the academies since the Middle Ages, for instance, the works of Teilhard de Chardin. Bergson's intention was to breathe 'life' into the life sciences, an objective which he pursued with outstanding literary skill, but no logical acumen, which is why his ideas are, from the point of view of the philosophy of the sciences, as dead as the dodo.

Bergson wrote *Creative Evolution* in order to reform biology, in which enterprise he did not succeed; the real biological advances of the twentieth century having been produced by precisely the kinds of people of whom he would have disapproved most strongly, i.e. the bio-mathematicians, population geneticists, etc. It seems to me equally open to question whether Bergsonian 'duration' (otherwise, life/process linked temporality) can be resurrected as a leading idea, not in vitalist biology, but in 'vitalist' social anthropology. Ingold wants to promote Bergsonian duration because this special-purpose temporality seems to underwrite his conviction that conscious (human/ social) beings are in some way *absolutely* different from other organisms, in having purposes, intuitions, understandings, etc.

Right or wrong, I feel that Ingold's project of defining the specificity of social being as against all other kinds of existence in the world, is ill-served by reliance on Bergson's distinction between 'abstract' mathematical-cum-physical time, which is merely a mental construct, and 'duration', which is 'real', experienced, lived-through time. It will be appreciated (in the light of Chapters 16–18 above) that Bergson's distinction is only a variant of the McTaggart distinction between A-series and B-series time, expressed in an excessively value-laden terms. Bergson was a prime A-theorist, whose work exercised a formative influence on contemporary A-theorists such as Mead, and McTaggart himself. Stripped of the imagery of creative evolution, Bergson is arguing for the primacy of A-series time, which can only be deduced from consciousness, over B-series time, which is a construct of mathematical reasoning, not 'life'. Enough space has been devoted to demolishing the logically purified form of A-theory put forward by McTaggart, so no purpose would be served by attempting to recapitulate the same argument in terms of the far murkier conceptual apparatus deployed by Bergson. And that is not the point I want to make, here, anyway. What I want to get at is the self-defeating nature of Ingold's appeal to Bergsonian duration in the context of his anthropological project, which is to identify the scope of anthropology with the elucidation of conscious, purposive action, as opposed to 'behaviour'.

In what way, I ask, is that project actually advanced by insisting on the special nature of humanly experienced time as opposed to any other kind of time? What more do we know, concerning who did what to whom, and why, by surrounding these doings and thinkings with a special kind of time whose primary characteristics are its ineffability, its never-to-be-repeated ebb and flux, and so forth? It is all very well to point to the fact that our uncertain experience of the world, and the confusion of our thoughts and motives as we grapple with the world, hardly give us any grounds for confidence in the adequacy of our unceasing efforts to impose order and assert control in practical life. But what is certain is that we do, always, attempt to impose order and assert control, and we live only in so far as we are successful in doing this. It may well be, as

Schutz has brilliantly shown in 'Choosing among Projects of Action' (1967), that ultimately we simply live through moments of decision, rather than deciding on the basis of an objective 'weighing' of each pro and con factor. But that does not alter the fact that we understand the decision-process (even in advance of the decision moment) only in so far as it is susceptible to analysis *ex post*, and that we understand no more about it (indeed we do not understand anything at all) referring it to the spontaneous evolution of the flow of consciousness.

The privileging to the A-series as 'real' and the downgrading of the B-series as 'intellectual reconstruction' ignores the fact that the structures of interpretation which guide us through the A-series flux are, precisely, internal 'reconstructions' (that is, maps of the world) of a B-series character. And it ignores the even more important fact that these structures of interpretation are efficacious only in so far as they are consistent with the truth of the world (though they may not be true themselves) and that this 'truth of the world' is the B-series truth, because only the B-series is capable of sustaining any system of truth and inference whatsoever. Theoretically, the A-series leads nowhere but down a logical cul-de-sac. The only consequence of Bergsonian subjectivism is to undercut the very possibility of describing the world at all, since to do so is always to engage in artifice, constructing models and setting lay-figures in motion on a mental stage, rather than communing on the level of ineffable spontaneity with the 'reality' of the Other.

Moreover, just as it is impossible to conceive of the activities of anthropologists as other than the recreation of social reality in B-series time (the time of maps and models, as opposed to the stream of consciousness) it is equally impossible to conceive of the mental life of agents, going about their own business (unlike anthropologists who go on about other people's business) as occurring entirely within 'lived' A-series temporality. We may be intellectually persuaded that the people we encounter in daily life are not 'actors' but possess the same spontaneous core of individuality as we experience ourselves as having, but the fact remains that we are obliged to treat them as actors. This arises from the fundamental principle of the reciprocity of perspectives; for me, the 'other' is the person I would be playing if I had been assigned his role in the play, and he mine. Even in the flow of daily life, the other is always an artificial creation of mine, and I also have to deal with the fact that, for the other, I am his artificial creation as well, so that for the purposes of determining my own conduct, I have to consider myself as an actor, too, since I am so considered by others. To have (as a human being) and intention *vis-à-vis* other human beings is to have an intention *vis-à-vis* a model of the other, not the other as he is to himself. This model of the other is (in terms of its inherent temporality) a B-series construct, from which A-series images may be drawn, as with any other kind of map; and the same applies to our models of the models others are presumed to entertain of us. In this sense, even our own inner life is a B-series construct, not a stream of consciousness.

The constructs which are evoked and exchanged in the flow of everyday interaction are drawn from the codified knowledge of social life maintained by the agent, who is a sociologist simply by virtue of having a social life. The more abstract, organized and comprehensive the sociological knowledge of the agent, the better he is positioned to realize his projects in the social world, as I hope the discussion of exchange in Chapter 27 may have served to illustrate. But social life, which is actually a play of constructs, images, discourses and models, conducted in the virtual space and time of the world synthesized, not by immediate experience but by reflective intelligence, cannot be accounted for by insisting on the primacy of A-series (experiential) time. The A-series, I have argued, is only a way-stage between the two B-series, the outer one of the real world and the inner one of mental models and maps. Experience, in other words, is only mediatory; what counts, and what deserves to be called truly 'real' is the B-series.

The arguments against privileging the A-series as 'human' time have been sufficiently rehearsed. What now needs to be done is to spell out the consequences of the philosophical approach adopted here (the 'moderate' B-series position derived from Mellor) for the practice of ethnographic description and analysis. In particular, what are the research implications of the theoretical demonstration that the B-series can be shown to encompass the A-series, giving rise to the theory of time-cognition outlined in Chapters 24–25? I would hope to draw a very specific lesson here, namely, that progress lies in the direction of bridging the gap between 'pure' B-theory approaches (such as Hägerstrand-style time geography; Chapter 20) and more cultural/cognitive approaches of the type more commonly favoured by anthropologists. It seems pointless to me to berate the geographers for their love of 'objectivist' cartographic exercises, and for not being phenomenonological or 'experiential' in what they do. It is much more likely, it seems to me, that the geographers' maps have profound but unexplored implications for the processes of human cognition. I look at time-geographic depictions of the choreography of everyday life with a marked sense of inward familiarity, for all that they represent data which could have been arrived at by studying the motions of human being as though they were ants in a nest. The methodology of data-gathering – between 'subjective' interviewing, projective tests, etc. and objective checklisting of movements, schedules, etc. – does not matter, because in the final analysis, what is internalized and cognized is pragmatically consistent what is objectively there. This may not seem always, or even usually, to be the case, but the much-advertised mismatch between the human/subjective world and the objective/scientific world is primarily an illusion stemming from the fact that models of the world do not have to be true 'absolutely'. They may well be false, but because false premises can be consistent with true inferences, models only need to have true inferential consequences in their specific contexts of application, i.e. practical ones.

Consequently, I believe that the foundations of time-anthropology ought to begin in the realm of time-geography and time-economics, 'objectively' understood. That is why I have not ignored these subjects in this book, though I am aware that in so doing I will have forfeited the sympathy of not a few anthropologists, particularly the more imaginative and intellectually ambitious ones, who have got into anthropology specifically in order to avoid doing economics and geography, and in the hopes of doing something much more akin to literary studies. I am also aware that (as has been pointed out to me by the editor of this series) the chapters of this book dealing with objectivist time anthropology and time economics are regrettably short of recognizably 'anthropological' examples and commentaries. This makes for a digressive presentation of these subjects, for which I apologize. But this defect in my presentation arises from the actual dearth of studies which integrate a sense of ethnographic cultural groundedness with the conceptual flexibility which, despite propaganda to the contrary, is abundantly present in objectivist styles of analysis. I insist that there is no contradiction of aims here, but a huge, and so far unexploited, series of intellectual opportunities.

There are no closed frontiers between intellectual approaches, only closed minds which refuse to cross them. That means that the time-anthropologists of the future must take models such as Becker's and Hägerstrand's (Chapters 20–22) and develop them in the same rigorous style, as well as learning to collect the appropriate categories of empirical data. It follows that time-budgeting studies must remain the basis of the investigative aspect of time-anthropology. The problem at the moment is that no real effort has been made to bridge the gap between time-budget studies (a pretty dull subject in the estimation of most anthropologists I know) and 'exciting' topics having to do with collective representations and the mediation of social processes.

I believe that the key idea which will enable this coming-together to occur is the idea of opportunity costs, currently only in common usage among economists, but one which deserves to be considered equally as important in social theory as, say, legitimacy. The concept of opportunity cost has no place in social theories which discount the calculated and intelligent characteristics of social action. This applies to the more extreme formulations of the theory of practice (Chapter 26). Opportunity cost also seems to imply a naive methodological individualism and an equally naive theory of actors' self-interest in maximizing individual utilities. However, there is no in-built conflict between the aims of the theory of practice (collectivity, *habitus*, sociality, etc.) and the concept of opportunity costs, because it is a matter of logical principle, not cultural design, that all actions have opportunity costs, and are meaningful to the agent in the light of these perceived costs. One cannot do *this*, without refraining from doing *that*, and 'this' (the meaning, value, attaching to the act, which is bound up with the action itself) cannot be grasped, except in conjunction with its corresponding 'that' – just as one cannot say 'dog' without saying not-cat, not-horse, etc.

The concept of opportunity cost is to the theory of action what the concept of context is to the theory of meaning. Or, to link these together, the meaning of an action is its anticipated outcome in the context of its anticipated opportunity cost. Opportunity costs are what make actions fateful and definitive. Moreover, if we think of actions always in the light of opportunity costs, we are able to overcome some of the aporias of freewill and determinism which divide social scientists into camps of determinists versus voluntarists. Because it is apparent that any action, however freely engaged in, has determined opportunity costs, which cannot be avoided by whatsoever act of freewill, and conversely, any action, however much coerced by factors other than the volition of the agent – as, for example, slave-labour – has an unwilled character only by virtue of the contrast with actions forgone, actions which (under other circumstances) would have been freely engaged in. As free agents we are enmeshed in the consequences of our actions, which operate always so as to limit our subsequent freedom of action, so that even if we are not enslaved by others, we enslave ourselves; and conversely, as creatures obliged to act under constraints not of our own making, we are unfree only to the extent that these constraints have alternatives – in other, feasible worlds – which are accessible to us in assigning meaning (i.e. opportunity cost) to our actions, but which are not realized.

Opportunity cost provides the bridging concept between subjectivity and objectivity in the sociological interpretation of action in the world. If there were not just one, real world, there would be no opportunity costs, because one could both perform and not perform the same action. But equally, it is only because, from the standpoint of the theory of meaningful action, this world lies at the centre of a penumbra of alternative possible worlds that opportunity costs arise, because the 'possibilities forgone' (which determine the nature and magnitude of opportunity costs) are computed not in terms of one world, but in terms of one (real) world and all of its accessible (unrealized) alternative worlds. The notion of opportunity costs implies both the primacy of the real world (and the inescapable causal texture of this primary world) and at the same time the fundamental proposition that as an object of thought, i.e. as the place we inhabit, in which we move about, and in which we realize projects of action, the 'real' world is just a member of the set of possible worlds (in fact, we do not even know which member of the set of possible worlds is the 'real' one).

Time-budget studies, time-geography and time-economics provide the basis for an objectivist analysis of the anthropology of time, but once the concept of opportunity costs is introduced, the objective study of the allocational possibilities of space-time 'resources' shades over into the study of culturally constructed, ethnographically grounded sets of possible worlds. As Bourdieu has shown, conventional attitudes constrain the agent's definition of the scope of the possibilities accessible to him. The ethnographic subject's definition of the possible (for him) may be perfectly at variance with the definition of his possibilities arrived at by an outside observer, who perceives possibilities of which the subject seems to rule out in advance, while the subject may anticipate the imminent possibility of states of affairs regarded as very remote contingencies by the observer. The explanation of the motives of the ethnographic subject has to be conducted in terms of his scheme of possibilities, because this scheme fixes his subjective opportunity costs, and hence the subjective value and meaning of his act; but the sociological understanding of the outcomes of acts is conducted in terms of the schema of possibilities operated by the observer, not the agent, because this schema fixes the opportunity costs of actions having real-world consequences. Subjective understanding of the motives of action is never sufficient, because the premise on which subjective understanding of the world is based is that the world is objective, that propositions entertained with respect to it are really true, or really false.

The fact that the ethnographic subject's map of the inherent possibilities of his world is not congruent with the observer's map, is the source of the problem of cultural relativism, which has surfaced repeatedly in the course of these pages. But the equally important fact that the ethnographic subject's map and the observer's map both aim to be true in one world, i.e. the real world, is the reason why cultural relativity does not pose an insoluble problem. It is necessary to provide an objectivist account of the temporally accessible (or spatio-temporally accessible) world of the ethnographic subject in order to apply the analysis of outcomes in terms of objective opportunity costs to his actions. The ethnographic subject's map of the world can only be evaluated (seen for what it is) in the light of the world to which it is supposed to refer, which is the real world, not an imaginary world which would be real were the ethnographic subject's map true (Chapter 6). It is merely patronizing to leave exotic ethnographic models of the world uncriticized, as if their possessors were children who could be left to play forever in an enchanted garden of their own devising. In practice, these maps survive because the only images which are drawn from them in their salient contexts of application are one which are experientially validated, but the objective opportunity costs entailed by the schemes of action these maps generate still accrue.

The sociological understanding of actions undertaken in the

light of culturally constituted maps of the world always implies of a critique of culture, whether or not this is acknowledged. We cannot make a choice between a 'friendly' account of cultural schemes of interpretation which takes them at their own (subjective) valuation, and a 'hard-nosed' one which confronts them with some externally defined reality, for the reason that there are no cultural scheme of interpretation which do not aim at realizing objective outcomes. In this respect the outside observer is never in a position to be more hard-nosed than his ethnographic subjects are themselves. But the outside observer in possession of codified knowledge amassed through objectivist research strategies is in a position, not exactly to transcend the native point of view, because this is not a matter of metaphysics, but to offer a rational critique of 'cultural reasons', from a standpoint inaccessible to those who simply operate cultural premises practically.

The anthropology of time ought ideally, therefore, to pursue a dual strategy of 'allocationalist' investigations of the inherent choreographical possibilities of social actions in their space-time frame, on the one hand, and on the other investigations leading towards the reconstruction, in model form, of the schemes of temporal interpretation, or internalized time-maps, of the ethnographic subjects. But in this plan of research, what is the status of collective representations? The earlier chapters of this book, dealing with the time-anthropology inspired by Durkheim, were aimed at criticizing the metaphysical exaggerations of the Durkheimian school, stemming from his misleading attempt to re-cast Kant in sociological terms (Chapters 1–3). The idea that the category time is created for us by the rhythms of social processes is fallacious. This is to identify time with what calibrates and measures it, as Bloch (1977) justifiably commented. But this is not to say that collective representations of time do not differ markedly in different cultural (and historical) contexts. Different productive regimes, for instance those that entail acute fluctuations in demand for labour or other resources at particular moments in the annual cycle, vs. equable regimes which do not do so, result in the development of very distinct kinds of cultural apparatus for handling time. I believe that these differences can best be explicated, as emphasized previously, by relating them to a notion of opportunity cost, and the cultural schemes and values in the light of which these opportunity costs are assessed. But analysis cannot anticipate ethnographic description, and where collective representations are concerned, a major source of difficulty lies in establishing their precise content and significance in the first place. How can the ethnographer identify the 'concept of time' in this or that culture?

To a considerable extent, Durkheimian anthropology has been preoccupied with concepts of time which surface in the context of ritual, notably calendrical festivals and life-crisis rites. As the analysis of Umeda ritual in Chapter 5 demonstrated, while it is certainly true that rituals dramatize time, and even manipulate it (in presenting models of life processes which may be modified or even inverted), this does not mean that calendrical festivals either create time or modify it, except rhetorically or symbolically. The interesting feature of rituals which seem to evoke, at will, aberrant time by showing aberrant processes, is the dialectical relation they bear to mundane temporality, where, by contrast to the ritual frame of reference, processes never occur except against resistance and with fateful consequences which ritual seeks to obviate. The elusive time which emerges from the analysis of ritual categories, in other words, cannot be detached from the ponderous entropic time of real-world events. From the standpoint of method, the investigation of ritual categories should not precede, but should follow, the investigation of the choreography of mundane social process, which form the background against which ritual reconstructs the world in the image of human desires. Ritual representations of time do not provide a 'world-view' but a series of special-purpose commentaries on a world, which cannot be defined in advance or once and for all, which have to be understood practically, not metaphysically.

Because ritual collective representations of time only cohere in the light of their implicit relation with the practical, they cannot be singled out as constituting the unique, culturally valid representations of time operated by members of a particular society. Instead, analysis of collective representations of time must proceed along a broad front, continually charting the interplay between systemic factors, deriving from the spatio-temporal layout of the practical world, and the wide variety of symbolic constructs which agents deploy in the course of handling their affairs. This interplay between objective and subjective aspects of temporality requires the development of a theory of time cognition. In Chapters 23–24 I have presented one such model, derived from Husserl and Neisser, but I would not of course claim that this model is definitive, especially since cognitive psychology is a fast-developing field whose true significance for social anthropology has not yet been fully realized or exploited. Much more work along these lines remains to be done, especially with regard to making models of cognitive processes which are more 'realistic' (i.e. true to the actual mechanics of thought-processes) than the very idealized picture that I have presented here. I also suspect that more work needs to be done on the relationship between the acquisition and use of language in relation to time cognition. I have dealt with these matters only briefly (Chapters 14–15), but I think that anyone who has the experience of learning a foreign language would be inclined to agree with me that tense, aspect and modality among the most complex grammatical features of natural languages, which always require detailed study and are often culturally illuminating as well. This is not to give assent to the 'strong' Whorf hypothesis, that language determines time cognition, but it is certainly demonstrable that different languages seem to highlight particular temporal/aspectual/modal relationships between events at the expense of others. And the historical principle, discussed in Chapter 15, that grammatical constructions are the congealed residue of what were once rhetorical tropes, means that grammar, in diachonic perspective, is never without cultural roots and cultural significance of its own.

Thus the recommended approach to the anthropology of time along a broad front, extended between time economics and geography on one wing, and on the other the symbolic processes of ritual, must include analysis of language and cognition as well. These disparate structures of temporality need to be integrated. One particularly promising way of encompassing this diversity is through the study of the emergence of differentiated structures of temporality in diverse domains during the course of socialization. Christina Toren (1990) has rightly emphasized the emergent and processual nature of Fijian concepts of hierarchy, and the same approach could, and should, be applied to the social cognition of time. I have not attempted this here, except in connection with Piaget's work (Chapter 13) and in relation to language acquisition (Chapter 15). At the moment we lack any ethnographic studies (apart from Piaget's) which focus specifically on the child's stage-by-stage construction of culturally grounded spatio-temporal categories. There seems to be scope for much more research into this topic. This would require not only naturalistic observation, but the greater use of projective tests and other methods borrowed from experimental psychology. The use of experimental manipulation need not be geared to the discovery of mechanistic 'laws of cognitive growth', but can be implemented simply to throw up richer and more interesting observational data which can be interpreted in many different ways.

Where, finally, does this leave the phenomenological approach to time? Currently, perhaps, it is the one that excites most interest among imaginative anthropologists and sociologists interested in 'human time', who can find, on the often obscure pages of Husserl and Heidegger, a sense of immediacy and relevance, which simply does not emerge from the equivalent pages of Mellor or Lucas, whatever the advantages possessed analytical philosophers in the matter of logical perspicacity. My position has been stated already, and it is that it is impossible to make a phenomenological analysis of human time except in the light of the outcome of logical analysis of time concepts. I am not at all opposed to phenomenology, but I am opposed to muddled phenomenology in which good 'humanist' intentions are confused with obscurantist and anti-rational denunciations of scientific objectivity. In this, I am certain that I am more aligned with the original intentions of Husserl and Schutz than many who have subsequently waved the banner of phenomenology more energetically that I have. I would claim, in fact, than the entire analysis is implicitly, if not explicitly, phenomenological, and that my psychological model derives directly from Husserl. I began this project under direct stimulus from Schutz, Husserl and Merleau-Ponty. Although the end-result may not look very phenomenological on the surface, the instructed will not be deceived into the belief that I have been their wholly unfaithful disciple.

In short, I believe that the time-anthropology of the future must be open-ended, eclectic, empirical, neither subservient to the prestige of the scientific method, nor so paranoid about science as to fail to see the virtues of objectivity, logic and soundly-based argument, lucidly set down on paper. Just because time is, as Lucas says, 'tenuous' does not give us the right to be obscure and baffling in what we choose to say about it. I have strenuously attempted not to be so, though with what degree of success I leave to the judgement of others.

# References

Altman, J. 1984. 'Hunter-gatherer subsistence in Arnheim land', *Mankind 14*, 199–21

Antonucci, F. and R. Miller 1976. 'How children talk about what happened', *Journal of Child Language 3*, 167–89

Appadurai, A. n.d. 'The problem of time among peasants in India', Paper delivered at New York University, Spring 1984

Arrow, K. 1951. 'Alternative approaches to the theory of choice in risk-taking situations', *Econometrica 19*: 4, 195–79

Attali, J. 1982. *L'Histoire du Temps*, Paris: Fayard

Austen, L. 1939. 'The seasonal gardening calendar on Kiriwina', *Oceania 9*, 237–53

—— 1950. 'A note on Dr. Leach's primitive calendars', *Oceania 20*, 333–5

Barnes, J. 1971. 'Time flies like an arrow', *Man* (n.s.) 6: 531–52

Barnes, R. 1974. *Kédang*, Oxford: Clarendon

Barth, F. 1959. 'Segmentary opposition and the theory of games', *Journal of the Royal Anthropological Institute 89*: 1, 5–23

Becker, G. 1965. 'A theory of the allocation of time', *Economic Journal 75*, 493–517

Berger, T. and Luckmann, J. 1966. *The Social Construction of Reality*, Harmondsworth: Penguin Books

Berlin, B. and Kay, P. 1969. *Basic Color Terms*, Berkeley: University of California Press

Bickerton, J. 1975. *Dynamics of a Creole System*, London and New York: Cambridge University Press

—— 1981. *The Roots of Language*, Ann Arbor, MI: Karoma

Bloch, M. 1977. 'The past in the present and the past', *Man* (n.s.) 12: 278–92

—— 1989. *Ritual History and Power*, London: Athlone Press

Borges, J. 1970. *Labyrinths*, Harmondsworth: Penguin Books

Bourdieu, P. 1963. 'The attitude of the Algerian peasant towards time', in J. Pitt-Rivers, (ed.) *Mediterranean Countrymen*, Paris: Recherches Mediterranéennes 1

—— 1977. *Towards a Theory of Practice*, Cambridge: Cambridge University Press

Bovet, C. 1975. 'Etude interculturelle de processus de raisonnement. Notions de quantité et relations spatio-temporelles', PhD thesis, University of Geneva

Bradley, R. and Swartz, N. 1979. *Possible Worlds*, Oxford: Basil Blackwell

Bronckart, J. and H. Sinclair 1973. 'Tense, time, and aspect', *Cognition* 2, 107–30

Brown, R. 1973. *A First Language*, Cambridge, MA: Harvard University Press

Brunton, R. 1980. 'Misconstrued order in Melanesian religion', *Man* (n.s.) *15*, 112–28

Burman, R. 1981. 'Time and socioeconomic change on Simbo', *Man* (n.s.) *16*, 251–67

Campbell, S. 1983. 'Kula in Vakuta', in J. Leach and E. Leach (eds). *The Kula*, Cambridge: Cambridge University Press.

Carlstein, T. 1982. *Time Resources, Ecology, and Society*, London: Allen & Unwin

—— Parkes, D. and Thrift, N. (eds) 1978. *Human Activity and Time Geography*, London: Edward Arnold

Carroll, J. (ed.) 1956. *Language, Thought and Reality: Selected writings of Benjamin Lee Whorf*, New York: Wiley

Carter, C., Meredith, G. and Shackle, G. (eds) 1957. *Uncertainty and Business Decisions*, (revised edn), Liverpool: Liverpool University Press

Church, J. 1976. *Language and the Discovery of Reality*, New York: Random House

Comrie, B. 1976. *Aspect*, Cambridge and New York: Cambridge University Press

—— 1985. *Tense*, Cambridge and New York: Cambridge University Press

Coseriu, E. 1958. *Sincronia, Diacronia, e Historia*, Montevideo: Universidad de la Republica

Cottle, T. 1974. *The Present of Things Future*, New York: Free Press

Damon, F. 1981. 'Calendars and calendrical rites of the northern side of the Kula ring', *Oceania 52*, 221–39

Davis, R. 1976. 'The northern Thai calendar and it uses', *Anthropos 71*, 3–32

Dummet, M. 1978. *Truth and other Enigmas*, London: Duckworth

—— and Lemmon, E. 1959. *Modal Logics between S.4 and S.5*, Zeitschrift für mathematische Logik, VEB Deutscher Verlag der Wissenschaften Berlin III

Durkheim, E. 1960. *The Division of Labor*, Glencoe, IL: The Free Press

—— 1915. *The Elementary Forms of the Religious Life*, London: Allen & Unwin

Endicott, K. 1979. *Batek Religion*, Oxford: Clarendon

Evans-Pritchard, E. 1939. 'Nuer time reckoning', *Africa 12*, 189–216
—— 1940. *The Nuer*, Oxford: Clarendon
—— 1965. *Theories of Primitive Religion*, Oxford: Clarendon
Findlay, J. 1975. 'Husserl's analysis of the internal time consciousness', *The Monist 69*
Fleischman, S. 1982. *The Future in Thought and Language*, Cambridge: Cambridge University Press
Fortes, M. 1945. *The Dynamics of Clanship*, London: International African Institute
Fortune, R. 1932. *Sorcerers of Dobu*, London: Routledge
Fraisse, P. 1964. *The Psychology of Time*, London: Routledge
Frazer, J. 1978. *Time as Conflict*, Basle: Birkhauer Verlag
Gale, R. (ed.) 1967. *The Philosophy of Time*, New York: Doubleday
—— 1968. *The Language of Time*, London: Routledge
Garfinkel, H. 1967. *Studies in Ethnomethodology*, Englewood Cliffs, NJ: Prentice-Hall
Geertz, C. 1973. *The Interpretation of Culture*, New York: Basic Books
Gell, A. 1975. *The Metamorphosis of the Cassowaries*, London: Athlone Press
—— 1982. 'The market wheel', *Man* (n.s.) *13*
—— 1985a. 'Style and meaning in Umeda dance', in P. Spencer (ed.) *Society and the Dance*, New York: Cambridge University Press
—— 1985b. 'How to read a map', *Man* n.s. *20*, 271–86
Girard, P. 1968–9. *Les Notions de nombre et de temps chez les Buang*, Paris: Societé d'Ethnographie de Paris
Givon, T. 1982. 'Tense–aspect–modality: the Creole prototype', in P. Hopper (ed.) *Tense–Aspect*, Amsterdam: Benjamin
Goff, T. 1980. *Marx and Mead*, London: Routledge
Gould, P. and R. Whyte 1974. *Mental Maps*, Harmondsworth: Penguin Books
Gregory, C. 1982. *Gifts and Commodities*, London: Academic Press
Gurvich, G. 1961. *The Spectrum of Social Time*, Dordrecht: Reidel
Halbwachs, M. 1925. *Les Cadres sociaux de la mémoire*, Travaux de l'année sociologique, Paris: Bibliothèque de philosophie contemporaine
Halliday, M. 1975. *Learning How to Mean*, London: Edward Arnold
Hallpike, C. 1972. *The Konso of Ethiopia*, Oxford: Clarendon
—— 1979. *Foundations of Primitive Thought*, Oxford: Clarendon
Harcourt, G. 1972. *Some Cambridge Controversies in the Theory of Capital*, Cambridge: Cambridge University Press
Heidegger, M. 1962. *Being and Time*, London: Macmillan
Héritier, F. 1981. *L'Exercise de la Parente*, Paris: Gallimard
Hintikka, K. 1969. *Models for Modalities*, Dordrecht: Reidel
Hobart, M. 1975. 'Orators and patrons: two types of political leaders in Balinese village society', in M. Bloch (ed.) *Political Oratory in Traditional Society*, London: Academic Press

Horton, R. and R. Finnegan (eds) 1973. *Modes of Thought*, London: Faber

Howe, L. 1981. 'The social determination of knowledge: Maurice Bloch and Balinese time', *Man* (n.s.) 16, 220–34

Husserl, E. 1966 [1887]. *The Phenomenology of Internal Time Consciousness*, Bloomington, INA: Midland Books

Ingold, T. 1986. *Evolution and Social Life*, Cambridge and New York: Cambridge University Press

Irwin, G. 1983. 'Chieftainship, Kula and trade', in J. Leach and E. Leach (eds) *The Kula*, Cambridge and New York: Cambridge University Press

James, W. 1963 [1890]. *Principles of Psychology*, Chicago: Great Books

Juillerat, B. 1980. 'Correspondence', *Man* (n.s.) 15, 732–34

Just, P. 1980. 'Time and leisure in the elaboration of culture', *Journal of Anthropological Research* 36, 105–15

Kant, I. 1929. *Critique of Pure Reason* (trans. N. Kemp-Smith), London: Macmillan

Kelly, R. 1977. *Etoro Social Structure*, Ann Arbor, MI: University of Michigan Press

Kriegel, J. 1970. *The Theory of Capital*, London: Macmillan

Leach, E. 1950. 'Primitive calendars', *Oceania* 20, 245–62

—— 1961. *Rethinking Anthropology*, London: Athlone Press

Leach, J. W. and Leach, E. 1983. *The Kula*, Cambridge: Cambridge University Press

Le Goff, J. 1980. *Time, Work and Culture in the Middle Ages*, Chicago: Chicago University Press

Lewis, D. 1973. *Counterfactuals*, Oxford: Basil Blackwell

Lévi-Strauss, C. 1948. *Race et Histoire*, Paris: Unesco

—— 1961. *Tristes tropiquez* [*A World on the Wane*, trans. J. Russel], London: Hutchinson

—— 1963. *Structural Anthropology*, New York: Basic Books

—— 1966. *The Savage Mind*, London: Weidenfeld & Nicolson

—— 1969. *The Elementary Structures of Kinship*, Boston: Beacon Press

Lévy-Bruhl, L. 1966 [1922]. *Primitive Mentality*, New York: Beacon Press

Linder, S. 1970. *The Harried Leisure Class*, New York: Columbia University Press

Lucas, J. 1973. *A Treatise on Time and Space*, London: Methuen

Lyons, J. 1977. *Semantics*, vol. 2, Cambridge: Cambridge University Press

Malinowski, B. 1922. *Argonauts of the Western Pacific*, London: Routledge

—— 1935. *Coral Gardens and their Magic*, vol. 1, London: Allen & Unwin

Malotki, E. 1983. *Hopi Time*, Berlin: Mouton

Marcus, G. and J. Fisher 1986. *Anthropology as Cultural Critique*, Chicago: Chicago University Press

Marr, D. 1983. *Vision*, Cambridge MA: MIT Press

McCloskey, M. 1983. 'Intuitive physics', *Scientific American*, April: 114–22

Mead, G. H. 1924. *Mind, Self and Society*, Chicago: Chicago University Press
—— 1959 [1925]. *The Philosophy of the Present*, La Salle: Open Court Press
Meggitt, M. 1976. 'Pigs are our hearts!' *Oceania 44*, 165–203
Mellor, D. 1981. *Real Time*, Cambridge: Cambridge University Press
Miller, G., E. Galanter and K. Pribram 1960. *Plans and the Structure of Behavior*, New York: Holt, Rinehart & Winston
Mimica, J. 1989. *Intimations of Infinity*, Oxford: Berg
Mountford, R. (ed.) 1960. *Records of the Australian–American Expedition to Arnheim Land*, vol. 2, Sydney: Sydney University Press
Munn, N. 1983. 'Gawan Kula', in J. Leach and E. Leach (eds) *The Kula*, Cambridge and New York: Cambridge University Press
—— 1986. *The Fame of Gawa*, Chicago: Chicago University Press
Needham, R. 1974. *Remarks and Inventions*, London: Tavistock
Neisser, U. 1976. *Cognition and Reality*, San Francisco: W. H. Freeman
Newton-Smith, W. 1980. *The Structure of Time*, London: Routledge
Ornstein, R. 1969. *On the Experience of Time*, Harmondsworth: Penguin Books
Palm, R. and A. Pred 1978. 'A time-geographic perspective on problems of the inequality of women', in K. Burnett (ed.) *A Social Geography of Women*, Chicago: Maarouta Press
Parkes, D. and N. Thrift 1980. *Times, Spaces, and Places*, Chichester: Wiley
Pelliot, P. 1929. 'Neuf notes sur questions d'Asie centrale', *T'oung Pao 26*
Piaget, J. 1970. *The Child's Conception of Time*, London: Routledge
Pitt-Rivers, J. 1963. *Mediterranean Countrymen*, Paris: Recherches Mediterranéennes, Etudes 1
Prior, A. 1966. *Past, Present, and Future*, Oxford: Clarendon
—— 1968. *Collected Papers on Time and Tense*, Oxford: Clarendon
Pryce-Williams, D. 1961. 'A study concerning concepts of conservation among primitive children', *Acta Psychologica 18*, 142–54
Reichenbach, H. 1947. *Elements of Symbolic Logic*, Berkeley: University of California Press
Rescher, N. 1968. *Topics in Philosophical Logic*, Dordrecht: Reidel
—— and A. Urquhart 1971. *Temporal Logic*, Vienna: Library of Exact Philosophy No. 3
Ryle, G. 1949. *The Concept of Mind*, Oxford: Clarendon
Sahlins, M. 1972. *Stone Age Economics*, Chicago: Aldine
—— 1985. *Islands of History*, Chicago: Chicago University Press
Schneider, D. 1963. 'Some muddles in the models', in *The Relevance of Models for Social Anthropology* (ASA 1) ed. M. Banton, London: Tavistock
Schutz, A. 1962. *Collected Papers*, vols 1 and 2, The Hague: Martinus Nijhoff
—— 1967. *The Phenomenology of the Social World*, Chicago: Northwestern University Press

Shackle, G. 1958. *Time in Economics*, Amsterdam: North-Holland
—— 1965. *A Scheme of Economic Theory*, Cambridge: Cambridge University Press
Smith, C. 1980. 'The acquisition of time-talk', *Journal of Child Language 7*, 263–78
Sorokin, P. and Berger, C. 1939. *Time Budgets of Human Behavior*, Cambridge, MA: Harvard University Press
Soule, G. 1955. *Time for Living*, New York: Viking Press
Spencer, P. 1965. *Samburu*, London: Routledge
Sperber, D. 1985. 'Anthropology and psychology. Towards an epidemiology of representations', *Man* (n.s.) *20*, 73–89
Sraffa, P. 1960. *The Production of Commodities by Means of Commodities*, Cambridge: Cambridge University Press
Stewart, F. 1977. *Fundamentals of Age Group Systems*, New York: Academic Press
Strathern, A. 1971. *The Rope of Moka*, London and New York: Cambridge University Press
Strehlow, T. 1947. *Aranda Traditions*, Melbourne: Melbourne University Press
Szalai, A. et al. (eds) 1972. *The Uses of Time*, The Hague: Mouton
Tannenbaum, S. 1988. 'The Shan calendrical system and its uses', *Mankind 18*, 14–26
Taylor, C. 1955. 'Spatial and temporal analogies to the concept of identity', *Journal of Philosophy 52*, 599–612
Thompson, E. P. 1967. 'Time, work-discipline, and industrial capitalism', *Past and Present 38*, 56–97
Tivers, J. 1977. *Constraints on Activity Patterns*, Occasional paper No. 6, Department of Geography, King's College, University of London
Toren, C. 1990. *Making Sense of Hierarchy*, London: Athlone
Turton, D. and Ruggles, C. 1978. 'Agreeing to disagree. The measurement of duration in a southwestern Ethiopian community', *Current Anthropology, 19*, 585–93.
Uberoi, J. 1962. *Politics of the Kula Ring*, Manchester: Manchester University Press
Werbner, R. 1984. 'Masking in a lowland New Guinea community', *Man* n.s. *19*
Weyl, H. 1949. *The Philosophy of Mathematics and the Natural Sciences*, Princeton, NJ: Princeton University Press
White, B. 1976. 'Population, involution, and employment in rural Java', *Development and Change 7*, 267–90
Wilkerson, T. 1976. *Kant's Critique of Pure Reason*, Oxford: Clarendon
Williams, B. 1957. 'Shackle's Ø-function and gambler indifference map', in Carter et al., *Uncertainty and Business Decisions*: 122–33, esp. Figures 1a and 1b
Wilson, B. 1971. *Rationality*, Oxford: Basil Blackwell

Woodburn, J. 1980. 'Hunters and gatherers today and the reconstruction of the past', in E. Gellner (ed.) *Soviet and Western Anthropology*, London: Duckworth

Zerubavel, E. 1981. *Hidden Rhythms*, Chicago: University of Chicago Press

# Index

Lightning Source UK Ltd.
Milton Keynes UK
UKOW03f1523120417
298982UK00001B/9/P